The Interpretation of
Diseased Dreams
- An introduction to the psychology of Delirium -

The Interpretation of
Diseased Dreams
- An introduction to the psychology of Delirium -

James M. FitzGerald

SPY MASTER PUBLICATIONS

2016

First Printing: 2016

ISBN-13: 978-1535042277
ISBN-10: 1535042273

Spy Master Publications, Republic of Ireland.

The Interpretation of Diseased Dreams

'Delirium has finally gotten the attention it deserves. FitzGerald's book is an original and solid contribution to the new psychodynamic neurology.'

J. Allan Hobson, MD
Professor of Psychiatry, Emeritus, Harvard Medical School
Professor, Department of Psychiatry,
Beth Israel Deaconess Medical Center

Contents

Acknowledgements

Gratitude is a virtue that is often neglected. Here I would like to express mine. I would like to thank Robert M. Kiely for editing this book and thus enabling me to write the book I always wanted. I would like to thank both Aaron K. Wiley and Bjarne Tungland for their graphic design skills.

I would like to thank J. Allan Hobson and Marian C. Diamond for inspiring me to write this book. I would like to dedicate this book to my parents who gave me the compassion to know what is right and the courage to do what is right. Finally, a special thanks to the rest of my family and friends, for without them dreams would not be possible.

List of Figures

Preface

A paradigm is the zeitgeist of science. Understanding it enables and emboldens us to identify its limitations, and experiment with expanding its frontier. A paradigm always appears to us as an external ordered agency. It is a form of secondary consciousness that is derived from us and through us yields its utility. This book explains how delirium overturns our assumptions about the perception of our current paradigm. The paradigm that we have hitherto used to describe the delirious psyche is one in which has an ever growing sclerotic boundary. A stagnancy of theory which inevitably leads to an inability to treat or prevent. How should this spirit of the age be confronted? In Nietzches' *Thus spake Zarathustra*, the reader is exposed to the three metamorphoses of the spirit. When we are born, we are a camel, and life puts a load onto us. It gives us a kick and sends us out into the wilderness of life. Within the desert we transform into a lion. The heavier the load, the more powerful the lion. The purpose of the lion is to kill a dragon, and deep within the desert this dragon dwells. This dragon is called 'thou shalt' and upon each of its scales is written in gold 'thou shalt'. The dragon confronts the lion and in defiance the spirit of the lion responds to the thousand years of values with 'I will'. When the lion kills the dragon it transforms into a child, a new beginning, a wheel running out of its centre (Nietzche, 1883-1885 [1917]).

In 1907, the psychiatrist Carl Gustav Jung published his book, *The Psychology of Dementia Praecox*. It was a meeting of modern psychology and clinical observation. It outlined how the psychology and neuroscience of the time could reconfigure how schizophrenia (then called *dementia praecox*) was studied. Beyond efforts to simply categorise its features into self-evident groups, he instead analysed the complex phenomenology in terms of how the human psyche operated both in health and disease (Jung, 1907). His book was a sensation and transformed how the field operated. The insights presented in that text still resonate over a century later. In 1999, the psychiatrist John Allan Hobson published his book, *Dreaming as Delirium*. Its aim was to comprehend these two major experiences of the human psyche and redefine the parameters of our paradigm (Hobson, 1999). However, Hobson's account was limited by the absence of in-depth delirium research, and hence the existence of a barrier to the full realisation of this formulation. Inspired by this spirit of inquiry, I dare to use, adapt, and develop the methods set out by these psychiatrists. If I fail to enhance, I endeavour at the very least not to disgrace this active participation in the life of the mind. For what could be more challenging and rewarding than to be an idealist in the life of the mind and a pragmatist in the world of action?

With the necessity of a new paradigm comes with it the identification and slaying of 'thou shalt'. This book is the product of the perceived historical trend from stagnant discourse to the precipice of an epistemological rupture. The complexity and magnitude of the work does not permit any final statement regarding treatment or theory, but to ignite a permanent theoretical revolution. This book has many aims. The first aim is to use the scientific understanding of dreaming to elucidate the structure and dynamics of the delirious psyche. The next aim is to introduce the theoretical and scientific challenges that delirium creates. This condition is as unique as the person who suffers from it and is thus an excellent opportunity to expand the limits of psychology. This book is not dedicated to the previous attempts to position delirium as a missing element into a structurally sound yet incomplete clinical edifice. This book is not an exact description of the other manuscripts on delirium, it seeks to integrate and internally criticise its assumptions, and hence push out the perimeter of our paradigm. My aim is not to transplant to the field of delirium the more structurally sound theories of dreaming. An effort to equate two mysteries. But it proposes to analyse the problems that delirium gives birth to, and to follow the logical and probable consequences of theories that can result from this interpretation. Hopefully this book will contribute to the much needed innovation in clinical theory and practice that is required to optimise psychiatry at a time when it has retreated into itself. There is something special about the boundary of the scientific paradigm and what could be more special than it not having any permanent boundaries at all?

Part I Introduction

1 The concept of delirium

1.1. What is delirium?

Somewhere between the dream and the void, when the psyche is in its twilight there exists a state known as delirium. What is delirium? In proposing this obvious question I am suddenly conscious of the challenge of an explanation. It is the ultimate paradox of medicine. At once universal to the human experience and unique to the individual life. It appears at different times, in different forms, to different people in different contexts. Mercurial to alchemists, divine to the devout, frightening to the ill and ignored by health care professionals; delirium casts a shadow over our lives and acts as the harbinger of our death. Theoretically and historically it is connected to the phenomenon of dreaming, both as its opposite in terms of purpose and equal in terms of experience. It evokes the spectre of a *dialectic in nature*. Today it is still an open question.

The demarcation between the origins of true madness is often divorced from the science constructed once this departure from normality occurs. This broken dialogue renders the language of medicine a monologue flanked by silence. In this book I shall endeavour to break this silence and give an account of the neurobiological and psychological relationship between dreaming and delirium. The psychological structures that serve us today are based on an evolutionary developed neural substrate that is in a dynamically reciprocal interaction with the environment. I will discuss the significance of the phenomena of dreams and delirious states, and elucidate the common source of their characteristic obscurity, the unconscious. Furthermore, I shall describe these underlying processes and how they relate to the forces involved in the human psyche.

To comprehensively organise my evidence I shall utilise the principle of consilience. This principle indicates, in explicit terms, that independent sources of evidence can converge to co-operatively identify an account of scientific knowledge (Wilson, 1998). I shall draw upon diverse disciplines of research, such as neuroscience, psychology, molecular biology, and evolutionary biology. Following this I will direct my investigation into more comprehensive and practical problems, which are inevitable as a result of engaging with the material that is beyond our immediate reflection.

I shall begin by giving an historical survey of the theoretical views that are now part of the contemporary discourse. The historical accounts of these topics are well beyond the scope of a single volume and are not the focus of this book. All societies have attempted to analyse the important and unique phenomena of dreaming and delirium. Identifying and analysing the commonalities that lead to unities between elements in the history of delirium must persuade us to question whether or not these categories are retrospectively fitted onto the historical pieces of evidence to manufacture a coherent whole. Such traditional values will have to be questioned as to their utility in forging a new paradigm or if indeed they are the very barriers that we must over-come. The answer that may become apparent is that each author reconstitutes these elements into groupings that fit within an accepted paradigm, the limits of which are ambiguously understood. This issue challenges assumptions made by calling into question whether or not the descriptions are attributable to a purely empirical entity known as delirium or an object constituted by a discourse that is based upon the paradigm. For the purposes of this work four domains will serve as the basis of our investigation. The four domains are 1) the source of dreams and delirious states, 2) the methods of interpreting these phenomena, 3) the meaning of these phenomena, and 4) their purpose in daily life. Each of these four domains are interrelated. By critically engaging with the assumed underlying unities between different elements of the delirium field, new continuities and connections can emerge which permit the development of a new paradigm.

1.2. The lexicon of delirium

Delirium then as now is a nebulous construct in medicine and the sciences that make up its theoretical foundation. Previous attempts at a history of delirium have imposed a coherent whole upon the repository of ideas and statements associated with our modern comprehension. According to Anthony Stevens, there is a developmental history to each medical science. There have been roughly five stages identified that compose this developmental sequence, 1) recognition of features, 2) defining the syndrome, 3) identification of tissue pathology, 4) demonstration of pathogenesis, and 5) discovery and development of cures and treatments (Stevens & Price, 2000: 5). Applying this structure to the conceptual development of delirium may yield a useful perspective when formulating hypothesis or analysing data pertaining to it. It can be stated confidently that these stages are not clear cut, but rather, are heuristic ideas that organise the history of these developments. When it comes to understanding delirium we can invoke the utility of this paradigmatic motif. However, we must be cognisant of how this conceptual analysis is used as a representation of a continuous historical investigation. Underscoring this position we must also remain aware of the transformation from one paradigm to another in order to question its procedure and theoretical foundation. We must depart from traditional perspectives on delirium that have presented it as an ahistorical entity, and one bordering on a transcendent ideal. Instead, we must focus upon the myriad mutations that have occurred throughout our recorded history of delirium. An interpretation that evokes questions on methods, theories, and limits.

If we accept that the first developmental stage of a medical science is dedicated to the recognition of specific features, then we can discern clearly that the majority of the conceptual history has been concerned with this first stage. Its multiple manifestations across different clinical settings, population, and periods in history support this proposition. The lack of a homogeneous terminology is the result of its peripheral status to medical fields. The lack of standardised terminology also reflects the heterogeneity of its phenotype and its temporal manifestation. There are more terms reflective of delirium than most researchers can imagine or accumulate. The word delirium itself is derived from the Latin *deliro/delirare* (de-lira, to go out of the furrow), put simply, to be crazy, to rave, to be deranged, to be out of one's wits (Lewis et al., 1879). It has a metaphorical dimension that links it to agriculture. It was first used by Celsus in the first century AD in his medical writing to describe mental disorders, both as a symptom and syndrome following head trauma or fever (Celsus 2.7). Celsus, who was not a physician, but an encyclopaedist, compiled the *Hippocratic Corpus*, translated it into Latin, and integrated it with his work *De Medicina*. He also identified it as a sign of approaching death (Celsus, 1935).

There is of course a plethora of other terms coined to try to capture this phenomena. The father of western medicine, Hippocrates of Cos believed in a materialistic account of mental disorders. Hippocrates established a rational system for medicine and organised disease in terms of categories, acute and chronic, endemic and epidemic. Other medical terms are attributed to him such as relapse, crisis, paroxysm, convalescence, and resolution (West, 2006; Fox, 2008). In keeping with his materialistic perspective, he believed that delirium was a disorder of the brain (Liposki, 1990: 5). Hippocrates never used the term delirium because it was a Latin word and he spoke/wrote in Greek. Instead, Hippocrates described delirium in terms of *lethargus* and *phrenitis*, the former referring to dulling of the senses and motor retardation, the latter referring to sleep disturbances, and the acute onset of cognitive and behavioural disturbances generally found in the context of fever. The fluctuation of *lethargus* and *phrenitis* was believed by Hippocrates to be a potential part of its clinical course (Lipourlis, 1983). Translations of Galen's works by Hynayn ibn Ishaq from Greek to Arabic enabled Islamic medicine to utilise his systematic and rational approach to medicine as a template for their future endeavours (French, 2003). The Arab Physician Najab ub din Unhammad in the 8th century, refers to a state of *souda* (mild delirium) as becoming *jannon* (severe delirium) associated with insomnia, restlessness, and agitation (Graham, 1967).

At the beginning of the 18th century, *phrensy/phrenesis* was separated from delirium, whereby, delirium was reserved for a state of brief madness, while *phrensy* and *phrenesis,* was associated with febrile conditions and related medical problems. To be more precise, *phrensy/phrenesis* and *paraphrenesis* were subdivided to refer to inflammation of the brain versus inflammation of the other organ systems respectively. Inconsistently, *paraphenesis* was also used to describe the prodromal or beginning stage of delirium (Adamis et al., 2007). The rise of epidemiology to tackle disease on a public scale, the role of micro-organisms to account for infection, and the continued enhancement of medical equipment all saw a sharp distinction in the quality of medicine in the 19th century (Porter, 1997). However, the 19th century developments in delirium research continued to employ terms with accumulating ambiguity. Linguistic dimensions of the words to describe delirium complicated the matter further, for instance, in French the word *delire* was employed to denote *phrenesis* and delusions (Berrios, 1981; Berrios & Porter, 1995). The term *confusion mentale* (Chaslin, 1895) was introduced to account for delirium as a result of organic causes, while other French authors employed terms such as *idiotisme asquis* (Pinel, 1809), *demence aigui* (Esquriols, 1814) and *stupidite* (Georgets, 1820). In German, the term *verwirrtheit* was used to describe features associated with delirium (Wille, 1888). In 1817, the main feature of delirium was proposed to be the clouding of consciousness. It was proposed that the state of fever induced disturbances in the organ of consciousness, the brain. The course and severity of delirium depended on this dynamic interplay between the fever and the brain. In clear terms, fever and consciousness fluctuated congruently whilst occasionally this was interrupted by lucid periods. It was also maintained that delirium was a state of dreaming whilst awake (Greiner, 1817). During the 1860s, John Hughlings Jackson continued research into the relationship between the clouding of consciousness and the psychopathology of delirium (Lipowski, 1990; 1991; Hogan & Kaiboriboon, 2003).

It was not until the end of the 19th century that many of the classical terms such as *lethargus, phrenitis, phrensy,* and *paraphrenesis* began to disappear from the medical discourse. The taxonomic preoccupation of this discourse was replaced with a focus on the disturbances of consciousness and its relationship to sleep and dreaming (Greiner, 1817). In the late 19th century, Emil Kraepelin described in the early edition textbooks on psychiatry, acute onset psychotic states with delusions, significant mood alterations, and vivid hallucinations that vanished abruptly. The term *period delirium* was introduced in the 4th edition of his textbook (Kraepelin, 1893).

The 5th edition saw *period delirium* turned into a subtype of delirious mania (Kraepelin, 1896). In the 6th edition manic depressive illness was integrated with delirious mania (Kraepelin, 1899). However, Kraepelin was aware that such conditions were not synonymous and explicitly stated that delirious mania 'must be classed with manic-depressive illness only with a certain reservation' (Kraepelin, 1904). However, in the 8th edition, Kraepelin removed the note and categorised both conditions together (Kraepelin 1913). In 1924, Carl Kleist, following on from the work of Carl Wernicke, coined the term *cycloid psychosis* to describe the phenomena that 'manifest themselves in multiple phases during life, come and go in an autochthonous way, often show antagonistic syndromes - confusion and stupor, hyperkinesis and akinesis - and do not lead to mental defects'. In addition, he described *cycloid psychosis* in terms of *confusional psychosis* and *motility psychosis*; such descriptions are arguably the same as the modern conception of delirium (Kleist, 1924; 1928). In 1962, Maurice Victor and Raymond Adams proposed the classification of *confusional states,* including *delirium, primary mental confusion*, and *beclouded dementia* (Victor & Adams, 1962). In the modern era, *ICU syndrome* or *ICU psychosis* became prevalent and was associated with both the ICU environment as well as underlying critical illness (McGuire et al., 2000). The term *oneirism* was used in the modern context to describe the alterations in behaviour and perception that resemble dreams during delirious states (Sellal & Collard, 2001). Delirium was until recently defined in the revised 4th edition of the Diagnostic and Statistical Manual of Mental Disorders (DSM-IV-TR) as a 'disturbance of consciousness with cognitive changes or perceptual disturbance, which has developed over a short period of time, and is caused by a general medical condition' (APA, 2000). With the publication of the new edition DSM-5, delirium is now redefined in terms of reduced awareness and inattention, while removing the term consciousness altogether. Such an alteration has been suggested to substantially impact both clinical care and research in the context of its interpretation (Meagher et al., 2014).

The terms used to denote delirium, including the word *delirium* itself, attempt to encapsulate at once the idea that it is a singular entity distinct from other phenomena. But such a word also tries to capture the notion that it is imbedded within a register of abnormal relations, without subscribing it to the status of an epiphenomenal entity.

1.3. Reconstituted origins of delirium

In defining the parameters that link the various constructs within a paradigm, one must be cognizant of the multitude of apparently peripheral aspects that in actuality form the nucleus out of which the paradigm operates; this focus is authority. An appreciation for the abstract authority that operates within a paradigm does not oblige us to merely rebel and reconstitute a new implicit authority, but rather to enable us to appreciate that the processes and rules of appropriation do not function on the basis of pure intentions. Dreaming and delirium have an intimate relationship to the subjective life of the individual, but an historical analysis of these entities is limited by our appreciation for their reconstructed origins in medicine. The following illustrations demonstrate how both dreams and delirious states have been associated with the prevailing world view of the time. Such beliefs have retained their potency in the imagination ever since and provide a conceptual link between the paradigms of science and the epistemological fields of discourse, in other words, hegemony.

Medicine as a discourse is always integrated with the prevailing world view of the time. Understanding how these other networks of relations connect to medicine further enhances our appreciation of how the phenomenological connection between dreaming and delirium operates. But the simple juxtaposition of empirical data coupled with the proximity of conceptual relations should not immediately lend itself to unconditional acceptance of their link. Instead the mapping out of the modes of discovery and enunciation should be utilised with a view to restructuring the delirium field and hence reformulating the much needed paradigm that delirium as a subject deserves.

In *The Dream in Primitive Cultures*, Jackson Steward Lincoln indicates that the dreams of 'primitive' peoples can be amenable to the same interpretation as modern people. Furthermore, he categorised dreams into 'big dreams' that had cultural significance, 'little dreams' that only had personal significance, 'medical dreams' that gave insight into the nature of disease, and 'prophetic dreams' that foretold the future (Lincoln, 1935). According to archaeological and anthropological evidence, shamans were the first humans who developed the capacity to heal people and dedicate their lives to doing so (Hoppál, 1987). The differentiation of a shaman as a distinct class from other members of society was typically based upon a sign of initiation, either derived from dreams and/or physical/spiritual illness, known as an initiatory crisis. This crisis drove the shaman to the edge of death and provided the transformative experience required to be a shaman. During this process the shaman made an introspective experiential journey to what was believed to be the underworld/spirit world and gained insight into their own crisis and thus, develop the capacity to heal others. There are many accounts of shamanic practices that illustrate this integrated practice and belief system. The consistent characteristics of these practices are to be found in ancient artefacts indicating minor surgical procedures (e.g. trepanning) and the distribution of herbal remedies (Eliade, 1972; Hoppál, 1987). Spells, amulets, and various means to alter consciousness were integrated with shamanistic medical advice (Hoppál, 1987). *Deliriogenic* substances were also associated with the tradition of shamanism. For example, in South America the Aztecs ritualistically used them in the temple dedicated to their Sun deity, and Peruvian shamans used a number of species of *Datura* in a mystery ritual for their youth (Radenkova et al., 2011). Shamans were believed to have made contact with the spirit world and acted as a conduit for the messages that nature had to offer humanity (Eliade, 1972; Whitehead, 2002). Dreams were interpreted in the same manner as all other hallucinations, including delirious states. Such traditions of interpretation and practice were disseminated through the generations orally (Butt, 1961). The experience of the shaman with his techniques of religious ecstasy can appear like a waking dream or delirious state, but should not be thought of as the same entity. Indeed, Mircea Eliade cautions against such an interpretation in his work, *Shamanism* (Eliade, 1972).

A paradigm can only become fully known retrospectively, and only when it has begun to suffer from diminished utility. The unitary cohesion of a field comprised of the concepts, explicit and implicit, about what is true and false, exhibits a stagnancy that no longer further generates propositions that can be rendered falsifiable. The paradigm in this sense operates as the mechanism that enables researchers to conduct themselves within their respective scientific field. Delirium challenges current anaemic paradigms, and urges upon the researcher the necessity of a new paradigm encompassing the myriad phenomenological features that emblazon themselves upon the psyche. Deeply connected to delirium and its meaning is the complex network of associations that it is imbedded within. Such an order enunciates this meaning.

Stevens in his work *Private Myths* outlines several developments for the early civilisations: (1) integration of dream interpretation (*oneirocritica*) into institutional religion, (2) deliberate induction of dreams for the service of divination, (3) recording of dreams and their interpretation, and (4) distinguishing between good and bad dreams and techniques of determining which category they are to be assigned (Stevens, 1997: 14). Civilisations such as the Babylonians and Egyptians indicate that dream interpretation had considerable cultural importance, as depicted by Egyptian hieroglyphs on scrolls such as the Chester Beatty papyrus and the written accounts of dream interpretation from *The Epic of Gilgamesh* (Thompson, 1930; George, 2003). According to Stevens, the ancient Egyptians were the first to practice systematic induction of dreams in people to divine the will of the gods and evoke answers to their personal problems and current illness. The Egyptian god of dreams, Serapis, had many temples (*serapeum*) erected throughout the Egyptian territory with the most famous being in Memphis in 3000 BC (Stevens, 1997: 15). In the ancient Greek tradition, Homers *Iliad* indicates that the sons of Asklepios were great doctors during the Trojan War. Asklepios becomes deified as the healing god and the erection of temples, referred to as *Asclepieia*, functioned as both shrines and medical centres for patients. At these temples patients would enter an altered state of consciousness of induced sleep (often as a result of opium consumption) referred to as *enkoimesis* and during this state they experience dreams that offered medical advice and prognosis. The experience of the dream itself or an adjunctive medical treatment or surgery cured the patient of their illness (Risse, 1990).

Plato's view of dreams was intimately connected with his conception of the human psyche. For Plato, the psyche was a tripartite system composed of the physiological desires (*apithymia*), the rational mind (*nous*), and high spirits (*thymos*) (Republic, 441a). Healthy growth and self-mastery meant the use of reason and art to harmonise these conflicted systems (*Republic*, 441e). In Plato's dialogues, *Phaedrus* and *Ion*, Socrates discusses the *Theia Mania*, a form of divine madness normally associated with the intervention and possession by a divine entity e.g. a god (Hackforth, 1972; Saunders, 1987). Socrates describes examples of deities bestowing the gift of insight upon people by inducing a state of frenzy and ecstasy. The most famous and important example of this *Theia Mania* is to be found in the oracle at Delphi (Foster & Lehoux, 2007). These particular examples illustrate how initial conceptualisations of the mind can extend beyond the individual and be applied to the wider culture.

It can therefore be acknowledged that paradigms are not just systems of thought or collections of texts, but are practices which have institutional, technological, and philosophical dimensions. The repeatable existence that characterises the paradigm has a paradoxical function of both generating specific hypotheses and general frameworks under which these can operate. The ideas about delirium can manifest, reproduce, be manipulated, combine, decompose, and transform all within this field. The terms used to describe them are invariably linked with accounts of those that are connected with the pathological features of the human subject.

1.4. Loci and regularities

We must resist the temptation to envision our engagement with the paradigm as an effort to travel from ideal to empirical, from internal to external, from the multiplicity of phenomenological subjectivity to unified truth, and instead recognise that we are all the while situated and emboldened to perpetuate a paradigm unto utter uselessness. A particularly interesting case of the operation of a paradigm is the Oracle at Delphi. This particular cultural phenonmenon, has been the subject of many interpretations down through the centuries. Each of these accounts is the result of the paradigm under which the authors operated. Historically, a great number of writers have discussed the oracle at Delphi and include, Plato, Aristotle, Herodotus, Pindar, Aeschylus, Euripides, Diodorus, Strabo, Ovid, Livy, Luke, Julian, Justin, and Plutarch (Foster & Lehoux, 2007). The discontinuous analysis renders it meaningful on several levels.

The oracle at Delphi, also known as the *Pythia,* was a priestess residing at the Temple of Apollo located in Delphi. Although the oracle at Delphi has been estimated to be established during the 8th century BC, it is believed to have a history stretching back into late Mycenaean era 1400 BC (Morgan, 1990; Dietrich, 1992). The rise of Christianity and its establishment as the official religion of the Roman Empire eventually led to zealous persecution and vandalism of many pagan sites, including the Oracle at Delphi. In 393 AD, Theodosius I ordered that the temple cease its operation (Brown, 2012). It has been proposed that the first deity to inspire these prophecies was Gaia, but eventually Apollo became the sole deity associated with this shrine (Fortenrose, 1974). The reattribution of the temple and holy site for Apollo is believed to be as a result of the rise of political influence of the Greek city of Corinth (Forrest, 1957). There are many stories to account for the origin of the oracle, but the account by Diodorus Siculus in the 1st century BC is striking. He cites the experience of a goat herder named Coretas who followed one of his goats after it fell into a chasm in the earth and started to act in a frenzied manner. He entered the chasm to rescue the goat and began to experience a divine inspiration and the ability to see both the past and the future. Word then spread of this discovery and after the shrine was erected at that site a young virgin was chosen as a mediator oracle to be exposed to these experiences and relay them to the public (Broad, 2007: 21).

It has been recorded that the oracle would undergo specialised purification rites each month which were composed of fasting and meditation in order to prepare her spirit. She would then bathe in the Castalian spring followed by drinking the waters of the Kassotis near the temple. It was believed a *naiad* (water nymph) with supernatural powers existed there. After these rites, she would mount her tripod seat within the *adyton* (Greek term to describe the 'inaccessible') and there she would hold laurel leaves, and a bowl containing water from the Kassotic into which she would see glimpses of prophecy. Pilgrims wishing to consult the oracle would bring the fee, an animal to sacrifice (the liver of the animal, normally a goat, was used to divine the auspiciousness of the moment), and a symbol of Apollo such as laurel branches (Broad, 2007: 34-36).

The historian Plutarch served as a priest at the shrine at the end of the 1st century and the start of 2nd century AD and observed that the life span of the oracle was significantly shortened. Such an early death was attributed to being in the service of Apollo (Plutarch, Trans 1936). There are several sources of evidence that indicate this. Plutarch describes how the oracle can mediate the revelations of Apollo following exposure to vapours from the Kerna spring waters that flowed under the temple and that there was a noticeable sweet smell when the deity Apollo was present (Broad, 2007: 38-40). However, from a modern perspective, it suggests that it was delirium as a result of *deliriogenic* substances, such as benzene and ethylene vapours, coming from the chasms. Some researchers such as Daryn Lehoux propose that ethylene and benzene were unlikely causes (Lehoux, 2007). Other researchers have proposed that the gas may be methane, carbonyl sulphide or hydrogen sulphide, hypothesising that the chasm might be as a result of seismic activity (Piccardi et al., 2008). In 1892, excavations at the site conducted by French archaeologist Theophile Homolle, did not find any such source of the fumes. In 1904, Adolphe Paul Oppe published an article outlining his claim that there were no vapours or extreme frenzied behaviour from the oracle and that such accounts were mere rumour and fabrication. In 1950, another French scholar, Pierre Amandry, corroborated these findings (Fontenrose, 1959). However, in the 1980s, a research team composed of an archaeologist John R. Hale, a geologist Jella Zeilina de Boer, a toxicologist Henry R. Spiller, and Jeffry P. Chanton, a forensic chemist explored the site at Delphi and found the fault lines and source of vapours attributed to the transformative state of the oracles consciousness. These findings have been recently confirmed by William Broad (Broad, 2007). Now it is well recognised that earthquakes in the region heated the bituminous deposit (estimated to contain a petrochemical content of 20%) which resulted in the production of fumes rising through the chasms and directly being absorbed by the oracle. In addition to these vapours, the waters of the Kerna springs have been shown to be contaminated with a high hydrocarbon content, thus adding to the psychoactive component of the oracles behaviour (De Boer & Hale, 2000). Modern research has suggested that exposure to these fumes can induce delirium as well as the frenzied motor behaviour that is characteristic of hyperactive motor clinical subtype of delirium (Lipowski, 1990).

The use of psychoactive components alone to bring about the oracles behaviour does not sufficiently account for everything. There are of course the cultural and thus psychological and mythological dimensions of this practice. Plutarch describes a situation when it was not a good time to consult the oracle, but the priests continued to consult the oracle despite the negative warning and the priests reacted in a highly anxious state leading to death shortly afterward (Plutarch, 1935). To our modern conception of psychology and mythological motifs, it might indicate that the power of suggestion that is characteristic of rituals coupled with the presence of sources of psycho-activity (the fumes and contaminated water) had thus exacerbated the oracles delirium.

According to West, the oracle has many of the same traits as shamanistic practices and proposes the hypothesis that this tradition may have been inherited from or alternatively influenced by similar practices in Central Asia (West, 1983). However, no evidence has been found to establish this fact. Perhaps this is evidence of inherited archetypal modes of human behaviour rather than as a result of cultural diffusion. In opposition to the traditional depiction of a history of ideas, which assumes that knowledge accumulates towards a historical conclusion, a detailed appreciation for the literature presents instead a discourse of signs that constitute an object. This discourse when actively engaged with is the system of practices out of which the object of their focus manifests.

1.5. Propositions and limitations

The functioning of a paradigm is not synonymous with the finite programme of hypotheses/propositions explicitly stated by researchers on their subject. Instead an implicit network of assumptions and conceptual biases exist under which a limitation principle can operate. This limitation allows hypotheses to be falsifiable and enables scientists to actively engage with the conceptual apparatus of self-limiting interpretation. The particular schemata that operates within a scientific paradigm are largely unconscious to us and permit us to focus exclusively on the object of our inquiry without being encumbered by the multitude of contextual associations, in other words, how science is embedded in cultural and societal forms and patterns. However, to reconstitute a new paradigm these otherwise unconscious dimensions need to be encountered in order to learn from the mistakes of the past and adapt to new systems of thought.

The key challenge to understanding delirium is the absence of any identifiable pathognomonic feature. Delirium is diagnosed in the clinical setting based on the therapeutic context, baseline cognition, a record of typical behaviour, and the detectable constellation of abnormal features that appear. This aspect of delirium research has focused on two domains. The first is the drafting of criteria to define what delirium is, and the second being the creation and validation of diagnostic scales to identify and differentiate delirium from similar conditions. Standardised criteria are warranted to enable health care professionals to detect and tackle this clinical problem. The established criteria for delirium were/are set out by the International Classification of Diseases (ICD) and the Diagnositic and Statistical Manual of mental disorders (DSM). The advent of the ICD, DSM, and other structured manuals/collaborative networks, enabled clinicians and researchers to strive towards an understanding of delirium. This consensus was and still is as a result of a combination of expert opinion and accumulated empirical evidence. According to the ICD-10, sleep-wake cycle and motor behaviour disturbances are explicitly mentioned as features of delirium, while the DSM-IV had a more broad ranging definition of features (APA, 1994). A number of studies have highlighted the lack of sensitivity for detecting delirium using the ICD-10 as opposed to the DSM-IV criteria (Cole et al., 2003; Laurila et al., 2004). A shortcoming of both criteria is the absence of grading the severity of delirium. A number of diagnostic scales such as the DRS-R98 and the Memorial Delirium Assessment Scale include measurements of severity when detecting and assessing delirium (Breitbart et al., 1996; Trezpacz et al., 2001).

Before the publication of the DSM III, the distinction between dementia and delirium in terms of diagnostic criteria were significantly lacking. This is not a surprising finding given that it has been reported that the comorbidity is so common that up to 89% of elderly patients in hospital with pre-existing dementia can develop delirium (Fick et al., 2002). Previous methods to taxonomise and differentiate between dementia and delirium rested upon the phenomena of *acuteness of onset* and its *temporal course*. However, such a distinction was not found to be reliable given that patients with Lewy body dementia (LBD) can have fluctuating features of cognitive impairment. Patients with delirium can also go on to experience persistent impairment of cognitive faculties (Wacker et al., 2006).

The publication of the DSM IV continued the neglect of the distinction between delirium and dementia, but complicated matters further by use of circular descriptions, for example, describing the diagnosis of dementia where 'deficits do not occur exclusively during the course of delirium' and describing the diagnosis of delirium as 'are not better accounted for by a pre-existing, established or evolving dementia' (APA, 1994). Sub-syndromal delirium (SSD), first proposed by Zbigniew Lipowski, is the presence of some features of delirium, but not enough of these features to be regarded as full syndromal delirium as set out by either the ICD or DSM criteria. SSD has been found to be associated with adverse outcomes and may provide an advantageous stage of addressing full delirium onset

(Levkoff et al., 1992; Marcantonio et al., 2002; Cole et al., 2003). In 2007, David Meagher and Paula Trzepacz proposed guidelines in order to improve understanding of the phenomenological distinctions between full-syndromal delirium, sub-syndromal delirium, and co-morbid dementia for the DSM 5. A key component of these guidelines was the use of psychometric instruments to quantitatively investigate the phenomenology of delirium in mixed neuropsychiatric populations.

There are a number of psychometric instruments that have been developed to operationalise the diagnostic criteria of delirium. According to one review, there are up to 24 different instruments to do this (Adamis et al., 2010). Arguably the most well validated and conceptually robust instrument to study delirium is the Delirium Rating Scale (DRS) and the revised version, the DRS-R98 (Trzepacz et al., 1988, 2001). These instruments have been used extensively in research and have been translated and revalidated numerous times for use internationally (Fonseca et al., 2005; de Rooij et al., 2006; de Negreiros et al., 2008; Huang et al., 2009; Kato et al., 2010; Lee et al., 2011). The major challenge to understanding the phenomenology of delirium is the accurate measurement of the fluctuating severity of its features, and so investigating the inter-rater reliability of assessment tools such as the DRS and the DRS-R98 is warranted as a suitable strategy to achieve this (Adamis et al., 2013).

In addition to the development of a number of tools to capture the cognitive and behavioural phenomenology of delirium, a complex set of methods for analysing this data had to be developed in order to tackle the temporal and transient time course of its manifestation. Statistical analysis of data must therefore be both cross sectional and longitudinal. According to Dimitrios Adamis, four different stages of development must be the central focus of analysing it, 1) the time period before the index episode, also known as the pre-delirious stage, 2) the index episode, defined as either, prodromal, sub-syndromal, or full syndromal stage, 3) the time period between the index episode and the follow-up assessment, and 4) the follow-up or outcome assessment(s) (Adamis, 2009). According to Graham Dunn, we can define the reliability of an instrument as the ratio of the true score variance to the observed score variance (Dunn, 1989). A key tenet of reliability, includes consistency in repeated testing and thus reproducibility. Use of reliable instruments in science enables researchers to calculate accurate sample sizes derived from populations of interest, which in turn allows researchers to determine the required power level to detect the effect size under examination (Fleiss et al., 2013). Instruments with low reliability obstruct the proper conduct of the scientific method and provide researchers with ultimately incorrect statistical inferences (Meyer, 2010). According to Adamis et al., estimation of reliability in tools to assess delirium must be able to fulfil a number of assumptions. The first being that errors must be mutually uncorrelated and the second being, that the errors must be uncorrelated to true scores. The third assumption is that there must be stability in true scores over the testing time periods for a delirium assessment tool to fulfil this assumption, assessment of delirium but be undertaken by both raters simultaneously. However, classical tests of reliability cannot be solely relied upon for delirium assessment due to the fact that the fluctuating changes in delirium will be detected as measured error which leads to underestimation of the actual reliability across time (Adamis et al., 2013). Furthermore, Adamis (2009) reviewed the wide variety of statistical methods that may be useful in analysing the data derived from delirium research and included well established tools from other fields of medical science such as survival analysis, path analysis, and structural equation modelling. The use of mixed effect regression modelling

(MRM) and generalised estimating equations (GEE) methods have especially been useful in understanding the intra subject and inter subject differences in the phenomenological profile of delirium (Liu & Hedeker, 2006). Applications of these methods have been incredibly useful in the context of staging delirium development. It has been reported that use of MRM has been applied to a wide variety of situations where analysis of intra subject variables pertaining to delirium are difficult to study. For example, as a result of applying MRM to delirium developmental stages, it has been reported that the emergence of post-operative delirium in children was significantly associated with their state of anxiety, that there is a significant increase in S100B during delirium, and that delirium can accelerate the long term trajectory of declining cognitive function in patients with Alzheimer's disease (Kain et al., 2004; Fong et al., 2009; Van Munster et al., 2009). In contrast, GEE has been found to have a better application for investigating population specific (marginal) patterns. Dolan et al., (2000) have used GEE to analysing two-year functional outcomes and its relationship to prognostic delirium. Pharmacological agents known to complicate delirium pathogenesis have also been investigated using GEE (Gaudreau et al., 2007). Application of GEE has also enabled research to understand the disturbed motor behaviour that is characteristic of delirium and establish in clear form the different motor subtypes, namely, hypoactive, hyperactive, mixed, and no clear subtype (Meagher et al., 2011).

Defining and recognising delirium is based on identifying consistently detectable core features (Trzepacz, 1999; Meagher et al., 2007). Statistical methods such as exploratory factor analysis (EFA) have been applied to an analysis of which features may form the underlying basis of the delirium phenotype. It has the capacity to do this due to its ability to analyse amongst a number of variables the inter-relationships. Once done, it can then identify a reduced number of factors that it can group those variables onto. A given factor is based on two things, the values obtained by the weighting of these variables and the inter-relationship between these variables within the groups. Another statistical method, confirmatory factor analysis (CFA), is required to validate (thus the confirmatory nature of it) these factors which have been identified (Byrne, 2005). Previous studies investigating the phenomenology of delirium using EFA have identified the core phenomenological features of delirium and proposed that these be organised into either two or three domains. According to Grover et al., (2011) using the DRS-R98 method of delirium phenomenology assessment, they found that there were two domains, 1) cognitive, sleep, and motor, and 2) thought, language, and fluctuations. While another study, identified two different domains, 1) cognitive, circadian, and psychosis, and 2) higher-order thinking (Mattoo et al., 2012). While a third study using the DRS-R98, found 3 domains 1) circadian integrity, 2) general cognition, and 3) higher order thinking. Circadian integrity is based upon the neural substrate that regulates circadian behaviour and physiological processes of the body. This circadian system is largely broken down into assessments of the sleep-wake cycle and motor activity. General cognition is based on a collection of psychological process such as attention, orientation, visual-spatial perception, long term memory, and short term memory. Higher order thinking is based upon language capacity and thought processes (Trzepacz & Meagher, 2008; Franco et al., 2009; Meagher et al., 2009; Kean et al., 2010)[see Fig 1. & Fig. 2].

Fig. 1 Three domain theory of delirium phenomenology

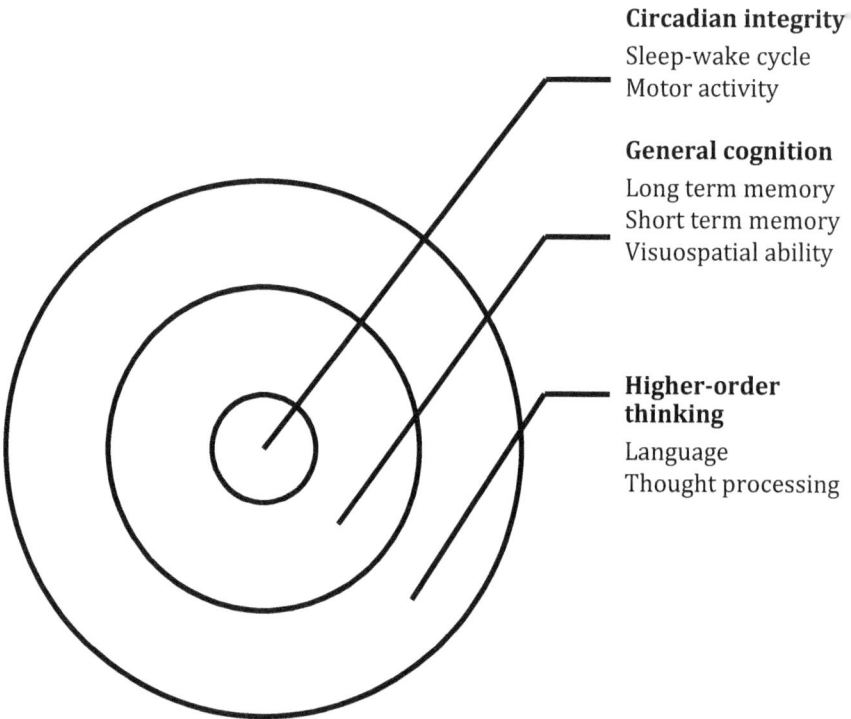

Circadian integrity
Sleep-wake cycle
Motor activity

General cognition
Long term memory
Short term memory
Visuospatial ability

Higher-order thinking
Language
Thought processing

Fig. 2 The three integrated domains of delirium phenomenology

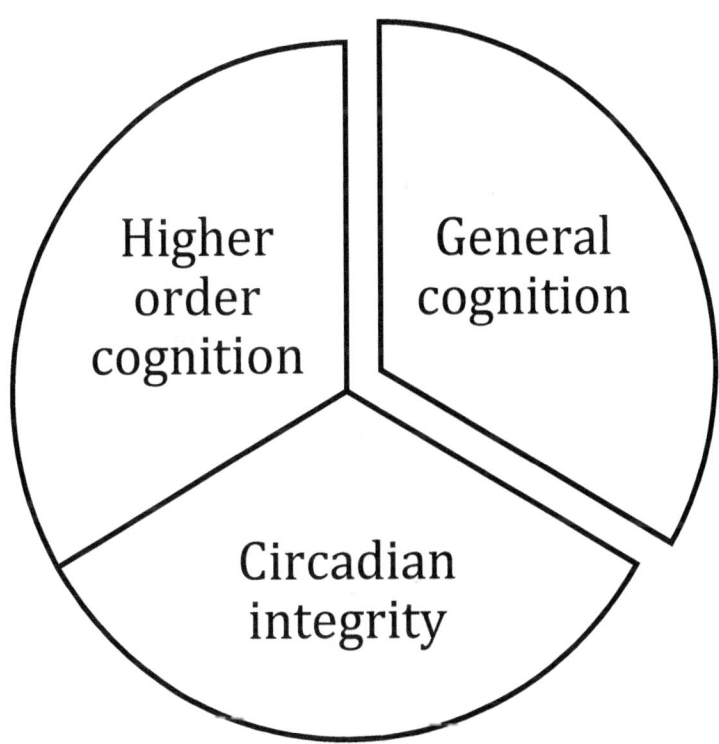

However, concepts such as general cognition and higher order thinking are by definition vague, and encapsulate a wide variety of overlapping neurocognitive processes. Despite the most stringent criteria set out, narrow limitations placed upon the identification of propositions as the sole function of the paradigm field, close it off, and render the paradigm ineffectual due to its inflexible boundaries between accepted concepts and the development of new ones. From the history of the following examples, we can appreciate the divergent trend between subjective phenomenology and an empirical method focusing upon the micro cosmos of the psyche as abstract methods. Such a system of processes forms the background for the equally limited mode by which parallel delirium research has progressed through.

As an initial point of departure, Aristotle's influence over science in our western tradition is unparalleled and therefore an exposition of his views is required to supplement many of the subsequent historical developments. In his system of philosophy all biological and natural processes were subject to formal causes. This principle of teleology runs through his entire perspective on biology and organises all life within the framework of the *scala naturae*, a great chain of being (Mayr, 1982; Mason, 1956). According to Aristotle, the human soul is a tripartite entity and composed of a vegetative soul for growth and reproduction, a rational soul for complex thought and reflection, and a sensitive soul governing the motor and sensory systems (Mayr, 1982). In contrast to his predecessors, Aristotle discounted the astrological or divine significance of dreams. Three works outlining his theories on the subject of sleep and dreams remain with us, *On Dreams*, *On Sleep and Waking*, and *On Prophecy in Sleep* (Stevens, 1997: 19). Aristotle's views on dreaming were congruent to his views on perception and part of his understanding of human psychology. In waking life, perception had the dimension of judgement to reflect and interpret it, while during dreaming, this critical faculty was suspended and the experience of dreaming then appeared as real as waking life. Aristotle was also aware of an in between transient state where judgement was retained, one which we might now refer to as lucid dreaming (Aristotle, *On Dreams*, 462: a5). Aristotle also believed that the content of hallucinations, illusions, fantasies, and dreams of people, both healthy and ill were analogous and derived from the same source.

After Aristotle died, the Lyceum, began the tradition of taking his theories as self evidently true without question (Annas, 1986). It is believed that this period of stagnancy in biology, and thus medicine, was practiced for almost 400 years, and it was not until the emergence of the City of Alexandria, more specifically, Claudius and the Ptolemies, that significant advancements were made in biology again. An underlying principle of classical medicine was the role air played as the essential principle of life. This idea is credited with Diogenes of Apollonia (5th century BC) and Anaximenes. The theory of the pneumatic current, which was derived from the belief that air (*pneuma*) was an essential life force, was followed by the Ptolemaic school of medicine in Alexandria. Herophilus of Chalcedon is recorded as the first established medical teacher in Alexandria and began to progress medicine in another direction. In contrast to Aristotle, who believed that the faculty of intelligence was attributed to the function of the heart, and the brain was merely a cooling system for the blood, Herophilus correctly attributed the faculty of intelligence, motor, and sensory functions to the brain. Herophilus organised the origin of dreams into those that were from God, those that were from the person's soul (*eidolon*) which were an image from the soul of what was to happen next, and the mixed dream (*synkramatikoi*) that arise spontaneously. These mixed dreams are the result of internal desire and influenced by external experience and images (von

Staden, 1989: 310). He also discovered the distinction between veins and arteries, with arteries having being known to have the capacity to pulse. The courses of the vasculature and nerves were mapped by Herophilus with the help of Erasistratus of Chios. Erasistratus examined the surface convolutions of many animal brains, including human brains, and suggested that increased convolutions were a characteristic foundation for the complexity of the mind. Both Herophilus and Erasistratus believed that air transformed into *pneuma*, and once inside the body, it then transformed to *pneuma zootikon* inside the heart, and then into *pneuma psychikon* in the brain (Kudlien, 1972). The flow of spirits and their relationship to the diseases of the soul was a major school of thought during the era of classical western medicine. In one experiment to provide evidence for the pneumatic theory, Erasistratus weighted caged birds before and after feeding to determine the weight loss birds might experience between feeding times (Fraser, 1969). This school of thought was the opposite of the predominantly physiological humoral theories established by Galen in the first and second centuries AD. Herophilus is also believed to be the discoverer of the pineal gland (Ariëns-kappers, 1979). He believed that this organ controlled the flow of *pneuma psichikon* from the medial to posterior cerebral ventricles (Kitay & Altschule, 1954). The aetiology of mental health problems, including neuropsychiatric disorders was thus based on a foundation of either one of these opposing theories and often a combination of the two. The relationship between delirium and the pineal gland and what would now be referred to as the circadian system has been part of these clinical observations since then.

Like many other Greek ideas and cultural behaviour, Greek medical concepts were adopted and adapted by the emerging Roman Empire. The humoral theories derive their origin from pre-Socratic philosophers such as Alcmaeon of Croton (540-500 B.C.), and Democritus of Abdera (460-370

B.C.) (Sherrington, 1946). Greek medicine was heavily dependent on the theory of the four humors and the Hippocratic School of medicine and the migration of Greek physicians from the Greek city states to Rome further solidified this influence. The Romans also governed the city of Alexandria, which included its libraries and universities. In particular at Alexandria, there was a great library which held multitudes of books and manuscripts on all of human knowledge, including medicine. Due to the permissive nature towards dissections there, doctors were also able to make many theoretical advances, including the discovery that the brain sends messages to the rest of the body (Mattern, 1999).

Galen of Pergamon (AD 129- 216) was a Greek physician who exerted a major influence over western medicine for centuries (Nutton, 1973). As a young man he served in the temple of Asclepius as a *therapeuties*, or attendant. In 162 AD when he moved to Rome, he began to lecture and made public performances of his knowledge of anatomy as derived from his animal dissections. He became such an authority on medicine that he was introduced to the Roman imperial court and eventually became the physician that would serve the great Roman emperor Marcus Aurelius (Mattern, 1999). Galen retained the notion that the flow of *pneuma psychikon* in the blood, then translated into Latin *spiritus animalis* was controlled by the brain as a pump and hence spreading *pneumatized* blood systemically (Hall, 1975; Swanson, 2007). Galen is credited with the first detailed anatomical account of the pineal gland (called *conarium*, from the Greek *konarium*, meaning pine cone). Galen gave the pineal gland a less glamorous role, denoting it a pseudo gland and having a role in the lymphatic system. Instead of the pineal gland acting as a valve, the vermis of the cerebellum was assigned the role of valve to the *pneuma psichikon* in the cerebral ventricles (García Ballester, 1972b; Zrenner, 1985). Regarding dreams and erotic dreams in particular, Galen proposed in his *On diagnosis from dreams,* that they were a manifestation of the patients current physiological state (Oberhelman, 1983: 46). Galen understood that delirium was secondary to disease and proposed the theory that it was as a result of an excess accumulation of yellow bile in the brain (Whitewell, 1937). The philosophy of the Stoics and the medical writings of the time focused upon the virtue of *sophrosyne* (moderation). Appetites and emotions according to the Stoics were categorised as primary emotions, such psychological processes that were not produced by the higher mind, but only experienced by it. The term *pathos*, first coined by the Greeks to encapsulate emotions, suffering and passion was held by the Stoics to be modifiable by judgements and the higher mind. Control over them was a method to achieve the goal of *apatheia*, or impassivity (Long & Sedley, 1987: 411). The fundamental principles of the materialist tradition in classical medicine are thus credited to Galen, who modified the pneumatic current theory and integrated it with the theory of humours. The materialist theory of the four humours would last from the classical era up till the 18th century (García Ballester, 1972a).

From these limited examples, it can be appreciated that medicine reorganises disease in terms of new patterns of syntax, new relationships between language and what it signifies, in relation to other structural changes in society, its practices, and institutions. The delirium that we now perceive as one form, results not only from our suspension of awareness of the disjointed concepts in history, but is also known by a comparison to the impossibility of the foreign attraction of a rejected system of thought. It operates like a distant memory from the history of science. It compels us to submit, to reflect, to resist, to recognise, and to finally act.

2 The representation of delirium

2.1. The measure of practicality

Psychology as a scientific enterprise will only be possible if it makes a return to a human condition of existence and to understand what is most human in man, namely his history. In 1890, William James wrote *The Principles of Psychology* and gave a detailed exposition of the brain-psyche unity (James, 1890). The absence of technology capable of being utilised to test psychological theories compelled the scientists of the time to engage mostly in theory building and an observation based evidence foundation for these theories. The first systematic theory that puts psychological disorders on a biological and consequently evolutionary foundation was Sigmund Freud. Building on this tradition, Freud and the network of collaborators and rivals would contribute to the psychoanalytical domain of psychology. The central preoccupation of this theoretical movement was the exploration of the unconscious psyche and its processes such as para-praxis, word association, memory systems, repression, hypnosis, and dreaming. The relationship between psychopathology and dreaming did not go unnoticed by Freud and became a constant source of evidence of the utility of dream analysis in the psychotherapy of patients (Freud, 1911). Unfortunately, the limitations of the time such as the cultural influence of a repressed and highly conservative Catholic Vienna rendered Freud's observations correct, but culturally skewed (Schwartz, 1999). The major emphasis that the phenomena of the psyche was founded upon a phylogenetic base is attributed to Carl Gustav Jung, and has enabled clinicians and researchers to identify many different, yet convergent, streams of psychological phenomena together e.g. dreams, culture, art, hallucinations, and mythology.

The origin and universality of these processes can be attributed to the archetypes of the collective unconscious (Campbell, 1976; Von Franz, 1999). These archetypes function as the structural and functional unit of the phylogenetic human psyche and enable humans to interact with their complex social and biological environment (Stevens, 2002). In 1907, Jung noted that the clinical picture of *dementia praecox* (now referred to as schizophrenia) was the same as dreaming and that the motor behaviour of the patient was such that they were acting out their dreams (Jung, 1907). Eugen Bleuler in his work, *Dementia Praecox*, also drew parallels between the cognitive processes of dreaming and patients with *dementia praecox* (Bleuler, 1911).

In reaction to these theories which attempted to establish a subjective account of the psyche, objective behaviourism emerged. For Burrhus Frederic Skinner, the psyche/brain was a *black box* where subjectivity could not be measured or accurately described and the experiences of the psyche were neither an appropriate object of scientific inquiry or even ineffable in principle. Language, symbolism, ideas, memory, affect, unconscious mental processes, and even the existence of the psyche itself have largely been ignored by this discipline. In the past century of academic psychology, there continued to be a tremendous disconnect between a psychology of objective behaviour and a psychology of subjective experience. Stevens uses the term *psychic agnosticism* to refer to theoretical perspectives that ignore the existence of the psyche (Stevens, 2002). Such a theoretical perspective is untenable with the continual progress of neuroscience, cognitive sciences, and other schools of psychology. Conversely, according to Peter Fonagy and Maria Tallindini-Shallice, psychoanalysis has engaged itself with the goal of establishing a psychological theory that has embraced the subjective experience (Fonagy & Tallindini-Shallice, 1993). Ideas initially discovered by psychoanalytical theory, such as repression, ego defence mechanisms, intra-psychic conflict, childhood sexual development, transference, and archetypes have all been found to be congruent and often rediscovered within the field of modern neuroscience and cognitive science (Mandler, 1975:3; Nesse & Lloyd, 1992: 601; Stevens, 2002). Behaviourism has retained its academic credibility due to its appeals to biological reductionism (also known as *neuromania*), in essence biased use of evidence derived from neuroscience to propose ultimately wrong positions (Tallis, 2012).

However, psychoanalytical theorists should not exist beyond the pale of criticism. The discipline of psychoanalysis has largely been based on *enumerate inductivism*, a process by which accumulated clinical examples are consistent with the model of the psyche that is being used. It is not capable of rejecting false positive observations and risks becoming an all-encompassing worldview. This situation negates any means of modifying theories or even rejecting aspects that are plainly incorrect. Such a state of affairs has been conceptualised as an epistemological breeding ground for opinions and theories to flourish and compete based on sophistry rather than evidence (Knox, 2003). This is a form of confirmation bias and is clearly poor scientific practice. The bias reaches a point where no objective evidence is capable of being determined. The models become sclerotic unto utter uselessness due to their inherent incapacity to be open systems of thought. For example, in a study of professional analysts engaged with the task of establishing a means of rating an analytic process, the researchers could not fulfil the task as there were no set criteria by which they could establish this fact (Vaughan et al., 1997).

Within the incomplete and fragmented science ofpsychology, one can situate the origin of the problems that plague delirium research. Cynicism resulting from the limitations of psychological theories has led to the mistaken belief that all theories and assumptions about the contents of consciousness can be excluded indefinitely. This is suggested by the removal of the term consciousness from the official criteria for delirium. The implicit principle now made manifest specifies a belief that when psychology is removed the innate structures and forms of the delirium phenomenon will be constituted by the account of disparate aspects of neuroscience to explain all possibilities of experience.

2.2. Composite empiricism

Our perception of the brain without a psyche, as the natural origin and distribution of delirium, is a space determined by the failure of previous researchers to define the object of their research and instead resort to a composite empiricism. In 1875, Richard Caton recorded the first ever electrical activity report of animal brains (Caton, 1875). In 1929, Hans Berger developed and discovered the method of electroencephalography (EEG) in humans (Berger, 1929). In 1937, these initial breakthroughs were applied by Loomis et al., (1937) to understand the activity of sleep. NREM sleep was characterised by sleep spindles, K complexes, vertex waves and delta slowing. In 1953, Nathanial Kleitman and Eugene Aserinsky discovered rapid eye movements (REM) in sleep and proposed that the REM sleep was associated with dreaming (Aserinsky & Kleitman, 1953). In 1957, William Dement and Kleitman organised sleep into four stages of NREM and 1 stage of REM sleep. Further developments into the human sleep cycle established that NREM was followed by REM in a cycle that repeated itself several times over the course of the night (Dement &

Kleitman, 1957). The discovery of the REM and NREM stages of sleep enabled researchers to accumulate enough evidence to substantiate the previous observations about the link between dreaming and the psychology of psychotic states. In 1927, Eugene Minkowski proposed that the sleeping state enables the manifestation of dreams with all their bizarre and irrational character. The inner life of desires manifested themselves in schizophrenia without the requirement of sleep (Minkowski, 1927). It has been proposed that REM sleep serves the function of restructuring the neocortical networks modified by the subjects experience during the day. Such a proposal is based upon REMs capacity to consolidate memories, in particular, relational memory and contextual memory, i.e. memory for organising encoded stimuli according to generalised similarities and to particular contexts of experience (Ellenbogen et al., 2007). The discovery and application of Lysergic acid diethylamide (LSD) to dream research and psychology in general were also an exciting avenue that has shed light onto the phenomena of the subjective psyche. The effects of LSD have also been shown to affect the serotonergic system, particularly as an antagonist of the 5HT1A receptor which in turn antagonises the brain stems serotonergic system. The decreased firing rate of the raphe nuclei coupled with the increase in frequency of the Ponto-geniculo-occipital (PGO) waves in the waking state is associated with the dreamlike state of hallucinations in waking consciousness. Hyper cholinergic activity in forebrain structures as well as decreased aminergic and serotonergic modulation are both demonstrated in dreaming states and psychosis (Benson & Zarcone, 2000; Bymaster et al., 2004; Gottesmann, 2006). It has also been found that there is a similarity between the physiology of the brain during REM and that of the psychotic state. Both states have significantly higher activity of the limbic systems coupled with hyperactivity of prefrontal cortex, in particular, the dorsolateral prefrontal cortex. Such enhanced emotional activity combined with dampened regulation of emotion leads to the experience of emotional lability observed in these states (Weinberger, 2002).

Understanding the regulation of these sleep/dreaming systems had also been part of this rapid history. The discovery of a functional neural substrate that mediates circadian behaviour had been discovered initially by the identification of the role the suprachiasmatic nucleus (SCN) plays in orchestrating the circadian timing system. In 1972, the elimination of circadian rhythms in neuroendocrine functions and motor behaviour were demonstrated in rats when their SCN was anatomically destroyed (Moore & Eichler, 1972; Stephen & Zucker, 1972). Such a finding may illuminate the link between disturbances in the circadian timing system and the motor subtypes of delirium. Robert Moore and Nicholas Lenn, discovered the existence of a retinohypothalamic tract that would act as a neural conduit for photic signals being detected in the retina and their resulting transduction to the hypothalamus, i.e. the SCN (Moore & Lenn, 1972). Later studies into the SCN identified various functions and behaviours such as the intrinsic rhythmicity of the neurons that make up the nucleus, the restoration of circadian rhythms with the reintroduction of a grafted SCN, and use of mutant strains of SCN to be implanted into host organism and resultant alterations in host circadian rhythms (DeCoursey & Buggy, 1988; Welsh et al., 1988; Ralph et al., 1990). In 1958, Melatonin was discovered in the pineal gland. In recent decades, melatonin synthesis has been shown to be derived from serotonin and regulated by ambient light (Axelrod & Weissbach, 1960; Fiske et al., 1960; Quay, 1960; Wurtman et al., 1964). The explanation of the circadian dysregulation of delirium has invoked the authority of many of these findings by singling out various particular findings and propping them up to explain the phenomenology of delirious experience as an epiphenomenon. In the absence of a robust paradigm, the use of a great many familiar similitudes of experience from the domain of medicine have been utilised to characterise our understanding of delirium.

The conceptual development of delirium has consistently recognised that it exists in the sole condition of extreme pathology. The interface between pathology and the human psyche requires an invocation of external elements that can impact upon the brain. It has long been recognised that cognitive dysfunction in humans can be induced by the administration of pro-inflammatory cytokines into the periphery. One model to explain the interactions between delirium manifestation and contributing factors is the sickness behaviour syndrome experience by humans. Significant alterations in mood, cognitive performance, and motivation can all be coordinated under a sickness behaviour response during an infection as described by Benjamin Hart. Behavioural aspects of this response include a change in motor activity with an altered directing of energy expenditure towards metabolic responses to sickness, i.e. fever, the humoral response, and social isolation (Hart, 1988). Biomolecules such as IL-1 RA and IGF-1, have also been found to be de-regulated in delirium (Wilson et al., 2005; Adamis et al., 2009a). Studies analysing blood and cerebrospinal fluid samples have suggested that such pro-inflammatory mediators impact upon the stress system (Pearson et al., 2010; Bisschop et al., 2011). A combination of impaired negative feedback functioning coupled with an aberrant stress response as a result of acute onset illness and infection has been observed as a general feature of the elevated cortisol seen in neurodegenerative diseases and the aging process in general. Cortisol has a negative impact upon mental status when pathologically elevated during responses to significantly demanding events such as surgery or illness (MacLullich, 2008). In elderly medical admissions and patients undergoing hip fracture repair, serum IL-6 and IL-8 has been found to be associated with the development of delirium, independent of baseline cognitive status or infection (de Rooij, 2007; Hall et al., 2011).

Patients suffering from delirium do so in the context of acute and critical illness and so direct research into this population is difficult. Instead similitudes of experience in the form of animal models have filled the theoretical void in order to furnish a more robust paradigm of delirium research. The development of animal models has seen the development of more lab-based models to test hypothesis pertaining to the pathogenesis of delirium. It has been proposed that the acute onset and measurability of severity render delirium an excellent target for the development of animal models, which have the added bonus of testing hypotheses, measuring clinically recognised precipitants, and risk factors directly (Cunningham & MacLullich, 2013). The first rodent model of delirium was composed of administering atropine (cholinergic muscarinic receptor antagonist) intraperitoneally, measuring its resulting slowing of EEG patterns, and observing acute onset cognitive impairment to tasks such as the blind alley maze (Leavitt et al., 1994). Later developments focused upon the role of pro-inflammatory processes and pro-inflammatory markers (e.g. lipopolysaccharide [LPS]) that would provide an animal model of severe sepsis. Cognitive functions have been shown to consistently detrimentally affect by challenges induced by inflammation, (Yirmiya & Goshen, 2011). However, the vast majority of these behaviour and cognitive studies have been based upon rodent models of these faculties and thus one must tread lightly when attempting to understand them in the context of human behaviour. In rodent models, for example, LPS has suppressive effects on motor activity, speed, and motivation which may be similar in humans, especially in the context of inflammation induced delirium (Cunningham &

Maclullich, 2013). Such models were done either by administering high doses of LPS to induce sepsis or surgically by caecal ligation and puncture which would in turn lead to sepsis due to poly-microbial infection. One such LPS induced delirium animal model showed the onset of acute alpha activity slowing in EEG (Semmler et al., 2008) Contextual memory is adversely effected by inflammation mediated by PGE2 and IL-1 (Hein et al., 2007; Frank et al., 2010). Cognitive flexibility tends to appear as the most labile and vulnerable faculties when exposed to systemic inflammation (Sparkman et al., 2006). However, other studies have highlighted how robust visuospatial memory and learning are when exposed to systemic infection (Jurgens et al., 2012).

Human studies of sickness behaviour have been conducted and confirm many of the findings from rodent modelling. Pro-inflammatory mediators such as LPS and INF-α (interferon alpha) have been shown to induce objectively behavioural and subjective emotional response of sickness (Grigoleit et al., 2011). Imaging studies have confirmed these subjective findings and observed neural changes implicated in these experiences of sickness (Harrison et al., 2009 a, b; Inagaki et al., 2012). However, what is less consistent is the variability of inflammation on cognitive performances in humans. If deficits manifest in otherwise healthy and young humans, the time course is very transient and compensatory mechanisms are believed to trigger a recovery response (Reichenberg et al., 2001; Grigoleit et al., 2010). Studies investigating the delirium-dementia continuum directly in humans have been very scarce and largely based on post mortem studies. Researchers have suggested that the mechanism that links these two phenomena may not be as a result of the typical pathophysiology of dementia (Davis et al., 2012). Elevated markers of CNS damage such as S100B have been found in hip fracture patients with states of active delirium

(Hall et al., 2013). Peripheral inflammation can often lead to infection of the CNS and lead to a condition referred to as septic encephalopathy. This can occur in all age groups and even in the absence of prior illness. The evidence would suggest that these extreme changes in behaviour do not fall within the spectrum of adaptive sickness behaviour. Human studies show that severe systemic infections are commonly associated with significant brain injury and long-term cognitive impairment in survivors (MacLullich et al., 2009; Iwashyna et al., 2010).

These studies broadly confirm the hypothesis that systemic inflammation increases the likelihood of delirium. An important caveat is that, apart from old age, prior cognitive impairment is the major risk factor for delirium, and such impairment may also be associated with higher levels of these cytokines (Lee et al., 2009). Indeed, in some studies, associations between proinflammatory cytokines such as IL-6 and delirium are lost when adjusted for prior cognitive impairment (van Munster et al., 2010). These data argue, like those of the ME7 animal model of delirium during dementia, that in humans, increased cytokines are associated with delirium, but may not be sufficient enough to induce delirium in the absence of prior vulnerability (Murray et al., 2012). If one accepts that there is utility in the findings from models of similitude, one must also recognise the significant gap between the experience of the delirious psyche and the source of its determinism. Drawing a parallel without a cohesive and robust theory limits the applicability of these separate experiments.

The latent grid of knowledge which organises every scientific discourse and defines what can or cannot be thought scientifically must also be combined with the active process of uncovering these levels. A constant and describable collection of concepts separated in time is a meaningless and ultimately useless constellation of features without a unifying understanding of how these can demonstrably be linked in a rational manner. Until the horizon of delirium research is expanded upon, the underlying paradigm will continue to exist in a mortified state and automatically disqualify its supporters from scientific discourse.

2.3. Plexus of significance

The paradigm is not only conditioned by the institutional inflections of society, but is also ordered by the idealised formal dimensions of the mind, i.e. the archetypes. The long ascending chain of knowledge progressively more detailed and laden with empiricism is a narrative composition laid out by the ego and hence held together by the proximity of logical relations. Dimensions of a paradigm can be transmitted. The narrower the gap between the historical loci, and hence paradigmatic experience, the more seamless the transition is. However, abrupt transformations can and do occur, which situate humanity in a place that is both familiar and alien; a position where one is confronted by the necessity of a detailed analysis of the existence of human nature. Understanding the various accounts of the significance of dreaming and delirium gives us key insights into the development of self-knowledge within scientific discourse.

These intimate experiences of life objectified by their universal form and personal content render them complex epistemological experiences that have undergone a multitude of interpretations. Let us furnish this exposition with fragmented historical examples from the literature on dreams. According to the ancient Greek literature discussing dreams, the meaning of dreams was not literal (Winkler, 1990: 27). A famous example from the *Histories* by Herodotus highlights this point. Hippias, the Greek traitor who served the Persians as their guide before they landed their army at Marathon, had a dream about sleeping with his mother and took it to mean that he would return to power in Athens after the war (Herodotus, History, 6.107). The maternal incest dreams of politicians were thought of as a good portent and indicated that the mother signified the nation-state and one's intercourse as signifying obedient and successful control over its executive institutions (Artemidorus, 1.79). However, in these early centuries empirical research was not entirely absent. *The Interpretation of Dreams (Oneirocritica)* was written by Artemidorus of Daldis around the 2nd Century AD. He wrote it after travelling for years doing field research in Greece, Italy, and many other regions (Stevens, 1997: 25). Artemidorus outlines his method for interpreting dreams, including categorising dreams into two broad groups, *enypnia* and *oneiroi*. *Enypnia* were manifestations of one's body state and its desires. *Oneiroi* were associated with the prophetic aspects of one's soul and being influenced by the gods. What is of interest is his observation that many dreams have complex cognitive structures such as linguistic devices involving puns, and a multifaceted relationship existed between dream images and their underlying meaning. He employed an empirical method that put dreams in the context of the dreamer's life (Stevens, 1997: 26).

Tertullian (c. 160-c. 225 AD), in his *Treatise on the Soul* (203 AD), believed that dreams came from three sources: God, nature (one's soul), and demons (Barnes, 1985). Therefore, dreams in this model existed independently of the will or the intention of the dreamer. During sleep, the soul leaves the body analogous to a brief death experience. St. Augustine also recognised the existence of the unconscious. St. Augustine refered to *illusio* (illusion), the term associated with the influence of demons over dreams, (Elliott, 1999:20). Gregory of Nyssa proposed that predominantly natural phenomena were capable of being understood psychologically, although God played a role in his model of the soul, as set out in his work entitled, *On the making of man*. The absurdity of dreams was due to the intellect and the senses being at rest when the person sleeps. The content of the dreams was composed of memories and the physiological state of the individual during sleep. Synesius of Cyrene proposed that there was a distinction between the mind and the soul and that the faculty of that fantasy acted as a mediator between these. The mind was the conscious domain of reality, the soul was a potentiality, and fantasy as a process of integration into consciousness. Stevens observes that these two early theorists foreshadow modern scientific theories regarding dreams proposed by Freud and Jung respectively (Stevens, 1997: 29).

Theoretical developments were not restricted to Christian Europe, but also existed in the Islamic world. According to Islamic medieval scholars, dreams could be organised into three different categories, the first being false dreams, the second being true dreams, and the third being patho-genetic dreams. The scholar Ibn Sirin (654-728) wrote two major works on dreams entitled, *Ta'bir al-Ru'ya* and *Muntakhab al-Kalam fi Tabir al-Ahlam*. He outlines his systematic method for interpreting dreams and promotes the practice of the public consulting of scholars (*Alim*) on their dreams. Other works by Islamic scholars included *On sleep and dreams* by Al-Kindus (801-873 AD), *On the cause of dreams* by Al-Farabi (872-951 AD), and *Muqaddimah* by Ibn Khaldun (1377 AD) (Khaldun et al., 1967; Haque, 2004).

Implicit in the dream theories of these scholars was the role of bad dreams, which may explain why bad and disturbing dreams, in other words, nightmares, has had sparse scholarship dedicated to it. Two major works in this area, one by Ernest Jones, *On the nightmare* (1971) and one by Wilhelm Heinrich Roscher, *Ephialtes* (1900) highlight the phenomena of nightmares being tied to a complex of conflicted eroticism since the ancient Greek world. According to Jones, this erotic dream-nightmare complex had a continuum of experiences from exclusively non-threatening erotic dreams to tense and tortuous erotically themed nightmares (Jones, 1971 [1931]: 42; 1974 [1932]: 111). Just as the theoretical frameworks developed moral dimensions, so too did treatment modalities. According to Michel Foucault, the content of dreams, especially erotic dreams, troubled ancient Greek and Roman physicians who prescribed a plethora of protocols to avoid their onset. Use of a lead plate to be placed besides one's testicles, having intercourse in the dark so that visual images associated with sex would not resurface during the dreaming state, and sleeping on one side were all examples of this aspect of preventive medicine (Foucault, 1986: 137). Other examples include, the Christian desire to indoctrinate the laity into the ascetic way of life and hence to resist sinful dreams ultimately lead to the publication of a number of penitential books. *The Irish penitential of Cummean* was modelled on Cassian's instructions for monks of the 5th century. Elaborate prayer formulas were introduced into the lives of Christians in an ever increasing attempt to exert control over it. The bed time prayer by Prudentius in his *Daily Round*, being an example of a method to ward off the sinful dream (Le Goff, 1988: 225; Prudentius, 1949).

A detailed understanding of nightmares later began to be imbued with Christian moral teachings. The ancient Greek term for nightmare was *ephialtes* meaning 'to jump on top of' (Chantaine, 1977). According to Roscher, the nightmare was imbued with an erotic dimension, and cites the identification of Pan with *ephialtes* in the ancient Greek mind, as cited by Artimedorus (Roscher, 1900). Themison of Laodicaea, the physician from

1st century AD, coined the term *pnigalion* (strangler) to refer to nightmares. Indeed, the Latin term *incubus* to refer to a demon that sleeps/lies upon the dreamer was coined at the beginning of the Common Era. The translation from *ephialtes* to *incubus* imbued with it the connotation of sexual activity, and provide a fine example of 'semantic contagion' (Hacking, 1995a). In 382 AD, Evagrius, an Egyptian monk, understood that the emotionally charged experiences stored in one's mind could be tapped into by demons and by doing so the demons could activate our sinful natures. The term *noonday demon* was used to describe boredom and despondency. The *noonday demon* would work against the intellect by partnering with the sensuous parts of one's soul (Evagrius, Praktikos, 36 [Guillaumont & Guillaumont, 1971]). He set out eight primal demons that are believed to be integrated with later theological thought as the seven mortal sins. What mattered most was their duration and if they were translated into action (Evagrius, Praktikos, 6 [Guillaumont & Guillaumont, 1971]). In the writings of Caelius Aurelianus, the *incubus* or the nightmare, was categorised as a sub-chapter with his chapter on madness and epilepsy. He proposed that if nightmares occurred frequently they were part of a chronic disease. He also highlights the experience of such nightmares as often being one of rape during sleep (On acute disease 1.3.56).

Paradigms are not characterless voids waiting to be stuffed with the accumulation of empirical findings to lay out their true form, but are constituted by the many hypotheses and theories that draw into its developing fold the desire of the researcher. In the context of delirium, the source of delirium was attributed to external physical causes. In the 5th Century Cassius Felix integrated the knowledge pertaining to the link between delirium and drunkenness (Lipowski, 1990: 12). In patients who were melancholic or mad, Chrysippus, theorised that there is a pronounced production of *phantasmata* (figments of one's imagination) from their minds. Such phenomena were distinguished from *phantasiai* (illusions based on real objects) (Long & Sedley, 1987: 237). The historian Procopius gave a detailed account of delirium in Constantinople in AD 542 during an epidemic of bubonic plague. His accounts resemble the modern description of hyperactive versus hypoactive delirium. Hyperactive delirium referring to insomnia, agitation, and sometimes violence while hypoactive was associated with prolonged sleeping and dulled cognition (Bury, 1958).

Moving forward to more familiar paradigms, we can perceive the Age of Enlightenment and the Renaissance as arguably the most important periods for the development of a scientific medicine. The mass production of publications, the growth of medical schools, and the rising power of the democratic state to usurp the previously held power of church and monarchy, all combined to contribute to its culmination. However, despite the new found enthronement of reason, challenges persisted. In the absence of robust paradigms, archetypal projections continued to dominate theoretical views on delirium and dreaming. The central position of reason made a scientific study of dreams rather unpalatable to researchers and thus, according to Freud in *The Interpretation of Dreams,* little had been done scientifically on dream theory due to its strong association with mysticism and religious ideas (Freud, 1900). Indeed according to Jones, approximately twenty-five works were published by physicians and scholars about the nightmare between 1650 and 1850 (Jones, 1971 [1931]: 14).

However, there was a slight shift in focus throughout this period. For instance, the meaning of the term *incubus* had changed from being a demonic presence to being an empirical set of physical perceptions imbued with medical explanations. In 1583, Weyer believed there was a physical explanation of the incubus phenomena, phlegm and melancholia may be contributory elements (Weyer, 1991 [1583]). In his *Anatomy of melancholy*, Burton attributes *'black meat'* (venison and hare) as being the source of these experiences (Burton, 1927 [1620]; 190). However, invocations of the supernatural continued to exist that complimented the descriptions of the nightmare which focused on somatic perceptions that accompanied its onset. Difficulty breathing, feeling a weight on one's chest, motor paralysis, and a sense of dread were and still are the most common experiences of its form. In the context of such a typical presentation of this parasomnia, the unconscious projected coherence onto these experiences in the form of the archetypal symbols of animals, people, elemental forces (humours), and demonic presences. In Andrew Baxter's work entitled, *Enquiry into the nature of the human soul* (1737), regarding nightmares, he reasons that since the human soul would not frighten itself that such bad dreams must be from the influence of external spirits (Ford, 1999: 178). In the medical literature of the 1760s, dreams with an erotic theme were categorised separately as part of medical doctrine on masturbation (Jaccard, 1975:11). Such dreams were a form of mental masturbation (*delectatio morosa*) (Ellis, 1936 (1898); Kinsey et al., 1948). John Waller describes the problematic existence of priapism as part of the nightmare experience (Waller, 1816:25). In congruence with this, Robert MacNish proposed that medical conditions such as angina, asthma and indigestion were possible causes of nightmares (MacNish 1830: 73, 124).

This trend is also apparent in the context of delirium. During the 16th century Ambroise Pare, a surgeon wrote about delirium as a complication of surgical procedures. He described delirium as a transient condition that commonly followed fever and pain due to wounds, gangrene, and operations involving severe bleeding of the patient (see Lipowski, 1990: 11). Thomas Willis the famous neuroanatomist is a key figure in the history of neuroscience and the medicine of the Enlightenment, and his most famous discovery was that of the circle of Willis; the cerebral vasculature of the brain. Willis departed sharply from the view held by the medical establishment of the humoral theory of mental health problems and psychological functioning. He did however, accept the theory that *phrenesis* and delirium were separate entities and were marked by the duration of psychological malfunctioning. One of his empirical observations (as a result of seeing an autopsy of an inflamed abscess within the diaphragm) had confirmed in his mind that the establishment theory of *paraphrenesis* (a type of pre-delirious state) was a result of an inflamed diaphragm. He also reported a number of pertinent risk factors such as old age, the severity of the febrile condition and the previous state of the patient's health as contributing to delirium pathogenesis (Eadie, 2003). However, despite his willingness to employ clinical observations to his discoveries in medicine, Willis believed that delirium was as a result of disturbed animal spirits. Such an account he believed explained delirium in the absence of fever (Eadie, 2003). Thomas Syndenham in the 17th century, applied empirical methods which led to the accumulated evidence to discredit the dominant humoral theory of disease. In the 17th century, the link between disturbed sleep, dreaming, and the circadian system became a more viable theory to account for delirium pathogenesis. Indeed, Richard Morton proposed that delirium was a state of a waking dream (Lipowski, 1990). The various terms dedicated to describing the delirious state were beginning to be differentiated and organised. Two important English medical dictionaries reflected another important shift in the 18th century. In 1719, Quincy stated in his English medical dictionary that 'delirium is the dreams of waking persons' (Quincy, 1719). In 1745, when James published his medical dictionary, the entry delirium, focused on the influence of the disturbed sleep-waking cycle to delirium (James, 1745). In 1749, hypnogogic and hynopompic states were described in the context of delirium by David Hartley. In 1794, symptoms such as altered states of consciousness and disorientation were introduced by Erasmus Darwin to differentiate delirium from so called *'madness'* (Hunter & Macalpine, 1963).

These now historical ontologies enable us to appreciate the interrelationship between the limits of knowledge, the absurd conclusions of a limited paradigm, and the dialectical nature of scientific discourse. The formalisation of knowledge that exists at the intersection of rationality and empiricism must all the while provide for itself opportunities to justify its methods and conclusions.

2.4. The interface between paradigms

The absence of scientific theory leads inexorably to the pure projection of archetypal motifs which imbue meaning onto the reductionist dimensions of empirical findings. These cruder cognitive processes operate and constitute elemental pattern recognition as part of the default mode of interpreting the world. The interface between paradigms is such an example of this circumstance, where projection exists and practices, such as alchemy and astrology, can exist congruently with the beginnings of a new paradigm, one in which would now be recognised as congruent with the contemporary scientific worldview. The clearest example of this is to be found in the interface between the middle ages and the Rennaissance.

At the fringes of orthodox medicine, folk medicine always dominated, and with it an emphasis on the supernatural dimension of things. Substances now known to be *deliriogenic* such as scopolamine, hyoscyamine, and atropine were utilised for folk medicinal purposes. Historically, many plants now considered to have *deliriogenic* properties, e.g. henbane (*Hyoscyamus niger*), deadly nightshade (*Atropa Belladonna*), and mandrake (*Mandragora officinarum*) were mixed together as potions. The potions were of such strength that they were regarded as magical and the experiential effects such as feelings of flying, and hallucinations of demons, snakes, and rats were associated with pagan witchcraft. Such potions served a wide variety of purposes, such as anaesthesia, as well as more exciting psychoactive-enabling properties. According to Richard Schultes, henbane has been used since recorded history for its pain relieving ability and was also used to relieve suffering brought by torture and death. It was noted that its major ability was not pain relief, but rather the induction of a state of oblivion wherein the individual did not recall the experience (Schultes & Smith, 1976). Deadly nightshade, also known as *Atropa belladonna* (meaning beautiful lady) gets its name due to the antiquated use of it by women to use the sap of the plant in order to dilate their pupils. In ancient Greek cultures during their ceremonial orgies, *Maenods* (women who were initiated into the cult rites of Dionysus) would dilate their eyes and proposition men. Many would enter a state of erotomania, and in their frenzied state dismembered the males. Roman priests often drank potions containing belladonna before their ceremonies honouring the god of war and seeking victory (Roberts & Wink, 1998).

Despite meagre attempts by folk medicine to tackle health problems, the Christian church as the sole authority over medicine, still cast suspicion upon these practices and relegated them to acts of witchcraft. For example, in the 13th century Bishop Albertus the Great reported that henbane was a substance commonly employed by necromancers to conjure demons. It was also recognised that for the initiation of new members into a witches' coven, the initiates would consume a potion containing henbane in order to perform the initiation rites of these groups. It had been observed that those who were intoxicated by this substance felt a sensation of someone forcing closed their eyelids and applying pressure to their head. Visual acuity became problematic and common objects had severely distorted shapes as well as experiencing powerful visual, gustatory, and olfactory hallucinations. The intoxication phase ended with sleep and during that sleep disturbed dreams continued to be experienced. These experiences have been researched extensively in the modern world and are coupled with other autonomic effects such as restlessness motor behaviour, tachycardia, vomiting, pupil dilation, and hyperpyrexia (Roberts & Wink, 1998). Here we can further juxtapose the differences in paradigms.

During the medieval period in Europe when witchcraft became more widespread it had been reported that belladonna was often mixed with henbane, mandrake, and the fat of a stillborn baby to produce a potent substance called 'witch's salve'. Such a concoction was applied to the skin or often inserted into the vagina for enhanced absorption. The witch's broomstick is believed to have been associated with this practice. Schultes cites an account of an investigation into witchcraft in 1324, which alleged that women accused of witchcraft often had pipes of ointment that they would use to smear the shaft of the broomstick and then would be held between their legs. Such reports were found to continue into the 15th century (Schultes & Smith, 1976). Witch-hunting manuals such as the *Malleus maleficarum*, depicted detailed accounts of the sexual assault on women by *incubi* and on men by *succubi*. (Kramer & Sprenger, 1970 [1486]). However, theologians of the Renaissance struggled with the reality of the accounts of demons and witches.

Another source of *deliriogenic* substances which gives us insight into the perspective of the period is the Mandrake root. This root had a significant role in the magical practices of Europe, primarily due to its psychoactive potency. Effects ranged from hallucinations, dream experiences and erotomania/aphrodisiac induction. Other elements of its significance included its resemblance to a human figure. Such similarities invoked the nature of *the doctrine of signatures* which was practiced in magic. Such a resemblance to the human body led many to believe that it had tremendous potential supernatural powers over the human both in mind and body, such as Pythagoras in 5th century BC. In the 3rd century BC, Theophrastus gave an account of elaborate rituals associated with the harvesting of this root. Josephus Flavius in the 1st century AD gives an account of taming the mandrake with urine and menstrual blood. Further myths indicated that at night the mandrake would shine like a star and could only be pulled from the ground by a black dog (a colour associated with evil and death). The mandrake would scream as it was being pulled out and it was dangerous for a human to try and extract it. Christian myths indicate that the mandrake was an early attempt by God to make a human. Roman magic practices began to associate its powers more with its actual psychoactive properties. Throughout medieval Europe it was believed that the mandrake would grow from the semen or urine of a hanged man. By the 16th century scholars began to be disenchanted by myths, but myths continued to be manifest well into the 19th century (Schultes & Smith, 1976).

A key compoenent to all paradigmatic shifts is the transformation of institutional practices. It was not until the founding of the medical college of Salerno in Italy in the 11th century that a systematic professional form of medicine re-emerged. The development of new schools continued throughout the 12th century and in the 13th century and the public was demanding that physicians have many years of training before they practice their art (Bowers, 2007). The Renaissance movement reignited the passion for critical and dynamic scholarship in Christian Europe. The translation of ancient texts from Greek and Arabic into modern Latin enabled European scholars to quickly accumulate knowledge from these sources and integrate them with the practical advances from Islamic culture and its scientific medicine. The advent of the experimental and observational methods that would become the hallmark of the scientific method grew during the later centuries of the Renaissance. Ancient taboos such as human cadaveric dissections were overcome and a wealth of medical knowledge was gleamed from this new human anatomical science (Getz, 1998). During the 16th century, Fracastoro described delirium in the context of disorientation in addition to other patient behaviours such as hyper vigilance or lassitude. Often these behaviours might exist in the same patient, sometimes alternating in the course of the day or alternating over a few days (Lipowski, 1990: 8). Vesalius investigated human anatomy and recorded details of the brain. It is believed that he corrected hundreds of mistakes made by Galen. However the true function of the brain was still largely unknown and attributed to the ventricular flow of energy and or humours (Bowers, 2007).

As is often the case that in the transition from one paradigm to another there is often a figure that is a combination of the two world views. Such a combination can lead to a dissonant view of the world and the self. Paracelsus is one such figure. Paracelsus (1493-1541 AD) who is regarded as the father of pharmacology and toxicology was also a highly zealous Christian alchemist. According to the psychiatrist Jung, Paracelsus was a man of two hearts. He was a combination of a Renaissance humanist and a materialist, but still subscribed to a world based on alchemical and mythological interpretations. He believed in a connection between the divine and the worldly, and his practice of medicine reflected that. He disdained cadaveric dissections in the absence of astrological consultation and decried classical empirical medical practitioners. He burned the published works of Hippocrates, Galen, and Avicenna and denied vehemently the humoral doctrine in medicine. He established the practice of iatro-medicine and the use of minerals as a treatment for many illnesses based primarily on his alchemical interpretation of nature and the human body. Paracelsus proposed that *phrenitis* (feverish delirium) was as a result of a deregulated *archeus*, a neural organiser of the will and a tripartite chemical system of salt, mercury, and sulphur (Montiel, 1998).

The interface between two paradigms is not restricted to distant history, but is an ongoing engagement with the limitations of our contemporary paradigm. A far less florid figure is John Allan Hobson, who can be regarded as one of the major modern theorists who has rigorously drawn parallels between the phenomenology and thus neurobiology of dreaming and delirium. In his 1999 book *Dreaming as delirium*, he acknowledged the role early theorists such as Jung, Freud, and Bleuler, in understanding dreaming and its relationship to delirium and psychosis in general. In contrast to psychoanalytic methods such as free association, active imagination, and amplification, Hobson examined the form of dreams rather than the content. Interestingly, Hobson choose as his instrument the mental state exam of medicine and applied it to dreams (Hobson, 1999). The same mental state exam, serves as the basis for the psychometric assessment tools for delirium, for example, the Delirium rating scale (DRS) and its revised version DRS-R98. Applying the comprehensive account of delirium as outlined in Lipowskis' work, Trespacs et al., developed a psychometric tool that would describe and measure the phenomenology of delirium, first with the delirium rating scales in 1988 and then a more revised version that tackled many of the previous versions short comings (Adamis et al., 2013). We can appreciate from this series of periods how the interaction at the most intimate level, the mind of the theorist, between the structural idealised forms of medical discourse and many of historical precedents from which inspiration if drawn. This offers a moment of light without effulgence to realise that the great epistemological obstacie is ourselves and how we situate ourselves not only in our current paradigm, but as a process of understanding previous paradigms.

2.5. Reconfiguration of death

Within medicine, there is the implicit belief that knowledge can progress towards an enhanced objectivity. Such is our paradigm, which has at its core the principle of learning from past discoveries and using them to inspire the development of a treatment strategy for delirium. To cluster them around the aim of inspiring a method by which medicine can address delirium, we must forsake the taboo of anachronism and accept that a configurational account of these treatments must be recognised as a reconstruction of a narrative that must be fabricated. Hence the cautious and punctuated tempo of this historical description. To state, to re-state, to circumambulate, to retrieve from the dustbin of history, all salient factors pertaining to delirium, and to reflect upon its relationship to cultural parallels, while being mindful of the ever pervasive temptation to join together these disparate elements to produce a seamless totality. It is these aspects that will be analysed here.

Treatment of delirium has always been largely focused on symptom based management and the modification of factors that may exacerbate delirium onset and duration (Meagher & Leonard, 2008). One of the earliest attempts to actively manage delirium was proposed by Aretaeus of Cappadocia, who is known in the history of medicine for first dividing diseases into acute and chronic. Furthermore, he distinguished the chronic condition dementia from the acute condition delirium (Lipowski, 1990: 6). He suggested putting the delirious patient in light if disturbed by the dark and in darkness if disturbed by the light. In order to induce sleep, he proposed the administration of a potion composed of poppy boiled in oil (Lipowski, 1990: 11).

The transition to more contemporary paradigms enables us to identify more familiar methods but identify consistent problems. The current treatment strategies often see delirium as a discrete entity that can be treated with a panacea. In 1914, pre-senile dementia and 'backward children' were alleged to be treated in a controlled trial with pineal extracts (Berkeley, 1914). Pineal extracts (referred to as Epiglandol) were administered to patients with acute psychosis (Bigelow, 1975). It is interesting to note that with the discovery of melatonin, the major hormone secreted by the pineal gland was found to have ubiquitous effects on the body, ostensibly confirming Descartes perspective on the pineal gland (Baker, 1985). Melatonin has also been shown to have a critical role in mental health problems such as affective disorders, schizophrenia, anxiety disorders and obsessive compulsive disorder, sleep and circadian rhythm disorders (McIntyre, 1990; Kennedy, 1994; Monteleone et al., 1994; Arendt, 1995; Zhdanova et al., 1995; Jan & O'Donnell, 1996; Karasek, 1999). The modern development of melatonergic drugs for delirium and dementia has continued this tradition to this day, even though it is based on more robust neuroscientific knowledge. Acknowledging the spectre of panacea enables us to broaden the self-imposed restrictions on our current treatment paradigm (de Roij et al., 2014).

In opposition to the panacea model, there exists the prophylactic model. The emergence of old age psychiatry in post WWII Britain was pioneered by Felix Post who established a tradition of precise diagnosis and provided prophylactic measures for patients admitted to acute hospital settings. Post proposed the role of acute physical illness as a major contributing factor to the induction of delirium. He stated that 'in avoiding breakdowns necessitating admission to a mental hospital, early recognition and treatment of physical illness and the provision of adequate nutrition as well as sleep are the main prophylactic measures.' (Post, 1962). The success of the prophylactic model will depend entirely on methods of identifying delirium. Therefore, the improved characterisation of its phenomenology has been proposed as a critical cornerstone of improved care and patient outcomes (Gupta et al., 2008). To put it more directly, we must achieve three goals, 1) have an evidence based theory of delirium, 2) how to differentiate it from other conditions that may share some of its diffuse features and co-exist conditions such as depression and dementia, and 3) identify its prodromal and sub syndromal dimensions so that it can be prevented. Between 1988 and 1990, Inouye et al., developed the Confusion Assessment Method (CAM) as an assessment tool that would greatly improve the recognition and identification of delirium. The success of this method is such that it is still the most widely utilised tool in delirium research. This is in part due to its ease of use and its robust validity (Inouye et al., 1990; Yang et al., 2013).

It is now recognised that as a complex neuropsychiatric syndrome, delirium's time-course is rendered heterogeneous. Previously held to be a transient disorder and one that is often self-limiting, delirium management is dependent upon treatment of the underlying pathological tributaries that contributed to the phenomenology of brain failure. Persistent delirium has been identified in approximately 20% of patients. Such persistent delirium is marked by having features of delirium (attention deficits and motor disturbances) for three and sometimes six months after the onset of the initial delirious state. This is a marked difference relative to the typical time-course of delirium which lasts from a few hours to a few weeks (Meagher et al., 2012). Notwithstanding the resolution of most delirium, these episodes have serious long term consequences. It is now known that delirium predicts multiple adverse outcomes, including increased length of stay, morbidity, institutionalisation, and mortality during admission and one year after discharge (Witlox et al., 2010). Moreover, in cognitively normal patients, an episode of delirium is associated with a higher risk of dementia in the years following the episode (MacLullich et al., 2009; Davis et al., 2012). Delirium is also often highly distressing for patients and carers and may result in post-traumatic stress disorder (Davydow et al., 2008; Fong et al., 2009).

According to a seminal paper by Sharon Inouye (1999), there has been the development of hospital wide programmes that tackle delirium at a systems level. This programme focuses on active screening and close monitoring of patients cognitive and behavioural status (Zaubler et al., 2013). According to a paper by MacLullich et al., (2013) the features of a delirium-friendly hospital were discussed as a means to tackle this problem which exists across all clinical settings. These characteristics included, 1) health care professionals possessing functional knowledge of delirium, 2) routine delirium screening, 3) available patient education on delirium for patients and their families, 4) existence of prevention measures both in treatment and in the environment, and 5) specialist care available.

The proportion of the world's population over 65 years old is increasing. As a syndrome that disproportionately affects elderly patients it is highly probable that the proportion of the population over 65 years old will increasingly become more exposed to this condition. Postoperative delirium is especially associated with significantly worse outcomes such as an increased risk for neurodegeneration, mortality, extended hospital stay, and increased health care costs (Marcantonio et al., 1994; Fong et al., 2009). Furthermore, as the number of citizens retiring increases, sources of revenue to fund public health services may be greatly diminished. Moreover, health care delivery systems have to radically adjust their priorities to meet the demand of this radical demographic shift (Getzen, 2014). To discover solutions we must recognise our capacity for historical hindsight and perhaps be bold enough to not wait for history to unfold before us. Instead, we can acknowledge the self-evident truth that prevention may be our best option instead of a cure.

Part II The structure and dynamics of the psyche

3 Ego and experience

3.1. The functions of the ego

We must confront a terrifying fact, as it is, delirium in its distressing volatility, in its elusive content, is a temporal horizon between meaning and nothingness. Understanding the content of delirium may reveal a superior understanding of its overall phenomenology, particularly if we are to improve the current scientific account of the neurocognitive processes that are characteristically lost with the onset of delirium. In theory, delirium can be understood to be a constellation of features which can be organised into objective signs and subjective symptoms (Franco et al., 2013).

The ego is the locus of all experience and is the focus of what we consider to be a key component of our consciousness. To understand the link between the different features of delirium a conceptual account of the ego must be undertaken. In *The Ego and the Id,* Freud summaries and develops the concept of the ego. The ego was theorised by Freud as a sense of I, and as an entity that enables a human to interact with the external world of the environment and the internal world of the psyche. The ego must not be conceived of as a corpuscular psychological entity, but as a complex of psychological processes that have both conscious and unconscious dimensions (Freud, 1923). The ego as a coherent whole pertains to a great number of interrelated psychological functions such as, 1) executive cognition, 2) psychological homeostasis, 3) social engagement and language, and 4) the developmental relationship between identify and the archetype of the Self. The final priorities of the ego are to signify the subject with cohesion and meaning, which is to say, the psyche can endure intolerable suffering regardless of the distance from the process of symbolisation. The most common altered state of consciousness encountered in society is unfortunately a pathological one, delirium. To understand the experience of delirium, its relationship to dreaming, and the underlying evolutionary derived neurobiology that links them both, it is imperative that the psychological agent of experience, the ego, is clearly understood. To that effect an account of what is experienced by both the ego of the patient and the health care professional is required. The unitary form delirium is therefore emboldened by the conceptually counterfeit separation of two loci of experience.

The experience of delirium by the health care professional has been codified systematically and investigated through the lens of scientifically derived instruments and theories. When analysing patients with delirium it has been found that they are at a significant risk of adverse and tragic clinical outcomes which oscillate between the foci of elevated morbidity and mortality (Kakuma et al., 2003; Leslie et al., 2005; Kiely et al., 2009). But despite its wide ranging implications for patients and the identifiable components of its aetiology, it is poorly recognised and worse still misdiagnosed in clinical practice (Kishi et al., 2007; Collins et al., 2010).

Delirium is a complex phenomenological entity that is as unique as the psyche that experiences it. Yet modern conceptualisations of delirium have been influenced by the tools used to assess, detect, and analyse its complex and transient nature (Adamis et al., 2010, 2013). Studies analysing the phenomenology of delirium have previously been based on cross sectional methods and have thus presented a static picture of delirium. Given that delirium is a fluctuating and reversible condition, an accurate analysis of its phenomenology must take into account these key features. Therefore, accurate characterisation of its nature must be based on longitudinal analysis of it (Adamis, 2009).

Disturbances of cognitive domains in delirium have been organised into general cognition (attention, orientation, affect lability, short term memory, and long term memory), and higher cognitive dysfunctions (language and thought disorder) (Franco et al., 2013). Although statistical analysis has indicated a rough organisation between general and higher cognition, these terms are very vague and are not isomorphic with clearly defined neurobiological substrates (Tittle & Burgess, 2011; Cabeza & Moscovitch, 2013). To put another way, the categories of general cognition and higher cognition are reflective of incomplete accounts of cognition, rather than reflective of empirical evidence gleaned from contemporary neuroscience and integrated to a refined theory of delirium cognitive dysfunction (Pessoa, 2008; Waring et al., 2010; Chou et al., 2013). One of the proposals that is laid out in this work is the re-examination of these cognitive domains in terms of primary and secondary consciousness and the development of assessments based on processes within those forms of consciousness.

3.2. Executive cognition

Executive cognition is a term used to describe those cognitive processes that require the ego in their performance. Attention and orientation are pivotal systems involved in executive cognition. The domain of executive cognition is one of the most complicated disturbances found in patients with delirium and is also pertinent to understanding the psychology of dreaming (Hobson, 1999). There is no one region dedicated to the phenomena of the ego, rather there are multiple regions and systems dedicated to the collection of processes, which together make up the ego (D'Argembeau, 2013). This is further proof that the ego is not a singular entity, but rather the agency of cohesion for these functions (Crone et al., 2013). The prefrontal cortex (PFC) is one of the phylogenetically youngest structures of the mammalian brain and given its high connectivity with the rest of the brain is it believed to be most suitable region to serve a number of the integrative functions of the ego (Kim & Johnson, 2014). The components' of this region of the brain serves executive cognition in the form of dissociable mechanisms with a broad degree of localisation to an underlying neuroanatomical region (Robbins, 1997; Aron et al., 2004). The PFC has also been implicated in complex integrative functions such as the regulation of emotions, memory retrieval, and social determinants of cognition (Gilbert & Burgess, 2008). Neuromodulation changes the dynamic nature of the brain and thus the psyche. For the purposes of clarity, neuromodulation refers to the complex interplay between various neurochemical systems that augment, enhance or diminish the otherwise fast electro-chemical signalling of neural networks (Sarter et al., 2005). Despite the on-going debate over the role of the PFC in executive cognition, it is known to have evolved and now functions as a regulatory region over the ascending neuromodulatory systems of dopamine (DA), norepinephrine (NE), serotonin or 5-hydroxytryptamine (5-HT), histamine, orexin, as well as acetylcholine (Ach), with some systems originating from the reticular regions of the brain stem and others from the mid brain and diencephalon (Amat et al., 2005; Robbins, 2005). Overall, these systems involved in neuromodulation have major roles in attention specifically augmenting the signal-to-noise ratio of encoding of neural representations. To further widen our understanding of executive cognition in delirium and dreaming, we must understand another principle function of the neuromodulatory effects upon the PFC. The Yerkes-Dodson, inverted U-shaped function which links the activity level of the ascending systems (mainly DA-ergic and NE-ergic) to the performance of executive cognition and its efficiency (Robbins, 2013a). Pharmacological investigations have largely revealed this inverted U dose effect (Gibbs & D'Esposito 2006).

Cholinergic neuromodulation from the basal forebrain cortico-petal system is the most rostral of the cortical systems. The entire neocortical mantle has its information processing modulated by this system and may provide insight into the unique human qualities of dreaming and delirium (Hedreen et al., 1984; Everitt & Robbins, 1997; Sarter & Bruno, 1997; Sarter et al., 2005). One hypothesis to account for the role of cholinergic neuromodulation is through signal-driven detection systems. The detection of signals that is required for attentional performance is dependent on the coherent quality of the cholinergic inputs to the neocortex. The properties of the signal (often referred to as signal driven) and the augmentation of signal detection are both mediated by this diffuse system. Such systems may elucidate the necessary integrative functions of amplified thalamo-cortical input and decreased associational informational encoding (Sarter et al., 2014).

Impaired cholinergic neuromodulation is a critical component to understanding delirium (Flacker et al., 1998; Flacker & Lipsitz, 1999; Trzepacz, 2000). Plasma and cerebrospinal fluid levels of acetylcholine have been reported in patients with delirium and have consistently been found to be significantly decreased (Golinger et al., 1987; Flacker & Wei, 2001; Plaschke et al., 2007). Age related changes in the cholinergic system may mediate the disturbance in executive cognition detected in delirium. Age related changes may manifest as decreased oxidative metabolism involved in Ach synthesis as well as the proposed hypothesis that the volume of Ach producing cells decreases with age, which may account for the advent of delirium in elderly patients (Gibson et al., 1981; Gibson & Peterson, 1981; 1983; Jansson et al., 2004).

In the context of delirium, attention is considered a core feature of delirium and is consistently kept as a cornerstone of its clinical diagnosis (Franco et al., 2013). Attention is dominated by two aspects, the first being external stimuli and the second being internal goals/bias (Noudoost et al., 2010). Selective attention is a cognitive faculty that enables the filtering out of irrelevant sensory information to further enhance our capacity to detect relevant information. It is one of the most well studied cognitive functions in neuroscience due to its role in many neuropsychiatric disorders (Robbins & Arnsten, 2009). Attention can be deployed to various characteristics such as specific locations in a space, a feature of the environment or an object (spatial, feature based, object-based attention respectively). Such deployment can be due to the voluntary, i.e. top-down, exogenous process or due to the salience of the stimuli, i.e. bottom up, endogenous (Noudoost et al., 2010). The majority of research has focused on the voluntary top down attention, however, both originating aspects of attention play a role in the execution of attention (Mirabella et al., 2007; Burrows & Moore, 2009).

The adaptive function of attention provides a process by which specific neural representations of features of sensation can be selected (and thus filtered) so that further processing can occur. The filtering process also involved the amplification of behaviour that is relevant to this information while directing behaviour away from irrelevant information. In other words, the main aim of attention is to increase the information output of specific populations of neurons that encode the relevant (selected representation of the sensation) to thus increase the signal-to- noise ratio of information input from the environment or internal milieu of the body (Noudoost et al., 2010).

The theoretical proposals of how neurons and thus the brain do this are many. The selected signals of information might be strengthened and thus enable their rapid progress to the more elaborate integrative processing stages of executive cognition. Accumulating evidence derived from electrophysiological studies indicates that the firing rate of neurons mediates the enhanced signal efficiency that is required and may do this via synchronising the neuronal populations that are encoding the information that is the focus of attention. One such example is the synchronisation of neuronal output of high frequency activity, which may have an effect on downstream areas and their respective spikes in activity (Salinas & Sejbiwski, 2001; Azouz & Gray, 2003; Tiesinga et al., 2008). Local field potentials (LFPs) and the inter/intra coherence amongst these spikes provides a mechanism by which phase locking amongst neurons occurs, thus leading to localised facilitation of integrating these spikes with the desired goal of encoding the information of attention and continuing the integration process via post synaptic signalling (Bichot et al., 2005; Taylor et al., 2005; Womelsdorf, 2006; Saalmann et al., 2007). The routing of information from the attention system enables the guiding of behaviour and decisions. Some studies have highlighted the existence of long range synchrony between groups of neurons. The link between these distant yet functional regions may provide the associated temporal reference domain that is required for integrative communication (Buschman & Miller, 2007; Saalmann et al., 2007; Gregoriou et al., 2009; Fries, 2009).

Orientation to time, place and person is a key component of robust cognitive functioning and hence must be considered intimately associated with attention. Indeed orientation is one of the first aspects of cognition that health care professionals test when patients are presenting with potential brain malfunction. In the hospital setting, patients can mistake the hospital for a more familiar place, such as a hotel or even their home, depending on the severity of their confusion. There is also marked exacerbation of orientation at night (associated with sundowning), thus suggesting a relationship between circadian rhythms, sleep systems, and orientation (Meagher & Trzepacz, 2009). When orientation is disturbed for instance, in recovery from electro-convulsive therapy (ECT), the post ECT delirium indicates that there is an order by which components of orientation return. The first being, person, then place, and finally time (Lipowski, 1990). Such an order continues to provide indirect evidence of orientation as a function of the ego due to the proximity of the cohesive sense of identity that the ego serves. Disturbances in orientation are part of the three domain theory of delirium while, lack of orientation is a consistent finding from dream reports. Hobson draws the parallel that the lack of orientation is based on a similar underlying neural substrate (Hobson, 1999). Orientation is not a solitary function and thus an attempt at understanding the underlying neural and psychological aspects of it require an understanding of what is the composition of the phenomenology of orientation. Orientation is composed of three broad based systems, the arousal system (often referred to as the level of consciousness), attention, and memory (Trzepacz, 1999). Orientation can be considered as a compound psychological function based upon attention and the autobiographical self. The autobiographical self is the aspect of the ego that is responsible for processing and encoding stimuli pertaining to one's identity and one's environment (Damasio, 2012). This aspect of identity has to be intimately bound with both explicit and implicit memory systems in order to retrieve and reproduce information about one's body, one's name and memories about one's life (Cabeza & St Jacques, 2007; Platek et al., 2008; Tacikowski et al., 2011). Studies investigating the neural correlates of these functions have been based on the theory of the 'self-referent effect', in other words, the psychological processing of differentiating others from one's self (Rogers et al., 1977). The neural structures implicated in the optimal functioning of this aspect of the ego are cortical midline structures which include the medial prefrontal cortex (MPFC), anterior cingulate cortex (ACC), and posteromedial cortices (PMCs) (Northoff et al., 2006).

However, one must blend this account with deeper evidence from other sources. The depth of neuroscientific detail to explain psychological processes should not forbid further inquiry into the content of delirium. Equally important to a more complete understanding is the role of the psychological processes required for furnishing the interior landscape of the psyche, its symbolism, its significances, and its self-imposed limitations upon experience.

3.3. Interpreting signs and symbols

The disturbed perceptual experiences of delirium, for instance hallucinations and delusions, have been shown to be significantly absent from those of more florid neuropsychiatric disturbances (Trzepacz et al., 2011). Such a difference is believed to be as a result of neurocognitive impairment resulting from failure of the patients generalised brain function (Carpenter, 2014). However, vivid dreams and nightmares are often associated with the onset of delirium (Koster et al., 2012). Therefore, the presence and or conspicuous absence of signs and symbols expressed by the patient's unconscious in dreams may enable health care professionals to identify the pernicious onset of subsyndromal delirium and perhaps differentiate it from full syndromal delirium. The reason being is that if the patient's psyche is capable of generating normal, healthy dreams, i.e. an intact virtual sensorium during sleep, then it would suggest their brain is optimally functional, given that dreaming serves as the basis of protoconsciousness (Hobson, 2009). As such, methods of interpreting the content of dreams may be applied to patients at risk of delirium to test any of these hypotheses.

Dream interpretation is haunted by the conceptual methods of hermeneutics that have composed the majority of its developmental legacy. Indeed, the term hermeneutics itself derived from the Greek messenger of the gods, Hermes, betray this scandalous origin in mysticism (Smythe, & Baydala, 2012). The interpretation of dream content has largely been based upon cultural interpretive methods such as the cipher method and the analogous symbolic method. The cipher method is based on the assumption that dream content is a code that can be understood by translating it into an already established code. Examples of this include the use of dream dictionaries. The analogous symbolic method is derived from the prophetic tradition of dream interpretation and serves to replace the dream content as a whole with an analogous intelligible comparison. Often this method focuses upon forecasting the future and many examples can be found in the Old Testament (Freud, 1900). In contrast to these pre-scientific methods, Freud proposes the use of free association. Free association is based upon the premise that the components of the dream have two dimensions, the manifest content and the latent content. The manifest content is that which is experienced by the dreamer when asleep. The latent content is the result of unconscious psychological processes such as condensation, displacement, (Freud, 1900). The latent content is unconscious, and hence is composed of processes, of which we are unaware, that are involved in producing the manifest content. The purpose of free association is to highlight the latent content and integrate it with consciousness so that it would add insight into the problems experienced by the patients.

The difference between symbols and signs in the experience of dreams also needs to be stated. The nature of signs is that they are codified elements that link and connect an element with another in a chain of association, encoded by our memory systems. Symbols have aspects of this sign encoding and processing, but have an additional dimension, a more affect driven dimension that is beyond conscious thought and experienced as numinous. Such symbols transcend the faculties of rational thought and connect the individual psyche with the ontological category of the transcendent (Beebe, 2004). In mythology, it is through the symbols that complexes which are unconscious can be understood by the conscious ego as well as by empirical observers (Cambray, 2001). Building upon the method of free association, Jung employed an expanded model of dream psychology. The methods and theory were derived from his conception of the psyche as a whole. Although free association enabled a patient and therapist to identify through the connecting of images and thoughts the structure and function of the unconscious complex, within the dream itself, there were dimensions of symbols that could not be traced back to memory experiences. They were by definition transcendent of the person's life. They were representing something new in the person's life, but old in the sense of being a phenomenological expression of the phylogenetic psyche. These symbols were based upon archetypes (Kubrick, 2008).

The archetype was an evolving concept to Jung and no clear definition of it exists (Hogenson 2004). Jung described them as forms without content, and environmentally dependent. He also made the distinction between archetypal expressions which were composed of archetypal images (and their ideas) and the *archetype as such*, which is described as the 'irrepresentable' existence of the archetypes (Jung, 1959). Modern researchers have redefined the archetype as an 'image schema', 'action pattern', 'domain specific algorithms', and 'mathematical principle of organization in a non-linear system' (Hogenson, 2001; McDowell, 2001; Knox, 2003; Hogenson, 2009; Stevens, 2013). Modern neuroscience talks of neurognosis in terms of the knowledge of our experience as being derived exclusively from the underlying neural substrate. The initial organisation of the brain mediates its functions of experience and cognition (Laughlin, 1996). The structural and functional components of the brain laid out during foetal and early infancy have significant genetic and molecular guidance. Given that these components are unknowable in and of themselves, only the temporal and perceptual dimensions of them can be known. This indicates that these inherited functional units are the neural substrate of the archetypes of the collective unconscious (Laughlin & Loubser, 2010). The neocortex being a complex neural system that is based upon a 'cognitive imperative' in turn composes a coherent understanding of all domains of experience (d'Aquili & Newburg, 1999). This cognitive imperative drives the neurognosis function by integrating altered states of consciousness with symbols from the collective unconscious to produce for example, mythological motifs (Laughlin, 1996).

According to Jean Knox, the 'irrepresentable' *archetype as such*, is based upon the neural substrate of the image schema. This construct develops from bodily experience, as encoded by multimodal imagoes in the ventro medial prefrontal cortex (VMPFC) and forms the foundation for abstract meanings. These schemas have the dual function of creating an interpretive order for the external world and the internal world of metaphor. These components, then serve as the abstract scaffolding by which images and other symbolic contents can then be integrated with to create the archetypal symbol. Such an account of archetypes negates Lamarkian explanations of the origin of these very real phenomena of the psyche (Knox, 1997, 2004). Encoding of stimuli that is highly affective to the ego complex involves roughly three main psychological processes. The first is internalisation, whereby abstract cognitive models of the external world are built up and amended over time. Such a complex connects the external world and the internal emotional responses. The second is identification, where the ego is altered due to the associative coding of the represented object from the environment where typical examples include authority figures such as parents and teachers (Sandler 2012). The third is introjection, which is dedicated to the development of internalised regulation of the ego via the superego (Perlow, 1995: 91). Although the existence of mythological motifs in culture and their parallel manifestation in the dreams of patients rendered this enough evidence for the existence of the archetypes, the reason behind the existence of particular mythological motifs is still the subject of active research (Jung, 1959; Goodwyn, 2013). For instance, cognitive anthropologists have attempted to account for the existence of cross-cultural mythological motifs and rituals within religion by examining the possible cognitive mechanisms that would be required in establishing these collective phenomena. Dan Sperber proposes that generational transmission through a culture of motifs is not an exact replication, but is complex and based upon the constraints of our neurobiology (Sperber, 2000; Sørensen 2007).

The inability of the ego to directly understand the archetypes is due to their expression through the non-ego neural substrates, namely the complexes (cognitive schemas). In dream symbolism there is a convergence of the personal and the collective. Personal in the sense that memory traces, encoded as imagoes (structural and functional units of complexes) by the

VMPFC and linked to unconscious psychological processing systems, are influenced by the self-reflective manifestation of the evolutionary derived psyche, the collective unconscious (Jung, 1959). As an analytical technique to understanding symbolism from the unconscious, amplification sets out a method to explicitly establish the parallels between archetypal symbols and mythological motifs. This of course is in stark contrast to the method of free association which links the images and symbols to personal experiences. The comparative study of myths enables the therapist to draw attention to the collective, and hence *evolutionary*, aspect of these symbols (Jones, 2003). This shift in focus both strengthens the therapeutic alliance and emboldens the patient to contextualise this particular experience with the rest of their life (Samuels et al., 1986; Cambray, 2001). In post-traumatic stress disorder resulting from florid delirium and associated nightmares about hospitals, such techniques may be part of an integrated therapeutic modality aimed at enhancing recovery from the patient's traumatic experience (Drews et al., 2014). At the very least such techniques may enhance contemporary attempts at a qualitative analysis of the phenomenology of delirium.

3.4. Psychological homeostasis

The human brain has both a system of compensatory mechanisms that restores balance and a neurodevelopmental programme for phenotypic expression. The human psyche can thus be considered a self-regulating system. The systems of compensatory mechanisms that maintain homeostasis in the psyche are composed of a number of unconscious neurocognitive processes known as ego defence mechanisms (EDM). EDM have been extensively studied over the past century and remain relevant theoretical constructs in modern psychiatry as affirmed by their inclusion in the DSM 5 (Vaillant, 2012). There are many definitions and terms associated with this complex theoretical construct. According to the previous DSM-IV-R, EDM are defined as 'automatic psychological processes that protect the individual against anxiety and from the awareness of internal or external dangers or stressors'. Individuals are semi-unaware of these processes as they operate unconsciously (APA, 2000: 807).

In *Delirium: Acute brain failure in man* by Lipowski (1980), EDM have been proposed to be altered as part of the generalised disturbance of neurocognitive processes in delirium. Indeed, more recent work has also suggested that such unconscious neurocognitive processes are involved in the brain failure that characterises delirium (Feinberg et al., 2013). The affective lability and altered emotional states of delirium may result from the disturbances of these EDM as part of a generalised disturbance of emotional regulation. While previous assessments of emotional states have been based upon clinical interviews and observer rated scales, the application of validated instruments that measure EDM (e.g. DSQ-40; DSQ-60) may reveal how neurocognitive disturbance and labile affect are related within the same pathological model.

Accumulated evidence has demonstrated a significant association between EDM and domains relevant to medicine and mental health problems such as physical health, psychological adjustment, and a robust therapeutic alliance (Vaillant & Vaillant, 1990; Maffei et al., 1995; Sammallahti & Aalberg, 1995; Blais et al., 1996; Watson, 2002; Bond & Perrry, 2004). An age-related use of EDM is considered to be part of a developmental stage of psychological growth (Labouvie-Vief et al., 1989). Individual mental health problems can also be identified by the use of EDMs, either via psychometric tools or clinical observation (Jacobs, 2010: 111). Research has also provided compelling evidence that EDM has a robust effect on adult functioning (Vaillant, 1976; Vaillant & Drake, 1985; Jacobsen et al., 1986; Perry & Cooper, 1986a; Vaillant et al., 1986; Perry & Cooper, 1989). EDMs are thus part of a system of psychological development and are a means of emotional homeostasis within the psyche (Bowins, 2004; Jacobs, 2010: 110).

The psychological systems involved in dreaming also include the use of these homeostatic EDM and serve the function of emotional regulation (Hartmann et al., 1991). There are many definitions for nightmares which include, a dream that frightens or disturbs the dreamer and is characterised by strong negative emotions that are experienced during dreaming, awake the sleeper and can be recalled (Hartmann, 1984; Wood & Bootzin, 1990; APA, 1994; Pagel, 2000). Nightmares are distinguished from sleep terror, with sleep terror being a fear based arousal from non-REM sleep coupled with no clear recall of mentation when awakened (Nielson & Levin, 2007). It has been found in a systematic review of the literature, that there is an intimate continuum between nightmares which wake people and bad dreams that do not disturb sleep (Zadra & Donderi, 1993, 2000). Nightmares in general are categorised into idiopathic nightmares where there is no single cause and post-traumatic nightmares which are as a result of traumatic experience and are often more intense. Such post-traumatic memories tend to be part of post-traumatic stress disorder (APA, 2000; ASDA, 2005).

The vast majority of people have experienced a nightmare at least once over the course of their life (Levin, 1994; Schredl et al., 1996). It has been found that in community based large scale epidemiological studies that 2%-6% of participants report weekly nightmare (Belicki & Belicki, 1982; Bixler et al., 1972; Haynes & Mooeny, 1975; Levin, 1994; Ohayon et al., 1997). The frequency and recall of nightmares have age related changes. In one study, 5%-30% of children experienced nightmares 'often or always' and 30%-90% 'at least sometimes'. In the comparative adult population, nightmares were expressed 'often or always' in 1%-5% and 'at least sometimes' in 60% (Partinen, 1994). The majority of studies has identified a general finding that children and adolescents experience a greater frequency of nightmares compared to adults (MacFarlane, 1962; Nielsen et al., 2000; Mindell & Barrett, 2002). However, this is not a complete or consistent finding (Simard et al., 2008; Agargun et al., 2004). In elderly populations, nightmares have been experienced less frequently (Salvio et al., 1992; Woods ct al., 1993; Niclson ct al., 2006).

According to Antti Revonsuo, dreaming can be understood, though the threat simulation theory (TST) (Revonsuo, 2000). During sleep a realistic simulation of threatening events is rehearsed and mastery behaviours are developed. The largely negative content that is experienced in nightmares is evidence of this theory. In terms of dreams that are not nightmares, the dream serves the function of revealing 'species specific survival skills' and depended on the environmental challenges that one must overcome. This theory also highlights the complex organisation of dream content and negates any presupposition that vivid dreaming is a result of random cortical activation during REM phase of sleep (Hobson & McCarley, 1977; Crick & Mitchinson, 1983, 1995; Hobson, & Pace-Schott, 2002). Given the deeply embedded nature of defence mechanisms within the unconscious of the individual, we can therefore, appreciate that delirium operates not only on a conscious level, but also at an unconscious level, thus reaffirming the well-established theory that delirium is reflective of generalised brain failure.

3.5. Personality and identity

The psyche and thus the individual ego do not exist in grand isolation, rather they are embedded in a complex social network that operates at both a conscious and unconscious level (Zhang et al., 2014). The psyche of the delirious patient is characterised by disturbances in self-referential encoding and processing (Partridge et al., 2013). The psyche in general has a dynamic axis that facilitates the social performance of the ego namely, the persona and the shadow. The shadow/persona axis is an archetype and as such cannot be known in and of itself (termed *archetype as such*), rather it manifests itself in temporal and cultural forms as archetypal symbols (Jung, 1951). These archetypal symbols reflect the diversity of human interaction, one's character, and significantly differs from society to society. The concept of the persona is derived by Jung from classical Greek theatre, initially referring to the mask worn by an actor (Stevens, 2013). In psychology, the persona is the role/mask we wear to serve social functions such as mother, father, sister, brother, lover, doctor, friend, teacher, and so forth (Jung, 1951). These signifiers operate within a networked system of meaning to enable us to communicate and understand the structure and dynamics of our society. This function of the human psyche operates both within the secondary order of consciousness and is shaped predominantly by the collective unconscious, in other words, the phenotype of the psyche. The repression of unacceptable ideas and feelings extends beyond overt traumatic experiences to aspects of one's own personality. The individual shadow is an archetypal organisation of all those repressed aspects of ourselves and therefore, operates autonomously within the psyche. The phenomenology of the shadow manifests as dark, mysterious, and same sex figures in dreams, visions, and fantasies (Stevens, 2013). In art, the shadow operates as a villain in plays and movies and often as a de-humanised monster. According to Von Franz, the process of dehumanisation is as a result of dissociation from ego consciousness. In other words, the more removed the encoded experiences are from being integrated into ego consciousness the more inhuman or elemental the figure or entity (Von Franz, 1974). In collective behaviour, the shadow manifests itself in the form of prejudice such as racism, homophobia, and sexism; whereby the repressed aspects of the group get projected onto a scapegoat such as those of Jewish descent, ethnic minorities, members of the LGBT community, and many other unfortunate examples of social hatred in society (Stevens, 2013).

The ego as a collection of psychological processes is also subject to being influenced by the orders of consciousness as a result of interacting with the external world. The most influential substructure is called the super ego (*uber ich*), which is itself embedded within two ordered dimensions of consciousness, and thus subdividing the super ego into the ego ideal and the ideal ego (Kohut, 2013). The ideal-ego, the interface between the ego and primary consciousness, can be understood in terms of any aspect of ourselves that we identify with, in essence a virtual representation of one's self (Rizzuto, 2014). The interface between secondary consciousness and the ego is referred to as the ego-ideal and functions as an abstract and often authoritative phenomenon that is perceived as radically alien to us (Chasseguet-Smirgel, 1985). In non-psychotic disorders that impact upon identity of the secondary order of consciousness is retained and the pronounced self-referential encoding is reflected back upon the virtual representation. Clear examples include body dysmorphic disorders such as anorexia nervosa and bulimia nervosa (Crerand & Sarwer, 2010). In the context of severe neuropsychiatric disorders where secondary consciousness is disturbed, the ego-ideal can operate within threatening delusional complexes in the form of the government, God, or in the hospital setting, being poisoned by health care staff (Siddle et al., 2002).

Although not entirely elucidated, there is an emerging picture of the neural substrates that perform these ego functions. The default mode network (DMN) has been proposed as the foundation of these processes, with cortical midline structures as being a specialised sub-system. These cortical midline structures have been proposed to be the integrative system that functions as the basis of encoding mentalisation (Qin & Northoff, 2011). In broad terms, mentalisation can be seen as the process by which encoded experiences of the self are processed in reference to others and itself (Frith & Frith, 2008; Izuma et al., 2008, 2010; Sugiura et al., 2012). The medial prefrontal cortex (MPFC) has been demonstrated to have an important role in the form of mentalisation both for social and individual function (Gallagher & Frith, 2003; Frith & Frith, 2006). In neuroimaging studies of facial recognition, the MPFC has been reported to activate as part of the mentalisation process, when the person is exposed to images of one's partner (Gobbini et al., 2004). The combined functional interaction between the MPFC and the lateral prefrontal cortex (LPFC) are implicated in processing the reflective self and form part of the coherent structure or narrative formation whereby, encoded memories of one's self are integrated with temporal memories of the past and intentions for the future (Gallagher, 2000).

In the context of delirium, fMRI analysis of the delirious state implicates the default mode network (DMN), this should not be surprising given the consistent findings from phenomenological reports on the experience of delirium. Examples of such findings include, clouding of thought processes or seeing the world through a fog or mist, intense emotional states (anger, fear, and anxiety), lack of control or self-agency, clouding of memory processes, and overt perceptual disturbances e.g. hallucinations and delusions (Schofield, 1997, McCurren & Cronin, 2003, Duppils & Wikblad, 2007). In particular, these overt perceptual disturbances involve other patients, health care staff, and deceased relatives (McCurren & Cronin, 2003, Stenwall et al., 2008a). Such a disconnect is inevitably linked to communication difficulties with patients reporting their feeling of alienation as a result of not being either understood or listened to (Granberg et al., 1998, Andersson et al., 2002, Duppils & Wikblad, 2007). Conversely, in healthy individuals, self-comparison exists as part of a perceptual system that compares an external experience of the self to internalised representations. Emotional expression of embarrassment can occur when there is a significant discrepancy. Such negative emotions are believed to act as part of a system that protects one's self from marked deviations that may be maladjusted, thus serving the integrity of the ego and its persona (Buss, 1980; Carver & Scheier, 1998). The anterior cingulate cortex (ACC) and anterior insular cortex (AIC) have been demonstrated to be key neural substrates of a wide variety of human emotions and also serve this function of regulating the self (Onoda et al., 2010; Moor et al., 2012). Self-recognition, autobiographical memory retrieval and known self-traits are all part of the self-agency function of the AIC (Farrer & Frith, 2002; Devue et al., 2007; Modinos et al., 2009). Self-referential encoded stimuli are processed by the ACC, with studies demonstrating modality's, such as auditory verbal feedback, and conceptual stimuli, such as short stories (McGuire et al., 1996; Vogeley et al., 2001). Based on neuro-imaging studies, the dissociated interaction between the AIC and ACC can be generalised in terms of self-referential processing. The subjective experience of embarrassment and recognition of alienation served by the right AIC and the functions of reflective self and contextual self-evaluation served by caudal ACC. Analysis of the functional connectivity between these regions has illustrated the integrated collective action of these regions. Functional connectivity analyses has revealed that the caudal subdivision of the ACC showed stronger connectivity with dorsal and ventral parts of the MPFC, and the left PFC, including the middle frontal gyrus (MFG), inferior frontal gyrus (IFG), and anterior insular cortex (AI), when viewing self-face images while being observed than when doing so without observation. In addition, the left AIC has showed a stronger connectivity with the left MFG, which is included in the above mentioned network centred on the caudal ACC (Morita et al., 2013). The DMN is believed to have a major role in mediating the experience of the internal environment and features such as social awareness, aspirations of the self (and its representations) integrated with memories of past experiences. This network has largely integrative and holistic function (Gusnard & Raichle, 2001; Buckner et al., 2008). Two subsystems are believed to reside within this network. The first is based on mnemonic processing and its neural substrates the hippocampus and entorhinal cortex, while the other subsystem deals with self-referential judgement functions and its neural substrate is the dorsal medial prefrontal cortex (Buckner et al., 2008). Both these subsystems converge on the posteromedial cortex (Fransson & Marrelec, 2008). During the memory encoding process the posteromedial cortex is de-activated but during the memory reconstruction and retrieval phase it is re-activated (Wager et al., 2009). Taken together the key contributory element of this integrative work results in our imagination, the phenomenological alteration and disintegration of which manifests with the experience of delirium.

4 Origin of reality and representation

4.1. Orders of consciousness

Delirium in its most pronounced state is a disorder of consciousness (Schiff & Plum, 2000). Consciousness, like delirium, is a graded phenomenon that can be described qualitatively and quantitatively (Gunther et al., 2007; Balduzzi et al., 2009). One of the three main domains of delirium phenomenology on which this work is based upon are the orders of consciousness which are functionally categorised as primary and secondary consciousness. Both primary and secondary orders of consciousness are also fundamental to understanding the relationship between dreaming and delirious states. Moreover, understanding consciousness in general would greatly improve the prospect of providing viable solutions to differentiating delirium from mixed neuropsychiatric conditions of which disorders of consciousness also feature (Fick et al., 2013).

A scientific account of consciousness must be based upon an evolutionary framework which rejects both dualism and the modern form of dualistic theory, epiphenomenalism (Chalmers, 2003). As such, Edelman bases his account of consciousness on three principles. The first is that consciousness in general is an emergent phenomenon that has been part of the evolutionary history of organisms. Neural Darwinism, is often used to describe Edelman's theory of neuronal group selection. This theory has three basic tenets, developmental selection, experiential selection, and re-entry (Edelman et al., 2013). Developmental selection refers to the dynamic relationship between the organism's genome and the resulting phenotype, the developing brain. Experiential selection refers to the continuous developmental processes of synaptic selection in the brain. To elucidate these processes, Edelman uses the analogy of how populations can change as a result of selection to explain how neuronal populations and their synaptic connections can be sculpted to form the dynamic brain (Rutishauser, & Edelman, 2012). Cell proliferation, cell migration, cell death, neuron arbor distribution, and neurite branching are also governed by similar selective processes (Edelman & Gally, 2013). Substrate adhesion molecules (SAMs) and cell adhesion molecules (CAMs) are situated as part of the complex cell to cell mechanism involved in the control of morphogenesis. The surface based molecules signal and modulate a well regulated formative programme of neuronal aggregation. In general terms, morphogenesis is mediated by these elements which are also dependent upon their reaction to epigenetic development (Horwitz, 2012). The final tenet is re-entry, which refers to the complex signalling between neuronal populations in the brain as a result of their reciprocal connections. Edelman describes this complex concept as a form of on-going higher-order selection that appears not only to be unique to animal brains, but that 'there is no other object in the known universe so completely distinguished by re-entrant circuitry as the human brain' (Edelman, 2006). Re-entry is proposed to mediate a coordinated neuronal activity in a wide variety of cortical regions. It is a ubiquitous form of signalling present in the telencephalon of most vertebrates and has many alternative names such as 'recurrent' and 'recursive' signalling (Edelman, 1993; Lamme & Roelfsema 2000; Edelman, & Gally, 2013). It should however be distinguished from the process of feedback. Feedback refers to a neuronal process that signals to other neurons with both a forward path signal and a pre-defined separate error pathway that has functions in control and correction (Popovych et al., 2006). In contrast, re-entrant signalling has as its most characteristic feature the simultaneous exchange of neuronal signals, which are regulated in a coordinated manner.

When integrated as a conceptual triad, these elements of the neural selection theory form part of the foundation for Edelman's theory of consciousness. Another part is based upon the second principle of consciousness which is founded upon a neurophysiological substrate which exists without the requirement of theological constructs such as a soul or spirit. The retention of the mind body dualism of the modern era is as a result of the philosophical inquiry of Rene Descartes. Consciousness itself interdependent from matter existed in a non-physical domain of reality the *res cognitans,* the realm of thought, while the human body and material world existed in the *res extensa*, the realm of extension. The pineal gland, found deep within the brain, was the point of connection between these two dimensions and thus the inter-point of the mind and body (Descartes, 1996 [1641]). It is recognised by modern neuroscientists that the brain and its counterpart the psyche are indeed two aspects of the same phenomena, analogous to light with its wave and corporeal form. According to James, consciousness is an emergent process that is a result of the interaction between the environment, the body, and the brain (Putnam, 1997). Early work into the neuroscientific account of consciousness proposed the hypothesis that the high frequency EEG oscillations are the ones that are most closely associated with consciousness. This hypothesis is generally attributed to the work of Christoph Von der Malsburg and Wolf Singer. Their major concern was the binding problem of conscious phenomena and how it is represented by the brain as a unified experience (Von der Malsburg & Singer, 1988). In a similar stream of thought, Rodolfo Llinás proposed the hypothesis that the thalamus and the neocortex of the brain had a system of recurrent signalling that would be sufficient to mediate consciousness (Llinás, 1988). However, many studies involving testing of the subject's awareness have indicated that the sensory neocortical regions implicated in this early hypothesis were not solely feasible for consciousness, for example, studies investigating cases of blind-sight, whereby aspects of visual perception are retained without any awareness, provided contradictory evidence (Weiskrantz & Carey, 1998).

Fig 1. Components of human consciousness.

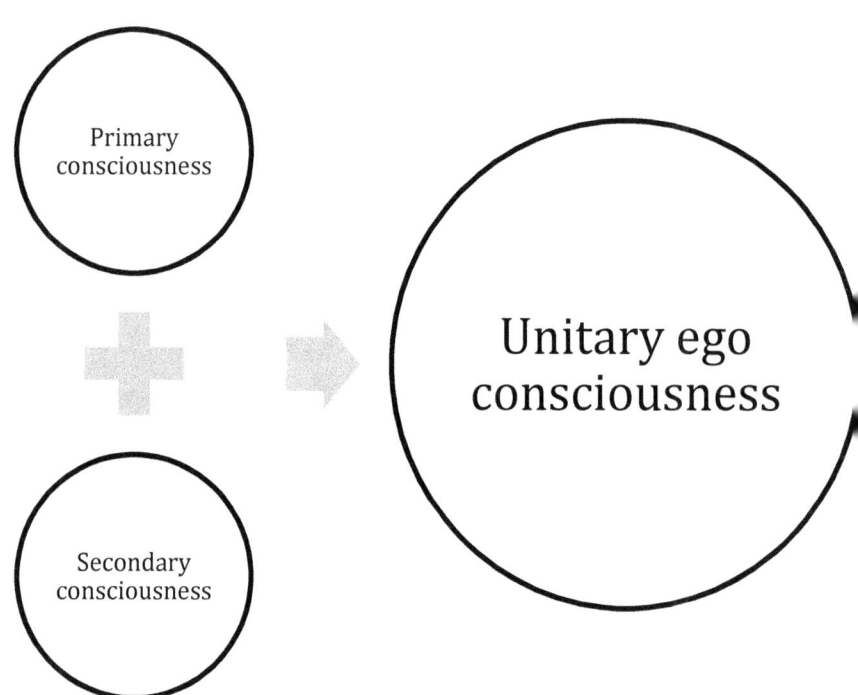

The unitary mode of consciousness as experienced by the ego can be conceptualised as being composed of a primary and secondary functional order. Primary consciousness is composed of sensation transformed into perceptual images and is thus a virtual abstract and multimodal based system. It has not only the function of being a mode of sensation, but can also integrate this state with memory, which consequently adds a temporal dimension to awareness, such that the present and immediate past are encompassed (Edelman, 2004). Due to the involvement of selective attention, this form of consciousness is itself composed of two components, the first being focal awareness which is the perceptual experience of attention by the ego and the second being peripheral awareness which is the phenomenal penumbra of this focus (Johanson et al., 2003). The neural substrate for primary consciousness is based on large systems. The integrated axis of the brainstem and limbic system sets out physiological drives for the organism and encodes a largely implicit foundation for experiencing the external world. The cerebral cortex-thalamic axis further encodes more diffuse memory systems and binds these with an awareness of the present. Edelman posits that it is the combination of perceptual awareness with conceptual memory that gives us the primary order of consciousness (Edelman, 2004). The third principle of consciousness is the intimate involvement of encoding sensory stimuli with conscious experience (Edelman, 2003). This third position is congruent with the theories of Merleu-Ponty, Jung, Beck, and Damasio and their accounts of the encoding of sensory stimuli into association based psychological constructs.

During the development of the adult psyche, secondary consciousness emerges as a vast mode of psychological being, whereby the functions of metacognition, language, and culture are born. In general, systems of communication exist as part of most animal behaviour as evidenced by the very simple range of signs, cues and stereotypical behaviours that they exhibit (Searcy & Nowicki, 2005). The most characteristic form of human communication is indeed language which is finitely complex and can embody our capacity for self-reflection (Jackendoff 2002; Pinker, 2007). Language is so central to the human subject that linguists such as Noam Chomsky have proposed the existence of a language acquisition device (LAD), an inherited and emergent system that executes a form of grammar which functions as the foundation by which specific languages can be acquired (Fodor, 1983; Cosmides & Tooby, 1992). Chomsky proposes that the LAD did not originate for the sole purpose of language, but is an example of exaptation, whereby the LAD has taken over neural systems that have been dedicated to other functions such as navigation (Hauser et al., 2002). Language and secondary consciousness are modalities which enable social attachment. During the first 9 months of an infant's life, the deictic relationship with the mother is the central focus. This relationship from the developmental point of the infant is termed primary intersubjectivity. From approximately 12 months, secondary intersubjectivity grows and with it a wider gaze upon the environment beyond that of the mother. This triadic relationship is often referred to as joint attention and serves as the basis for the expansion of the infant's vocabulary (Trevarthen, 1998).

Awareness of one's self is an emergent process of the developing ego and as such it is influenced by both primary and secondary consciousness. The most well researched method to investigate the primary emergent mode of this type of awareness is through the mirror self-recognition (MSR) test. This test demonstrates the existence of self-consciousness in animals including humans. For example, chimpanzees pass this test by recognising themselves while other primates do not (Asendorpf et al., 1996). The findings from the MSR test are the empirical basis of Jacque Lacan's theory of reality and its relationship to the ego. The phenomenological descriptions of the imaginary order and the symbolic order are congruent with those of primary and secondary consciousness respectively. According to Lacan, the human ego is an agency that gives coherency and masks the underlying fragmentary nature of the body (Lacan, 1953). In modern psychological terminology imbued with evidence from neuroscience, we can identify this phenomenon with the individuals' experience of the multitude of underlying neuropsychological process that exists beyond the threshold of consciousness. The ego gives coherency as part of the emergent properties of executive cognitive functions that the ego has evolved to serve. The central functional locus of this agency is the concept of the core self. The core self is composed of features such as, affective regulation and motivated patterns of behaviour and as such, has been implicated as an integrative function of the cortical midline structures and the subcortical midline structures of the brain (Panksepp, 1998, Panksepp & Northoff, 2009). The connection between the cortical and subcortical midline structures and the mirror neuron systems have been proposed to be integrated by a multitude of neural pathways and critical relay centres (Uddin et al., 2007). An example of a critical relay centre is the insular cortex, which functions as a structure for interoceptive processes which have been encoded, processed, and relayed from the mirror neuron system to the cortical and subcortical midline structures (Rizzolatti & Luppino, 2001).

The abstract nature of dreaming with its enhanced cognitive associations and limited mode of self-agency highlights its pronounced primary consciousness and significantly altered secondary consciousness (Spitzer et al., 1991; Hobson, 2009). In this state of dominant primary consciousness the existence of primary process functioning is made manifest. Such primary processing as evidenced by fallacious interpretations of reality is based largely upon labile affect. This same neurocognitive processing is also the central feature of magical thinking in the waking state and serves as the wish based experience of dreaming. This wish is founded upon the content and direction of the dissociated complexes forcing upon the ego aspects of oneself that have been dissociated. Therefore, the wish of the dream must not be considered identical as the term wish as used in common language, whereby the intentionality of the wish is associated with the ego, rather than the unconscious psyche. The qualitative change of the dream experience has been attributed to shifts in neuromodulation from the amine-ergic systems diminished influence to a state of dopaminergic and cholinergic dominated influence (Hobson et al., 2000; Solms, 2000). This hyper dopaminergic state is consistently attributed to the pleasure seeking primary processing and is believed to be implicated in the wish aspect of dreaming (Solms, 2014). The characteristic disturbances in consciousness that patients with delirium experience parallel this distinction between primary and secondary consciousness. In delirium functions of secondary consciousness such as language, metacognition, and orientation are all disturbed and as such, patients report severe disorientation and alienation from social interaction during a delirious episode (Partridge et al., 2013). The smooth regulation of selective attention is based upon the interface between the executive function of the ego and the complexes that orchestrate attention in the waking state. When primary consciousness dominates the major deficits in attention are consistently detected as a central feature of delirium. The reason is that attention itself is still present as a cognitive system given that it is subject to the graded phenomena of consciousness (Sanders, 2011; Spreng et al., 2013). In delirium, this dysfunction of attention is a reflection of the breakdown in cohesion between the orders of consciousness and executive cognition, and reprioritises inattention as the degree of functional integrity in the brain.

4.2. The unconscious

Previous accounts of delirium have largely focused upon describing in rudimentary form the ego consciousness of the delirious state. Such accounts have also neglected a robust account of the origin of the contents of this heterogeneous phenomenology, namely the unconscious. Therefore, an account of the reciprocal and mutual relationship between ego consciousness and the unconscious is warranted in order to inform a more complete understanding of the experience of delirium. It is a common conception that is rendered false by empirical evidence, that only what is psychological must also be conscious and consequently only that which is conscious is rendered the sole topic or subject of psychology. Understudied phenomena such as hallucinations, hypnosis, and dreams were the first elements of the emerging science of psychology that inspired researchers to accept that beyond the pale of what is now referred to as ego consciousness, there is an entire system outside of our immediate awareness, the unconscious (Levin et al., 2011).

The relationship between ego consciousness and the unconscious is based upon repression and dissociation. With a major example of a disorder of these systems being post-traumatic stress disorder (PTSD), which is also a complication of delirium (Jackson et al., 2014). Repression is an unconscious neurocognitive process involved in removing conscious awareness of stimuli that induce severe anxiety (Rofé, 2008; Raz, 2011). It is a multidimensional concept which refers to a broad range of ego defence mechanisms and coping strategies that impact upon memory, and has a major role to play in the pathogenesis of many mental health disorders. In the context of conversion disorders, previously referred to as hysteria, Freud proposed that traumatic memories have their affect repressed and transformed into features of bodily distortion (Freud, 1962). Studies investigating the neural correlates of such a mechanism, i.e. the neurobiology of repression, have identified the key role of the dorsolateral prefrontal cortex (DLPFC) in the activation and resultant deactivation of the explicit encoding of memories by the hippocampus. Recent work has illustrated that during a model of memory suppression, patients exhibit decreased left hippocampal activity resulting from significant increased left DLPFC. The right superior supplementary motor area (SMA) and temporo-parietal junction (TPJ) were also found to have increased activity relative to controls. Moreover, it was noted that patients were unable to activate the right inferior frontal cortex (IFC) during these tasks. Connectivity between motor areas, such as the SMA, the cerebellum, and the amygdala, were also found to be enhanced in patients. Taken together, this evidence suggests that there is indeed a neural mechanism that links repression with emotional and motor behaviour (Aybek et al., 2013).

Repression and dissociation are intimately linked in the psyche. The experience of trauma is a common feature of human life. The most common form of trauma is relational trauma (trauma resulting from destructive relationships between people) and has been experienced by two thirds of the adult population (Bureau et al., 2010; van der Kolk & d'Andrea, 2010) The area of relational trauma is emerging as a robust field of neuroscientific inquiry with recent work emphasising the causative role of relational trauma to processes involved in memory and affect regulation (Bremner, 2010; Lanius et al., 2010). If repression can be considered a broad term used to describe the ego defence mechanisms (EDM) that separates potentially traumatic affect from images and ideas, then dissociation can be considered the normal state of psychological functioning within the unconscious (Knox, 2013). Dissociation is the method by which complexes can re-arrange to adapt to new encoding sensory inputs in order to enhance and maintain adaptation to the environment. However, in the absence of the ego's ability to appropriate aspects of the complexes to serve identity and behaviour, the complexes can function in an autonomous manner and manifest as compulsions (Brooke, 1991). The abnormal sensory encoding, resulting from trauma can often manifest in severely debilitating conditions such as PTSD. Individuals with PTSD report vivid flashbacks that are multimodal and originate from the un-integrated encoded experiences (van der Kolk & Fisler, 1995). In particular the experience of trauma dissociates the encoding of emotional states as separate from verbal memories (Schmahl, et al., 2010). Environmental cues that are perceived as associative can activate these repressed autonomous complexes resulting in the terrifying experience of flashbacks (Brewin et al., 1996). The disturbances in language associated with the experience are present, for example, when one has extreme difficulty in finding the words to describe the trauma (Moores et al., 2008). Neurodevelopmental disorders such as Tourette's syndrome highlight this functional and structural defect between unconscious thought processes mediated by the complexes and incomplete control over them by the ego. Such problems are exacerbated by the presence of high emotionality and stress (Coffey & Park, 1997). According to Lanius et al., (2002) dissociation has two forms. The first form is the hyper-arousal state whereby the Hypothalamic-Pituitary-Adrenal (HPA) axis in concert with the autonomic nervous system (ANS) and limbic system are activated by trauma. The higher cortical regions such as the anterior cingulate cortex (ACC) and the medial prefrontal cortex (MPFC) have been 'shut down' in this state resulting in unregulated emotional responses and encoding. Such a scenario serves as the neurobiology for the occurrence of flashbacks, nightmares, and hyper vigilance that often constellates anxiety disorders and PTSD. The second form of dissociation is marked by hypo-arousal, whereby there is significantly increased activation of the ACC and MPFC which inhibits emotional responses with characterised features such as de-realisation, disengagement from emotional dimensions of memory and experience (Schmahl et al., 2010: 182). EDM (originating in PFC regions) keep these distressing encoded experiences separate and further dissociated from ego consciousness (Bowlby, 1980; Dozier et al., 2001). The persistence of this exclusionary encoding process is further complicated by the breakdown in functioning complexes, which can lead to the emergence of un-integrated systems to influence our behaviour in ways that are highly maladjusted and problematic (Bretherton, 1995; Fraley & Shaver, 1999). In its most extreme manifestation, these subsystems can organise into dissociated personalities and alter an individual's self-agency, for instance, in dissociated personality disorders (Sinason, 2002; Van der Hart et al., 2006). It has been reported that these alternative personalities are organised according to attachment figures that one has experienced (Loewnstein & Welzant, 2010).

Another example of problematic unconscious processing is the existence of nightmares. Nightmares are often part of the phenotype of delirium and may even herald the onset of delirium (Loster et al., 2012). Nightmares can be considered in terms of states and traits, whereby, the state refers to the continuity between the dreamer's emotional state and the emotions present in dreams and particularly nightmares, and the traits refer to the specific components that contributes to nightmare onset such as mental health problems, and demographic features such as gender and age

(Schredl, 2003). Nightmares are also part of the homeostasis of emotion that is conducted by the psyche, with the major emotions during nightmares being intense fear, anger, and disgust (Zadra & Donderi, 2000). Nightmares can be proposed as breakdowns in the optimal regulation of emotion that is normally conducted during dreaming. According to Freud, nightmares serve the function of integrating repressed encoded stimuli (anxious and traumatic experiences) into consciousness (Freud, 1900). Evidence from neuroscientific studies of sleep, dreaming, and human cognitive functions have begun to confirm many tenets of the theoretical hypothesis of nightmares as first proposed by the psychoanalysis of dreams (Greenberg et al., 1972; Lansky & Bley, 1995). One such stream of evidence is the role of dopaminergic pathways during REM sleep stage and its proposed basis of expressing affective concerns during dreaming. Significantly elevated dopaminergic signalling during this mode of behaviour has been associated with the onset and experience of nightmares (Solms, 2000).

A clear example to prove the role of nightmares as processes of integration is to be found in the treatment of patients with post-traumatic nightmares. During the course of successful psychotherapy, patients experience dream motifs that increasingly present themes of self-mastery (Germain et al., 2004). According to Hartmann, there are specific processes serving emotional regulation in dreaming and nightmare experiences (Hartmann, 1996; Hartmann, 1998). The nightmare experience has been proposed to be the result the contextualisation of the person's emotional concerns. In non-distressing dreams, emotions tend to be more mosaic, and diffuse and thus a clear understanding of the contextualisation process is difficult to analyse in isolation. The contextualisation process of nightmares would enable the establishment of new associations to an emotion with a view to adapting to this emotion (Hartmann, 1998b). This hypothesis would further demonstrate that dreaming serves a purpose. An integrative model has been proposed to gather together both the psychological and neurological aspects of dreaming in order to provide a working model for nightmares. The affect network dysfunction (AND) model is one such model that has made a major effort at this (Nielson & Levin, 2007). Its theoretical foundation is based on studies investigating neuroimaging of PTSD patients, anxiety disorder patients, and neurophysiological profiles of personality and combined with the AMPHAC (amygdala, medial prefrontal cortex, hippocampus, and anterior cingulate cortex) model of nightmare formation (Levin & Nielson, 2007). The central position of this theory is that nightmares originate from an innate adaptive function of the affective systems dedicated to fear memory extinction.

The reproduction of fear extinction memories during dreaming is believed to be a result of three main processes. The first is element activation whereby the hyper-associative state of sleep enables enhanced access to dissociated aspects of episodic memories, often de-contextualised from real world occurrences. The second is element recombination, where each of these now recruited elements are reorganised and integrated with recently encoded contextualised memories. The third is emotional expression, whereby the now recombined memories are engaged with during the experience of dreaming as part of the integration process. The affect distress factor determines the severity and frequency of the nightmare and is a developmental trait often as a result of trauma and relational neglect. According to Nielson and Levin, (2007) this process is dependent on the concept of affect load, the state factor that is a combination of an individual's capacity to regulate emotions and experience of stressful occurrences. The affect load is challenged by the requirements to develop and grow the psyche by integrating dissociated and often repressed encoded stimuli within the unconscious psyche. Application of this model to delirium may yield novel insights into disturbances of affect regulation that often form as part of delirium phenomenology.

4.3. Memory and learning

The growth and development of the psyche is based on learning which in turn is based on its functional units, the memory systems (Meyer et al., 2013). An account of the role of the memory systems and their relationship to the phenomenological disturbances of delirium may provide assessment targets for differentiating delirium from mixed neuropsychiatric disturbances that also have impairments in memory (Osse et al., 2013). The memory systems of the human brain interact within multiple brain regions and neuromodulatory interconnections between these regions (Rugg, 2013). In particular, the cholinergic system has been found to have wide neuromodulatory effects which connect together the neural substrates that serve attention, memory, arousal and REM sleep (Sarter & Bruno, 1999). Such processes are all disturbed in the delirious state (Maldonado, 2008). Dreaming and sleep has long been considered integral processes involved in memory augmentation, consolidation, and integration (Winson, 1985, 2002; Kali & Dayan 2004; Winson, 2004). Human memory systems are divided into conscious and unconscious sub systems, and are often referred to as explicit memory and implicit memory. Testing these subsystems requires memory performance tasks and neuroimaging studies of task specific reactivated areas (Buckner et al., 1996; Cabeza & Nyberg, 1997; Buckner et al., 1998; Grill-Spector et al., 2006). The reproductive retrieval of memory is based upon the reconstruction of the context by which the imago (qualia) was encoded (Kahn et al., 2004). Numerous neuroimaging studies of various sense modalities have reported such findings through the detected activation of association cortical areas (Nyberg et al., 2000; Persson & Nyberg, 2000; Wheeler et al., 2000; Nyberg et al., 2001; Vaidya et al., 2002; Woodruff et al., 2005; Wheeler et al., 2006). For example, spatial and object encoded experiences require the recruitment of neural regions, such as the parietal and fusiform cortices, in memory retrieval (Köhler et al., 1998b; Sala et al., 2003). Implicit memory has been proposed to be independent of the hippocampus and related regional activity, for example, the entorhinal cortex and the para-hippocampal gyrus (Cave & Squire, 1992; Knowlton & Squire, 1994). However, this is not a clear cut finding, with the hippocampus having a role in implicit spatial memory retrieval (Chun and Phelps, 1999; Park et al., 2004). Stress is a major modulator of memory encoding and reconstruction with many neural structures (hippocampal formation and prefrontal cortex) that mediate these functions, and possess a dense concentration of glucocorticoid receptors (Payne et al., 2002, 2004). Cortisol, being the most significant neuroendocrine meditator involved in the stress response, has broad based effects on attention, alertness, and waking states (McEwan, 2000, 2007). It is also impacted upon by circadian integrity (Fitzgerald et al., 2013). It has been proposed that cortisol is a key determinant in the functional status of the hippocampal formation and the prefrontal cortex and their involvement in memory (Lupien et al., 2009). The hippocampal-adrenal network has been proposed to amplify the effects of *deliriogenic* factors (Brown, 2000). Such hippocampal dysfunction has been suggested to result in the confabulation of delirious patients (Jacobsen & Sapolsky, 1991; de Kloet et al., 1998). The apparent dissociation between the explicit and implicit memory subsystems has been accounted for by a number of theoretical frameworks. For example, the declarative-nondeclarative theory posited that the retrieval of episodic memory is dependent on the interconnected subsystems of the prefrontal cortex and the medial temporal lobe (MTL), while the retrieval of implicit memories was dependent on brain regions implicated in motor behaviour and skill encoding e.g. the basal ganglia (Squire et al., 1993; Knowlton et al., 1996). However, a clear distinction between what is categorised as either conscious or unconscious memory systems has not been found to be a consistent finding in neuroimaging studies, for example, the PFC has regions that are dedicated to both explicit and implicit memory tasks, the MTL also has roles in both processes, (Fletcher & Henson, 2001; Badre & Wagner, 2007; Henke, 2010; Dew & Cabeza, 2011).

Further theoretical developments utilised the dichotomy between conception and perception to account for the interaction between neural regions, resulting in conscious and unconscious memory processing. It has been suggested that hypotheses pertaining to auxiliary functions of neural regions should be included in the conceptual-perceptual theory, and that there should be an alignment between conceptual memories and the neural substrates that function in semantic processing. The same should hold true for perceptual memories and regions implicated in sensory processing (Roskies, 2009). However, it has been found that such an assumption is too simplistic to account for complexities of cortical regions, such as the left anterior ventrolateral prefrontal cortex (LAVL-PFC) and left lateral temporal cortex (LLTC), that have both conceptual and perceptual processing in semantic and episodic memories (Prince et al., 2007; Binder et al., 2009).

Memories have emotional dimensions and are encoded in the context of positive and negative experiences. Such memory systems find their structural and functional locus within the amygdala complex, including its efferents and afferents (McGaugh, 2000; Buchanan & Lovallo, 2001). There is consistent evidence gleaned from studies investigating memory as a reconstruction rather than reproductive process (Neisser & Winograd, 1988; Schacter, 1995; Roediger, 1996). Memories change as a function of time and provide the underlying assumption that it is a reconstructive rather than reproductive process (Murray et al., 2002; Payne et al., 2002, 2004, 2006). Memory consolidation is often defined as the process that integrates and stabilises newly acquired information from short term into long term forms (McGaugh, 2000). The mechanism of repression can therefore be conceptualised as a particular form of memory consolidation for the encoded stimuli of traumatic experiences. Sleep has a role in the consolidation of a wide variety of memory forms attributed to its complex phases, namely REM and NREM sleep (Yaroush & Sullivan, 1971; Barrett & Ekstrand, 1972; Fowler et al., 1973). Emotional memory consolidation is served by the REM phase of sleep (Maquet et al. 1996; Walker, 2009). Moreover, emotionally charged episodic memories may rely on both REM sleep and SWS for their consolidation (Ellenbogen et al., 2006; Marshall and Born, 2007; Payne et al., 2007). Theories surrounding sleep based memory consolidation feature a two-step process which initially involves the hippocampal encoding of neural representations of stimuli and then a gradual encoding upon the neocortex through bi-directional signalling between the two structures (McClelland et al., 1995; Buzsaki, 1998). Synchronization between these structures is proposed to be mediated by slow oscillations (1 Hz) and consequently temporally align sleep spindles (Siapas and Wilson, 1998; Sirota et al., 2003; Diekelmann and Born, 2010). Such aligned activity indicates that this is the measurable effect of the neuro-plasticity of the neocortical-hippocampal memory consolidation process (Schabus et al., 2004; Clemens et al., 2005; Schmidt et al., 2006).

The disturbances of memory in delirium are further complicated by phenomenological dysfunctions in circadian integrity and language. Indeed, both language and the circadian system have undergone a complicated evolutionary development. While the phylogenetic history of the circadian system has been roughly traced from cyanobacteria to our species, the evolution of language is still a topic of speculation (Collier et al., 2014; Hauser et al., 2014). Understanding the link between circadian integrity and language should enable us to appreciate the isomorphism between the human brain and psyche. Broad ranging studies looking at the circadian influence upon language have yielded encouraging results. In a study that compared linguistically healthy versus linguistically impaired speech processing of children, i.e. the domains of sentence comprehension and pre-lexical access to syllables, there was a circadian impact upon performance. The non-impaired children exhibited optimal performances in these linguistic tests, e.g. syllabic repetition and sentence comprehension, at approximately 19:30h and 9:00h respectively (Reinberg et al., 1988). Other components of language such as semantic processing have been demonstrated to have more optimum performance in the morning hours and decline as the day goes on (Folkard, 1975). In a study of patients with dementia, measures of word fluency have identified evening hours (17:00 and 18:00h) as times of optimum performance (Yaretsky et al., 1996). Many other studies have highlighted the diurnal variation of language components such as voice processing, spelling proficiency and syntax processing (Morton & Diubaldo, 1993, 1995; Dietrich, 2006).

However, methodological challenges arise when conducting and interpreting the results of such tests, with many factors such as food, energy levels, exposure to light, and unconscious processes of motivation all potentially confounding the influence of the circadian system (Herzog & Muglia, 2006; Hirayama et al., 2007). Constant routine protocols have been developed in order to remove many of these complicating issues (Blatter & Cajochen, 2007).

The relationship between language and dreaming can be conceptualised on two fronts, the first is the cognitive processing of language during the wake phase of the circadian cycle, and the second being the content of dreaming that is related to language components. The first area concerns itself with studies looking at learning in the context of cognitive processing during sleep. Early studies indicate that dreaming itself does not impact upon linguistic ability, but rather language processing, particularly during REM sleep, can impact upon dreaming (De Koninck et al., 1988; 1995). There is a significant increase of REM sleep when subjects have experienced increased language learning performance tasks, reflecting the role of language processing during this phase of sleep (De Koninck et al., 1988; 1989; 1990).

The influence of language upon the content of dreaming has a long conceptual history going back to Artemidorus and has a central position in the free association technique of psychoanalytical methods of dream interpretation. In cognitive studies investigating the content of dreams, it has been found that 80% to 100% of 'medium to long REM dreams have reported some form of speech (Snyder, 1970). Speech in dreams is not generally distorted, but reflective of grammatical and contextually robust dimensions (Heynick, 1983). In a study of bilingualism in dream content, it was found that bilingualism does not disturb the robust language faculty during dreaming, the use of language in vivid dreaming is secondary to the initial manifestation of the dreaming imagery and the language selected is reflective of its role in dream processing of language during REM sleep

(Foulkes et al., 1993). Previous work of examining the domains of delirium phenomenology has grouped attention, orientation, and memory together under rubric of general cognition and language and thought disorder as higher cognitive disturbances (Trzepacz & Meagher, 2008). Typically, the faculties of attention and orientation are guided by unconscious processes and thus bound to the faculty of language. During his training at the Burghölzli, Jung applied the techniques of the word association test, Galvanic skin response and other physiological measures to investigate the complexes of the unconscious psyche. A patient was connected to these machines and then a list of words was said to them, at which point they would respond to each word and the response time was measured. The recorded responses would indicate one or more themes. Most of the words would have little emotional impact, but certain words would elicit a pause, an extended response time, and a change in a number of physiological measures (Jung, 1904). Such features (referred to as complex indicators) were evidence of complexes, feeling toned affective structures that were bound with images and thoughts in the mind of the patient (Jung, 1907). The use and description of complexes became a cornerstone of psychoanalytical theory and were re-discovered in other fields of psychology for example, cognitive schemas. According to Aaron Beck, schemas are defined as 'a structure for screening, coding, and evaluating the stimuli that impinges on the organism. On the basis of the matrix of schemas, the individual is able to orient himself in relation to time and space, and to categorize and interpret experiences in a meaningful way' (Beck, 1967: 283). Subsequent theoretical developments have integrated findings from neuroscience to expand the theory of schemas to include its multimodal representation (James et al., 2007). Many attempts at investigating complexes from a neurophysiological perspective were performed during the 1980's using Quantitative

ElectroEncephaloGraph (QEEG) techniques (Petchkovsky et al., 2013). More recent studies have reported that the process of attention was significantly improved when a complex was activated. Subject performance on implicit learning tasks also improved when a complex was activated (Shin et al., 2005). Such a finding confirmed Jung's reports that complexes had a directional influence upon attention (Jung, 1904). It has been demonstrated in a study comparing the fMRI activation pattern of 'complexed responses' to 'neutral responses' that there is a specific neural circuit implicated in its response to the word association test. This study highlight structures implicated in the resonance circuitry of functions such as empathy (awareness of other), and mindfulness (awareness of self). It also found the activation pattern initiated by these processes combined with a broad based inter hemispheric dialogue (Petchkovsky et al., 2013).

According to Allan Shore, the right hemisphere has a role largely in implicit (unconscious) processing of functions such as communication, affect, cognition, communication, and regulative integration of these domains. These processes converge together to provide the neural correlates of the unconscious aspects of the ego (Schore, 1994, 2003a) This system is also developmentally regulated and is impacted upon by the tremendous influence of early infancy and care-giver relations. Such an influence impacts upon the encoding of unconscious processing involved in complex repetitive interaction, para-linguistic functions, expression of emotions, and non-verbal cues (Schore, 2003b, 2004). However, it has been proposed that the distinction between implicit and explicit psychological functioning is much less distinct (Bucci, 2004). The multiple code theory proposes that the psyche is founded on a multiformated cognitive-emotional system. The formats of sub-symbolic and symbolic used to process that which is analogical and continuous are opposed to the symbolic format which processes according to discrete dimensions (Bucci, 1985, 1997, 2001). The subsymbolic format functions as part of implicit processing, the symbolic format which can be further divided into verbal and non-verbal sub-formats, operates as part of explicit processing (Bucci, 2002). The non-verbal symbolic encodes images that are multimodal and serves as the structural and functional units (imagos/qualia) of the complexes.

The congruent encoding of the external and internal world represents and gives credence to the requirement of complex social behaviour that is exhibited by animals, namely attachment and bonding. Attachment has been identified as an inter-dependent motivational system which enables the social dimensions of animal and human behaviour (Bowlby, 1988: 20-38). The internal objects are organised into 'internal working models'. These attachment complexes are built up over time and form the foundation for social behaviour throughout life. These complexes have been referred to as 'representations of interactions that have been generalised' (RIGs) and encapsulate patterns of relationships rather than singular relationship episodes (Stern, 1985: 97; Fonagy, 1999).

The ego is the most integrative and dominant complex which attempts to execute its functions via the bi-directional input from the complexes. However, given the overlap and high density integration of these complexes, the difference between the ego and the other complexes in the healthy individual must be minimal. Indeed, studies conducting memory performance tasks and measuring the difference between self and other have demonstrated that there are reduced differences when the other is closer to one's self e.g. friends and family (Markus & Kitayama, 1991; Symons & Johnson, 1997). Regions dedicated to this task have been associated with the prefrontal cortex and the cortical midline structures (Parvizi et al., 2006; Hagmann et al., 2008). Neuroimaging studies have reported that the cortical midline structures have activation patterns that reflect this. In particular, the medial prefrontal cortex (MPFC) exhibits similar neural activity when traits of self and a close other are being tested. The reverse has also been demonstrated (Ochsner et al., 2005). It has also been proposed that the MPFC is differentially activated by self and others, with the most ventral areas more active for self and more dorsal areas more active for other (Amodio & Frith, 2006).

Studies investigating the neural correlates of executive decision making coupled with affect regulation have provided a rudimentary model of interactive regions. Decision making is mediated through the activation of the MPFC to signal to the amygdala complex and nucleus accumbens, which are in turn modulated by the encoded psychological complexes. This functions in behaviour as motivation and arousal towards the stimuli. Signalling can also exist between the MPFC and the ventrolateral prefrontal cortex (VLPFC), with the VLPFC signalling to the dorsal striatum resulting in altered responses to stimuli. The VLPFC may have roles in regulating both emotions and executive decisions by influencing the ACC, the AI, the amygdala, and the temporal cortex. A dorsal subsystem exists for conflict resolution via relays from the dorso-medial prefrontal cortex (DMPFC) to the dorso-lateral prefrontal cortex (DLPFC) where selective attention processes are executed. The DLPFC in turn has influenced signalling over the sub systems required for processing of temporal cortex functioning (semantic associations, encoded response options, and reinforced behaviour). The encoded imagos of these complexes exist in a mutually inhibitory manner with modulatory signalling from the amygdala and MPFC and DACC (amplifying the amygdala response) (Levins et al., 2014; Clarke et al., 2015). The complexes therefore serve as the emotional foundation for the individual's sense of bodily self across the variety of experiences in both health and disease.

4.4. Contents of the unconscious

The unconscious should not be perceived as a repository of useless processes out of which ego consciousness emerges, but as a highly sophisticated arousal system that enables the optimal orchestration between the intent of the ego and the Self; the crossroads between the will and destiny. The human CNS and hence psyche has multiple functions for regulating the arousal system, as mediated through the complexes. The thalamus has been proposed as a critical modulator for selective attention due to its wide variety of neurochemical inputs such as serotonin, histamine, acetylcholine and norepinephrine from their respective nuclei. The selective neocortical activation that is served by the respective relay thalamic nuclei, such as the reticular nuclei, have significant inhibitory (GABAergic) impact upon the sensory relay of stimuli from the environment. Certain stimuli can then be prevented from reaching higher cortical cognitive integration via thalamocortical pathways (Muller, & Destexhe, 2012; Poulet et al., 2012). The neocortex also has major roles in regulating arousal in a top down fashion. One of the most concentrated convergent regions of the arousal system is the medial prefrontal cortex, which has the ability to signal via descending pathways to the brainstem, the hypothalamus, and the basal forebrain (Hurley et al., 2004; Aston-Jones & Cohen, 2005).

Dreaming, delirium, and the waking state are all different global states, but all three have a coherent and unitary form of brain functioning as constituted though different neuromodulators and arousal systems (Hobson et al., 2014). Prominent examples include the robust activity of the aminergic group, e.g. histamine, serotonin and norepinephrine, during the wake state and cholinergic activity during dream states (Orem, 2012). Moreover, delirium is believed to be characterised by a mixed extreme of hyper and hypo dopaminergic states coupled with hypocholinergic signalling (Maldonado et al., 2013). Although attributing broad based neurosignalling systems to these brain states may orientate research towards identifying the precise neural phenotype of these states, such characterisation requires a detailed account of the phenomenology. Otherwise, ambiguous attributions may stifle progress in research by retaining a disguised form of the prescientific humoral theory of brain function.

Understanding the contents of delirium requires understanding the environmental influences that may impact upon the unconscious psyche of the patient in the clinical setting. Over the past few decades, there has been an increase in research focused on patient's experiences of the intensive care unit (ICU). Studies have focused on environmental stressors such as pain, mechanical ventilation, and the patient's emotional responses to these experiences (Bergborn-Engberg & Haljamae, 1989; Compton, 1991; Granberg et al., 1998). Longitudinal studies have highlighted recollections of negative memories and vivid nightmares, and their subsequent detrimental impact upon socio-adaptive functioning (Daffurn et al., 1994; Jones et al., 2000). The term 'unreal experiences' has been used to refer to the collection of 'visual and/or auditory phenomena, which appear in a condition experienced as totally wakeful or in a condition between wakefulness and sleep' (Granberg et al., 1999: 29-30). The convergence of stressors such as intubation and critical illness onset is believed to induce states of delirium and this potentially prodromal phase of 'unreal experiences' or dream like experience (Rotondi et al., 2002). When investigating patient experiences of the ICU, it was found that 38% of patients reported a dream like experience. This dreaming experience was further subdivided into hallucinations and or delusions (14%), unpleasant dreams or nightmares (18%) and other dreams (6%) (Rundshagen et al., 2002). Patients staying less than 24 hours in the ICU reported less dreaming (8%) and more recall of factual events (20%). Traumatic memories are often recalled by patients after discharge from ICU, with up to 91% recalling traumatic experiences and approximately 50% experiencing pain, respiratory distress, and anxiety. The nature of the traumatic memories is most revealing, with the majority (75%) being nightmares, with a smaller number (22%) experiencing these up to the time of being interviewed (Stoll et al., 1999). The content of these vivid experiences is not entirely derived from real life events, but rather originate from within the unconscious psyche (Jones et al., 2000; Skirrow et al., 2002).

The emergence of hallucinations is the result of typical neural activity patterns (Moss, 2014). Concerning auditory verbal hallucinations, there have three dimensions identified. The first is the linguistic complexity, which is based upon the range of single words to complete conversations. The second is the attribution to the subject, the difference between attribution to other or self, in other words, the perception of the origin of the auditory hallucination. The third is the spatial locality, which is also divided into inner and outer, considered another way, the origin of these perceptions either from outside of one's head or hearing voices from inside oneself (Stéphane et al., 2003). Henri Ey provides the theory that hallucinations are as a result of the disintegration of the mental life. The disintegration refers especially to consciousness and the resulting hallucination revealing the underlying unconscious processes (Ey, 1973b: 1341). The hallucination therefore diverges from normal waking experience, whereby the orders of consciousness with a maintained integrity have shaped the experience of the external world in such a way as is experienced as reality. Such a breakdown is potentially to account for the diminished cognitive self-monitoring and dysfunctional thought bias attributed to these hallucinations (Frith et al., 2000; Larøi, & Woodward, 2007). In order to further develop the significance of dysfunctional cognitive functioning, one must situate these aberrations within the qualitative mode of the ego.

In health and disease, the ego bears witness to the union of the perceptual dimensions of the unconscious and conscious aspects of the psyche, and in doing so, balances the ontology of the world within an experiential system of meaning. In *The phenomenology of perception*, Maurice Merleu-Ponty explains that experience of the external world (reality) is not merely a result of perceived images (called *perceptum*, 'what is seen') based solely upon sensory detection. The subject that perceives these images is bound to the experience (called *percipiens*, 'he who is seeing'). The *perceptum* and *percipiens* are both aspects of the same seamless phenomenon, due in part because the construct of the subject is based upon sensation, perception, and the cohesion of the experienced body as performed by the ego. The perception of external reality is not merely a reproduction of objective findings, but is shaped by the subject as it is sensed. This is further reinforced if one considers that cognitive processes are not isolated from emotions and affect, but are bound by them as part of optimal behavioural functioning (Merleau-Ponty, 1945/1962). In the context of ego defence mechanisms the separation and reattachment can occur as part of an unconscious strategy to alleviate anxiety and prevent the experience of trauma. It is reasonable therefore to propose this in light of the interconnected neural systems that link executive cognition to the HPA axis due to its role as a functional locus and orchestrator of widespread physiological systems (Gilbert, 2001).

The hallucination is not based solely on an externally derived sensorium. An instance that may clear the ground is the existence of auditory hallucinations in people who are congenitally mute. Their auditory register has not been activated in the manner that our presuppositions posits, but gives credence to the theory that these hallucinations are shaped by internally derived cognitive processes that give cohesion and meaning (Atkinson, 2006). This process operates at a foundational level within the primary order of consciousness to provide a delineated and cohesive experience of reality. It is the secondary order of consciousness that adds the structured, signification and symbolic dimensions to the experience of reality (Lacan 1977; Fink, 1996, 2011). To therefore understand cognitive dysfunctions, such as the hallucination, we must invert the focus from the *percipiens* manifesting a hallucinated object (*perceptum*) to the effect of the *perceptum* on the *percipiens*. In so doing, we can link and contextualise the relationship between the processes of perception and the mechanisms of significance and symbolisation, namely the metaphorical activity of the unconscious.

The metaphorical manifestation of the phenomenology of dreaming has always been a contentious issue in dream research. However, since the publication of Freud's *The Interpretation of Dreams*, it continues to be developed with accumulating evidence indicating that the metaphorical imagery is based on the affective states of the dreamer (Hartmann, 1998). During dreaming, contextualisation processes manifest as contextualising images. These signs and symbols are poignant dream images which are associated with discernible emotions of a specific concern. The content or type of signs and symbols are associated with different events and dream sequences. The existence of these contextualising images has been confirmed in studies looking at the dreams of subjects with recent traumatic experiences. Contextualising images increase in intensity and frequency after a distant or recent traumatic event (Hartmann et al., 2001b; Hartman, 2007). Many of these findings have been independently validated (Walk et al., 2002; Levin & Basile, 2003; Davidson et al., 2005). Such phenomenological findings are congruent with evidence from neuroscientific analysis of dreaming, particularly REM sleep, and its hyper associative and labile emotional state (Stickgold et al., 1999). The concept of the central image has been proposed to psychometrically assess this entity in dreams (Hartmann et al., 1997; Hartman et al., 1998). Investigating contextual images in the delirious subject may identify a novel method of assessing the severity of delirium and its relationship to the complex phenomena of hallucinations, nightmares, and delusions. Typically, hallucinations, delusions, and nightmares do not share exactly the same structure and dynamics, but all share some key characteristics such as their origin, the unconscious psyche. Jung often proposed the hypothesis that dreaming, hallucinations, and other narrative products of the unconscious had a compensatory effect upon the ego. The compensation was a function of the adaptation required for optimal psychological well-being, as well as, enabling the growth of the psyche (Jung, 1934). The dialectic that is played out in the conscious aspect of the mind then reveals the significance of what is happening within the psyche of the dreamer.

4.5. Transformation of ego consciousness

The life of the organism is directed towards increasing complexity. However, organisms resist the natural development towards disorder and are subject to the free energy principle (Ashby, 1947). The brain is also an agent of order and actively engages in maintaining order by resisting the entropy generated from the environment (Friston, 2010). This complexity is best expressed through the growth and development of consciousness which is the foundation of the individuation process (Jung, 1963; Semetsky, 2004). Psychological growth is in essence an open system and one that is a function of time (Brent, 1978; Prigogine, 1980). Such a breakdown in the functional cohesion between increasing complexity and regulating order may indeed be the foundation for delirium onset given the convergence of risk factors such as, age, deregulated stress responses, and reduced neurocognitive reserve to buffer these insults (Sanders, 2011; Maldonado, 2013). The growth of consciousness is not an archaic and outdated mystical idea, but founded on empirical neuroscientific evidence. Early theorists such as Hudson Hoagland, proposed that time perception is a function of the rate of oxidation in the brain (Hoagland, 1933; 1966). Roland Fraisse asserted that the perception of time is a function of human consciousness. This awareness of time was determined by the awareness of capacity during a changing event (Fraisse, 1966). Robert Goldstone provided evidence derived from studying individuals in different metabolic states that this perceptual time function was driven by a biological mechanism (Goldstone, 1967). Peter Ornstein further elucidated the role of awareness of time as a function of consciousness and furnished this theory with evidence to propose the theory that estimation of time was the key to understanding this phenomena. It was found that large amounts of information, such as one might experience during emotionally potent events, renders the perception of time as fast, but in events where stimuli were largely minute, such as travelling a new route, time was perceived as very slow (Ornstein, 1969). For Itzhak Bentov, life and consciousness were interrelated. Consciousness according to Bentov, is the capacity of a system to interpret and respond to stimuli, and can be measured by time. Time as an index of consciousness can be understood as the ratio of subjective time divided by objective time. The life process is seen as a progressive one, whereby higher forms of consciousness are attained (Bentov, 1977; Newman, 1995). Aging is therefore seen as one in which increasing complexity is afforded the consciousness of the individual. Indeed, this time index and hence the expansion of consciousness have been shown to dramatically increase as a temporal function (Newmann, 1999). Chris Newman attempted to further draw a relationship between content, awareness, and perception, and proposed that perception was equal to awareness divided by content. Perception of time was not a function of psychological processing, but rather emotional dimensions function as a dilatation of time. This dilatation of time is the mode by which dreams and altered states of consciousness such a meditation function. Small changes can be seen with the state of mind-wandering or day dreaming, but markedly different during dreams. The subjective experience of time increases as one ages and may suggest age related growth of consciousness (Newman, 1982). According to Michel Jouvet, the purpose of REM sleep was to enhance the rehearsal and thus learning of instinctual behaviour with more recent theorists proposing that it is involved in threat stimulation (Revonsuo & Valli, 2008; Revonsuo, 2014). Sleep and hence dreaming are considered in terms of minimization of free energy (Friston, 2010). The cholinergic and aminergic systems that originate in the brainstem act as the main neuromodulatory systems involved in the encoding of perceptual experiences, with REM and NREM encoding different stimuli. The REM sleep system has been proposed to be involved in the development of various neuronal systems, especially the visual system (Frank, 2011; Bókkon, & Mallick, 2012). More generally, Hobson proposes that the function of dreaming is in the formation of protoconsciousness. To quote Hobson, '…REM sleep may constitute a protoconscious state, providing a virtual reality model of the world that is of functional use to the development and maintenance of waking consciousness.'(Hobson, 2009). It has also been theorised that REM sleep provides a functional connection between explicit and implicit memory systems (Bókkon, 2005). Indeed, the evolution of homeothermic status (of which REM sleep has been proposed to be evolutionary derived from) of animals, such as birds and mammals, has been linked with the development of explicit memory systems (Bókkon, 2005; Diekelmann, & Born, 2010). According to Revonsuo, dreaming 'reveals consciousness in a very special, pure, and isolated form', in essence 'the ontology of dreams is the ontology of consciousness' (Revonsuo, 2006). Insights gained from dreaming and its explanatory power of consciousness have high yield for a superior account of delirium onset and resolution. Many authors have integrated the theoretical framework of entropy and free energy to enable researchers to develop a model of interaction between the external world and the psyche of the individual (Friston, 2010; Gallese, 2013). Ego consciousness is based upon its integration within primary and secondary modes of consciousness. Primary consciousness is the preverbal and pre-ego state of consciousness of humans, and it is with the development of ego cohesion, as measured by self-identification, that a functioning ego is said to exist (Carhart-Harris, & Friston, 2010). Primary consciousness carries with it a relatively large amount of entropy and it is only with the development of secondary consciousness that this disorder can be curtailed. Secondary consciousness integrates uniquely human psychological constructs and constrains our experience of reality through structured and coherent systems (Friston, 2010; Hobson et al., 2014). The secondary order of consciousness enables the individual to suppress and mitigate the accumulation of entropy and in doing so enable a semi-permanent state of realism; a unitary mode of consciousness. This structuring enables the psyche to exist in a state of order and thus to bring fourth an approximation of what is experienced as consensus reality (Friston, 2010).

In neuropsychiatric conditions, such as delirium, there is a breakdown in this secondary consciousness and whatever components of it are intact reconfigure to create new experiences of reality, for example hallucinations and delusions, albeit with neurocognitive deficits. The diffuse brain failure of delirium is such that such processes can continue to disintegrate and with it the subject descends into a state of stupor and eventually coma (Trzepacz et al., 2011). In contrast, the secondary consciousness of the dreaming state is reconfigured and transformed as part of the general growth and development of ego consciousness. The internally generated dreamscape is reflective of the growth of the psyche, particularly, when one examines its content. The biographical content of everyday life conforms to the continuity hypothesis whereby dream content reflects everyday encoded experiences and integrates them with unconscious schemas. These schemas are modulated by archetypes which represent through symbolic forms something new and when activated have a more numinous effect upon the dreamer (Kluger, 1975; Laughlin, & Tiberia, 2012). Such a theory can also be found in the deliberate activation of archetypal dimensions of the psyche through the use of psychoactive substances. For example, potent 5HT2A R agonists (classical psychedelics), such as LSD and psylocibin have been shown to have a catalysing effect upon the growth and development of the psyche by transforming consciousness in a similar manner to dreaming and other healthy altered states of consciousness e.g. hypnosis/lucid dreaming. In contrast, *deliriogenic* substances also activate these archetypal dimensions, but as their name suggests induce a potent and traumatic delirium (Novak, 1997). Therefore, the role of neurodevelopment with its functional forms of recovery and preparation can be recast as the theory of how dreaming and delirium impacts upon individuation through their respective transformations of ego consciousness.

5 Growth and adaptation

5.1. Circadian integrity

A robust scientific account of delirium must include a perspective from evolutionary biology. In general, the suitable adaptation of the organism to its environment is the central tenet of evolutionary biology. The organism typically has to adapt to two types of niche. The first type is the spacial niche (biotope), comprised of different ecological and biological systems, e.g. desert, forest, ocean, etc. The second type is the temporal niche (chronotopes), comprising systems of time, e.g. day-night cycle, seasonal cycle, and moon cycle (Roenneberg, 1992). In order to successfully adapt to chronotopes, all organisms require rhythmic functions that operate in an endogenous and exogenous capacity. Exogenous rhythms require an external pacemaking signal to drive them. Endogenous rhythms are continuously cycling in the absence of an external signal and are referred to as free running. Such endogenous rhythms often have a periodic function parallel to an external stimulus, and although they exist in the absence of external stimuli they can be influenced by one (Halberg, 1959). Internalised clock/pacemaker/ endogenous oscillating systems enable cyclic behaviour to be driven in the absence of external stimuli. It is these internalised clocks that become synchronised with an environmental stimulus (Zeit-geber/time giver). This is a complex biochemical process called *entrainment* (Roenneberg et al., 2003b). A wide range of biological responses to the chronotope have been found to exist, such as the synthesis and degradation of specified molecules or particular patterns of behavioural responses entrained to a temporal stimulus. Rhythmicity is categorised according to a temporal cycle. Ultradian rhythms are biological rhythms found to be shorter than one day (<24h). While infradian rhythms are biological rhythms found to be longer than one day (>24h). The circadian rhythms are biological rhythms that occur with a periodicity of approximately 24 hours (Gerkema, 2002). Although the circadian phenomenology has been consistently recognised as part of the phenotype of delirium, it is only in recent decades that the neural substrate is being investigated.

The generation and regulation of circadian rhythms in humans is a function of a specific neural system, the circadian timing system (CTS) (Moore, 1997). This complex system acts as a central gatekeeper in the temporal regulation of vital functions such as sleep-wake patterns, reproduction, the stress response, hormone plasma concentrations and cognition (Reppert & Wever, 2002). A primary function of the CTS is to allow the organism as a whole to anticipate and adapt to the changing challenges of the environment (Schibler & Sassone-Corsi, 2002). This allows for optimal functional engagement with the environment and at a physiological level allows for a synchronisation of biological processes thus enable the efficient use of biological pathways. As an example, the circadian mechanisms possessed by hepatocytes promote glycolysis during the daytime and gluconeogenesis nocturnally (Asher & Schibler, 2011). The CTS is composed of three functional elements, (1) a pacemaker, (2) entrainment mechanisms, and (3) effector systems that regulate biological rhythms (Moore, 1997) [see Fig 2.].

Fig. 2 Model of the circadian timing system (CTS)

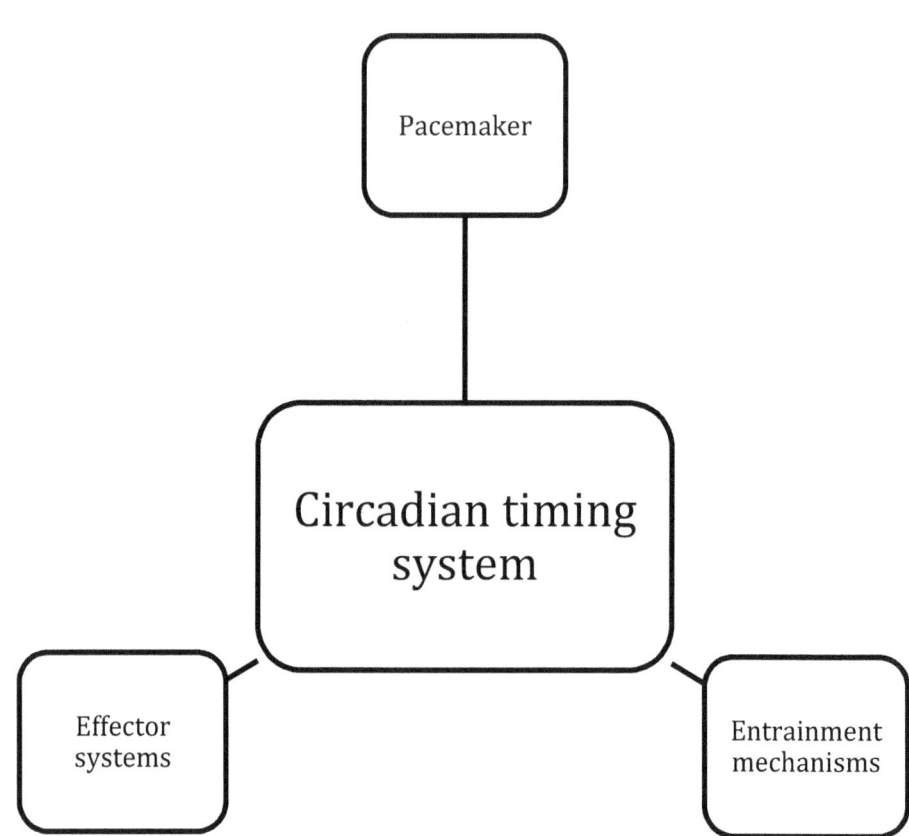

The suprachiasmatic nucleus (SCN) functions as the circadian pacemaker that directs or drives rhythms. The SCN has been found to be composed of two bilaterally symmetrical nuclei located within the anterior hypothalamus and each nuclei is estimated to have approximately 10,000 neurons (Reppert & Weaver, 2001; Antle & Silver, 2005). SCN ablation results in the elimination of circadian rhythms while transplantation of an SCN restores circadian rhythms to the donor (Ralph et al., 1990). It has been reported that the primary photoreceptors for the CTS system are a small population of retinal ganglion cells in the retina which express melanopsin (Provencio et al., 2000; Berson et al., 2002). Photons of light are transduced by these cells (non-rod, non-cone, retinal ganglion cells) and directly innervates the SCN via the retinohypothalamic tract. The circadian system is capable of integrating intensity, duration, and the spectral composition of photic signaling, which enables the integration of a temporal dimension to vision (Berson et al., 2002).

It has been demonstrated that in vitro dissociated SCN neurons can continue firing for several weeks (Welsh, 1995). To do this, SCN neurons require a system of synchronisation amongst its population. It has been proposed that GABA and VIP may have a role in this synchronisation system (Liu & Reppert, 2000; Colwell et al., 2003; Cutler et al., 2003). Each SCN nuclei can be further subdivided into a shell and core region (Lee et al., 2003; Hastings & Herzog, 2004). It has been reported that the neurons of the shell exhibit endogenous rhythmicity while the neurons of the core exhibit exogenous rhythmicity (Moore et al., 2002; Tanaka et al, 1997). Moreover, the core neurons have been found to gate photic signalling and are thus implicated in the control of rhythmic phase shifts in the neurons of the shell (Antle & Silver, 2005).

Previous theories held that acetylcholine mediated a direct light entrainment mechanism through nicotinic acetylcholine receptors (nAChRs) located on SCN neurons (Zatz & Brownstein, 1979; Zatz & Herkenham, 1981; Zhang et al., 1993). However, glutamate was found to be the major neurotransmitter in the SCN influenced by light. A subsequent discovery has found that forebrain cholinergic neurons (medial septum, nucleus basalis, diagonal band, substantia inominata, and the brainstem cholinergic neurons of the pedunculopontine, laterodorsal tegmental and parabigeminal) all signal with neurons in the SCN (Bina et al., 1993). The influence of acetylcholine over the SCN remain unclear, but muscarinic receptors (M1-5) rather than nicotinic receptors appear to be the major receptor type found in the SCN and respond to forebrain cholinergic signalling (Fuchs & Hoppens, 1987; Artinian et al., 2001; Yang et al., 2010). The SCN is coupled to an effector system which involves rhythmic release of melatonin from the pineal gland. In humans, melatonin receptors are present in most physiological systems such as the reproductive, renal and immune systems and are thus thought to be regulated by melatonergic mechanisms (Maestroni, 1993; Reiter et al., 2004). Two types of melatonin receptors (MT1 and MT2) are involved in sleep regulation, principally through their influence upon the timing of sleep (Caumo et al., 2007).

Clock genes regulate the loop of circadian rhythmicity, with positive regulators including the proteins Clock and BMAL1 (Brain and Muscle Arnt-Like protein 1), while Per1, Per2, Per3, Cry1 (Cryptochrome) and Cry2 are involved in negative feedback in the circadian clock (Dunlap, 1999; Hastings et al., 2003). Clock genes are also expressed in peripheral tissues and thus most cells possess an intrinsic capacity for circadian rhythmicity (Boivin et al., 2003; Azama et al., 2007). In addition, the SCN also has the capacity to synchronize the many biological clocks found in peripheral tissues to a circadian rhythm by the CTS (Reppert & Weaver,

2002; Hastings et al., 2003; Gachon et al., 2004). Peripheral clocks provide an ubiquitous system that regulates physiological functions such as body temperature, cortisol synthesis/release, and hepatic control over gluconeogensis, glycolysis, and lipid metabolism (Aschoff & Wever, 1981; Buijs & Kalsbeek, 2001). Although the SCN entrains these peripheral clocks, it is not entirely required for the circadian rhythm of the peripheral clocks (Balsalobre et al., 2000a, 2000b; Abe et al., 2002; Yoo et al., 2004). For example, it has been hypothesised that certain peripheral clocks can be entrained by food. Such a clock has been referred to as the food entrainable oscillator (FEO) (Stephen, 2002).

In humans, light is a pivotal zeitgeber (environmental time signalling stimulus) that allows for the entrainment or synchronisation of circadian rhythms to the 24 hour cycle (Duffy & Wright, 2005). Other (non-photic) environmental factors such as social exchanges / schedules, physical activity and availability of food can also act as zeitgebers but appear less potent (Wever, 1970; Mieda et al., 2006). The SCN adjusts clock phase through different neurobiological substrates according to either the daytime or night time domain (Gillette & Mitchell, 2002). The sensitivity of the SCN at night is mediated by glutatmate and subsequent intracellular elevations of Ca2+ and cyclic GMP (Honma & Honma, 2003). The sensitivity of the SCN during the day is mediated by pituitary adenylyl cyclase-activating peptide (PACAP) (Hannibal et al., 1997). During the twilight phase the sensitivity and responsiveness of the SCN is mediated by melatonin, which is produced during the night (Liu et al., 1997; Macchi & Bruce, 2004).

To explain such phenomena, it has been proposed that there was a Morning-Evening (M-E) oscillator within the SCN. These two distinct internalised clocks respond to light in accordance to the time of day. One internalised clock is responsive to morning light and the other to evening light. It was further postulated that such a system would have the capacity to respond to seasonal changes of light (Pittendrigh & Daan (1976b). It has been demonstrated that the molecular clock (Per1 & Cry1 and Per2 & Cry2) has the capacity to form two distinct internalised clocks (Daan, et al., 2001). The former in response to morning light and the latter responding to evening light. Such findings have been confirmed in mouse and Drosophila models of the human SCN (Jagota et al., 2000; Grima et al, 2004; Stoleru et al., 2004). Phase response curves for humans indicate that there is no 'dead zone' whereby the internalised clock is not responsive to photic stimuli (Jewett et al, 1997). The spectral composition of light also has an effect on entrainment (Duffy & Wright 2005). Melatonin is suppressed during exposure to short wavelenght (blue) light (Thapan et al., 2001). Such short wavelenght light has been shown relative to long wavelenght light to produce phase shifts (Lockley et al., 2003; Warman et al, 2003). Given that the twilight period of day consists predominantly of short wavelenght light, it has been proposed that this transition time between day and night, has a critical role in influencing the entrainment mechanism (Roenneberg & Foster, 1997).

Neuroscientific research implicating the role of circadian integrity in health has led to the proposal of a 'circadian resonance hypothesis' which refers to findings that health is optimised by the precise congruence between the environment and the CTS. A transient state of desynchrony between endogenous circadian oscillators and environmental cues is evident in animals and humans undergoing either phase-shifts or shift-work. Sometimes when the entrainment of endogenous circadian pacemakers to its systemic oscillators does not entrain to environmental cues, a desynchronised rhythm occurs and is referred to as a state of internal desynchrony (ID). Such a desynchronised state impacts upon the phase and amplitude relationships between the sleep drive, motor activity, core body temperature and hormone release (Reid et al., 2004; Haus & Smolensky, 2006; Salgado-Delgado et al., 2010). Such temporary desynchrony requires several cycles of re-entrainment for restoration of the circadian rhythym.

Chronic Circadian desynchrony (CCD), has been observed in shift workers undergoing sustained work schedules that significantly disrupt circadian entrainment. Such a desynchrony can lead to a variety of health problems such as obesity, diabetes, infertility, and cardiovascular disease (Knutsson, 2003; Folkard & Akerstedt, 2004; Haus & Smolensky, 2006; Waage et al., 2009; Lange et al., 2010). Circadian Rhythm Disorders (CRDs) reflect a chronic dysregulation of the CTS, with the misalignment between the endogenous CTSs and the 24 hour rhythm of the external environment (Wever, 1997). For example, in optimal environmental conditions, the day/night cycle resets the circadian biological clocks to achieve 24h cycles. In conditions with no external zeitgeber (e.g. constant darkness/light), the normal cycle of 24h is absent and a free running period occurs. The integrity of the circadian rhythm system can be measured by identifying the timing of peak melatonin concentrations and / or estimation of the time at which core body temperature reaches a nadir. This is typically around 5am or two hours prior to natural waking (Schultz & Steimer, 2009).

The most common CRDs relate to shift work, jet lag, and delayed sleep phase syndrome (Turek & Gilette, 2004; Srinivasan et al., 2008). Of note, these conditions highlight how disruptions to circadian rhythms include additional problems with cognitive functioning, motor activity and affective disturbances. The so-called *sundowning syndrome* has received particular attention as an example of the link between dyregulated circadian systems and the occurrence of neuropsychiatric disturbances that may be relevant to delirious states (de Jonghe et al., 2010). Sundowning syndrome is a CRD characterised by phase delay with severe behavioural disturbances that are linked to the degree of circadian disruption (Volicer et al., 2001). The disruption of circadian rhythms has been linked to pathological changes in the SCN in Alzheimers disease [AD] (Stopa et al., 1999). Moreover, factors such as daylight exposure, medication and active medical morbidity have all been observed to impact upon the behavioural symptoms of sundowning syndrome (Volicer et al., 2001; Staedt & Stoppe, 2005; Bachman & Rabins, 2006). Similar studies involving patients with AD have reported significant restlessness and deregulated core body temperature during sleep (Ghali, 1996; Satlin, et al., 1996). The molecular basis of these disorders is attributed to Clock genes and their polymorphisms (SNPs) (Piggins, 2002; Archer et al., 2003; Pereira et al., 2005). Patients with affective disorders, including bipolar disorder and major depression, have also been found to have detrimental polymorphic clock genes (e.g. hPer2 and hClock) implicated in the deregulation of affect (Desan et al., 2000; Shiino et al., 2003). Lack of substantial evidence has failed to significantly explain the role of deregulated clock genes in CRDs and delirium. Detailed investigation of the phases of the circadian cycle may reveal the underlying mechanism of delirium phenomenology as impacted upon by circadian disturbances [see Fig. 3.].

Fig 3. Model of the relationship between delirium and circadian mechanism.

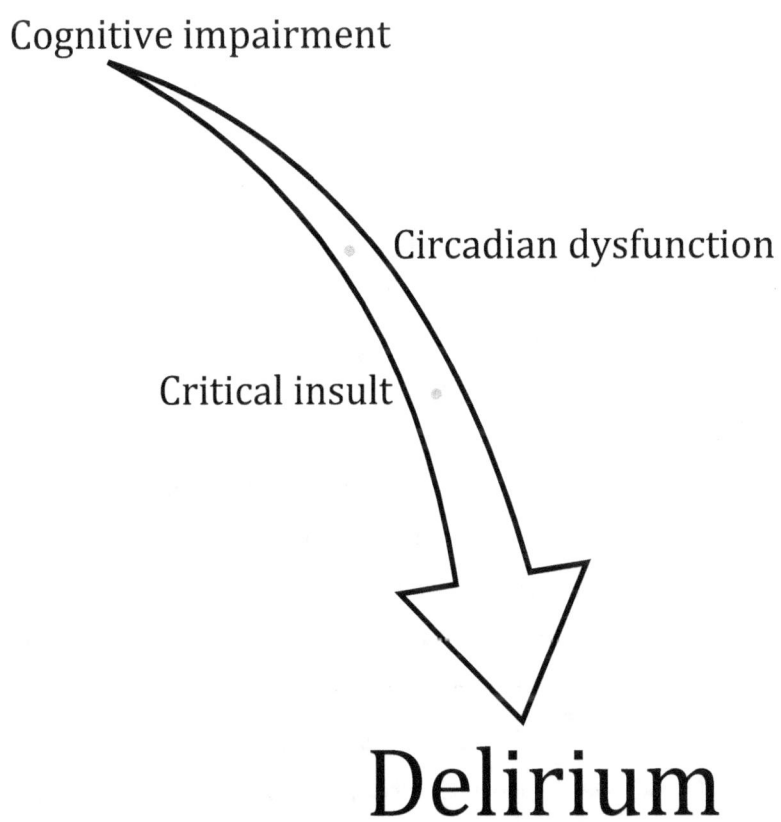

5.2. The sleep-wake interface

It has been consistently remarked upon that during the clinical encounter with delirium, one of the most characteristic features noted is the apparent existence of the patient in both the sleep and wake phases of the circadian cycle (Jacobson et al., 2008). To be sure, empirical evidence from EEG studies suggests that there is a parallel between the subtypes of delirium (hypoactive and hyperactive) and stages of sleep (NREM and REM) (Greenberg & Pearlman, 1967; Kojima et al., 1981; Jacobson & Jerrier, 2000). Perhaps a breakdown in the integrity of the neural systems regulating the different phases of the circadian cycle and hence the different stages of sleep may explain the apparent phenomenon of delirious patients existing in multiple stages of the circadian cycle at once. In order to tackle such issues, an overview of both sleep and wake phase neurobiology is required.

Contrary to popular conception, sleep is a rhythmic and active behaviour that enables the organism to engage in a process of periodic recovery. The circadian regulation of sleep optimises its evolutionary function. Sleep has been found to have influences over many CNS functions such as learning, memory, cognition and energy conservation in the body (Maquet, 2001; Hobson & Pace-Schott, 2002). Initial research into the neural networks underlying sleep and consciousness was catalysed by the discovery of the relationship between desynchronised EEG neocortical activity (arousal) and electrical stimulation of the paramedian reticular formation, with caudal midbrain and rostral pons involved in maintaining the aroused and attentive state (Moruzzi & Magoun, 1949; Lindsley et al., 1949). Sleep has also been broadly categorised into two main phases,

NREM (non-rapid eye movement) and REM (rapid eye movement). The first phase of NREM sleep comprises 75% to 80% of sleep and is associated with the presence of musculoskeletal muscle twitch, large-amplitude low-frequency EEG oscillations and non-florid dreams (Maquet 2001). The second phase of REM sleep comprises 20% to 25% of sleep and characterised by rapid movement of the eyes, low-amplitude, fast electroencephalographic (EEG) oscillations, absence of active motor activity and high cerebral activity such as vivid dreaming (Aserinsky & Kleitman, 1953; Hobson & Pace-Schott, 2002; Pace-Schott & Hobson, 2002). The phases are generally subdivided into stages. The first four stages correspond to the NREM phase from initiation of sleep in stage 1, light sleep in stage 2 and deep sleep in stage 3 and 4. The fifth stage corresponds with REM. Overall the stages and phases have been found to occur periodically, for example stage 1, 2, 3, 4, REM (5), 2... etc. NREM lasts from between 60 to 90 minutes (each stage approximately 5-15 minutes in duration), while REM lasts 5 to 15 minutes. These different stages of sleep have been characterised by unique polysomnographic measurements (Pace-Schott & Hobson, 2002).

The phases of REM and NREM sleep are both based on a complex interplay of subsystems that maintain sleep in general, but enable activation of different neural networks to induce their respective dreaming forms. Slow wave sleep (SWS) is the deepest of the NREM phases and is the phase from which people have the most difficulty being awakened. The vast majority of SWS (80%) is experienced during the first half of the average night's sleep (8hours). The NREM sleep promoting network is composed of the ventrolateral preoptic nucleus (VLPO) which innervates the histaminergic neuronal population of the tubomammillary nucleus (TMN). They exert their effect via the somnogen (sleep promoting peptides/ligands), galanin, and GABA, which impacts upon the arousal system structures (LC, RN, PAG, LH, PBN,) (Sherin et al., 1998; Lu et al., 2000). Although they, like many of the neuronal populations of the hypothalamus have complex and often contradictory roles in neuroregulation, the VLPO generally exerts a sleep promotion pathway (Takahashi et al., 2009). Lesions of this area have indicated that there is a decrease of total sleep by 50% and the majority of NREM sleep, but not REM sleep can be retained by the function of the extended VLPO (Lu et al., 2000). The second half of the night has significantly more REM sleep. Within the sleep system itself, the REM-off and REM-on system of the mesopontine tegmentum, is also structured and functionally related in this mutually inhibitory (GABAergic signalling) manner (Verret et al., 2006; Sapin et al., 2009). REM sleep occurs when activity in the aminergic system (comprised of histamine, serotonin and norepinephrine) has decreased enough to allow the reticular system to escape its inhibitory influence (Hobson et al. 1975, 1998). The cholinergic neurons are to be found in the pedunculopontine (PPT) and lateral tegmental nuclei (LDT). These subsystems signals to the lateral hypothalamus, basal forebrain, intra-laminar, reticular thalamic nuclei and prefrontal cortex (Satoh & Fibiger, 1986; Hallanger et al., 1987). Neuronal firing from these regions is most rapid during REM sleep, during the wake state less so, and during NREM sleep the slowest (El Mansari et al., 1989). The monaminergic neurons are to be found in the mesopontine region and are subdivided into median and dorsal raphe nuclei (serotonin) and the LC (norepinephrine) (Aston-Jones & Bloom, 1981; Kocsis et al., 2006). Other minor monaminergic signalling is derived from small populations of dopaminergic neurons in close proximity to the dorsal raphe nucleus (Lu et al., 2006a). Higher up in the hypothalamic region, the TMN synthesises and releases histamine (Steininger et al., 1999). In contrast to the cholinergic neurons, the monoaminergic system has little to no activity during REM and NREM sleep, but they are most active during the wake state (Kocsis et al., 2006; Takahashi et al., 2010). Smaller regions that contribute to the wake promoting monoaminergic system are the GABAergic neurons of the basal forebrain, glutamatergic populations of neurons in the parabrachial nucleus and precoeruleus region and the orexinergic/hypocretin system (Lu et al., 2006; Yoshida et al., 2006).

Initially believed to be derived from the cholinergic signalling of the PPT and LDT nuclei after the establishment of the NREM sleep phase and the subsequent advent of PGO waves (Sakai & Jouvet, 1980; El Mansari et al., 1989). The transition of the LC, the DRN, and the TMN into a state of silence during REM sleep implicates an inhibitory function bestowed upon cholinergic signalling over monaminergic signalling to transition from NREM sleep to REM sleep, thus establishing a reciprocal inhibitory system (Hobson et al., 1975; Aston-Jones & Bloom, 1981; Takahasi et al., 2010). Lesions of the PPT in animal models (cats and rats) have found that the REM system is minimally effected (Wenster & Jones, 1988; Lu et al., 2006b). Overall, it has been realised that the monoaminergic and cholinergic systems may only have a role in modulating REM rather than direct onset of it. More detailed research aimed at identifying small regions that regulate REM sleep using Fos immunoreactivity measures have found that the sublaterodorsal nucleus, precoeruleus region, and the medial parabrachial nucleus are all part of the REM system. Use of the GABA antagonist, bicuculline has shown that it disinhibits the sublaterodorsal nucleus and heralds the onset of REM sleep (Boissard et al., 2002).

However, the sleep-wake interface is not based solely on cognitive processes, but also incorporates motor behaviour. Indeed, motor activity profiles are more characteristic of a clear demarcation between the sleep and wake phases of the circadian cycle. The intimate relationship between the cognitive systems and the motor systems is such that it may reveal the phenotype of the clinical motor subtypes of delirium (Meagher, 2009). Such an intimate connection between cognition and motor behaviour is dependent upon the arousal system. The arousal system is a functionally related constellation of structures that synthesise and release a number of neurochemicals that signal to sleep-wake regulatory regions upstream during the awake phase of the circadian cycle (Jones, 2003). Although these subsystems are activated to promote wakefulness, they are also involved in the modulated higher cognitive systems such as the stress response and the reward/motivational system as modulated by the hypothalamic-pituitary-adrenal (HPA) Axis-limbic system interface, to name just a few pertinent examples (Shansky, & Lipps, 2013). Mental health problems, such as anxiety disorders, these systems serve as the neural substrate for their respective phenotypes (Itoi & Sugimoto, 2010). Within and between these structures, based on their respective afferent (input) and efferent (output), their functions must have a more refined basis of operation.

The two most well researched and conceptually influential systems impacting upon the wake phase are the norepinephrine and hypocretin systems. The norepinephrine (NE) system is found normally adjacent to the fourth ventricle in the brain stem and has its condensed origin as a structure known as the locus coeruleus (LC) (Berridge & Waterhouse, 2003; Weissman et al., 2011). The LC makes up about 50% of the total production of NE (the rest is divided amongst significantly smaller and diverse regions), and it is believed to be the only region with NE signalling to the neocortex (Berridge & Waterhouse, 2003; Aston-Jones & Cohen, 2005; Sara, 2009). NE executes its functions via adrenoceptors of which there are a wide variety (Weissman et al., 2011; Berridge & Waterhouse, 2003).

During the wake phase these neurons tonically fire at approximately 1-3Hz and phasically at 8-10Hz, depending on the experience of the salient stimuli. They have little to no activity during REM sleep while they retain minimal activity during NREM sleep (Hobson et al., 1975; Aston-Jones & Bloom, 1981). The LC system also has the capacity to maintain an increased membrane potential of neocortical neurons during the wake phase (Constantinople & Bruno, 2011).

The other major constituent of the wake phase promoting system, is the hypocretin system. This system has a typical condensed origin in a contiguous band of nuclei spread from the dorsomedial, lateral hypothalamus (LH) and perifornical regions with a rough population of 80,000 hypocretin/dynorphin/glutamatergic synthesising neurons. The hypocretin (often referred to as orexin) neuropeptides have been identified as a pair (hypocretin 1 & 2), which are derived (cleaved) from the same genetic sequence (De Lecea et al., 1998). They execute their effects via receptors, hypocretin 1 receptor and hypocretin 2 receptor, with different affinities (Sakurai et al., 1998). This neural system whose origin is small, has a wide diversity of psychological effects (De Lecea et al., 1998; Sakurai et al., 1998). Efferents of the hypocretin system are to be found in the entire cerebral cortex, the basal forebrain, tubomamillary nuclei and the brain stem, particularly the locus ceruleus, as well as the intralaminer nuclei of the thalamus, and anteroventral thalamic nucleus (Peyron et al., 1998). Significant afferents to this system includes the LC, dorsal raphe nuclei, parabrachial nucleus, central nucleus of the amygdala, ventral tegmental and the medial prefrontal cerebral cortex (Yoshida et al., 2006). These neurons have been reported to have significantly greater discharge activity during functions such as reward and goal directed behaviour and are collectively referred to as *physiological integrators* (Lecea et al., 2002; Hassani et al.,

2009). The neural substrate that mediates this wide variety of functions has been shown to reflect a medial to lateral difference across this population of neurons, with lateral neurons being more associated with reward behaviour and medial neurons closely aligned with stress and arousal systems (Harris & Aston-Jones, 2006). It has been proposed that given their activity during the wake phase of the circadian cycle, these neurons modulate the arousal state required for an organism to engage in goal oriented behaviour. Hypocretin are also implicated in the modulation of food intake due to their influence over leptin and glucose, both indicative of the metabolic status of the organism (Sweet et al., 1999).

The transition between the sleep and wake phases of the circadian cycle must be rapid and precise so that an animal once asleep and in a vulnerable position can wake rapidly and escape potential danger. The transition from waking to sleep is much slower, at approximately 10 minutes in humans. As measured by EEG there is a transition from low voltage, high frequency waves of the wake state to the high voltage slow waves of the NREM sleep phase (Takahashi et al., 2009). During NREM sleep, the progression is to gradually slower waves until slow wave sleep (0.5-4Hz) is dominant (Philips et al., 2010). The transition from NREM to REM sleep is also rapid with a progressive decrease in voltage and increase in frequency of neuronal activity coupled with significant theta activity. In particular, during human REM sleep there is much more pronounced activity in the hippocampus and neocortex. To account for the mutually inhibitory relationship between these two phases of sleep, the flip-flop switch model was proposed to tie together the neural subsystems that served sleep behaviour (Saper et al., 2001; Mano & Kime, 2004). This relationship insures a rapid and relatively complete transition between the states of sleep and awake. The CTS controls these phases and sleep disorders are as a result of disturbed circadian integrity.

There are two main theories to account for the relationship between the CTS and sleep. The first is the temporal regulation of sleep while the other is the *restorative sleep theory*. In reality, however, it has been found that both components are correct and are congruent with sleep as both a conserver of energy and as a homeostatic drive (Pinel, 2001; Daan & Beersma, 1984). In fact a two process model of sleep regulation has been proposed to explain the relationship between the CTS and sleep (Borbly, 1982; Daan et al., 1984). There are two oscillators controlling this dynamic process, the circadian oscillator (CO) which controls wake propensity, while the homeostatic oscillator (HO) controls the homeostatic components of sleep (Dijk & Czeisler, 1994). This model proposes that wake propensity decreases in line with melatonin onset (Claustrat et al., 2005). Once HO has established the onset of sleep, the sleep drive is then controlled by the CO for the duration of the night (which is controlled by HO (Dijk & Czeisler, 1994). The gating model of sleep is thus proposed to be dependent on the phase relationship between these two oscillators (CO and HO) (Daan et al., 1984). Several neurotransmitter systems have been implicated in this integrated system. Adenosine has been proposed as the major molecule for the promotion of sleep through a negative feedback cycle on neuronal populations associated with wakefulness (Porkka-Heiskanen et al., 2002). While hypocretin/orexin has been proposed as a major molecule involved in wakefulness (Pace-Schott & Hobson, 2002). Accumulating evidence indicates that there is age related loss of hypocretin neurons (Kotz et al., 2005; Kessler et al., 2011). Such an age related change may implicate its role in the onset of delirium. With relevance to delirium phenomenology, the hypocretin system (with its connections to the basal forebrain and prefrontal cerebral cortex efferents) has an emerging role to play in cognitive functioning, both in healthy subjects and with an age related decline. Typically hypocretins increase cortical release of acetylcholine as a result of increasing the firing rate of basal forebrain cholinergic signalling neurons (Fadel & Federick-Duus, 2008; Arrigoni et al., 2010).

5.3. Dreaming and adaptation

Although delirium is considered to be a neuropsychiatric syndrome, the focus upon pathology has neglected any consideration of what role it plays within the wider life of the individual, as reflected in the evolutionary history of humanity. The phenomenology of delirium particularly lends itself to an analysis from the perspective of evolutionary biology. The experience of delirium is plagued by a breakdown of circadian functioning and social cohesion. The significance of delirium phenomenology can further be enhanced by invoking the theoretical accounts of dreaming as it pertains to the life of the individual. There are a plethora of theories to describe and account for the existence of dreaming, and as valiant an effort as they have been they have largely been based on folk psychological frameworks (Turner, 2013). To understand this from our scientifically informed perspective, we would do best to start our reflection based initially upon an evolutionary neurobiological framework, both in terms of the environmental adaptation to the environment and social functioning.

Our understanding of the evolution of sleep systems is largely based upon comparative studies looking at the existence of REM, NREM, and thermoregulation in other species of animals (Stickgold, & Walker, 2013). There is a tenuous link between the development of language, brain maturity, the growth of consciousness, and REM sleep. The dreams of children, which are largely static and visual experiences, reflect this development (Domhoff, 2001; Hobson, 2009). One of the most conserved features of the neurobiology of the psyche is the role of the circadian system, whose phylogenetic history goes back as far as cyanobacteria (Johnson et al., 2011). In mammals, the circadian influence upon the neuronal activity of the neocortex has been proposed as the viable candidate to explain the promotion of dreaming in general (Wamsley et al., 2007). Early work highlighted the relationship between the phase delays of circadian signals and their resultant effect upon dream recall. It was found that the dream reports of delayed dreams were more intense visually and detailed overall. In general, it was found that the ultradian and circadian influences upon sleep and dreaming were independent, but also additive in their respective effects upon dreaming (Antrobus et al., 1995). The propensity to enter REM sleep during nocturnal sleep is also found to be regulated in a circadian manner with REM consistently occuring during the early morning hours before awakening (Dijk, & Cajochen, 1997).

In the broader context of investigating delirium neurobiology, understanding the neurobiology of the different sleep subsystems may elucidate the phenomenological parallel between delirium and dreaming. In studies of dream recall, it is estimated that awakenings from REM sleep, yield about 60% to 90%, while those from NREM yield a much lower range of 25% to 50% (Nielsen, 2000). Based upon the current evidence, functional neuroimaging to characterise the neural correlates of dreams has largely only been conducted during REM sleep (Kussé et al., 2010). Regional brain activity has been linked to REM sleep in the following areas: the amygdaloid complexes, hippocampal formation, and anterior cingulate cortex (ACC), as well as the pontine tegmentum, thalamus, and basal forebrain. While a number of regions such as the dorsolateral prefrontal cortex (DLPFC), orbitofrontal cortex, posterior cingulate gyrus, precuneus, and the inferior parietal cortex has been demonstrated to be hypoactive (Maquet et al., 1996; Braun et al., 1997; Nofzinger et al., 1997; Maquet, 2000). Such a constellation of activity suggests that there is a distinct role attributable to REM sleep for emotional memory processing and consolidation (Wagner et al., 2001; Sterpenich et al., 2009; Nishida et al., 2011). The dominance of negative emotion over positive emotion is a consistent trait of dreaming, with aggression and fear being the most represented (Hall & Van de Castle, 1966; Strauch & Meier, 1996). The specific form of deactivated neural regions (relative to the waking state) may illustrate the removal of executive functions such as repression and the return of many of the repressed encoded features that constellate the overwhelming majority of dreams (Nofzinger et al., 1997; Braun et al., 1997; Maquet, 2001; Maquet et al., 2005).

Conversely, NREM sleep is associated with widespread cerebral deactivation, including the pontine brainstem, the orbito-frontal cortex, and the anterior cingular cortex (Braun et al., 1997; Hofle et al., 1997). In contrast, REM sleep is linked to the activation of these same regions (Maquet et al., 2005). This NREM sleep-driven deactivation thus reflects the continuous decline in the activation of the reticular activating system (RAS), and results in the disfacilitation of thalamocortical relay neurons, which then allows the emergence of thalamocortical oscillations (Steriade & Timofeev, 2003). NREM deactivation of the ascending arousal systems, may have the effect of significantly reducing forebrain neural activity and hence impact cognition negatively (Hofle et al., 1997; Maquet et al., 2005). Moreover, the deactivation of limbic structures, such as the anterior cingulate, may hinder this emotional salience as compared to REM sleep (Hofle et al., 1997; Hobson et al., 1998).

The role of dreaming in adaptation is based upon the role sleep plays upon neurodevelopment, and in the context of humans, the role of culture and mental health. Human culture can be conceived of as a combination of the arts and the sciences, and it is well recognised that dreaming has played a significant role in the inspiration and thus the birth of new ideas within these domains of human culture (Barrett, 2001; Hartmann, 1998). Indeed, transitions in one's life can activate archetypes (image schemas) to provide a framework by which new behaviour and experiences can be integrated into ego consciousness. Another example is to be found in the life of the individual whereby dreams can be utilised as part of psychotherapy and as a source of self reflection (Hartmann, 1995, 1998). Dreaming has largely a compensatory and growth based function. This can clearly be seen in the context of dream experiences after real life occurrences of trauma. In trauma a new experience penetrates the apparent unitary form of consciousness and forces the person to experience something radically new and therefore threatening. Initial stages of these experiences are repressed and dissociated from the rest of ego consciousness in order to reduce the onset of an anxious state that would otherwise hinder the optimal behavioural functioning. Given that such an experience is radically new, it is encoded and represented in a symbolic form so that it can be integrated into the modality of consciousness. This serves the dual function of enabling an individual to remain an autonomous subject, but also a social subject integrated into a social network of human interaction, i.e. culture and social attachment.

However, culture and social cohesion are largely made possible by repressing that which is socially unacceptable and often at odds with our own desires. Dreaming helps regulate part of this complex process. Negative occurrences in dreaming have been estimated to be seven times more likely to occur than positive occurrences, with 70% of those negative experiences being directed at the individual dreamer (Hall & Van de Castle, 1966; Domhoff & Hall, 1996). Such negative phenomenal figures plague the psyche of the delirious subject, perhaps symbolically representing the threat that the patient is experiencing during critical illness and, more ominously, as a portent of an increased risk of mortality (Goodwyn, 2012). The manifestations of negative phenomenal figures are reflective of anthropomorphic and non-anthropomorphic images of the shadow archetype. Indeed, these threatening phenomenal figures often dominant dreaming with aggression accounting for 45% of social interaction in dreams, with the dreamer often finding themselves as the victim of aggression (Hall & Van de Castle, 1966; Domhoff & Hall, 1996; Strauch & Meier, 1996). The archetypal motif of the shadow, who has a central core of destruction, can also be seen in the evolutionary light of an adaptive function for anti-social behavior, including murder. Other studies of recognising self versus non self, and in group versus out group recognition, all serve social cohesion and are the cultural inflection of the phenomenology of the shadow archetypal motif, as evidenced by the appearance of an enemy and/or a stranger. (Tajfel, 1984; Öhman et al., 2001b; Bernstein et al., 2008). In particular, the symbolic image of the trickster who defies social norms, finds its role congruent with one that represents the unwanted feelings and repressed aspects of encoded experiences that reemerge in new forms (Jung 1959b; Von Franz, 1964; Duntley & Buss, 2011).

If all experience can be proposed to be a virtual simulation of the perceptual world, generated internally with enhanced contribution from external physical stimuli, then surely this same principle operates in dreaming and delirium (Revonsuo, & Salmivalli, 1995). Through our perceptual systems, an abstraction of the environment is what is encoded and from that the constellation of complexes that have encoded these abstract imagos shapes our motivation but also reality via attentional systems. This primary perceptual system exists in order to enhance our adaptation to the environment. The secondary mode of consciousness enhances both adaptation and alienation, with the functions of language, symbolism, and communication, thus preventing humans from having a direct experience of nature (Lacan, 1988). Therefore, adaptation is not merely a reactive system of homeostasis. The human is not in some state of harmony with the world around it, nor can it ever achieve such a state. Although there is a system that enables us to respond to the challenges of the environment psychologically, such as the employment of ego defence mechanisms, the environment as sculpted by our perception of reality is one which is subject to change. The reality that is experienced by the ego is but a product of the ego by its perceptual projections coupled with the function of differentiating the subject from the object and self from others. Alienation from the environment occurs when the functional integrity of these integrated systems breaks down. Delirium in this sense is alienation.

In the clinical moment that abetted and protected delirium, the return to first principles is in fact the first organisation of a medical field dedicated entirely to delirium. One that is composed of empiricism and fundamental in its rationalism, a medley for scientific reformulation. In its everyday practice, the delirious experience resembles the rest of the structural edifice that it is embedded in. A clouding of consciousness, an absence or presence of behaviour that is clinically defined, but fundamental, because like the rest of medicine, it is an enigma that has consequences. When dissipated it is forgotten or ignored, but for many it can remain as a dysfunctional form; a trauma and its dissociation. This PTSD, this domain of reconstituted truth, encroaches upon life and upon the convenience of the psyche in a comparable way to new experiences. Overloaded by definition, defaulting by design, the naïve ego observes through a fog of language, clinical settings and clinical dogma a transmission of meaning from the patient to the health care professional; an open confession of a nightmare.

5.4. Day dreaming and delirium

Evidence from non-task oriented trials and reports of inattention during mind wandering/day dreaming, enable one to draw the conclusion that it serves as a useful model for delirium and thus an understanding of its underlying neurophysiology may yield insight into its heterogeneous phenomenology (Christoff et al., 2011; Domhoff, 2011; Pace-Schott, 2011). In accordance with the isomorphism theory, it should not be a surprise to find that the neural substrates mediating mind wandering and dreaming during sleep have also been found to be highly congruous (Fosse & Domhoff, 2007; Pace-Shott, 2007; Nir & Tononi, 2010; Pace-Shott, 2011). In general, dreaming/mind wandering mentation can serve as an experimental model for psychotic cognitive states (Hobson, 2004; Robbins, 2013). In the modern scientific era, Freud drew parallels between sleep-dreaming, day dreaming/mind wandering, and creative activity. He proposed that all three modes are derived from similar psychological processes and find their origin in the unconscious (Freud, 1908). Other contributing elements of the evidence that waking conscious thought, day dreaming, and dreaming proper are part of a continuum are found in the reports of nightmares. It has been reported that subjects reporting a high frequency of nightmares also have similarly frightening day dreams (Van der Kolk et al., 1984).

The phenomenology of mind-wandering and dreaming have been consistently been reported as being very similar. Early studies conducted into reports of mind-wandering reported the experience of it as being qualitatively similar to dreaming in 19% to 24% of cases (Foulkes & Scott, 1973; Foulkes & Fleisher, 1975). More recent evidence indicates that dreaming during sleep and daydreaming during quiet wakefulness share similar features such as emotional salience and the projection of past events onto our conceptions of the future (Wamsley et al., 2010). The congruence of phenomenology is further evidenced by analysis of key domains. The first is perception, which is the foundation of experience and is predominantly visual and auditory with other senses, such vestibular sensation (flying, falling, and acceleration) playing a much smaller role (Klinger & Cox, 1987; Stawarczyk et al., 2011). This audio-visual predominance in dreams has been known since the writing of *The Oneirocritica* by Artemidorus and experimentally confirmed in modern times from an exploration of individuals manifest dream content (Schwartz, 2000; Schredl, 2010; Harris-McCoy, 2012). However, other studies have highlighted that the manner in which one investigates sensation in the manifest dream content determines some of the results, for example, when investigators specifically looked for bodily/somatic sensation such as pain, subjects would report more detailed dream content. The next domain is that of enhanced emotion whereby approximately 70% to 75% of adults report an emotional component to their manifest dream content (Domhoff, 2011). The dominance of positive and negative emotions within dreams has yielded conflicting findings and reflect the complex contextual nature of the dream and the underlying psychological state of the individual (Fosse et al., 2003;

Schdrel, 2010). However, it is generally believed since Freud that negative emotions and in particular, anxiety, dominate emotional dream experiences. In 69% of mind wandering reports, enhanced emotion is present and recounted as positive in 42.5% and 26.5% of cases, with 31% of such experiences being reported as emotionally neutral (Killingsworth & Gilbert, 2010). Another domain is bizarreness/irrationality, which is characterised by disturbances, including large shifts in time, incongruous elements of a situation or people or impossible feats of action. However, defining these features remains a subject of debate (Zadra & Domhoff, 2011). For example, in dreaming reports there has been found to be the existence of bizarre elements in 32% to 71% of cases, as scored on a simple scale aimed at capturing a sense of strangeness from phenomenal elements that appear surprising and/or illogical to the subject (Stenstrom, 2006; Schredl, 2010). In reports of spontaneous thoughts, it has been found that 20% of these reports are scored as bizarre/irrational on a (Klinger, 2008). In a study that looked at these elements in both dreaming and spontaneous thoughts, (within the same subjects), it was found that bizarre elements, were twice as likely to occur in dreams compared to mind wandering (Williams et al., 1992). The phenomenal feature of bizarreness during REM dreaming has been proposed to be as a result of extensive cholinergic activity in the PFC coupled with alternating dopaminergic activity in the mesolimbic and mesocortical subsystems (Solms, 1997; Hobson et al., 2000; Gottesmann, 2006). Cognitive bizarreness is also a shared feature with the waking experience of patients with psychotic disorders (Scarone, 2008).

The identification of a continuum of these phenomenological states indicates that it is reasonable to suggest that disorders of secondary consciousness would be highly congruent to the phenomenology of dreaming (Hartmann, 1996; Windt, 2014). Indeed many authors, from the distant past up to the present day, draw parallels between neuropsychiatric disorders, such as schizophrenia and psychosis in general, and propose that such a state is one of being in-between distinct sleep or waking modes. Such an indeterminate mode of consciousness in healthy individuals has been associated with lucid dreaming and hypnosis. Hypnosis and lucid dreaming can be considered similar, if not identical states of consciousness. Both states have characteristic features of dissociability, ease of thoughts, robust attention and self agency. Individuals are subject to auto-suggestion and can enhance both self hypnotic induction and lucid dreaming. According to Hobson (2014), lucid dreaming can be a useful model for the neurobiological mechanism of hypnosis. The issue now appears to be empirically addressable. In fact, studies investigating the neurophysiology of hypnosis have in clear terms attributed it largely to the DMN. Thus, vindicating the position that these continuous modes of consciousness are associated with each of these categorical states of phenomenology. Yet a major challenge still confronts these novel empirical and theoretical proposals; can they help define novel diagnostic or therapeutic tools?

In its essence, delirium is something that humanity does not control. Everywhere we remain chained to evolution, whether we deny or affirm it. Delirium is replete with formal structures of meaning, which is to say that a comprehensive analysis of it must be performed upon the theoretical basis that delirium exists within a newly defined horizon of experience. Beneath these structures lie a hidden truth, that defies our otherwise almost organic appreciation for our experience in the world. Beneath the processes of the ego, the constellations of the complexes, the archetypes, right down to the formal unity of the unconscious itself and beyond, is the void, the contradiction of immanence and transcendence, the foundation out of which our psyche exists and back into which it descends. A human life is no longer delirious on account of the inevitability of death, but because death lies in the heart of delirium itself. The delirious psyche is occupied by a radiated series of phenomenological reconstituted features from the structure of the brain. It is surrounded at all times by encoded memories, it transmits these encoded features back into the world from which it experienced them. The ego wounded and attempting to resuscitate itself, necessitates its role as the centre out of which meaningful relations are concentrated, and from them, are perpetually reflected upon. The configurations of a unitary cohesion are these processes, a series of phenomenal mutations resulting from generalised neural dysfunction, an empirical exposure divorced from health and optimal well-being.

Part III The phenotypic basis of delirium

6 Developmental chacteristics

6.1. Narrative structures

In congruence to dreaming, understanding the narrative forms of hallucinations and delusions in delirium requires an account of what psychological processes are involved in their manifestation. Only a few studies have been undertaken to understand the narrative structures of the delirious state (Patridge et al., 2013). The rate of recall of delusions in the ICU setting has been found to range from 47% to 73% (Jones et al., 2001; Capuzzo et al., 2002). However, it is recognised that narrative delusions are often absent from severely delirious patients and it has been proposed that such a deficit is due to widespread cognitive impairment (Trzepacz, 1994). In particular, the less structured delusions of delirium are as a result of left cerebral hemispheric dysfunction (Cutting, 1987). Thought disorder and its communicative medium of language are typically assessed by the health care professional at the bedside. However, quantitative speech analysis has emerged as a viable technique to analyse language and hence thought disorder from patients, particularly in the context of dream reports. Application of language analysis methods to graph theory has yielded encouraging results (Cabana et al., 2011; Mota et al., 2014). Typically, graph based representations of language are done so with nodes representing words and the edges between the words representing the grammatical and semantic relationships (Bollobás, 1998; Bullmore & Sporns, 2009). More recent work has identified the congruent structural graph forms between dream reports and the thought disorder of patients diagnosed with schizophrenia (Mota et al., 2012; 2014). Perhaps an appreciation for other methods of dream analysis may furnish us with the theoretical capacity to understand the narrative structures of delirium?

The main psychological process that is implicated in the experiential form of narrative is projection. Projection is the psychological process whereby aspects of one's psyche are imbued with objects in the environment, but perceived as existing entirely separable from the psyche. Projection was initially devised as a concept from the early work of psychotherapists using psychoanalytically informed models of the mind. It is thus based primarily on clinical observations (Von Franz, 1985). In the clinical setting, patients presented with the phenomena of misjudgments and of ultimately not comprehending the origin of these. Childhood and parental interaction sculpts and shapes a significant portion of the process of projection. Emotionally charged experiences encoded in the psyche are directed towards figures and objects which have analogous characteristics. The projection cannot be reduced to an implicit memory encoded by the amygdala complex, but rather it is a sum of the characteristic features that constitute a component of the object perceived. The difference between an illusion and misperception is that the cognitive error can be resolved easily, while with a projection ego defence mechanisms such as rationalisation may take place in order to justify the perception. Given that the person is unaware of the origin of these projections, it is reasonable to state that they are indeed largely unconscious processes (Samuals et al., 1986; Walker, 2014). According to Von Franz (1985), projection refers to facts that are easily demonstrated, but encroach upon psychological areas that are still unresolved. The neural basis of projection can be discerned from the involvement of self versus non-self processing by the cortical midline structure system (Qin & Northoff, 2011; Moran et al., 2013).

In general, robust narrative structures are an emergent property of the developing psyche. It has been reported that the narrative structure attributed to adult dreaming only manifests between 5 and 8 years of age. Before that, the dream of a child is based on simple wishes and archetypal motifs reflective of the developing brain (Foulkes, 1982; Resnick et al., 1994). From approximately 6 years onwards, the narrative structure becomes more robust, and 'give evidence that the mind has a need for orientation in terms of space, time, social context, and ongoing events' (Chafe 1990: 97). This is evidenced by dream narratives that begin with 'a statement of the particular place, time, characters, and background activity against which the events of the narrative proper then unfold' (Chafe 1990: 94). Although dreaming and delusions may share a common point of origin, the apparent coherency of the narrative is an illusion. Instead, both narrative structures result from a multitude of processes that create a mode of reality that serves their respective functions. The function of dreaming can be seen as part of the neurodevelopment of the subject, a modality of individuation, and a function of protoconsciousness (Hobson & Friston, 2012). The function of a delusion can be seen as constructing a form of meaning in the presence of a lesion or dysregulated integrative cognitive and perceptual systems (Freeman et al., 2002; Gerrans, 2013). Freud's interpretative method for dreams also reflects this fact, but from a more elementary position. The manifest content is what is apparent to the dreamer and is reflective of the complex dream work. This complex processing is comprised of condensation, displacement, considerations of representability, and a secondary revision (Freud, 1900: 486). The successful dream analysis is based not on reductionist translations of either the manifest or latent content, but on an understanding of the psychological processes (associations) involved in creating dream phenomenology (Jung, 1945). The basis of the first order revision, namely condensation and displacement, are set out by the AMPFC system and the hyper associative state of REM sleep (Nielson & Levin, 2007; Murkar et al., 2014). Here the encoded fragments of the day are processed with existing encoded experiences according to emotional and conceptual associations. These encoded elements are then bound together in a provisional manner (Nielson & Levin, 2007). During the first order revision, the representability of these encoded stimuli is processed both in terms of their primary sensory modality, but also other modalities, according to how congruent schemes have been integrated (Freud, 1900; Murkar, 2014). An example of this being a thought integrated with an image or sound. Processes best understood in terms such as metaphor, metonymy, and punning illustrate the rich linguistic dimension of these processes (Kilroe, 1997, 1998, 1999a). Both metaphor and metonymy are constituents of the signification process. For metaphor, one signifier is substituted for another in a chain of signification, i.e. vertical relations, while metonymy is involved in the linkage and combination of signifiers in a signifying chain, i.e. horizontal relations (Evans, 2006). This enables us to understand that there must be a perceived association between a projection and the object upon which we project.

Lacan finds a convergence between the process of condensation and displacement in the respective linguistic mechanisms of metaphor and metonymy (Lacan, 1977: 164). He further proposes that repression involves the processes of metaphor (Lacan, 1977: 175). This parallel is useful as it enables us to draw upon the findings from cognitive linguistics to explain the relationship between the complexes and archetypes, but on a grander scale analyse the cohesion of narrative structures. The origin of metaphor during the dream can be seen with the hyper-associative neurocognitive model of dreaming (Nielson & Levin, 2009). In repression, the hippocampal explicit memory system is downplayed, but the amygdala based implicit system continues to exert its influence upon experience (Han & Shi, 2013; Markowitsch, & Staniloiu, 2013). The external experience is encoded into a condensed representation of the multimodal stimuli, and given its separation from ego consciousness, is represented symbolically and referred to as *the return of the repressed*. Therefore the return of the repressed, as is seen in nightmares and delirium can be understood as a metaphor (Evans, 2006). Metonymy can be considered as a linguistic form of displacement when a signifier is combined or linked to another object without direct literal inference. Metonymy, based upon a sole source domain is considered to be cognitively subsidiary to metaphor which relies on a number of domains. However, the metonymy process can expand into a metaphorical process in the same manner that displacement in dreams can be part of the condensation function (Lacan, 1977; Ruis de Mendoza Ibáñez, 1998, 2001; 2003). The secondary revision is the process by which aberrant and often contradictory aspects of concepts and images in dreams are bound together in a seamless manner (Freud, 1900: 537). This function is largely as a result of the deficits in meta-awareness/reality testing within secondary order consciousness and gives us the characteristic experience of the oneiric state (Hobson, 2009). In his work *On the nature of Dreams*, Jung (1945) applies a narrative structure to the phenomenology of dreams. The dream begins with an exposition of time, place, and situation of the dreamer; a plastic mode of orientation. The plot then develops before the protagonist. Then a *peripeteia* or change in circumstances manifests. The dream typically ends with a *lysis* or solution (Jung 1974: 80-1). The narrative structure of the dreams is not an *a priori* fact. It is a faculty of the ego and hence based on the projection of a comprehensive structure upon the dream (Foulkes 1982: 276). According to Ernest Hartmann, 'though we are often forced to work with verbal dream reports we need to keep in mind that these are only attempts to render the dream experience in a preservable and reproducible form.' (Hartmann, 1996:12). Fortunately, accumulated studies have indicated that dream reports are reliable representations of dreams (Taub et al., 1978; Kramer, 1993). During REM sleep the intensity of the REM has been shown to be aligned with the activity of the dreamer, and the stimuli presented to the dreamer are often incorporated into dream experiences and reports (Roffwarg et al., 1962; Kramer et al., 1983). The dream report also co-varies with the intensity of the experience during REM sleep (Kramer et al., 1975; Kramer, 2006). The coherent narrative structure and its imagery is therefore not the result of random processes coupled together, but are in fact convergent in a highly orchestrated integrative system, particularly, in the forebrain (Solms, 2000). Therefore, an appreciation of narrative structures may highlight the function, but also reveal the deficits in the integrity of systems required for orientation that are lost during the development of delirium; deficits in integrity that construct a terrifying new reality.

The dignity of meaning has final priority within the psyche, which is to say, we can endure intolerable distance from meaning and retain even minimal attachment with an obscure glimmer of it. The structural forms of delusions have been recognised as residing within cerebral dysfunction, more particularly, left cerebral hemispheric delusions are associated with poly-thematic delusions, that are characterised broadly by experiencing a *separate reality* marked by florid events and individuals. The converse of this of course is that monothematic delusions result from right hemispheric dysfunction (Coltheart, 2015). In the context of delirium, these less structured delusions are resulting from left cerebral hemispheric dysfunction (Cutting, 1987). Unfortunately, there is a paucity of research pertaining to hemispheric dysfunction in delirium, however, the invocation of the isomorphism theory can furnish us with propositions that can be rendered falsifiable. According to a systematic review of the delirious experience, one can identify that delirium is marked by florid, polythematic delusions (Partridge et al., 2013). However, the single biggest obstacle to a full integration of these narrative accounts is the absence of psychometric measures of delirium severity. It is reasonable to propose that milder forms of full syndromal delirium, sub syndromal delirium, and prodromal delirium have preserved hemispheric functioning which enables the reconstruction of polythematic delusions, while more severe types of delirium are resulting from more widespread neural dysfunction and as such, monothematic and non-cohesive delusions are present.

6.2. Archetypal motifs

Projections originate in archetypes and complexes. The existence of recurrent motifs has been the hallmark characteristic of archetypes. Indeed, in the absence of neuroscientific evidence the parallels between isolated cultures and their mythological themes, characters, and systems of thought all provided the empirical evidence necessary to propose their existence (Haule, 2011). Archetypes are at all times structuring the experiential phenomena of life, including illness. Although by definition they cannot be experienced in and of themselves, their formal identity can be discerned from a careful study of perceptual experience (Smith, 1984). The existence of archetypal motifs in critically ill patients is largely understudied but promises to be a fruitful area of research. In a study looking at the experience of patients in the ICU, their dreams were reported as having four main themes, 1) transformations of perception, 2) aloneness, 3) death/rebirth, and 4) transformations of life.

It has been found that the poignancy of pre-death visions/dreams can be attributed to the general principle that dreams become more vivid and intense during transition stages (Barrett, 2001). Unfortunately, the most consistent and problematic experience of delirium and the ICU in general is the manifestation of nightmares. The origin and content of nightmares have been described and attributed to archetypal motifs, particularly, symbols of the shadow. The modern conceptualisation of the shadow archetypal image is congruent with the experience of dark and threatening figures experienced either in the dream state or the perceptually disturbed onset of delirium (Stevens, 2013). In different cultures and languages the words used to describe the nightmare have separated the bad dream from its cause as being one derived from an animal, person, demon etc. The typical words for nightmare in German are *Alp* (elf), *Alptraum* (elf dream), and *Alpdruck* (Elf pressure). In French, the word *cauchemar* refers to 'oppressive fiend', with the mar(e) element being derived from mythological figures of the ghost, the vampire, and the water monster, to name a few examples (Gamillsches, 1969). The dictionary of Dr. Johnson refers to the term *mara* as coming from Northern European mythology to describe a spirit that 'was said to torment or suffocate sleeper' (Johnson, 2003 [1755]). It is from this Scandinavian motif, that our English term nightmare comes from (Tillhagen, 1960; Frayling, 1996: 8).

The consistency of the description and conservation of the forms denotes what Bastion would refer to as the *elementargedanken*, the elementary idea, while the cultural manifestation would have been referred to as the *volkergedanken* or folk idea (Koepping, 1983). However, the existence of recurrent motifs is not sufficient to prove the existence of archetypes and as a consequence other pieces of evidence must be gathered in order to bolster this valuable theory (Pietikainen 1998; Goodwyn, 2013). The first point of evidence comes from Jung, whereby, the archetypes are not inherited images of symbols, but rather organising principles of images and ideas that are structured as a narrative, thus the reason why myths, dreams, and all other productions of the unconscious psyche often have a comprehensive structure (Jung, 1956). The archetype becomes activated in the context of environmental cues. Such cues can be referred to as *archegens*. These can be defined as archetypal generators and have the function of activating archetypes when encountered. This connection to the environment can be seen in the analogous behavioural patterns of other organisms which enable the organism to maintain its adaptive function within the environment, and as part of its life development (Stevens, 2013). When activated the archetype can induce numinous and powerful affective states coupled with striking imagery and ideas (Jung, 1959: para 99-103). However, such a theory, although robust and useful does not explain the content of the re-current motifs (Goodwyn, 2013).

The most compelling theoretical account of the archetype is from Knox, who identifies the *archetype as such*, the irrepresentable dimension of the archetype as being based on an emergent neural substrate, the image schema. Previous attempts to explain the underlying biology of the archetype have resorted to identifying analogous structures and patterns in animals. The proposed innate or pre-existent nature of these structures is their theoretical foundation (Stevens, 2013). However, according to Knox (2003), these theories fail to appreciate the role of epigenetics in the development of the psyche. Developmental organisation in early life sets the stage for the range of possibilities and the trajectory for the new developmental phase. Epigenetic processes of development are driving the developmental trajectory and are by definition a product of environmental and executive functions of the organism's genome. The epigenesis of developmental processes initiates a relatively wide range of plasticity but through environmental interaction that plasticity range reduces and the possible trajectories of development reduce in number (Sinha, 2005). As maturation continues these developmental organisations become more refined and established.

The convergent development of the retino-topic visual regions and the REM dreaming system may enhance our understanding of how dreaming may provide a method by which protoconsciousness can be formed. Lower level V1 and V2 visual areas are crucial to the formation of functions associated with executive cognition and some retino-topic areas can be found in the pre frontal cortex (Slotnik, 2001; Muckli, 2010). Such a visual dominance in dreams is reflected in the dreams of children whereby the visual imagery is present while an agentic mode of movement during such dreams is consistently absent (Domhoff, 2001). The developmental absence of episodic memories, autobiographical memories and linguistic skills also impacts upon the narrative structure of a child's dream (Foulkes, 1999). According to Yuval Nir and Giulio Tononi (2010), 'overall, dreaming appears to be a gradual cognitive development that is tightly linked to the development of visual imagination.' Moreover, the physiological and hence the psychological processes required for REM sleep have been demonstrated to share great similarities with visual imagery of waking experience (Llina & Ribary, 1993; Cantero et al., 2000; Ogawa et al., 2006).

Image schema can be considered as preconceptual abstract knowledge structures and are moulded by recurrent patterns of experience (complexes). The use of these archetypes extends into abstract reasoning and interpretation, thus the reason why in the absence of new information human cognition projects, symbols or preconceived notions i.e. archetypal motifs, to sustain their ontology. The reality that is perceived is coherent despite the absence of new information (Lakoff, 1987, 1989). Image schemas have consistently been found to be the structural foundation for metaphor (Lakoff & Johnson, 1980, Ruiz de Mendoza Ibáñez, 1998; Lakoff & Johnson, 1999; Hampe & Grady, 2005). At a more cognitive level, the invariance principle states that the relationship between these phenomena is one in which the source domain of the metaphor must be preserved and consistently linked to the structure of the target domain. The relationship between metaphor as coming from a complex and the archetype as a structuring pattern resolves the interface between an ostensibly evolutionary derived brain and an extremely complex environment. The neural substrate of the shadow archetypal image is the connection between the image schema system and the generalised schemes that have been repressed within the unconscious psyche. The particular form of what has been repressed is represented symbolically in the archetypal image of the shadow (Goodwyn, 2012). In other words, the archetype merely provides a structure, but our lives evoke its potential manifestation. To be more precise, the underlying cognitive processes involved in the formation of these constructs shapes our reality both in health and disease.

6.3. Emergence of senescence

An account of delirium would be incomplete without an overview of age-related neurocognitive decline in general and chronic neurocognitive failure (dementia) in particular. In biology, aging is composed of two features, a rise in risk of mortality and/or the decrease in fecundity, with both as a product of chronological time (Finch, 1990; Baudisch, 2011). Senescence, otherwise known as the biological process of aging, is a dual process combining both endogenous and exogenous aspects. The accumulative changes are inwrought at the level of the whole organism and at the molecular and cellular level. Senescence poses a conceptual challenge to the theory of evolution because the destination and goal of this process is death. Major theories in this area can be organised into two broad categories for simplicity. The first being that senescence is merely a general breakdown in the physiological function of the organism, ultimately heralding death and the other theory proposes that old age is a specific stage of development in the life span of the organism (Monaco et al., 2012). The existence of a specific developmental stage dedicated to senescence indicates that there must be an underlying molecular programme that is activated during this last chapter of life.

Age related neurocognitive decline has been observed to exist in many mammalian species such as rodents and primates (Gallagher & Rapp, 1997; Devan et al., 2014). The development of dementia as the inevitable result of age related decline in the CNS is still an uncertainty. In past centuries, clinicians' referred to the existence of *senile dementia*. However, dementia can often occur in the relatively young adult population (Reiman et al., 2004). The most famous case report, of course, being made by Alois Alzheimer in 1908 with a 51 year old female with *pre-senile dementia*. During the post mortem examination, her brain was discovered to have degenerated severely, and at a neuronal level, there was the presence of neuritic plaques (NPs) and neurofibrillary tangles (NFTs) (Kuchibhotla, 2013). Such a case report became recognised as the discovery of what is now known as Alzheimer's disease (AD).

It is consistently found that dementia (of which AD makes up 60% to 70%) is an exponential function of age, especially from the age of 65 onwards (Jorm & Jolley, 1998; Fratiglioni et al., 2000; Tom et al., 2014). Up to the ages of 95 it has been shown that the pathological profile of developing NPs and NFTs continues to increase as a function of age (Braak & Braak, 1997). Within the age range of 65 to 90 years, the incidence of AD, roughly doubles and studies examining the pattern beyond 90 years have highlighted the significant interpretive restrictions due to small sample sizes (Ankri & Poupard, 2003). Findings from studies have suggested conflicting results, with either some groups presenting with a plateau incidence rate while other groups continuing on an inevitable trajectory towards dementia (Matthews & Brayne, 2005). A study entitled: 'The 90+ Study', has attempted to add clarity to the issue. This study followed 330 people (aged 90+) with no dementia at the time of the study and measured their dementia status longitudinally. This study found that the incidence rate of dementia continues exponentially after 90 years of age (Corrada et al., 2010).

The transformation in perspective from dementia as being part of the aging process, to a discrete pathological entity, has ushered in a major movement to discover treatments targeting the underlying phenotype (Albert et al., 2011; Nelson et al., 2011). AD is believed to be human specific, with no clear evidence that it exists in other mammals, not even other primates. Initially held hypotheses to explain this situation included the maladaptive neuroplasticity hypothesis (Neill, 2012). The maladaptive neuroplasticity system, combined with the aging human brain, converged to produce the pathological entity known as AD. This maladaptive state is a result of the unique evolutionary adaptations that compose human neuroplastic potential. This potential when functioning optimally has robust compensatory mechanisms to restore and maintain a certain level of neuronal integrity and functioning (Fjell, 2014). However, age related changes can occur in certain populations of vulnerable neurons, such as the down-regulation of net glutamatergic excitation signals to this group. Since both mechanisms occur in normal aging and are associated, the onset of AD could be seen as a continuum of ageing, rather than as a discrete pathological entity (Berchtold, 2013).

The inherent dynamic nature of neuronal synapses enables the human brain to establish a system of compensatory measures to maintain homeostasis. They also serve homeostasis over the course of one's life by maintaining a congruence between the accumulated experience of the past and the on-going experiential influence of the present (Cheetham et al., 2008; Butz et al., 2009). The onset of age-related and exogenous traumatic insults activate the compensatory system that initiates and mediates repair mechanisms (Bertoni-Freddari et al., 2002; Selzer et al., 2014). However, emerging evidence indicates that the compensatory nature of synaptic plasticity may not have entirely benign effects and may be implicated in the pathogenesis of AD (Huang & Mucke, 2012; Santos et al., 2014). It has been proposed that one of the main contributing factors to NP formation would be the result of abnormalities in the compensatory responses of neuronal re-sprouting. Some researchers have even positioned neuroplasticity as the primary aetiological factor in the pathology of AD (Neill, 2012; Santos et al., 2014).

Originally it was theorised that this pathological mechanism involved two phases. The first or initiatory phase was characterised by the loss of synapses at the onset of senescence throughout the default mode network. The most vulnerable region to this form of decline is the posteromedial cortex, resulting in the onset of the second phase or propagation phase. Given its key role in the default mode network, impaired functioning of the posteromedial cortex leads to down regulation of glutamatergic excitatory signalling to the entorhinal cortex. Such a loss is accompanied by dentritic spines from layer 2 of the entorhinal cortex. The rest of the neuronal system begins to initiate the compensatory mechanisms which attempt to restore functional integrity in this region. However, this process results in the death of the neurons of layer 2 and the formation of NFTs (Neill, 2012).

Age related regressive changes have been observed to occur in the dendritic spines and arbours of neocortical pyramidal neurons in non-human primate and human cortices (Anderson & Rutledge, 1996; Duan et al., 2003). The importance attributed to the involvement of dendritic spines in the post synaptic stage of excitatory signalling may explain the characteristic decline of the cortico-cortico pyramidal inter neuronal signalling required for higher cognitive functioning (Nimchinsky et al., 2002). One of the most distinguished regions of change is in the prefrontal cortex of non-human primates and the respective degeneration in layer 1. In addition to marked morphological changes in terminal dendrites, there has been an observed reduction of 30% to 60% in the synaptic densities (Peters et al., 1998). In human studies age related changes have been found to manifest as an approximate decrease in dendritic spine densities of approximately 46% in adults over 50, compared to a much younger cohort (Jacobs et al., 1997). Similar findings have been observed in non-human primates, indicating that these changes are a conserved feature of age related decline in the primate brain (Nimchinsky et al., 2002).

Other vulnerable structures of neurodegeneration are the projections linking the dentate gyrus and pyramidal cells (CA1) of the hippocampal formation of the entorhinal cortex, leading to the characteristic deficits in the episodic memory system (Morrison & Hof, 1997; Hof & Morrison, 2004). The cotico-cortico projections between the pyramidal neurons of the association cortices of the prefrontal, the temporal cortex, and the parietal cortex are also significantly vulnerable due to the absence of a robust compensatory mechanism when insulted/degenerated (Bussiere et al., 2003; Hof & Morrison, 2004). In particular, pyramidal neurons of the 3rd and 5th layer of the neocortex are densely populated by somato-dendritic, non-phosphorylated neurofilament proteins (npNFP) which have been reported to be specifically vulnerable, as part of the progression of AD (Rudrabhatla, 2014). Such a widespread integrative failure may elucidate the specific regional formation of NFTs, and the resulting phenotypic progression from memory deficits to a more generalised neurocognitive failure seen in late dementia (Hof & Morrison, 2004).

Studies examining the prefrontal cortices of aged macaque monkeys have found significant alterations in NMDA receptor numbers (Bai et al., 2004; Hof & Morrison, 2004). At a molecular level, AMPA and NMDA receptor subunit proteins (GluR2 and NR1) have been reported to significantly decline in numbers as a function of age, particularly, in cortical circuits linking frontal and temporal association cortices implicated in integrative cognitive functions (Dickstein et al., 2013). The hippocampus shares many of the same vulnerabilities as the neocortex does with age related decline and during the progression of AD the NR1 levels of the neurons of the dentate gyrus have a consistent profile of age related decreases in aged macaque monkeys (Mishra & Gazzaley, 2014). Pre-synaptic markers of synaptic functional integrity have also been noted to have age related changes. The protein synaptophysin has been reported to decline in an age related manner, particularly in the dentate gyrus, resulting in spatial memory deficits (Smith et al., 2000). Within the hippocampus there is reported selective vulnerability within the molecular profile of synapses in the CA1 region (Rosenzweig & Barnes, 2003). Such age related changes in grey matter are accompanied by white matter changes as well, and with demyelination of the subcortical tracts of these cortices, so too a functional decline in the measure of cognitive skills and visuo-spatial ability (Peters, 2002).

The decline of cortico-cortical systems is not solely due to neurodegeneration, but to a loss in neurochemical functional integrity. These systems are linked to sub-cortical modulatory systems involved in widespread cholinergic and monoaminergic signalling. There is accumulating evidence to implicate these modulatory systems as being under duress of age related functional decline (Prauss et al., 2014). As a general finding in aged rats, the metabolite concentrations of dopamine and norepinephrine have been found to be significantly depleted in neocortical regions (Allerd et al., 2011). Congruently, pharmacological targeting of D1 receptor and A2 receptor systems in animal models has illustrated improvements in prefrontal cognitive functions. This finding has been found in aged animals, but no such effect in younger animals, illustrating that these agents are acting as enhancers in a system that is capable of enhancing, or has pre-existing deficits (Arroyo et al., 2014; Robbins & Cools, 2014).

Examples of age related changes and eventual degeneration illustrate how the elderly brain is at significant risk of developing delirium. The complex compensatory mechanisms coupled with highly vulnerable neuronal regions render it a challenging system to maintain longitudinally. It has been proposed that based upon its clinical profile, the degenerative mechanisms of delirium are probably unique to delirium and largely determined by the critical illness that is inducing its onset (Popp, 2013).

6.4. Delirium clinical motor subtypes

Clinical motor subtypes (hyperactive and hypoactive) of delirium have been consistently recognised as key phenomenal features of delirium (Bynum, 2000). According to Lipowski, a third category of a mixed subtype can be used to describe a heterogeneous motor subtype with no dominance of either hyper or hypoactivity (Lipowski, 1989). Empirical studies have highlighted the consistent finding that delirium manifests with these distinctive motor activity profiles (Boettger & Breitbart, 2011; Slor et al., 2014). The use of these subtypes is believed to enhance not only a better conceptual understanding of delirium, but provide new targets for treating the underlying disturbed neurophysiology (Van der Cammen et al., 2006). A number of studies have provided evidence that there may be a link between these subtypes and a number of clinical features such as the aetiology of delirium, the severity of non-motor features in delirium, prognosis, and the treatment experience of delirium (Meagher et al., 1996; Olofsson et al., 1996; Marcantonio et al., 2003). Studies investigating delirium as a result of alcohol withdrawal have noted that hyperactive subtypes tend to dominate while delirium as a result of conditions such as hepatic insufficiency tends towards hypoactive delirium (Ross et al., 1991). It has been proposed that the pronounced CNS activity during alcohol withdrawal is the origin of the hyperactive subtype as measured by fast-wave activity and increased cerebral blood flow (Engel & Rosenbaum, 1945).

The different subtypes have been proposed to be reflective of different neurochemical systems disturbed during delirium pathogenesis (Trzepacz, 1999). Anticholinergic states as a result of traumatic brain injury, hypoglycaemia, thiamine deficiency, cerebrovascular accidents, and hypoxia have all been implicated in the onset of delirium, but studies linking these conditions to motor subtypes have been lacking (Trzepacz, 1994). The suprachiasmatic nucleus (SCN) has extensive connections with cholinergic forebrain structures (e.g., nucleus basalis) but their precise function remains unclear. Brain stem cholinergic projections to the thalamus and mid-brain have a key role in the regulation of the sleep wake cycle, including REM and NREM dreaming phases with increased cholinergic activity during wakefulness and REM sleep (Reinoso-Suarez et al., 2001; Pepeu & Giovannini, 2004). In addition, the release of acetylcholine at sites that serve key cognitive functions (e.g. hippocampus) follows a circadian rhythm that is modified by activity. Acetylcholine and cholinergic agonists (e.g., carbachol) can induce phase-shifting of the circadian cycle while acetylcholinesterase inhibitors can improve sleep architecture in elderly patients with or without dementia (Cooke et al., 2006; Moraes et al, 2006; Jiang et al., 2014). There are also significant interactions between cholinergic and melatonergic mechanisms. Melatonin induces increased acetylcholine release at the nucleus accumbens that is associated with increased motor activity and nicotinic receptor efficiency (Paredes et al., 1999). In short, evidence points to a complex and bilateral communication between cholinergic activity and circadian mechanisms, although their relevance to the pathophysiology of delirium requires more direct investigation. Other studies have highlighted the role of GABAergic activity due to the link between delirium onset, alcohol withdrawal and patient exposure to GABAergic agents such as benzodiazepines (Trzepacz, 1994). GABAergic mechanisms implicated in delirium include the up-regulation of GABA-A receptors, the increased synthesis of endogenous GABA agonists and stimulation from exogenous GABA agonists (Sanders, 2011). Similar mechanisms have been speculated in alcohol withdrawal delirium, although existing evidence indicates that there is a considerable difference between the pathophysiology of alcohol-withdrawal delirium and other causes. GABAergic neurotransmission is also key to the optimal function of the SCN and hence circadian integrity (Liu and Reppert, 2000; Mintz et al., 2002; Wang et al., 2003; Caputo & Bernardi, 2010).

Although the relationship between *deliriogenic* factors and motor subtypes has been identified, methodological inconsistencies have been a major obstacle to this and hence an account of the underlying neurophysiology is lacking in understanding these motor subtypes (Meagher, 2009). Examining neural systems that integrate cognition with motor behaviour such as self-agency may further enhance our understanding of delirium. Self-agency is an important aspect of ego functioning, both as a developmental mode of growth, but also as an integrated domain of cognition coupling for motor behaviour (Sato, & Yasuda, 2005; Knox, 2010). Self-agency is a developmental dimension of the process of individuation which is itself based upon the dialectical relationship between the ego and the Self. The emergence of self-agency initially stabilises the ego, but also develops an ego that is more compassionate and less egocentric. According to Freud, the ego is first and foremost a bodily ego (Freud, 1923). Part of such an identity can be partially attributed to the cortical somato-motor homunculus on the motor cortices and the spacio-temporal experiences of one's self mediated by the precuneus cortex (Solms, 2011). From early childhood physical contingency and its associated connections with the mirror neuron system have been proposed as viable neural substrates for the development of self-agency (Gergely & Watson, 1996; Knox, 2009). According to Gallese and Lakoff, abstract thought and imagination share a convergent neural substrate with imagination being conceptualised as a form of stimulated action (Gallese & Lakoff, 2005: 2). The development of the cortical motor system and its resultant de-coupling of primary from the secondary motor system enable a partial but incomplete separation between action and thought (Knox, 2013).

The role of the ego in terms of self-agency, and in the broader developmental scheme of individuation, can be understood by examining agentive judgement and agentive experience. Agentive judgements and agentive experiences are intimately linked in both execution and content (Pacherie et al., 2006). Electrical stimulation of the supplementary motor area can often elicit a subjective experience of the urge to perform motor behaviour (Fried et al., 1991). It has been proposed that the generation of accurate kinematic and temporal prediction, essentially how and in what manner should the body behave, are based upon concordance with efferent and afferent signals (Haggard et al., 2002; Tsakiris et al., 2005). In particular, self-agency is based upon *intentional binding* whereby the perception of motor behaviours and motor intention are experienced as being closely matched in subjective time (Haggard & Clark, 2003; Haggard & Chambon, 2012). In REM sleep behaviour disorder, there is specific degeneration of an otherwise robust regulation of motor and cognitive systems. One of the key features of REM sleep behaviour disorder is the loss of atonia during the REM stage of sleep (Schenck & Mahowald, 2002). In 1965 Jouvert and Delorme, reported lesions in the peri-locus ceruleus area and the resulting dream enactment behaviour during REM stage sleep that followed (Jouvet & Delorme, 1965). Studies using animal models have implicated lesions in other regions involved in sleep such as the medullary and pontine areas (Luppi et al., 2011). More recent work has found the existence of ponto-geniculo-occipital (PGO) waves in REM sleep which have been demonstrated to be correlated with memory processing (Conduit et al., 2004; Datta et al., 2008). In particular, the pontine component of the PGO waves (the p waves) have a wide functional role in the neurodevelopment of the amygdala complex, the hippocampus, and the visual systems (Frank et al., 2001; Dang-Vu et al., 2006; Guzman-Marin & McGinty, 2006).

These wide ranging compositie empirical findings require a broader theory to encapsulate their critical role in the pathogenesis of delirium. There are two main dimensions to the theory of delirium pathogenesis according to Robert Sanders. The first is the state of CNS integrity of the patient at risk for delirium. Such a patient has an age related decline of CNS cyto-architecture and neurocognitive reserve. This state of pre-existing CNS integrity is a result of the life trajectory of the patient and their particular state of senescence. The key component to delirium onset is a GABAergic mediated pathway. The onset of delirium is due to the rise of inhibitory tone (GABAergic mediated) to further break down pre-existing impaired integrity of the aged brain (Sanders, 2011). Taking these streams of evidence together, an enhanced account of the phenotype of delirium is emerging which bridges the phenomenological with the neurophysiological.

6.5. Terminal dreams

Death and dying is a painful reminder of the finiteness of life. End of life dreams and visions are the most poignant form of end of life experiences (Gurney et al., 1886; Barrett, 1926; Wills-Brandon, 2000; Fenwick et al., 2007). Common experiences include the description of religious figures, deceased friends, and family (Houran & Lange, 1997; Fenwick & Brayne, 2011; Kellehear et al., 2011). The prevalence of these experiences of conscious dying patients has been estimated to be between 50% and 60% and there is accumulating evidence that highlights the therapeutic value of these experiences (Mazzarino-Willett, 2010). These experiences are often part of the dying process and bring a meaningful and easier mode of dying (Wills-Brandon, 2000; Lawrence & Repede, 2013). However, these experiences are often ignored or rationalised by health care professionals as epiphenomena resulting from intoxication, delirium or dementia (Betty, 2006; Mazzarino-Willett, 2010). One of the consequences of such numinous experiences in the context of cynicism has been the under reporting of end of life experiences by health care professionals, families, friends and even the patients themselves due to a perception that they may be a source of ridicule (Brayne et al., 2006).

Within the current scientific paradigm a more comprehensive account of the relationship between dreaming and delirium is manifesting. In the paper, *On the nature of dreams,* Jung describes the difference between the purpose that dreams serve and the false teleological interpretations ascribed to it (Jung, 1945). Hobson, in a number of books and papers, highlights a neural basis of such finality by ascribing dreaming as a process involved in the growth of consciousness, the so called protoconsciousness theory (Hobson, 2014). The most challenging obstacle to a fuller appreciation of the interrelationship of these entities is the absence of an account of their purpose or a sense of their finality. Given the role of archetypes in the developmental process of the human life, it should not be surprising that the great problems of life are to be represented by archetypal motifs (Jung, 1921: 373). According to Edward Whitmont, archetypes can be activated during three conditions. The first being the clinical situation between the psychotherapist and patient, when analysis turns from biographical details to more collective life themes. The second is during the manifestation of psychosis, particularly delusions and hallucinations. The third can be broadly conceptualised as 'when inner or outer events which are particularly stark, threatening or powerful must be faced, when there is a state of psychic or physical emergency' in clear terms, a transition stage from one developmental stage to another (Whitmont, 1969: 74). Jung identified three major transition periods in the life of humans, puberty (transition from child to adult), midlife (transition from material to spiritual), and end of life with the inevitable culmination in death. In delirium, we can see that the activation of the archetypal motifs is associated with two confluent factors, the psychosis resulting from cognitive impairment of critical illness and the terminal stage of illness/life that is often characterised by elderly patients. Studies looking at the end of life dreams and visions (ELDVs) have been found to typically manifest in patients who have robust cognition, including orientation to their surroundings, i.e. a non-delirious state (Osis & Haraldsson, 1997; Brayne et al., 2006). The difference between ELDVs and pathological experiences such as hallucinations and delirium resides in the qualitative experiences of the patients, for instance, the non-pathological state of the ELDVS render the patient into a state of inner peace and a sense of peaceful impending death (Brayne et al., 2008; Barbato, 2009; Mazzarino-Willett, 2009). However, these non-pathological processes can often be medicated as they are understood to be delirious and hence, deprive the patient of much needed, meaning and ease their suffering at this final stage of their life (Mazzarino-Willett, 2009, Fenwick, & Brayne, 2010).

The impact of age related changes of the CNS upon dreaming may also yield interesting findings for a fuller understanding of delirium. In young subjects dream recall after NREM sleep was found to be inversely linked to

12-15.5Hz range associated with centro-parietal spindle and 1-3Hz range associated with frontal delta activity (Chellappa et al., 2011). It has been proposed that this relationship is the result of the activity (reduce neuronal membrane potential) of the intrinsic thalamo-cortical neural network during the NREM phase of sleep (Steriade et al., 1993; Timofeev et al., 2001). In general, dream recall decreases with aging (Zanasi et al., 2005). Age related changes in the circadian system have been proposed to mediate this. The attenuated amplitude of the melatonergic functions, such as core body temperature rhythmicity, are characteristic of the aging process, with other age related changes, including a decrease in the amplitude of circadian signals involved in the drive for wakefulness towards the end of the sleep phase of the circadian rhythm (Münch et al., 2005). The initial discovery of REM sleep associated it solely with the psychological processes of dreaming (Aserinsky & Kleitman, 1953). However the psychological processes of dreaming are recognised in all other stages of sleep, including sleep onset, NREM1, NREM2, and NREM3/4 i.e. Slow Wave Sleep (Fosse et al., 2004; Nielson, 2000; Nielson et al., 2006;). Different psychological processes occurring during the different phases of sleep reflect the differences in dreams reported from these phases (Kaufman et al., 2006). In particular, the neural basis of REM sleep and dreaming have been proposed to be doubly dissociable but highly correlated (70%-90%) (Domhoff, 2005; Solms, 2011; Oudiette et al., 2012). However, definitive relationships are difficult to tie down due to the principled position that dreaming is also associated with neocortical activity (Antrobus et al., 1995; Foulkes, 1999). The most well defined accounts in the literature suggest that REM involves robust activation of the limbic system. In particular, the amygdala and the dorsolateral prefrontal cortex are activated, both of which are implicated in executive cognition and the function of repression (Maquet, et al., 1996; Miyauchi et al., 2009).

In a study that directly investigated patients dreams in a palliative care setting, it was found that end of life experiences had a prevalence of 87%, with 59% of these experiences having the theme of 'preparing to go somewhere' (Kerr et al., 2014). In Freud's *Beyond the Pleasure Principle,* he sets out an account of a psychotropism towards death, which is later called *thanatos*. This growth response towards death is dialectically bound with the psychotropism for life, e*ros* (Freud, 1920). A growth response towards death would seem antithetical to an evolutionary perspective when all other physiological functions including the vast array of psychological compensation mechanisms are dedicated towards growth and life. According to Von Franz (1986), the unconscious aspect of the psyche behaves as if the psyche is immortal and that death is but an illusion. Such evidence can be gleamed from the vast cultural artefacts of a belief in the afterlife. At an individual level, death is conceived of as a part of the life experience and gives the psyche its dynamism (Laub & Lee, 2003). At a cultural level, *thanatos* can be evidenced by the mass destruction of humans both between warring factions and upon themselves with the worsening climate change crisis (Hedges, 2002). However, according to Lacan, *thanatos* works solely as a function of the symbolic order and clear distinctions must be made to differentiate it from abstract theological notions of the Nirvana principle, where the organism seeks a return to an organic state or state of non-suffering. The repetition that is characteristic of *thanatos* is built into the function of the drive and motivation. The drive functions as a means of desire which has its goal not solely directed at an object, but also takes itself as an object; a perpetual cycle of desire. Such a cycle may actually exist in the context of the neural substrate of the drive systems in the CNS, with built in regulatory systems to break the cycle and instil a sensation of satiety. Breakdown in these satiation systems induces perpetual motivational behaviour towards the objects of desire. According to Lacan, the drives as a functional component of the psyches' motivational system contains within it *thanatos*, by which he states that the drive is insatiable (Lacan, 1988). Such insatiable drives can be seen with the behaviour to repeat or in the disturbances of neural drive systems continually seeking for the object to satiate the drive. Disorders with disturbances in satiation signals include addiction and substance abuse (Rose & Walters, 2012). Patients with dementia and delirium often have significant disturbances in physiological drives including hunger, sex, and sleep (Krishnamoorthy, & Anderson, 2011). Perhaps one can draw a parallel between the breakdown in these drive systems as evidence of *thanatos* in humans.

The underlying reason for this conspicuous absence of a comprehensive account of *thanatos* are the philosophical issues, once rendered intimately associated with the principle of teleology and now relegated to being beyond the pale of scientific enquiry. To infer precise end designs or purposes to living organisms is to give credence to the long discredited theory of intelligent design or Aristoteleon notions of teleology (Gotthelf, 2012). We must immediately concede that delirium as such cannot be considered to have a purpose as it is not an autonomous entity, but rather a breakdown in CNS integrity that ensures a coherent regulation of interaction between unconscious psychological activity and conscious activity that is required for living. Although dreaming may have a specific function, rendering it under the rubric of teleology is false. Instead the function of ELDVs even in the context of delirium may provide solace to the dying and may enlighten the role of delirium in the span of human life (Kerr, 2014).

7 Convergence between dementia and dreaming

7.1. Cognitive failure

Delirium is an evolutionary fact for which assistance must be given while it exists. Its occurrence requires a suitable response from family and health care professionals. The hospital is a complex solution for the care of the elderly. On the one hand, it has all the requirements for optimal physiological resuscitation and management, while on the other, it is a functional domain of stigmatization.This is partly due to the unsupported and exhausted staff who are continually exposed to the prospect of death. This prospect acts as a threshold for action and beyond it the empathic transference of the therapeutic alliance, in all its structural heterogeneity. Although the neural substrate of delirium is ill defined, an understanding of dementia and neurodegeneration furnishes us with the conceptual apparatus to address this issue and to enhance our ability to comprehend the delirium-dementia continuum. Beyond the modes of similitude enacted by discarded parts of science, the establishment of relations between one pathology and another enables one to identify parallels and divergences between both. There are many common neurodegenerative diseases affecting millions of individuals globally. Parkinson's disease (PD) is believed to be caused by the loss of dopaminergic neurons in the substantia nigra pars compacta. Dopamine is a major neurotransmitter in the brain that has roles in motivation, pleasure, and cognition (Dalvi et al., 2014; Surmeier et al., 2014). The substantia nigra pars compacta is a region of dopaminergic neurons that is functionally associated with the basal ganglia. The basal ganglia is a system that integrates the behaviours of motivation, emotion, and movement. CNS regions affected by PD, have many consequences on major aspects of the peripheral nervous system. Basic daily activities such as speech and motor function can become burdensome due to the chronic nature of this disorder (Lim, & Lang, 2010). Major signs include muscle rigidity, slowing of movement, and a persistent tremor at rest. There is also a plethora of other features all associated with the skeleto-musculature of the body, which are part of this short list. Overall, the patient's life expectancy is shortened dramatically due to auxiliary symptoms (DiStefano et al., 2011).

The striatum is a sub-cortical region and is composed of the caudate and the putamen. Histologically, the cellular bridges connecting the putamen and the caudate appear as striations and thus give the striatum its name. The striatum is a unique region of the basal ganglia as it receives most of its inputs (Gottfried, & Haber, 2011; Haber, 2011). Huntington's disease (HD) is initially associated with neurodegeneration of these regions (Pavese, & Brooks, 2013). HD is a neurodegenerative disorder of the striatum and many regions of the basal ganglia. Its mean age of onset is during the fourth or fifth decade of life. HD is highly progressive and the mean age of survival is 15-20 years (Harrington et al., 2014). There is no known therapeutic approach which is successful in treating this disorder, but many believe that stem cells may be a viable option (Kordasiewicz et al., 2012; Pardo, & Saura Antolín, 2014). HD is caused by a mutation which encodes an irregular expansion of the CAG-encoded poly-glutamine repeats as a protein (huntingtin). HD is unique among the major neurodegenerative disorders since most of its exact genetic mechanism is well characterised (Aronin, & DiFiglia, 2014).

Alzheimer's disease (AD) is quite different, it is believed to be a degeneration of mainly higher cortical and sub-cortical areas that govern cognitive processing, memory, and executive cognition. Degeneration of these regions leads to dementia with progressive memory loss (Ahn, et al., 2011; Possin et al., 2011). However, it is worth noting that neurodegeneration can occur in various other regions such as the entorrhinal cortex, which causes loss of smell in patients (Hirni et al., 2013).

Due to the wide variety of the structural and functional variation of neurons in the CNS, it is not surprising to find that degeneration of neurons can exist in isolated regions. However, this is in stark contrast to regions of neurons that are linked by broader regulated pathways. Degeneration in these regions can lead to a wide range of problems. The hippocampus is a subcortical region of the brain linked bi-directionally to the hypothalamic-pituitary-adrenal (HPA) axis and has a significant role in the limbic system. Its main role is in memory processing, primarily declarative, and spatial memory. AD is a neurodegenerative disorder whose initial site of neurodegeneration is the hippocampus (Lee et al., 2014). AD is a disabling neurodegenerative disorder that progressively worsens with age. Difficulty in diagnosing this disease is due in part to the pernicious cognitive loss from this disease (Lee et al., 2013). Initial symptoms of this disease are similar to an adverse stress reaction, for example, poor concentration and memory problems. However, there are distinct features of AD that indicate its neurodegenerative characteristics such as the persistence and progression of cognitive loss (Middleton et al., 2001; Zhang et al., 2011). Neurodegeneration in AD is normally restricted to cortical and subcortial regions, for example, frontal cortices, temporal cortices, parietal cortices, cingulate gyri and subcortical regions such as the hippocampus (Jack Jr., et al., 2013; Ryman et al., 2014). AD and PD affect different areas of the CNS and thus, patients present different pathological characteristics. There is a growing body of literature indicating that there may be a large quantity of common characteristics in the biochemical processing underlying neurodegeneration (Soto, 2013; Wardlaw et al., 2013; Xie et al., 2014).

The convergence between the developmental programme of the human aging brain and the phenotype of AD allows us to understand the molecular and genetic components of both these phenomena. The genetics of AD could reveal the genetics of the aging human brain, albeit in an earlier and aggressive form. According to Christoff, (2012) such genetic programs have been organised into two groups. The first group is composed of those regulatory genetic programs that control the rate of senescence development. The second group is involved in the modification of distinct age related pathologies of the brain. The broad focus of the first group renders such an ill-defined group as being the subject of speculation and rudimentary hypothesis formation (Kirkwood, 1977, 2002). However, gene regulatory networks (GRNs) have been proposed to be the molecular basis for the stage of senescence (Davidson, 2010; Neill et al., 2011; Wang, 2013). In contrast to theories dedicated to senescence as a distinct genetically controlled stage of development, there is a position that holds that the aged brain is as a consequence of an overall accumulation of age related changes in other systems with no over-arching *plan* for old age. Genes that may be part of the GRNs include known causative genes such as PS1, PS2, and APP. While genes such as APO-E, CR1, BIN1, and PICALM may be useful as examples of genes in group two. Unfortunately, no distinct GRN have been identified as part of AD pathogenesis, but perhaps a GRN may have to include other epigenetic dimensions such as micro RNA sequences to give a more holistic view of the molecular orchestration (Schonrock et al., 2012; Zhang et al., 2013). Senescence has been attributed as the process most implicated for the initiation phase of AD pathogenesis. This process largely involves a gradual breakdown in metabolic efficiency as a function of time (Braak, & Del Tredici, 2011). The evolutionary progression of the human brain is based upon the specificity of vulnerable neurons, whereby, the neurofibrillary tangle (NFT) formation is a result of a new glutatmatergic excitatory signalling decrease and eventual loss. In particular, Layer II of the entorhinal region typically loses glutatmatergic signalling from the posteromedial cortices first. Consequently, there is loss of glutatmatergic signalling to the CA1 of the subiculum and hippocampus (Axelsen et al., 2011). The initiation phase is also marked by the buffering capacity of the CNS compensatory neuroplastic processes. However, the transition from initiation phase to propagation phase overcomes these compensatory mechanisms (Thal et al., 2002). Amyloid deposition has been found to have high specificity for the entorhinal cortex, the neocortex, and a number of critical regions of the default mode network (Buckner et al., 2009; Sperling et al., 2009; Vlassenko et al., 2011). Moreover, amyloid deposition has been proposed to be as a result of APP up-regulation, while environmentally derived protective factors include exercise, cardio protective diet, and education (Luchsinger, & Mayeux, 2004; Rossi et al., 2008; Migliore, & Coppedè, 2009).

7.2. Delirium-dementia continuum

Cognitive failure is a term used to refer to functional loss as a result of brain failure. Given the isomorphism of these entities, brain failure is cognitive failure. Like all organ systems, the brain can fail and manifest as severe pathology. In addition, this failure can have acute and chronic presentations. For the purposes of this work delirium is conceptualised as an acute onset brain failure and dementia as a form of chronic brain failure. Delirium itself has been proposed as the first sign of a negative decline in patient well-being (Freter et al., 2005). However, to complicate things further, both these conditions can co-occur. In the community and in the hospital, the prevalence of delirium superimposed on dementia (DSD) has been estimated to be within the range of 21% to 89% (Fick et al., 2002). Psychological disorders, such as depression, can also complicate the clinical differentiation between delirium and dementia, with the reported prevalence being approximately 28% (Edlund et al., 2001). Based upon extrapolation figures for the growth of the aging population in the United States, it has been estimated that there will potentially be 14 million patients with these co-occurring conditions (Norton et al., 2014). It is therefore crucial that assessment tools are capable of differentiating between these co-occurring conditions. EEG serial assessment has been proposed as a viable candidate for detecting delirium, however, the sensitivity for delirium in the context of dementia is found to be low, even though it has a high specificity for delirium (Tussey et al., 2010; Hall et al., 2012).

At the centre point of this problem is the grim spectre of neurodegenration that determines the severity of these conditions. Neurodegeneration is a broad term that applies to both the beneficial and the dysfunctional processes. As a beneficial process, it is the primary cause by which the central nervous system (CNS) as a whole can allow synaptic plasticity, anatomical sculpting of the brain during development, and clearance of dysfunctional cells in the CNS. This allows the organism to maintain its optimum adaptability within the environment. Dysfunctional neurodegeneration can be a multi-factorial problem and have severe consequences on the body as a whole (Son et al., 2012). One of the most studied neurodegenerative diseases, for example PD, is believed to have a hereditary, environmental, and age related aetiology which initially affects the motor system. This form of neurodegeneration affects normal control of skeletal muscles. This can have obvious implications for the quality of life of the individual with this disease and their families.

Neurodegeneration must be considered as an inherent function of the nervous system as it allows the CNS to adapt to environmental changes both internally and externally of the organism. Neurodegeneration can be categorised as acute or chronic. Acute neurodegeneration may be the result of a stroke or head trauma. AD and PD are normally associated with chronic neurodegeneration (Cruts et al., 2012). The specific aetiology of these diseases is not known (Weintraub, et al., 2011). However, various hypotheses and functionally dysregulated pathways are involved (Wingo et al., 2012). During the prodromal phase of AD pathogenesis, glucose metabolism has been selectively demonstrated to reduce in the postero-medial cortex, while amyloid deposition is reported to be increased (Dickerson et al., 2009; Pan et al., 2011). Age related and pathological failures of the deactivation process of the postero-medial cortex have been reported during the memory encoding phase and such failures lead to demonstrable worse memory performance (Lustig et al., 2003; Pihlajamaki et al., 2010).

It has been proposed that there is an incongruence between early onset dementia and loss of basal cholinergic neurons. Indeed, features such as loss of appetite, decreased intake of food and thus weight loss may precede this cognitive decline. Such a finding may indicate the role of the orexinergic/hypocretin system (Hirshkowitz, & Sharafkhaneh, 2005; Wakefulness, 2012). The orexin system modulates attention via the septo-hippocampal cholinergic system (Sakurai et al., 2010). Orexins are beginning to be conceptualised as having direct roles in cognition that go beyond their impact upon arousal. Attentional demands as executed by the medial prefrontal cortex (MPFC) have been improved when OxB is infused into this region (Lambe et al., 2005). Administration of an Ox1R antagonist either through the basal forebrain or systemically has been demonstrated to impair attention performance (Boschen et al., 2009; Fadel, & Burk, 2010).

More interestingly is their role in sleep regulation and hence it is reasonable to suggest they impact upon delirium. During sleep the hypocretin system has initially very little activity, in particular during NREM sleep, but with the onset of REM sleep these neurons are reactivated again as part of the transition from sleep to wake. Obstructing their function renders it extremely difficult for animals, including humans, to emerge from anaesthesia or to remain alert and awake (Sakurai, 2007). The condition narcolepsy marked by cataplexy and a sudden shift into sleep (particularly REM sleep due to its regular function of suppressing REM sleep) is believed to be as a result of an autoimmune induced neurodegeneration of these neuronal populations (Peyron et al., 2000; Sehgal & Mignot, 2011). Narcolepsy is a disorder characterised by significantly lower numbers of orexin neurons and cognitive dysfunction (Rieger et al., 2003; Naumann et al., 2006). More particularly, there is reduced orexinergic signalling to the septo-hippocampal pathway and this combined with the reduced postsynaptic responsiveness to orexinergic signalling is suggested to contribute to deficits in arousal, learning, and memory associated with optimal hippocampal functioning. Neuroscientific and psychometric measures of the sleep wake transition have been found to be lacking due to the rapidity of the transition. One study highlights the use of state space analysis techniques, examining the labile transitions between sleep and wake states in orexin knockout mice. They found that mice spent more time in the transition state between sleep and wake rather than deep delta NREM sleep or theta rich wake state (Behn et al., 2010).

The age related breakdown of orexinergic signalling to the septo-hippocampal cholinergic system has been proposed to be a critical aspect of the cognitive dysfunction experienced by mammals as they age. The relationship between GABAergic signalling and hypocretin activity is pertinent to delirium. It has been reported that fragmentation of the sleep wake cycle (without disturbing the duration of sleep/wake time) has been induced by selectively disinhibiting the genes for GABA b receptor in hypocretin neurons (Matsuki et al., 2009). Such a finding suggests that the selective sleep-wake cycle fragmentation may be as a result of the normally induced genetic disinhibition of hypocretin neurons.

The relationship between dreaming and cognitive failure may further be elucidated by an account of REM sleep behaviour disorder (RBD). The loss of atonia during REM sleep is one of the cardinal features of REM sleep (Schenck & Mahowald, 2002). Indeed, RBD has many similar features with delirium and dementia, including, dysfunctional arousal and cognitive deficits (AASD, 2005; Iranzo & Santamaria, 2005). The onset of idiopathic RBD is found to begin between the ages of 50 to 70 (Teman et al., 2009). Prevalence estimates derived from population studies suggest that it is experienced by 0.38% to 0.5% of adults (Ohayon & Guilleminault, 2005).

The paucity of studies pertaining to RBD render it a condition with a largely speculative pathophysiology. In human studies, RBD has been associated with a wide variety of disorders such as Guillain-Barre syndrome, narcolepsy, and limbic encephalitis, as well as pharmacological entities such as, alcohol, beta blockers, SSRIs, and SNRIs (Gagnon et al., 2006a, 2006b). The strongest connection of RDB to other disorders is the class of neurodegenerative conditions known as synucleopathies (Postuma et al., 2012). In a systematic review, Postuma et al., provides two main streams of evidence to connect RBD with Parkinson's disease and further proposes it to be a robust predictor of its onset. It has been estimated that the risk of developing a neurodegenerative condition can be as high as 65% at 10 years (Latreille et al., 2014). It has been found that the clinical latency of the neurodegenerative disease between these conditions is much longer than in other attempts at predictive screen, for example RBD has a clinical latency of 13 years compared to PET scans of the substantia nigra and its associated premotor features which is 4-7 years (Morrish et al., 1998; Hilker et al., 2005).

The loss of atonia is often accompanied by dream enactment behaviour, however, studies have not consistently been able to connect dream enactment behaviour to dream content, largely due to problems with dream recall by subjects in studies (Iranzo et al., 2009). Dream enactment behaviour has been identified in RBD patients in the range of 64% to 95% (Sfora et al., 1997; Olson et al., 2000; Iranzo et al., 2005). Interestingly, motor behaviour as measured by the Trunk Control Test (a validated measure of the subjects' ability to control trunk position) has been proposed as a distinguishing test for dementia on its own from DSD (Bellelli et al., 2011). However, further studies are required to establish the precise nature of motor disturbances that may distinguish these phenomena.

Understanding the molecular pathogenesis of neurodegeneration gives us insight into the complex orchestration of genome activity in the emerging phenotype. In recent years the discovery of miRNAs, small RNAs that have roles in the regulation of levels of target mRNA transcripts and the translation process, have lead to a greater appreciation for the molecular mechanisms underlying optimal human CNS functioning (Ambros, 2004;

Krol et al., 2010; Czech & Hannon, 2011). These molecules originate in the nucleus of the cell, and are generated due to the cleavage by the microprocessor Drosha/DGCR8. Once in the cytoplasm, the pre miRNA is further cleaved by DICER to generate the double stranded miRNA biomolecule. One of these strands typically gets degraded while the other binds to the Ago region to become the miRNA Silencing Complex (miRISC). It is estimated that most protein encoded genes have one or more miRNA associated with them. MiRNA and neural morphogenesis are closely linked. Early experiments with knock out of global biogenesis of these molecules halted the neuralation process of embryonic CNS development (Bernstein et al., 2003). Subsequent studies have demonstrated roles of DICER in proliferation, neuronal migration and age related integrity (Schaefer et al., 2007; Damiani et al., 2008; Davis et al., 2008; McLoughlin et al., 2012). Despite the largely sporadic existence of Alzheimer's disease (AD), a comprehensive account of its molecular pathogenesis is emerging (Hampel, 2013). The characteristic features of AD, at a molecular and cellular level, are the deregulated amyloid beta clearance and disturbances in gamma secretase and beta site APP cleaving enzyme 1 (BACE1) (Lu et al., 2013). In AD patients with elevated BACE1, miRNA-29a/b has been proposed as part of disturbed process of amyloidogenic peptide accumulation (Hébert et al., 2008). Other examples of disturbed miRNA subsystems involved in AD pathogenesis include, miRNA-15 family in Tau kinase molecular disturbances and miR-16, miR-101, miRNA-106a which are associated with APP regulation (Long & Lahiri, 2011; Liang et al., 2012; Long et al., 2012). MiR-34b has been shown to be elevated in HD patients (Gaughwin et al., 2011). While the premotor stage of PD has been shown to demonstrate downregulation of miR-34b/c and subsequent mitochondrial dysfunction, many of the miRNA have been proposed as potential biomarkers of the aging process (Miñones-Moyano et al., 2011; Abe & Bonini, 2013).

Despite its occurrence, delirium is largely under-reported and under-detected in the clinical setting. The co-occurance of dementia and delirium carry with it the simple yet complex problem of devising tests and methods of differentiating these entities. Use of a molecular and cellular framework may enable researchers and clinicians to differentiate and detect the pernicious presentation of prodromal and subsyndromal delirium.

7.3. Interpreting the unitary syndrome

Previous attempts have been made to identify the pathognomonic feature that would make delirium stand out from dementia, but unfortunately the global neural dysfunction of both disorders has made the establishment of a direct measurement difficult (Meagher et al., 2010; Morandi et al., 2012; Leonard et al., 2013). The robust rating scale for delirium phenomenology, the Delirium Rating Scale-Revised-98 (DRS-R98), combined with longitudinal and factor analytical methods that have been used to confirm the hypothetical existence of a three domain theory for the phenotype of delirium. This three domain theory has been conceptualised as being composed of, 1) general cognition, 2) higher level cognition, and 3) circadian integrity (Trzepacz & Meagher, 2008; Franco et al., 2009; Meagher & Trzepacz, 2009; Kean et al., 2010). This work proposes that although these findings are approximating the empirical state of delirium, an appreciation for the logical and probable consequences of the underlying theory is significantly lacking. Therefore, the three domain theory should be reconstituted into a multidimensional model of delirium.

Cognitive efficiency is a central part of the pathology of cognitive failure and therefore measures of this efficiency would indicate in clear terms the progress and remission of such a failure. Visuospatial processing and working memory are well recognised functions linked to the domain of executive cognition and assessing age related declines in cognition in general (Fisk et al., 1996; Brennan et al., 1997; Robbins et al., 1998; Van der Linden, 1998). In elderly populations, patients with Alzheimer's disease have been shown to have significant deficits in visuospatial processing and working memory (Money et al., 1992; Morris, 1994; Cornoldi & Vecchi, 2003 Thompson et al., 2006). Assessing visuospatial processing can be done using the spatial span subtest derived from the Wechsler Memory scale which states that its purpose is a measure that 'taps an examinee's ability to hold a visual spatial sequence of locations in working memory and then reproduce the sequence' (Bo et al., 2009). The concept *dysexecutive syndrome* has been used to account for this age related and pathological dysfunction between these functional systems as measured by spatial span tests (Baddeley, 1991).

The spatial span forwards (SSF) and spatial span backwards (SSB) are based upon measures of the integrity of the virtual sensorium of the individual. One's generation of a virtual representation of the interface between the external world as transduced by the senses and reprocessed by the CNS. This virtual representation is founded upon the primary and secondary modes of consciousness and the perceptual and conceptual systems that reside within them. The primary mode of consciousness functions as a mediator for the perceptual abstraction of the real world. While the secondary mode of consciousness binds this with a much wider experience encoded within metacognitive domains of executive cognition. Indeed, visuospatial manipulation requires at least some pivotal role and influence of the processes of executive cognition (Curtiss et al., 2001; Dobbs et al., 2001).

Attention is consistently found to be a key feature of delirium phenomenology and has a strong association with other features in delirium, according to the data (Meagher et al., 2007, 2010). However, deficits in attention also exist in chronic conditions such as dementia with Lewy bodies and late stage Alzheimers disease (Metzler-Baddeley, 2007; Kolanowski et al., 2012). The use of the Edinburgh Delirium Test Box has demonstrated that measures of sustained visual attention may be more specific in distinguishing delirium from dementia and cognitively normal populations (Brown et al., 2011). Use of eye tracking technology and oculomotor analysis have also provided novel ways in which the attention deficits of delirium can be assessed (Exton & Leonard, 2009; van der Kooi et al., 2014).

However, attention is not a singular function, but is the foundation for executive cognition (Cowan, 1999). Working memory can be conceived as being a component of ego consciousness which enables the binding together of transient functions of working memory, e.g. visuospatial sketchpath, the phonological loop, and episodic buffer. These transient functions are also working in concert with more established systems such as long term memory, language, and visual semantics. It is the breakdown in this system that SSF and SSB have attempted to measure. In the context of delirium, it has been found that the SSB may be useful in differentiating delirium from dementia due to the preserved short term features of certain forms of dementia. Moreover, the SSF which is also a pattern recognition test has also been shown to be discriminatory for delirium with its functional emphasis on attention over working memory (MacLullich et al., 2013).

Subsyndromal delirium (SSD) is a state characterised by the presence of delirium features, but without full syndromal delirium (FSD) criteria. It is associated with outcomes intermediate between FSD and no delirium (Dosa et al, 2007; Cole et al, 2008, 2013). Although it is thought to include many features of FSD, such as disturbances in motor behaviour, consciousness and sleep-wake rhythmicity, a comprehensive account has been impeded by the lack of clear criteria. However, recent work has applied a discriminate analysis approach and multinomial logistic regression methods to the phenomenological profiles of delirious and non-delirious cases to generate a conceptual phenotype of SSD. It was found that an intermediate severity of a range of neurocognitive features attributed to the FSD phenotype characterised SSD (Trzepacz et al., 2012). Other work has suggested a definition of SSD that can allow for reliable and consistent diagnosis (Osse et al., 2009; Trzepacz et al., 2011).

Although the frequency of delirium has been reported to occur in 11% to 42% of medical inpatients, the frequency of SSD is less well defined and is estimated to occur in approximately 7% to 45% of patients, according to the clinical cohort and diagnostic measures to define it (Ouimet et al, 2007; Voyer et al, 2009; Bond et al, 2012). Further investigations into the phenomenology of SSD may enable researchers and clinicians to tackle the many negative outcomes, for instance, elevated mortality, increased length of stay and reduced socioadaptive functioning, of this intermediate state (Marcantonio et al., 2002, 2005; Cole et al., 2003, 2008; Bourdel-Marchasson et al., 2004).

However, disparities of up to a third of delirium status attribution, namely full syndromal delirium (FSD) or subsyndromal delirium (SSD), by validated instruments Confusion assessment method (CAM) and the DRS-R98 have indicated that the neurobehavioural interface of what can be diagnosed as delirium requires more focused research. Moreover, the recent publication of the DSM-5 criteria for delirium has marginally altered the previous DSM-IV criteria with a focus upon inattention with vague terms such as consciousness downplayed (APA, 2013). Such an alteration has been found to be restrictive and thus impact upon delirium case identification. Indeed, recent work using pooled data set and retrospective study design has indicated that there is a varied concordance (30% to 89%) between DSM IV and DSM-5 attributed cases. Such a discrepancy was due to interpreting key phenomenological features such as orientation, acute onset, and fluctuating course (Meagher et al., 2014).

7.4. Neuropathologies of the self

To understand the role of the ego and executive cognition in delirium we must draw upon comparative features from the neuropathologies of the self (NPS). NPS have increasingly been found to be associated with neurodevelopmental and degenerative syndromes, such as dementia. Specific examples of the NPS include the often revised category of delusional misidentification syndromes (DMS) which further demonstrate a state of pronounced separation of the functional aspects of the ego (Feinberg, 2011). DMS co-occur with about 38% to 78.3% of Lewy body dementia and Capgras syndrome (CS) patients in particular, show a typical manifestation in AD with a range of 25% to 47% cases reported (Feinberg et al., 2005). DMS were initially conceived of as a set of four disorders.

However, subsequent developments have reorganised this taxonomy. This group is organised hierarchically to describe the various levels of disturbances of the self that may be reflective of the severity of cognitive impairment. In particular, the first level is centred on severe cognitive deficits, which are all either contributory to delirium or are different terms to describe delirium (Feinberg, 2011). DMS are also particularly important as they are often found in the context of severe neurocognitive impairment, such as dementia, and would highlight their shared neurocognitive features with delirium.

The central feature of DMS is the misidentification or perceived duplication of places, persons, object, and events that are closely associated with the patient. The misidentification is due to lesions found in neural substrates which serve as subsystems involved in integrating the encoded memories of the misidentified subject with the nebulous ego of the individual. The perception of double has been found to be a universal feature and is reflective of two dimensions of the psyche (Kohut, 2013). The first is the reflection of the different registers of the ego, namely the ideal-ego/persona, and given its universality it is an archetypal phenomenon. The dialectic between the persona and the shadow becomes more pronounced with these syndromes. The more dissociated the persona gets from the shadow, either by trauma related dissociation or by more long term neural lesions, the more the polarisation between these subsystems induces a strong emotional affectation associated with each.

In the context of CS, a familiar person is believed to be replaced with an imposter. The disconnection is based exclusively on persons, and even objects and animals with which one has a strong emotional and associative bond (Paille`re-Martinot et al., 1994; Young et al., 1994). The reaction to this new imposter entity is deemed threatening and suspicious. CS exists in terms of both acute and chronic CNS disorders. Chronic CNS disorders include the broad syndromes of schizophrenia and its related sub phenotypical disorders. Acute CNS disorders include cerebrovascular disease, subarachnoid haemorrhage, head injury, epilepsy, pituitary tumour, pseudohypoparathyroidism, and myxoedema (Preskorn & Reveley, 1978; Summers, 1984; Bouckoms et al., 1986; Lewis, 1987; Santiago et al., 1987; Feinberg et al., 1999; Collins et al., 1990). Fergoli syndrome (FS) can be considered the converse of CS and has the central feature of 'hyperidentification', in essence the misidentification is reversed whereby non familiar places, objects, and people are identified as familiar to the person (Feinberg et al., 1999). Another example of DMS is phantom boarder syndrome, the belief that there is an uninvited person living in the same home as them. Here we can see the shadow in action, the phenomenology of the shadow is projected onto this perceived and conceptual threat. Open hostility, aggressive behaviour, and violence towards the perceived threat render these DMS very challenging. It has been found that neural lesions have been associated with the onset of each of these syndromes. The regions of these lesions, is not surprisingly associated with the neural substrate of identification of self and other (Feinberg, 2011).

To be sure, the difference between the emergences of the archetypal images of the shadow in dreams is fundamentally different to CNS disorders. In the context of dreams, the repressed and dissociated aspects of one's self re-emerges as part of the process of integration and growth that the dreaming catalyses. In CNS disorders, the otherwise robust higher cortical structures that maintain the dissociation of repressed aspects breaks down due to permanent or transient CNS insults. For example, men with histories of aggressive behaviour, social withdrawal, and substance abuse become consistently violent when they develop CS (Bourget, &

Whitehurst, 2004). In this instance, the shadow is given free rein to control their behaviour which is well planned and very dangerous. CS and related DMSs have been shown to have unilateral brain lesions, particularly in the right hemisphere, typically in the frontal cortex. The overlap with the proposed neural substrate for dissociation and repression should therefore not be surprising (Feinberg & Shapiro, 1989; Devinsky, 2000; Feinberg et al., 2005). The misidentification of familiar places as foreign has been observed to be a highly prevalent feature of patients with neurodegenerative disorders affecting both the frontal and temporal cortices. In particular, disturbances in familiarity in both FS and CS have been associated with functional over and under activity of the peri-rhinal cortex respectively (Devinsky, 2009). The prevalence of facial processing and recognition disturbances in CS may be accounted for by the selective right hemispheric deficits of these patients. In essence, the CS patient can recognise a face, but such perception is not integrated with emotive encoded associations that give one a sense of familiarity, and the complex pertaining to that person is structurally dissociated (Breen et al., 2000). Detailed research into the fusiform gyrus has further elucidated the reason behind this dysfunction and disconnect between familiarity and recognition (Alexander et al., 1979).

According to Robyn Langdon and Max Colheart, there is a two factor account for the activation of delusional complexes (Langdon & Coltheart, 2000; Coltheart et al., 2011). These two factors are, 1) the neural insult that affects the psychological processing which generates the content of the delusion, for instance a lesion in the neural substrate involved in face processing can generate the phenomenology of mirrored-self misidentification delusion, and, 2) a functional deficit in belief evaluation, which is a major contributing element to maintaining the delusion (Breen et al., 2001; Coltheart, 2007). This factor resolves the issue of patients having similar lesions, but different delusional forms (Connors & Coltheart, 2011). Therefore, patients require both elements to generate delusional phenomenology. Delusional misidentification co-occurring with Alzheimer's disease has been seen to be resulting from hypo-perfusion of the inferior and superior temporal lobes. These regions broadly confirm the disturbances in parahippocampal and fusiform regions and thus explain the disturbances in associative place and face encoding (Starksteain et al., 1994). According to Garry Young, the delusional belief is a compensatory mechanism, in other words, an attempt by the individual to comprehend the dissociation between encoded representations of the objects and place with the real-time experience of it. The delusion, now part of the *percepiens*, structures the experience of the object as foreign, yet intimately linked (Oyebode, 2008; Young, 2008).

The mean time of onset of DMS in the context of AD has been reported to be 3.5 years and approximately 27% develop at least one form of DMS within the first year of AD. DMS increases a doubling of risk of aggressive behaviour by patients with AD even when paranoid delusions are accounted for (Tsai et al., 1996; Cook et al., 2003). The left medial temporal regions, orbitofrontal cortex, and cingulate cortices have been demonstrated to have significant hypo-metabolism in this patient population. PET studies have further highlighted the deficits in functional connectivity between the dorsolateral prefrontal cortex (DLPFC), paralimbic structures (orbitofrontal cortex [OFC] and anterior cingulate cortex [ACC]), and multimodal association cortices all implicated in the manifestation of DMS in patients with AD (Mentis et al., 1995). A smaller number of studies have confirmed a similar pattern of neuronal functional disturbances in dementia with lewy bodies co-occuring with DMS, thus confirming a consistent neuronal pathology (Nagahama et al., 2010; Thaipisuttikul et al., 2012). Therefore, applying the relationship between phenomenology and neural substrate in DMS to delirium may enhance our understanding of its pathogenesis. However, these findings do not substitute for novel studies, but map out the range of findings that we may come to expect from an exploration of delirium. An appreciation of the subtle perceptual transformations, the differences between the different forms and the hermeneutical foundation on which all these pathological facts are built upon, all alter our experience of delirium. We are therefore required to measure its variations, the cognitive defects, the behavioural excesses, and the experiential mutation that all join as the unitary form of delirium.

7.5. Hypnosis and cognitive impairment

The aging population brings with it the increased exposure to invasive medical and surgical procedures. To be sure, the convergence of polypharmacy, bedside restrictions and the employment of surgical interventions are all important risk factors for developing delirium. With delirium there is a rediscovery of the patient. The traditional perception of pathology was one in which the patient as an individual was removed from the pathological scope and in its place a constellation of aberrant features circumscribed the clinical encounter. To render delirium an area of optimal medical care, health care professionals must strive to restore authenticity to the patient. To provide the patient with a depth and breadth to describing and understanding their experience, with all the pain, the gestures of significance, and the deluge of complaints that emanate from being critically ill.

Hypnosis offers an adjunctive approach to enhancing the care of the terminally ill and the elderly. With no overt side effects and as a non phramacological method, it is a highly sought modality for elderly patients who are often managed through polypharmacy. The use of hypnosis in the elderly has seen tremendous benefits when applied to a wide variety of clinical problems such as chronic pain condition (e.g. osteoarthritis) and its management (Gay et al., 2002; Morone & Greco, 2007). It has also been used as an adjuvant during medical procedures such as colonoscopy (Elkins et al., 2006; Lutgendorf et al., 2007). Hypnosis can be defined as 'an alternative state of awareness and alertness characterized by heightened and focused concentration that is achieved in order to actualize a particular goal or latent potential' and it has been known about in various forms for thousands of years (Erickson, 1970; Kohen & Olness, 2012). In 1784, the Marquis de Puysequr, discovered that the trance state that follows hypnotic suggestions such that 'changes in sensation, perception, cognition, or control over motor behaviour' that leads to an altered state often described as a 'normal state of focused attention'. The term hypnotism itself was coined by James Braid who believed that the hypnotic trance was due to eye muscle fatigue (Kirsch et al., 1997). Medical hypnosis gained favour in Europe with the help of pioneering clinicians such as Jean-Martin Charcot and Hippolyte Bernheim. Freud started using hypnosis but later developed the technique of free association as an alternative but an analogous mode of gaining insight into the unconscious psychological processing of his patients. After the revival of medical hypnosis by Clarke Hull, Milton Erickson (one of Halls' students) began to develop a systematic and applicable method for clinical hypnosis or hypnotherapy. On the basis of his approach, six identifiable steps in the therapeutic process of hypnosis have been established, 1) trance induction, 2) transition into trance, 3) metaphorical or anecdotal guidance,

4) direct statements or suggestions, 5) trance termination, and 6) follow-up evaluation (Havens & Walters, 2002).

Accumulated work has focused on an investigation into the phenomenology and neurophysiology of hypnosis (Vanhaudenhuyse et al., 2014). Hypnosis is proposed to be a state of focused attention involving focal concentration, enhanced absorption, and a relative suspension of peripheral awareness. It has three components to its phenomenology (Spiegel, 1991). These cardinal features are, 1) The tendency to become fully involved in perceptual and imaginative experience, referred to as absorption, 2) a mental separation of the otherwise unitary cohesion of experience, known as dissociation, and 3) an enhanced compliance with instructions and a suspension of critical judgement, known as suggestibility (Demertzi et al., 2013). In particular, ego consciousness is significantly altered with enhanced mental ease and ego-centric automaticity, in other words, ideas and thoughts flow more easily and without deliberate will (Rainville & Price, 2003). Neuroimaging and EEG studies have begun to piece together the underlying neural substrate of this phenomena. Not surprising the neural substrate is also derived largely from the default mode network (Demertzi et al., 2013; Vanhaudenhuyse et al., 2014).

It has been consistently demonstrated that the hypnotisability of the subject determines the effectiveness of hypnosis. Elderly patients with cognitive impairment have been proposed to be unsuitable for hypnosis and the differences between the responses of younger subjects compared to older subjects may reflect this (Milling, Coursen, Shores, & Waszkiewicz, 2010). Patients with cognitive impairment and AD have been shown to have attention deficits, often as a result of degeneration of regions implicated in attention such as the anterior cingulate gyrus, right partietal, and frontal cortices (Faymonville et al., 2006). So while there may be preconceived notions about elderly cognitive capacity, the impact of age upon the trait of hypnotisability is not confirmed by the evidence. One study has reported a fluctuation of the trait of hypnotisability as decreasing from ages 17 to 40, but then a general trend towards an increase and ultimately stabilisation of it as a function of age (Page & Green, 2007). However, cognitive impairment may impact upon hypnosis, given that hypnosis has been described as a process involving 'attentive receptive concentration' and neurophysiological mechanisms that serve attention are involved in hypnosis (Raz et al., 2006).

The extent of typical sleep disturbance in the elderly population is such that it is a clinical problem generally treated with sleep inducing medications (Crowley, 2011). In particular, the reduction in slow wave sleep (SWS) is specifically associated with neocortical thinning, PFC atrophy, and mild dementia (Mander et al., 2013; Sanchez-Espinosa et al., 2014). This is further complicated by the administration of sleeping tablets which have been shown to detrimentally impact the occurrence of SWS, not to mention a whole catalogue of adverse side effects from these substances (Riemann & Perlis, 2009). The research on hypnosis in sleep is in its infancy, but offers promising results. A recent placebo-controlled crossover study into the sleep elderly female cohort exposed to hypnosis reported many positive findings. One key finding was a 57% increase in SWS in the treatment group and this was followed by the enhanced functioning of the prefrontal cortex (Condi et al., 2015).

The induction of altered states of consciousness by hypnosis has highlighted its utility in clinical and research contexts such that it can be used as a robust method to create and model transient CNS disorders (Oakley & Halligan, 2011, Woody & Szechtman, 2011; Oakley & Halligan, 2011). Mirrored-self misidentification, an NPS that reflects a monothematic disturbance that gives the patient the belief that their reflection in the mirror is not theirs, is often a feature of the prodromal phase of dementia and advanced global dementia (Connors et al., 2012). The shared phenomenology between hypnosis and delusions is striking, with both states significantly altering perceptual experiences despite the presentation of contrary evidence (Connors et al., 2014). According to the two-factor theory of delusion formation, disruptions to cognition that shape the delusion can do so regardless of damage to the neural substrate that mediates these processes. They are secondary and compensatory (Colheart, 2015). This finding can serve as the theoretical basis of using hypnosis to model the delusional state without any detrimental impact upon research subjects. To be considered a viable candidate for being a successful analogue, the model needs to be able to re-create the features of the research condition and also be able to demonstrate the convergence of the same mechanisms causing the pathological condition in detail (Oakley & Halligan, 2011, 2013). Taking all these streams of evidence and drawing upon the neurocognitive impairment that is seen in delirium onset, hypnosis might provide a valuable method for studying delirium phenomenology.

In psychotherapeutic strategies for anxiety disorders, many cognitively orientated treatments have begun to integrate hypnosis based modalities to include, mindfulness, motivational interviewing, well-being therapy, and relaxation (Roemer & Orsillo, 2007; Ruini & Fava, 2009; Westra et al., 2009). Hypnotherapy, the clinical adaptation of hypnosis has its efficacy extensively investigated and reflected upon (Flammer & Bongartz, 2003). The essential format of hypnotherapy is the integration of the therapeutic alliance with clear goals pertaining to affective recognition and modulation, not to mention, mastery practice upon affective and cognitive issues. Hypnotherapy can be utilised to alleviate the anxiety and in particular, individuals can be taught self-hypnotherapy as part of a direct psychotherapeutic programme. Such formats of self-hypnosis can enhance self-mastery and control over their symptoms and alleviate the stress and impairment of their condition (Baker & Nash, 2008).

Guided imagery as a treatment modality to alter the aberrant bodily sensations of being critically unwell may provide a useful adjunct to patients at risk of developing delirium. Such a strategy may be based upon codifying bodily stimuli in a manner that is more pleasant rather than being interpreted as threatening. For example prodromal, sub-syndromal, and at risk patients guided visually by suggesting that the sensation of being critically unwell are comforting sensations, preventing these new sensations as being threatening and being perceived as snakes, spiders or ghosts or a nightmare. Guided imagery in nightmare syndromes has shown encouraging results. According to a systematic review of non-pharmacological treatments of nightmare disorders, a number of treatment modalities involving forms of hypnosis and relaxation have been shown to have robust positive effects against nightmares. However, as is characteristic of studies involving hypnosis, inconsistent methodologies and terminology make data rather opaque to interpret (Aurora et al., 2010). Enhanced orientation strategies combined with hypnosis and guided imagery may stabilize and rehabilitate the dysfunction in the virtual sensorium that is being disintegrated by the pro inflammatory state of critical illness. Although it may not subside the inflammatory process it may act prophylactically against the development of PTSD by preventing the onset of delusional and hallucinogenic compensations from the unconscious and serve to guide patients towards sustaining a more comforting reality.

It seems quite clear that no reform of medical teaching on delirium is possible without the realisation that the current practice of medicine is the problem which masquerades as a solution. The practice of medicine must carry with it a sense of doubt, not of the utility of the practice itself, but of the epistemological authority on which practice subscribes, does one treat patients in terms of soothing the conscience of the practitioner, *the family*, or the patient themselves. From where does the locus of duty originate and gravitate towards? What makes delirium comprehensive in the corpus of clinical knowledge to all practitioners is its immediate relationship with the nature of the psyche. Instead of being the locus of a bland behaviourism, a new depth psychology would have to be imbibed. There one would learn about delirium, not what old conceptualisations espoused, but a new formal paradigm that opens itself up to everyday practice.

8 Multidimensional model of delirium

8.1. Divergence between dreaming and delirium

Delirium is a complex syndromal phenomenon reflective of generalised neural dysfunction and thus lacks a pathognomonic feature. To be sure, its phenomenological complexity renders it a clinical challenge as evidenced by the often misdiagnosed and undetected episodes, with the possibility that up to 2/3 of cases are missed (Kishi et al., 2007; Collin et al., 2010). Therefore, clear and concise diagnostic criteria are fundamental to improving detection and management. Initially the advent of clear diagnostic criteria from the DSM-III, DSM-IIIR, and DSM-IV supported the formation of a theoretical framework to enable researchers to significantly expand the field of delirium (APA, 1980, 1987, 1994; Meagher, 2009). In particular, the DSM-IV delirium criteria have become the gold standard by providing researchers and clinicians with a highly inclusive description (Morandi et al., 2013). Unfortunately, researchers have identified disparities between the DSM based delirium criteria and the ICD-10 based criteria (Cole et al., 2003; Laurila et al., 2004; Cole et al., 2007; Kazmierski et al., 2008). The DSM-5 has sought to build upon the success of the DSM-IV criteria by integrating it with contemporary research. A concordance study examining the retrospective application of DSM-5 and DSM-IV criteria to a pooled database, identified that the use of either strict or inclusive DSM-5 criteria significantly altered the concordance with DSM-IV criteria. Key phenomenological features such as disorientation, acute onset of features, and the fluctuating course of features, were the subject of this challenging variation (Meagher et al., 2014).

The development of validated tools such as the Memorial Delirium Assessment Scale [MDAS], the Revised Delirium Rating Scale [DRS-R98], and the Cognitive Test for Delirium [CTD] to assess the phenomenology of delirium enabled researchers to overcome the previous absence of robust instrumentation that was required to capture the breadth of delirium as a syndrome (Blazer & Nieuwenhuizen, 2012). Such instruments enabled researchers to present the heterogenous phenomenology of delirium as a cohesive entity. However, a distinction has been made between core features which are believed to be invariant, such as inattention and sleep-wake cycle disturbances, and non-core features, such as labile affect and perceptual disturbances, which have a highly heterogeneous manifestation (Jabbar et al, 2011; Mattoo et al, 2012; Meagher et al, 2012). As a consequence, current phenomenological models of delirium suggest three principal domains, generalized disturbance of cognition with disproportionate impairment of attention, disorganization of higher-order thinking, and alterations to sleep-wake cycle and motor activity [see Fig 1]. Indeed, the application of factor analysis has identified the cognitive and neurobehavioural range of features of delirium. Previous work has suggested the individual features of delirium follow separate trajectories. For example a prospective study exploring delirium in stem cell transplantation patients found that the early stages of delirium were dominated by non-cognitive features and after the one week mark cognitive impairment peaked and dominated the phenomenological state of the psyche (Fann et al., 2005). Other work found in the palliative care population that disorientation was a less consistent feature than other related cognitive elements over the 24 hour period (Meagher et al., 2007). Subsequent work has demonstrated that inattention is a dominant and consistent feature of a delirious episode (Leonard et al., 2007). Trezpacz and Meagher set out a programme of research to perform phenomenological studies aimed at targeting the relationship with these features and investigate causation, pathophysiology, treatment needs, and prognosis of delirium. It was found that although certain subtypes of delirium are associated with clinical outcome and underlying pathophysiological states, the conceptual framework of delirium pathogenesis remains incomplete. A re-examination of delirium phenomenology is warranted. Integrating the qualitative and quantitative forms of phenomenology enables one to identify a parallel with the underlying neurophysiology and confront us with an under-appreciated form of consilience. The three domain theory is incomplete, inaccurate, and requires further development. Based upon a more inclusive integration of current delirium literature, an updated multidimensional theory of delirium phenomenology is required (Hobson & Voss, 2011; Franco et al., 2013; Leonard et al., 2013; Edwin van Dellen et al., 2014). Instead of three main domains of delirium phenomenology there are, in fact, four dimensions; 1) circadian integrity, 2) executive cognition, 3) orders of consciousness, and 4) temporality. Circadian integrity is composed of two sub domains, motor behaviour and disturbances in the sleep wake cycle. Marked disturbances of this domain manifests as reversals of the sleep wake phases of behaviour and extremes of motor disturbance, for example, hypoactive, hyperactive and mixed motor behaviour profiles (Fitzgerald et al., 2013). Executive cognition is a term used to describe those cognitive processes that require the ego as the functional locus of performance. Despite the illusion of coherency, there is no one region dedicated to the phenomenon of the ego, rather there are multiple regions and systems that together make up the ego (Maniadakis et al., 2011; Rizzolatti, et al., 2014). The third domain, the orders of consciousness are the functional modes by which executive cognition is enabled. They are divided into primary and secondary consciousness, but exist as an integrated whole, and thus serve as the modalities by which delirium, waking and sleep consciousness possess a unitary phenomenology, (Grinde, 2013). The fourth dimension is temporality and results from the convergence between the neurocognitive reserve of the subject and the influence of pathological processes upon this reserve [see Fig 4].

Fig 1. Model of factors involes in temporal dimension of delirium phenomenology

Figure 2. Multidimensional model of delirium phenomenology

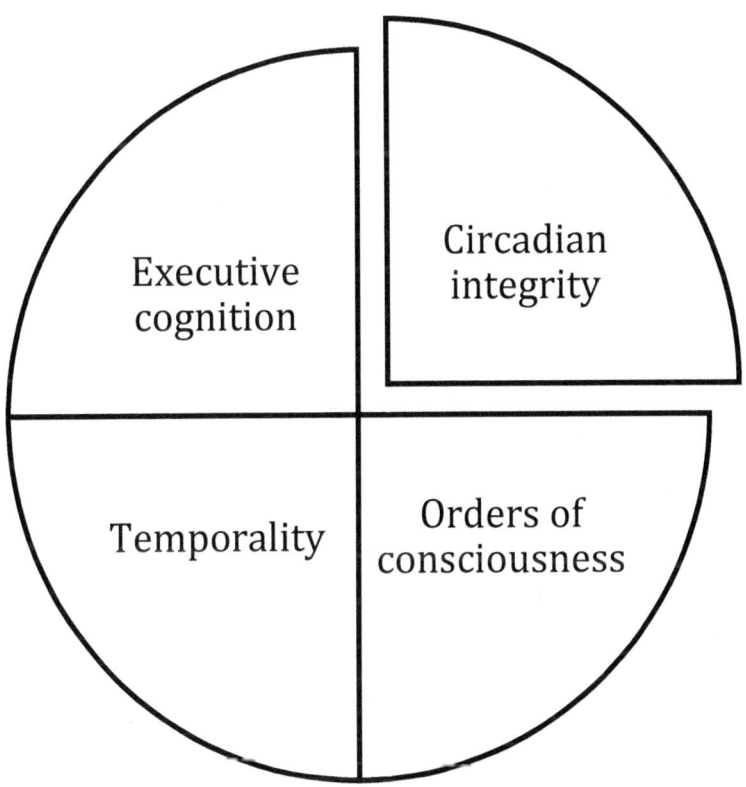

This new theory can be further enhanced by the application of findings from dream research. The convergent phenomenology of dreaming and delirium is in turn informed by the isomorphism theory. In essence, this theory posits that the psyche and brain are one and the same entity, with the logical implication being that comparative phenomenology is reflective of shared neurobiological processes. However, the precise manner in which the phenomena can be understood as reflective of one another is still a matter of debate (Gómez-Ramirez, 2014; Stoyanov, 2014). More complex still is the functional role dreaming plays in the context of sleep and cognitive mechanisms. Current neurobiological theories of dreaming propose that it is a means by which the psyche reactivates, consolidates, and integrates salient encoded stimuli with waking experience (Wamsley et al., 2010; Desseilles & Duclos, 2013; Wamsley, 2014). The dream itself represents the isolated elements of encoded stimuli of the unconscious psyche, and integrates these with newly encoded features of waking experience in order to develop the internalised cognitive representations of the individual's life (Schwartz et al., 2002). Another aspect of this theory is the function of growth, more particularly the role dreaming plays in emotional homeostasis and threat resolution (Hoss. 2013; Svennson et al., 2013).

The phenomenology of delirium can be comprehended by examining the relationship between the congruence of the states of dreaming and delirium with a particular analysis of key phenomenological domains. The first is perception, which is the foundation of experience and in dreaming there is a predominance of visual and auditory stimuli while other senses, such as vestibular sensation (flying, falling, and acceleration) playing a much less significant role (Klinger & Cox, 1987, 1988; Stawarczyk et al., 2011). This audio-visual predominance in dreams is a consistent finding from *The Oneirocritica* by Artemidorus and experimentally confirmed in modern times by dream reports (Schwartz, 2000; Schredl, 2010; Harris-McCoy, 2012). However, other studies have highlighted that the manner in which one investigates sensation in the manifest dream content determines some of the results, for example, when investigators specifically looked for bodily/somatic sensation such as pain, subjects would report more detailed dream content (Schredl, 2010). Such enhanced sensitivity and pronounced perceptual dominance can be seen in the delirious state (Boettger, et al., 2014). The next domain is that of enhanced emotion whereby, approximately 70% to 75% of adults report an emotional component to their manifest dream content (Domhoff, 2011). The dominance of positive and negative emotions within dreams has yielded conflicting findings and both reflect the complex contextual nature of the dream and the underlying psychological state of the individual (Fosse et al., 2003; Schredl, 2010). However, it is generally believed, since Freud, that negative emotion and in particular anxiety dominates emotional dream experiences. In mind wandering reports, enhanced emotion is present and recounted as positive in 42.5% of cases and negative in 26.5% of cases, with the remainder of cases being reported as emotionally neutral (Killingsworth & Gilbert, 2010). This affective lability is another significant feature of delirium phenomenology, with a significant proportion of patients expressing depressive symptoms (O'Sullivan et al., 2014). Another domain is bizarreness/irrationality, which is characterised by disturbances, including large shifts in time and incongruous elements of a situation or people or impossible feats of action. However, defining these features remains a subject of debate (Zadra & Domhoff, 2011). For example, in dreaming reports there has been found to be the existence of bizarre elements in 32% to 71% of cases (Schredl, 2010). In reports of spontaneous thoughts it has been found that 20% of these are scored as bizarre/irrational on standardised scales (Klinger, 2009). In a study that looked at these elements in both dreaming and spontaneous thoughts (within the same subjects) found that bizarre elements were twice as likely to occur in dreams compared to mind wandering (Williams et al., 1992). Similar disturbances in cognition both involved in general neural processing and higher cognitive processing are well established domains of delirium (Partridge et al., 2013; Grover et al., 2014).

The recent advances of neuroscience and psychology have made it possible to give a scientific account of the relationship between dreaming and delirium. Previous accounts of delirium have largely focused upon describing in rudimentary form the ego consciousness of the delirious state. Such accounts have also neglected a robust account of the source of the contents of this heterogeneous phenomenology, namely the unconscious (Hobson, 1999). Therefore, an account of the reciprocal and mutual relationship between ego consciousness and the unconscious is necessary to form a more complete understanding of the experience of delirium. However, despite the enthusiasm for identifying the convergence of neurophysiology and phenomenology of these states an account of their differences is warranted in order to be able to formulate coherent hypotheses and theories. The most obvious difference between dreaming and delirium is the origin of these phenomena. Delirium is an acute onset brain failure and results from the convergence of a number of pathological occurrences such as a deregulated HPA axis and a fluctuating pro inflammatory CNS state which all set upon a vulnerable age related brain (Maldonado, 2013). Based upon the data we can also draw another conclusion from measures of delirium phenomenology, that in addition to measuring these features individually, these features are bound together with the functional integrity of the CNS into a cohesive unitary syndrome (Leonard et al., 2013). In delirium, the pro-inflammatory state of the CNS transiently disturbs this integrity as evidenced by the fluctuating severity of the features. This CNS fluctuation is due to the dialectical interaction between the pathological processes and the compensatory mechanisms, i.e. neurocognitive reserve. In dementia, we can see this on a larger and more apparent scale, particularly in vascular dementia (Rockwood, 2002). Dreaming results from the neurophysiology of sleep, and has two main forms reflective of that sleep, NREM and REM dreaming. Dreaming is a critical component to the development and growth of consciousness and hence the individuation of the psyche as a totality. In addition, dreaming finds itself as part of a continuum with the conscious life of the individual as can be evidenced by the plethora of studies investigating the continuity hypothesis. Dreaming is part of the process of growth and hence life. On the other hand, delirium is an acute onset and often reversible state of brain death, although it can be experienced as an oneiric state with the manifest content of archetypal motifs and biographical details furnishing it. Understanding the phenomenology, neurochemistry, and pharmacology used to tackle its distressing features further highlights the relationship between these complex states of consciousness. Although the phenomenology of dreaming and delirium are close, delirium is more congruent to nightmares given the overwhelming evidence that finds the experience of delirium to be negative and often traumatic. The experience of delirium may be the psyche's attempt to integrate and understand its own destruction. The critical state of the unwell individual experiencing delirium enacts an abberant stress response and pro inflammatory state that can be perceived as a major threat. Indeed, it is a major threat, as the psyche is approaching its potential end.

8.2. Circadian integrity in delirium

In the context of delirium, circadian integrity refers to the integrity of the sleep-wake cycle and motor behaviour which operates in a circadian manner [see Fig 3.]. The causal relationship between sleep disturbances and the occurrence of delirium is less clear, but studies consistently implicate prior sleep disturbances as a risk factor for developing delirium (Heller et al, 1970; Sveinsson, 1975; Özyurtkan et al., 2010). Prospective studies indicate a close correlation between reduced nocturnal and excessive daytime sleep and post-operative delirium risk, and identify sleep-disturbance as an indicator of prodromal or early delirium (Kaneko et al., 1997; Fann et al., 2005). A small study of postoperative patients in the ICU using polysomnography found that sleep disturbances preceded the emergence of delirium (Trompeo et al., 2011). Matsushima et al., (1997) prospectively found prodromal changes of background slowing on EEG (theta/alpha ratio) and sleep disturbance associated with changing consciousness in CCU patients developing delirium. Moreover, sleep enhancement strategies and avoidance of hypnotics can reduce delirium risk (Inouye et al 1999; Flaherty et al., 2003). Investigations into the sleep-wake cycle of delirious patients have identified the different measurable dysfunctions found in delirium. Disturbances of the sleep-wake cycle have been found to exist in the range of 73% to 99% of patients even in the absence of dementia (Jabbar et al., 2011; Mattoo et al., 2012). Insomnia, increased somnolence, and varying degrees of fragmentation have been found to be the patterns of the altered sleep-wake cycle of delirium. The most striking element and one that may reveal the interconnections between dreaming and delirium is the degree of sleep-wake fragmentation and its observable reversibility in patients who are delirious (Gupta et al., 2008). Thus, there is a link between sleep disturbances and delirium, but it remains unclear whether sleep disturbances cause delirium or simply reflect the emergence of delirium, or perhaps both contribute to an escalating cycle of delirium and disturbed circadian integrity.

The human CNS and hence psyche has multiple functions for regulating the arousal system and its functions related to motor activity systems. The arousal system is itself a functionally related constellation of structures, that synthesize and releases a number of neurochemicals that signal to sleep-wake regulatory regions upstream during the awake phase of the circadian cycle (Jones, 2003). The neocortex has major roles in regulating arousal and attention in a top down fashion. One of the most concentrated convergent regions of the arousal system is the medial prefrontal cortex, which has the ability to signal via descending pathways to the brainstem, the hypothalamus, and the basal forebrain (Hurley et al., 1991; Aston-Jones & Cohen, 2005). The thalamus has been proposed as a critical modulator for selective attention due to its wide variety of neurochemical inputs such as serotonin, histamine, acetylcholine, and norepinephrine, from their respective nuclei. The selective neocortical activation that is served by the respective relay thalamic nuclei, such as the reticular nuclei, have significant inhibitory (GABAergic) impact upon the sensory relay of stimuli from the environment. Certain stimuli can then be prevented from reaching higher cortical cognitive integration via thalamocortical pathways (Manning et al., 1996; Parent & Descarries, 2008).

The majority of patients with delirium demonstrate discernible alterations in their motor activity profiles, including loss of control/self-agency and/or exhibit motor activity that is inappropriate in its timing (e.g., daytime somnolence, and nocturnal agitation). Such disturbances are reflective of a dysfunction of the temporal regulation of motor behaviour (Yang et al., 2009). Disturbances of motor activity can include hypoactive and/ or hyperactive presentations, with some *mixed subtype* patients exhibiting features of both within short time frames. What underlies these patterns and their clinical significance remains uncertain, but they may reflect the influence of differing aetiologies, treatment exposures, and individual patient characteristics such as genetics, frailty, age, and prior cognitive functioning (Kiely et al., 2007). Relative hypoactivity is linked to frailty, severity of physical illness, comorbid dementia, and older age, while hyperactivity is linked to metabolic conditions, including drug withdrawal and intoxication (Camus et al., 2000; Meagher et al., 2011). More recent work reflects the integration of the sleep-wake cycle and motor behaviour under the phenomenological dimension of circadian integrity. Such work also provides insight into the relationship between dreaming and delirium. Phenomenological work has highlighted the differences between motor subtypes in the degree of sleep-wake cycle disruption and identified through factor analysis their intimate association (Boettger & Breitbart, 2011). Neurobiological work has demonstrated that physical activity and motor behaviour are subject to circadian regulation and fluctuation. However, there have been limited direct studies of the processes that regulate circadian activity in delirious patients, but two indicated disruptions to melatonergic function (urinary 6-SMT) according to motor subtypes of delirium (Balan et al., 2003; 2014). Moreover, empirical evidence from EEG studies suggests that there is a parallel between the subtypes of delirium (hypoactive and hyperactive) and stages of sleep (NREM and REM) (Jacobson et al., 2008). In dreaming, motor behaviour is significantly altered. In NREM, there is hypotonia but retention of motor activity, albeit in reduced form. In REM sleep there is complete atonia, but in the context of dreaming there is significantly more self-agency, i.e. internalised representations of the motor activity, in other words, the person exists as a movable persona within the dream landscape (McNamara et al., 2007).

Typically, the regulated circadian integrity of sleep-wake cycle and motor activity enables humans to adapt and interact with the two functional domains of their psyche, the ego-consciousness of the external world and the internal world of the unconscious (Contelmo et al., 2014). It has been proposed that the degree of lucidity and individual motor autonomy in dreaming has been found to be more congruous to that of waking experience than the more popularly believed accounts (Barrett, & McNamara, 2012; Schredl, 2014). Investigative observations based on this assumption have led to identifying the psychological interface between the internal and external world and termed it *boundary thickness* (Hartman, 2011). Such boundaries refer to the degree of marked separation between waking and sleeping states (Blagrove, & Pace-Schott, 2010). Cognition of thick boundaries tends to be more orientated towards serial thought processes, clearly dichotomous cognition and the qualitative less influence of unconscious affective states upon ego consciousness (Hartmann, 2011). Perhaps a breakdown in the integrity of the neural systems regulating the different phases of the circadian cycle and hence the different stages of sleep may explain the apparent phenomenon of delirious patients existing in multiple stages of the circadian cycle at once.

8.3. Orders of consciousness in delirium

Delirium in its most pronounced state is a disorder of consciousness (Schiff & Plum, 2000). The unitary mode of consciousness as experienced by the ego is composed of a primary and secondary functional order. Primary consciousness is the preverbal and pre-ego state of consciousness of humans, and it is with the development of ego cohesion as measured by self-identification, that a functioning ego is said to exist (Hobson & Voss, 2011). Primary consciousness is composed of sensation transformed into perceptual images and is thus a virtual abstract and multimodal based system. It has not only the function of being a mode of sensation but can also integrate this state with memory which consequently adds a temporal dimension to awareness such that the present and immediate past are encompassed (Boly et al., 2013). Secondary consciousness integrates uniquely human psychological constructs and constrains our experience of reality through structured and coherent systems (Edelman & Tononi, 2013). Primary consciousness carries with it a relatively large amount of entropy and it is only with the development of secondary consciousness that this disorder can be curtailed. This structuring enables the psyche to exist in a state of order and thus to bring forth an approximation of what is experienced as consensus reality (Edelman et al., 2011).

The characteristic disturbances in consciousness that patients with delirium experience parallel this distinction between primary and secondary consciousness. In delirium, functions of secondary consciousness, such as language, metacognition and orientation are all disturbed and as such patients report severe disorientation and alienation from social interaction during a delirious episode (Partridge et al., 2013). In prodromal, sub/full syndromal delirious states, there is an acute onset yet graded qualitative and quantitative breakdown in the functional integrity of the CNS. Such a breakdown is marked by a compensatory reconfiguration of the remnants of primary and secondary consciousness as experienced by the typical virtual sensorium: the unitary syndrome of delirium. Only a few studies have been undertaken to understand the narrative structures of the delirious state (Grover & Shah, 2011; Grover et al., 2014). It is recognised that complex and systematic, i.e. narrative delusions are often missing from severely delirious patients and it has been proposed that such a deficit is due to widespread cognitive impairment (Trzepacz et al., 2011). However, patients' recall of delusions during their ICU stay has been found to range from 47% to 73% (Capuzzo et al., 2003; Jones et al., 2001). In particular, the less structured delusions of delirium are as a result of left cerebral hemispheric dysfunction (Heilman & Valenstein, 2011). In general, robust narrative structures are an emergent property of the developing psyche (Foulkes, 1982; Resnick et al., 1994). Although dreaming and delusions may share a common point of origin, the apparent coherency of the narrative is an illusion. Instead, both narrative structures are resulting from a multitude of processes that create a mode of reality that serves their respective functions. The function of dreaming can be seen as part of the neurodevelopment of the subject, a modality of individuation and a function of proto-consciousness (Hobson, 2009). The function of a delusion can be seen as constructing a form of meaning in the presence of a lesion or disintegration of integrating cognitive and perceptual systems (Coltheart et al., 2011). This unitary syndrome is the result of the reconfigured experiences of reality as abstractly encoded by the neural network of complexes and the retained perceptual system of the psyche. Such a constellation of experiences shapes motivation and hence guides the attention and orientation systems through the interface of ego consciousness.

A breakdown of this interface is detected as the heterogeneous phenomenology that is pronounced in delirium, typically inattention and disorientation.

Central to a clearer understanding of these dysfunctions is the role of mind wandering and its phenomenological congruence to dreaming, as well as the underlying cortical mechanism accounting for the mnemonic processes, in other words, the default mode network (DMN) (Mason et al., 2007; Vanhaudenhuyse et al., 2010; Wamsley et al., 2010). The DMN is composed of functionally and anatomically connected neural regions (Greicius et al., 2009). These regions include the dorsal and ventral medial prefrontal cortex, the retrospenial cortex, the inferior parietal lobule, the posterior cingulate cortex, the lateral temporal cortex, the precuneus cortex, the hippocampal formation, and the surrounding parahippocampal cortex (Parvizi et al., 2006). This is all the more relevant considering that recent neuroimaging research has found that the distinct disturbances in the neural substrate of delirium are to be attributed to the DMN (Christoff et al., 2011; Domhoff, 2011). The DMN was initially proposed as a model of the brain in a state of non-task orientated cognitive functioning (Gusnard & Raichle, 2001; Raichle & Snyder, 2007). However, this initial formulation has grown to include the engagement with past experiences or future possibilities as well as reflecting on the perspectives of other individuals (Buckner & Carroll, 2007). This nebulous construct attempts to capture the true nature of undirected cognition and therefore contribute to the current discussion. One such experimental concept is spontaneous thought which has the characteristic feature of effortless and undirected thought. Such a function is similar and often used synonymously with day dreaming (Klinger, 2009). Another useful concept is stimulus independent thought (SIT). Again SIT and day dreaming both constitute a situation whereby a person is meant to be performing a task and the resulting deviated cognition (Christoff et al., 2009, 2012). Despite the unclear and often used synonymous terms, it is apparent that the neural substrates underlying these concepts are indeed similar (Christoff et al., 2004; Stawarczyk et al., 2011).

Ego defence mechanisms (EDM) have long been suggested to be part of the disturbances in neuro-cognitive processing of the delirious state (Lipowski, 1990; Feinberg, 2011). This of course is in the general context of the relationship between ego consciousness and the unconscious as based upon repression and dissociation (Summers, 2014). If dissociation can be considered the normal state of psychological functioning within the unconscious, then repression can be considered as a broad term used to describe the EDMs that separates potentially traumatic affects from images and ideas (Boag, 2012). This is particularly important because dissociation is the method by which complexes can re-arrange to adapt to new encoding sensory inputs in order to enhance and maintain adaptation to the environment. Put another way, this process is integral to reducing the predictive error that exists within the functional inference mechanisms of the psyche.

Fig 3. Perception as interface between top-down expectations and sensory driven analysis.

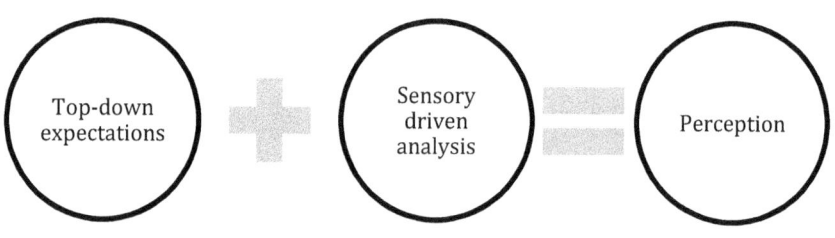

Fig 4. Model of prediction error (free energy) minimization.

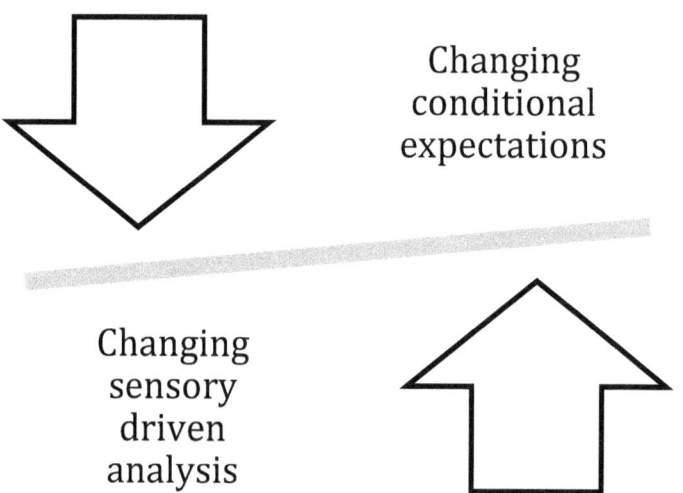

Disorders in these functions include PTSD, and it has consistently been reported that patients develop PTSD features from their delirious experience. More particularly, and in the absence of the ego's ability to appropriate aspects of the complexes to serve identity and behaviour, the complexes can function in an autonomous manner and manifest as compulsions and stereotypical behaviour (Belli, 2014). The abnormal sensory encoding resulting from trauma, can then manifest in severely debilitating conditions such as PTSD. Individuals with PTSD report vivid flashbacks that are multimodal and originate from the un-integrated encoded experiences (van der Kolk et al., 2012). This pathological state is the result of dysfunctional inference mechanisms that narrow the gap between incoming sensory stimuli and encoded experiences. One's experience of the external world is abberant due to this disconnect and further escalates the cycle of mismatch between what we are experiencing and what we expect to experience as encoded by the unconscious. A disconnect that further sets the stage for delusions and hallucinations.

8.4. Executive cognition in delirium

At the phenomenological level, executive cognition is the most complex functional disturbance in delirium and dreaming (Domhoff, 2011; Terzaghi et al., 2014). The distinguishing features of each is difficult to determine, because they are profoundly based upon functional modalities which include language, thought processes, perception, emotional homeostasis, attention, orientation, memory processes, and self/other inferential processing. Indeed, at the centre point of the experience of the ego is the theory of the *self-referent effect*, in other words, the psychological processing of differentiating others from one's self, and the growing number of studies performed to elucidate the neurobiological dimensions to each (Rogers et al., 1977). A particular focus is played in the role of the cortical midline structures such as the medial prefrontal cortex (MPFC), anterior cingulate cortex (ACC), and posteromedial cortices (PMCs), and how they together contribute to the ego (Northoff et al., 2006).

One of the theoretical loci that unite modern research into delirium and dreaming is the role of orientation and attention. Attention is consistently found to be a key feature of delirium phenomenology and has a strong association with other features in delirium, according to the data (Meagher et al., 2007, 2010). However, deficits in attention also exist in chronic conditions such as dementia with Lewy bodies and late stage Alzheimer's disease (Metzler-Baddeley, 2007; Kolanowski et al., 2012). In order to optimally function, attention must pay tribute to two dimensions of the stimuli, external stimuli from the environment and internal psychological goals/bias (Noudoost & Moore, 2011). The emergence of selective attention as a cognitive faculty that enables the filtering out of irrelevant sensory information further enhances the ego's capacity to identify relevant information. But the selective characterisation of attention must not misguide us into thinking that it is a single well circumscribed system, but rather it is the result of the interface between between executive cognition, the arousal systems, and the network of unconscious complexes/schemas (Bucci, 2011; Cohen, 2014). In dreams there is a discernible pronouncement of the emotional impact of these unconscious schemas in the shaping of the dream work (Selterman et al., 2013). Such emotionality may act as an analogous model for how affective lability manifests in delirium. Another more impressive model would be the dysfunction of executive cognition in the context of nightmares. Nightmares exist within the continuum of waking experience and are congruent with the rest of dreaming, except in the dimension of emotion (Schredl, 2003). Hence, nightmares are also part of the homeostasis of emotion that is conducted by the psyche. The emotions during nightmares tends to be intense fear, anger and disgust (Zadra et al., 2006; Robert & Zadra, 2013). Nightmares can be proposed as breakdowns in the regulation of emotion that is normally conducted during dreaming. According to Freud, nightmares serve the function of integrating repressed anxiety into consciousness and thus overcoming shameful and traumatic experiences (Freud, 1900). This general finding has been confirmed by other studies (Greenberg et al., 1972; Lansky et al., 1995). Evidence from neuroscientific studies of sleep, dreaming, and human cognitive functions have begun to confirm many tenets of the theoretical hypothesis of nightmares as first proposed by the psychoanalysis of dreams. One such stream of evidence is the role of continuing activity of dopaminergic pathways during REM sleep stage and its proposed basis of expressing affective concerns during dreaming. Significantly elevated dopaminergic signalling during this mode of behaviour has been associated with the onset and experience of nightmares (Solms, 2000).

The emotional regulation in dreaming is served by several processes that contribute to the form and content of dreaming experience (Hartmann, 1998; 2007). The critical process is that of the contextualisation of the person's emotional concerns. In non-distressing dreams, emotions tend to be more mosaic, and diffuse, and thus a clear understanding of the contextualisation process is difficult to analyse in isolation. The contextualisation process of nightmares would enable the establishment of new associations to an emotion with a view of adaptation to the emotion

(Hartmann, 1998b). This hypothesis would tie together the dimensions of nightmare phenomenology and further demonstrate that they serve a purpose. An integrative model has been proposed to gather together both the psychological and neurological aspects of dreaming in order to provide a working model for nightmares. The affect network dysfunction (AND) model is one such model that has made a major effort at this (Nielson & Levin, 2007). Its theoretical foundation is based on studies investigating neuro-imaging, PTSD patients, anxiety disorder patients, and neurophysiological profiles of personality and combined with the AMPHAC (amygdala, medial prefrontal cortex, hippocampus and anterior cingulate cortex) model of nightmare formation (Levin & Nielson, 2009). The central concept of this theory is that nightmares originate from an innate adaptive function of the affective systems dedicated to fear memory extinction.

Disorientation is a pronounced feature of delirium and much of dreaming. More specifically, disorientation in the context of dreaming is based upon cortisol modulation of the cognitive functions of the PFC serving orientation (Perogamvros, & Schwartz, 2012). Orientation is composed of three broad based systems, the arousal system (often referred to as the level of consciousness), attention, and memory (Trzepacz et al., 2011). It can also be considered as a compound psychological function based upon attention and the autobiographical self. The autobiographical self is the aspect of the ego that is responsible for processing and encoding stimuli pertaining to one's identity and one's environment (Damasio, 2012). This aspect of identity has to be intimately bound with both explicit and implicit memory systems in order to retrieve and reproduce information about one's body, one's name, memories about one's life, etc. (Cabeza & St Jacques, 2007; Platek et al., 2008; Tacikowski et al., 2011).

Sleep and dreaming have long been recognised as being integral processes involved in memory augmentation, consolidation, and integration (Winson, 1985, 2002, 2004; Kali & Dayan 2004). The complex phases of sleep, namely REM and NREM have particular memories attributed to their consolidation (Ackermann, & Rasch, 2014; Murkar et al., 2014). Examples include, emotional memory consolidation is governed by the REM phase of sleep (Maquet et al. 1996; Walker, 2009). However, it is increasingly recognised that emotionally charged episodic memories may rely on both REM sleep and SWS for their consolidation (Ellenbogen et al., 2006; Marshall & Born, 2007; Payne et al., 2007). These findings are relevant to the role memory and sleep play in delirium, with age-related decline of cognitive integrity being the most significant aspect related to the reduced REM sleep time of patients with delirium (Weinhouse et al., 2009).

8.5. Model of dreaming and delirium interface

With all its sorrow and relief, delirium forms the boundary between the living psyche and the void; it is the compensatory psyche upon the precipice of death. Its pathogenesis equally complex is underlain by a myriad accumulation of aetiological factors which converge to precipitate the noxious stimuli that initiates the psyches decline. To be sure, one particular area that requires further inquiry is the pathophysiological basis of the phenomenological fluctuation of delirium. It is reasonable to propose that it results from two major components, neurocognitive reserve and the time course/interaction of pathological processes upon this reserve. The first, neurocognitive reserve is the structural and functional reserve of the human

CNS and its capacity to buffer insults (Jones et al., 2010). As the term suggests neurocognitive reserve is conceptualised in terms of brain reserve and cognitive reserve, whereby brain reserve refers to the capacity of CNS to function despite on-going pathological changes. Examples of markers of this include synaptic density and premorbid neuronal parenchymal integrity. In congruence with that, cognitive reserve refers to capacity of alternative cognitive systems to be recruited and compensate for diminished optimal cognitive functioning. Examples of this include economic status, educational achievement, and stimulating occupation (Jicha & Rentz, 2013; Wilson et al., 2013). In keeping with the isomorphism theory, they are two aspects of the same phenomenon. Most of the research has been focused on long term cognitive failure, i.e. dementia, however, the same model has been applied to delirium with the view that some patients have the capacity to overcome stressors, for instance, the hospital setting and acute illness (Saczynski et al., 2014). Previous work has identified that educational achievement and increased activity participation are protective against developing delirium in the hospital setting (Scmitt et al., 2012; Inouye et al., 2014). More recent work looking at markers for neurocognitive reserve in delirium have found that many of the established markers for reserve, with the exception of vocabulary knowledge, were not associated with an increased risk of developing delirium and thus, proposed that these factors are relevant for long term compensatory capacity rather than acute onset and may be further reflective of post delirious episode outcome i.e. how fast and to what degree patients recover from delirium (Saczynski et al., 2014). There is of course an intimate relationship between neurocognitive reserve and inference functions within the human CNS. Early research into this particular area suggests that in the neuroimaging of subjects with age related cognitive impairment it was found that this impairment reflective of different neural regions of the CNS. There are two major views on this. Firstly, it is speculated that these different regions or different activity is reflective of the impairment in and of itself. While the converse is that this differential activity is reflective of the neurobiological changes that occur over time which include compensatory and organizational mechanisms, hence resculpting the neural networks required for optimal cognitive functioning during the transition into senescence.

The Bayesian inference framework is useful to model the structure and function of psychological schemas (complexes) and to their resulting psychotic features, namely delusions, hallucinations. The central theme is that of perception as a form of unconscious inference (Von Helmholtz, 1871; Barlow, 1990). It can best be summarised as 'incoming information is interpreted in light of our prior expectations' (Corlett et al., 2009). Learning and experience are therefore modulated by mismatches between expected and actual sensory stimuli, this mismatch is referred to as predictive error or free energy. The optimal psyche will attempt where ever possible to narrow the error to enhance the organism's capacity to adapt and respond to the environment. To do this new information must be coded efficiently into preexisting models of the world, i.e. complexes. Congruent to existing accounts of the neurobiology of memory encoding, a three level analysis as proposed by David Marr (1982). Firstly, there is the computational level whereby sensory inputs are predicted to enable the optimum adaptation response to the environment. Next is the algorithmic level, which exhibits a hierarchical Bayesian strategy to derive this prediction. Finally, the implementation level seeks to integrate this series of predictions. Such a system of processes has been proposed to be governed by glutamatergic signalling (NMDA for feedback and AMPA for feed-forward signalling.

The impact of these processes is modulated by key neurotransmistters systems, particularly dopaminergic and cholinergic subsystems (Corlett et al., 2009).

The second dimensional basis for fluctuation is the time course/interaction of the pathological process with neurocognitive reserve. Recent work looking at the neuro-immuno axis indicates that the impact of acute onset insults deregulates the HPA axis and its extended integration with neuroendocrine and immunomodulatory functions within the CNS. Such a complex system of interconnections may be the explanatory model required to explain the onset of delirium, its fluctuating time course, and its resolution/persistence. The most well studied area is sepsis associated delirium and the impact of cytokines on neuromodulatory systems such as acetylcholine (Osorio et al., 2015). In particular the role of cytokines (TNF α) can remain (sometimes for months) raised within the CNS and are associated microglial activation (Perry, 2004; Qin et al., 2007). In general, microglia have roles in phagocyctosis, antigen presentation, secretion of pro inflammatory biochemical (chemokines, proteases, and cytokines) and rapid proliferation (Perry, 2004; Teeling & Perry, 2009) Microglia act as a critical component of the innate immune response system in the brain and are normally in a quiescent state. However production of the pro-inflammatory mediators have effects on astrocyte tight junctions which disturb the integrity of the blood brain barrier and thus expose the neural tissue to further insult (Garden & Möller, 2006). Such microglial activation leads to exacerbate neuroinflammation and subsequent degeneration of the CNS. After systematic infection disturbances in neural function can arise from these detrimentally deregulated mediators and manifest in the behavioural changes seen in infection (Garden & Möller, 2006; Ebersoldt et al., 2007). The neuroinflammatry state in the CNS is a result of microglial activation which leads to degeneration of basal forebrain cholinergic signalling (Willard et al., 1999; Teeling & Perry, 2009). There are even reports of age related factors such as up regulation of inflammatory responses and implicated in the pathogenesis of dementia (Hoozemans et al., 2006; Franceschi et al., 2007).

The innate immune system can respond differently depending on its stimulation. Primed microglia, in other words, microglia that have been activated by initial factor(s) leads to them being capable of an enhanced inflammatory responses and worsening consequences (Perry, 2004). Evidence from postmortem studies of brains of elderly patients who had sepsis exhibit increased CD68 expression on their microglia. This finding was also associated with increased numbers of microglia in the grey tissue of the CNS indicating a more widespread inflammatory response (Panda, 2009). There is also modest evidence to indicate that cholinergic neurmodulation has effects upon the innate immune response and thus on attenuating effect on the inflammatory response in the CNS (Tracey, 2002; Quan & Banks, 2007). Impaired cholinergic regulation of microglia may render susceptible patients to developing delirium or worse dementia (De Simone et al., 2005).

The fluctuating lucidity of the delirious episode is understood to be resulting from the psychological function of boundary thickness. Psychometric assessments (using the Boundary Questionnaire) of thick boundaried subjects to thin-boundaried subjects have indicated that the dreams of thick boundaried subjects score similar to day dreams of thin boundaries subjects in terms of dream phenomenology such as bizarreness and metaphorical imagery (Kunzendorf, et al., 1997). This would suggest that waking cognition and day dreams are more continuous with dreaming during sleep than conventional wisdom discerns. There is an obvious continuum between these categories of thin and thick boundaries with a normal distribution of scores (Hartmann, & Kunzendorf, 2006). The central point of these findings must compel one to understand the sleep-wake cycle in terms of ego consciousness and its plethora of cognitive processes and motor behaviour that is more characteristic of a clear demarcation between the sleep and wake phase of the circadian cycle. Examining the subjective reports on the phenomenology of delirium, there is a consistent theme of patients experience an inability to distinguish between reality and imagination and sleep and wake state (Partridge et al., 2013). The onset of delirium may be marked by a propensity towards diminished sleep-wake boundaries.

The ego gives coherency as part of the emergent properties of executive cognitive functions that the ego has evolved to serve. The central functional locus of this agency is the concept of the core self. This element is composed of features such as, affective regulation, and motivated patterns of behaviour and as such have been implicated as an integrative function of the cortical midline structures and the subcortical midline structures of the brain (Panksepp, 1998, Panksepp & Northoff, 2009). The connection between the cortical and subcortical midline structures and the mirror neuron systems is the result of a multitude of neural pathways based upon critical relay centres (Uddin et al., 2007). An example of a critical relay centre is the insular cortex which functions as a structure for interoceptive processes which have been encoded, processed and relayed from the mirror neuron system to the cortical and subcortical midline structures (Rizzolatti & Luppino, 2001).

If one accepts the threat simulation theory of Revonsuo, the dream is a realistic simulation of threatening events that are rehearsed and ultimately mastered. This is supported by the vast majority of dreams exhibiting negative content and challenging scenarios. The dream has an evolutionary function which reveals 'species specific survival skills' and is therefore dependent on the environmental challenges that one must overcome. This theory also highlights the complex organisation of dream content and negates any presupposition that vivid dreaming is a result of random cortical activation during REM phase of sleep (Crick & Mitchinson, 1983, 1995; Singer, 2014). A key compensatory aspect of the dream is the reproduction of fear extinction memories. Such a process has three main stages to it. The first is element activation where the hyper-associative state of sleep enables the access to dissociated aspects of episodic memories, often de-contextualised from real world occurrences. The second is element recombination, where each of these now recruited elements are reorganised and integrated with recently encoded contextualised memories. The third is emotional expression, whereby the now recombined memories are engaged with during the experience of dreaming as part of the integration process. The affect distress factor determines the severity and frequency of the nightmare and is a developmental trait often as a result of experiencing trauma, and abuse experiences such as neglect. According to Nielson & Levin (2009), this process is dependent on the concept of affect load, the state factor that is a combination of an individual's capacity to regulate emotions and experience of stressful occurrences. The affect load is challenged by the requirements to develop and grow the psyche by integrating dissociated and often repressed encoded stimuli within the unconscious psyche.

More generally, Hobson proposes that the function of dreaming is in the formation of protoconsciousness. In line with the distinction between primary and secondary consciousness, Hobson proposes that dreaming, particularly during REM sleep has pronounced features of primary consciousness. He also highlights the qualitative decrease of features of secondary consciousness in dreaming and further proposes that disturbances in secondary consciousness are the foundation for the uniquely human neuropsychiatric conditions including delirium (Hobson, 2009). This is not surprising given the plethora of evidence that illustrates that psychotic states and dreaming share many neurobiological substrates (Pappert et al., 1999; Weinberger & McClure, 2002; Gottesmann, 2006). Indeed, both reveal the intimate drama between the unconscious complexes and the ego which they relate. One can discern, at this rudimentary stage of research that a working framework is beginning to emerge. A key aspect is the application of findings from inference models of neurobiology as empirical evidence of the dynamic behaviour of the unconscious as it impacts upon ego consciousness. The constellation of cell to cell signalling modulated by excitatory and inhibitory feedback loops, coupled with modulatory neurotransmission systems all furnish this emerging account.

Delirium occurs in states of dopaminergic dysregulation, both hypodopaminergic and hyperdopaminergic (Trzepacz et al., 2010). Plasma and CSF levels of the DA metabolite Homovanillic Acid (HVA) are altered in delirium, with greater dopaminergic disturbance in those with psychosis (Ramirez-Bermudez et al., 2008; van der Cammen et al., 2006). Dopamine-blocking antipsychotic agents are the first line pharmacological intervention for both prophylaxis and treatment of delirium and are thought to act by correcting imbalance between dopaminergic and cholinergic systems (Meagher, 2010; NICE, 2010). Circadian variation in dopamine receptor sensitivity, striatal dopamine turnover, and plasma HVA concentration occurs in healthy humans and is thought to be mediated by striatal dopamine-melatonin interactions (Doran et al 1990; Eisenberg et al, 2010; Zisapel, 2001). Melatonin has complex interaction with dopaminergic systems, both directly inhibiting postsynaptic striatal dopaminergic signalling and promoting presynaptic dopamine neuronal integrity (Zisapel, 2001; Venero et al., 2003; Eisenberg et al., 2010). These effects are site-specific, for example, melatonin inhibiting DA release in hippocampal and hypothalamic centres, while dopamine and melatonin act as mutually inhibitory signalling molecules of day/night status in the retina (Parades et al., 1999; Guido et al, 2010). Patients with mixed and hyperactive delirium have been observed to have greater exposure to psychotropic agents and greater use of antipsychotic medications (Godfrey et al., 2010). Conversely, there may be a parallel between the hypoactive and hypodopaminergic state and dreaming during NREM sleep.

In clinical theory, delirium necessitates forms and features that differentiate it from other pathologies. Delirium has a savage nature which obscures its true identity by intervening into the trajectory of critical illness. It mutates the regular ordered, almost vegetal existence of internal medicine and its myriad applications. The denatured position of pathology worsens in the context of unrecognised delirium. The complexity escalates beyond the simplest behavioural models of healthcare professionals and situates it beyond their comprehension to the point of ignorance and worse still fatalism. The field of interventional medicine gets obstructed by the intermingling of the indistinct phenomenal features of delirium pathogenesis. However, the co-occurrence of delirium with chronic diseases exposes the impotency of current theories of delirium to analyse its nature. A multidimensional theory of delirium, which seeks to circumscribe the boundary of the delirious psyche will therefore go along way to restoring a sense of progress to medicine.

Part IV Conclusion

9 Research and recommendations

9.1. Overview of medical management

Due to its prevalence, incidence, cost, and complications, delirium is a major target for improved health care delivery (Inouye et al., 2014). The optimum management of delirium relies on several principles. The first is the understanding of factors that culminate with the onset of delirium. It is a general finding that delirium does not result from a sole factor, but its pathogenesis is a mosaic of active factors. These factors can broadly be categorized into those that predispose patients to developing delirium, such as old age and critical illness, and precipitating factors, such as polypharmacy and patient immobility, which act synergistically with the predisposing factors to propel a patient into a state of delirium. Logically an understanding of the interaction between these factors enables health care professionals to actively engage with interventions that disrupt the convergence of these negative factors. According to Marcantonio (2011), this approach when understood fully has four main points, 1) addressing the cause(s) of delirium, 2) maintenance of behavioural integrity using either/or a combination of behavioural and pharmacological strategies, 3) an active prevention strategy for delirium complications, and 4) extensive support for rehabilitation and maintenance of social-adaptive functioning. However, novel approaches aimed at phenomenological domains may be more efficacious.

The recognition that up to 22% of patients with delirium develop persistent delirium and the extensive morbidity associated with having developed delirium has induced researchers to propose that delirium may indeed be a clinical entity managed by active treatment (Meagher et al.,

2012). Active treatment may also be informed by incorporating two key elements into its theoretical framework. The first is the critical period hypothesis which proposes that illnesses are more responsive to treatment in the prodromal or initial stages of the illness, rather than the later phases of the condition. This critical period hypothesis needs to be further developed and supported by data to determine the critical periods of delirium and help provide health care professionals with an improved appreciation for factors such as relapse rates and forms of recovery. The second related concept is the role of the duration of untreated delirium. This is the period between the onset of delirium and initiation of treatment. This is particularly relevant in the palliative care setting, where in the days and hours before death, there is a reported delirium prevalence of 88%. However, the continual usage of vague nomenclature such as *terminal anguish*, *terminal restlessness*, and *terminal agitation* all present real obstacles to optimising patient welfare. The assumed naturalness of the co-occurrence of death and delirium may promote a therapeutic approach that is fatalistic and simply ignore the potential development of strategies to reverse this *terminal delirium* (Bush et al., 2013). Unfortunately, there is no consensus for the development or licensing of a treatment for delirium and high quality evidence for strategies such as pharmacotherapy are lacking (Lacasse et al., 2006). In a systematic review of anti-psychotic pharmacotherapy in delirium, Meagher et al., (2013) highlight that in the absence of high quality evidence and standardized clinical management, the treatment of delirium is guided by low quality evidence and empirical management. This is very problematic, particularly in the context of deliriums' heterogeneous phenomenology, including its fluctuating time course, and the wide variety of complex patient populations who are at an increased risk of developing it (Fong et al., 2015). Fortunately, the scientific evidence for the beneficial efficacy of pharmacotherapy used both in a prophylactic approach and a routine active management basis is growing (Inouye et al., 2014).

Pharmacotherapeutic interventions for delirium are dependent upon the clinical context of the patient. Antipsychotics are divided into two groups, namely first generation antipsychotics (FGA) and second generation antipsychotics (SGA). Each of these categories has side effect profiles that correlate with the relative affinities for specific receptors. Initially haloperidol, an FGA, has been commonly administered to patients as a first line treatment for cases of ICU delirium. In addition to having serious side effects such as neuroleptic malignant syndrome and *torsades de pointes*, there is little evidence reporting its capacity to reduce the incidence of delirium in this patient population (Meyer-Masetti, 2011). Since previous guidelines promoting haloperidol as first line treatment were published in 2002 (Jacobi et al., 2002), the pain, agitation, and delirium guidelines have been published which downgraded the recommendation of haloperidol treatment for cases of delirium (Barr et al., 2013). There has been a gradual replacement of haloperidol with SGA with the view to enhancing efficacy and reducing the risk of adverse side effects. Unfortunately, there exists a paucity of research to demonstrate the superiority of these drugs (Devlin et al., 2010). Active treatment approaches in the palliative care setting are composed of many conflicting elements from family, medical ethics, and duty of care for patients. More specifically, end of life care needs to address the patient's goals of care whereby, treatment is matched to the patient's values. This can be achieved through advanced discussion with patients and the establishment of a substitute decision maker when the patient's capacity to make informed decisions is absence e.g. during an episode of delirium. The patient's goals of care may not conform to healthcare professional's goals of care, especially when it comes to the issue of delirium reversibility versus minimal sedation and reduction of symptoms of discomfort. It has been found that with current palliative care approximately 50% of delirium cannot be reversed (Lawlor et al., 2000). Therefore, approaches such as medication profile review with the purpose of reducing *deliriogenic* medications may optimise patient's well-being and reduce the risk of delirium where possible.

The evidence base has also not been able to address more complex issues in delirium phenomenology such as the clinical motor subtypes or the comorbid conditions that cohabitate the psyche of the patient e.g. dementia. Understanding the phenomenological domains of delirium may indicate how best to approach the challenge of delirium as a heterogeneous entity. The aim of pharmacotherapy is to reduce agitation and distress induced by delirium through sedation (antagonism at H1 receptors). The role of sedation is controversial as excess sedation can negatively impact upon neurocognitive functioning. Conversely, the positive effects of sedation are proposed to be due to the promotion of sleep and regulating the sleep-wake cycle in an effort to optimise circadian integrity. The emerging role of the sleep/circadian timing system as a pathological domain in delirium renders it an interesting target for novel candidate therapies. Benzodiazepines and other hypnotic medications can increase the total sleep time, but they interfere with the natural progression of sleep phases and decrease the duration spent in the most restorative phase of sleep (Mistraletti et al., 2008). Conversely, melatonin has been shown to be a relatively safe and an inexpensive drug, especially for elderly and cognitively impaired patients (Baskett et al., 2001; Zhdanova et al., 2001; Leger et al., 2004; Karasek, 2007). Early reports that melatonin can have positive effects in the treatment of postoperative delirium have been supplemented by randomized controlled trials indicating a significant prophylactic effect in elderly medical/surgical patients and post-operatively in children (Kain et al., 2009; Sultan, 2010; Al-Aama et al., 2011). Thus, the selective regulation of sleep may provide a means of treating other patients with delirium (de Jonghe et al., 2010). Although the range of symptoms that occur in delirium is similar for different age groups, younger patients present with greater symptom fluctuation and more marked disturbances of the sleep - wake cycle (Martin et al., 2014). Melatonin is well tolerated in children and may be a suitable therapeutic agent also for young people with delirium (Buck, 2003). Furthermore, given the significant interrelationship between depressive illness, delirium, and circadian disturbance, pharmacological agents that have overlapping influences on these clinical entities may provide novel drug therapies for delirium (Leonard et al., 2009). For example, melatonin agonists such as agomelatine have antidepressant qualities and can synchronize and regulate circadian rhythms in patients with depressive illness (Heun et al., 2013). In addition, another melatonin agonist ramelteon is an effective hypnotic agent (Richardson et al., 2008; Kuriyama et al., 2014). Thus, these agents may provide a means of restoring circadian dysregulation in patients with delirium.

Alternatively, we are faced with several lines of evidence that suggest that pharmacological strategies may not be suitable. The use of non-pharmacological methods and strategies to reduce poly-pharmacy may provide robust adjuvants to successfully managing delirium (Hein et al., 2014). There is insufficient evidence for the use of phototherapy for patients with dementia (Forbes et al., 2014). Other preliminary work has indicated that bright light therapy may be a useful therapeutic intervention for delirium (Taguchi, 2013). Finally, exercise has demonstrated preventative effects and may provide a possible treatment option for patients with delirium. It was reported that significant protection against delirium is possible when elderly patients engaged in regular exercise (Yang et al., 2008; Tatematsu et al., 2011). This may operate through synchronizing the circadian timing system and encouraging the normal sleep-wake cycle by preventing extended periods of patient immobility (Balas et al., 2014). Physical exercise during the evening delays melatonin secretion and suggests that exercise is a recognized zeitgeber (Atkinson et al., 2007). In the ICU, preventive strategies consist mainly of nonpharmacological interventions aimed at reductions in noise, light, and other sources of sleep disturbances (Kamder & Needha, 2014). However, more studies are required to build upon these initiatives in order to optimise patient rehabilitation in the ICU setting.

It is clear from the literature that the onset of delirium is rarely dominated by a single factor and instead delirium is often a result of a multitude of risk factors converging upon the CNS of a vulnerable patient (Inouye et al., 2014). Therefore, it is reasonable to suggest that targeting modifiable risk factors through a multicomponent approach may be the most suitable solution to ameliorating this impending public health crisis. First developed in Yale University medical school, the Hospital Elder Life Program (HELP) has been proposed as a major strategy against delirium. Indeed, it is a multicomponent intervention that focuses on several domains, including cognitive impairment, sleep deprivation, immobility, visual impairment, hearing impairment, and dehydration. The initial selection of such domains was based upon both the evidence based risk of their impact upon delirium and the modifiable nature of these risk factors, in other words, how these domains are amenable to standardized interventions and routine outcome measurements (Strijbos et al., 2013). HELP has been implemented in hundreds of hospitals in the United States and Europe and consistently demonstrates significant improvements in medical care with the added bonus of reducing cost (SteelFisher et al., 2011; Akunne et al., 2012). Strategies for immobility, visual impairment, hearing impairment, and dehydration has been found to be elegant methods to reduce the risk of delirium. However, the domains of cognitive impairment and sleep deprivation are still capable of being enhanced. Despite the fact that delirium has an acute onset, there is an emerging emphasis in the literature concerning itself with the prodromal phase of its onset and the subsyndromal form of its phenomenology. Such phases would provide valuable targets for clinical interventions aimed at preventing full syndromal delirium. Such an integrated strategy may lead to a significant improvement in overall clinical care and more importantly a dramatic enhancement of quality of life for patients, staff, and families.

9.2. Rehabilitation of the psyche

The psyche is the always presupposed foundation of reality, its meaning, and its organisation. Recovery from delirium is paramount to alleviating the risk of developing dementia and a host of mental health problems resulting from the often terrifying experience of delirium. Although it is proposed that delirium is often reversible, more recent evidence suggests that it is marked by incomplete recovery (Witlox et al., 2010). Current treatment strategies aimed at delirium focus upon both pharmacological and non-pharmacological based modalities (Eubank, & Covinsky, 2014; Javedan, & Tulebaev, 2014). Given the complicated state of this condition more research has focused upon integrated clinical strategies, for example, cognitive focused interventions for dementia and

HELP programmes for patients at risk of delirium, both with promising results (Rubin et al., 2011; Strijbos et al., 2013). Cognitive focused interventions exclusively target indirect and direct optimal cognitive functioning domains such as orientation, attention, and memory (Clare et al., 2013; Giebel, & Challis, 2014). It has been suggested that cognitive focused interventions be divided into two broad categories (Clare, 2003; Clare et al., 2004). The first is cognitive training which aims at improving or maintaining patient cognitive functions through standardized tasks and come in various media e.g. analog and computerized forms (Bahar-Fuchs et al., 2013). The tasks can be tailored to suit the needs and ability of the patient (Papp et al., 2009; Owen et al., 2010; Peretz et al., 2011). However, the evidence has not established the efficacy of these interventions beyond the training context. This provides a serious challenge to future efforts at task and intervention design (Papp et al., 2009; Jaeggi et al., 2010; Owen et al., 2010). In addition, the research has also integrated these strategies with pharmacological based interventions as well as other cognitive exercises e.g. visual imagery (Quayhagen et al., 2000; Koltai et al., 2001; Cahn-Weiner et al., 2003; Gates et al., 2011). The second form of cognitive focused interventions is cognitive rehabilitation, which aims at improving or maintaining an 'optimal level of physical, psychological and social functioning' of impairments resulting from injury and/or illness (Mclellan, 2012). The conceptual framework of cognitive rehabilitation has evolved considerably from previous work which aimed at restoring optimal functioning in younger patients with brain injury to explore how enhancing cognitive performance can be done within a supportive network of patients and their families working in a therapeutic alliance with healthcare professionals (Wilson, 2002; Koehler et al., 2011). In contrast to cognitive training, rehabilitation emphasizes the enhancement of performance in the everyday living setting. Rehabilitation strategies are aimed more specifically to target impairments that are most relevant to the real-life context of the patient's life. Therefore, the goals of rehabilitation interventions are based on collaboration and are patient specific (Clare et al., 2003). The majority of research has focused upon dementia and according to a Cochrane review of patients with mild and moderate dementia, these interventions have consistently efficacious improvement of generalized cognition and quality of life (Woods et al., 2012).

As research continues on treatment modalities for dementia, challenges persists. The most significant challenge is the inconsistent study design, particularly establishing adequate sample sizes and randomization employed in clinical trials (Bahar-Fuchs et al., 2013). A more important core challenge is the use of specific standardized routine outcomes. Measuring the efficacy or having a clear conceptual framework for assessing what the goals of rehabilitation are is necessary to determine which strategies work and which do not. Standardized routine outcome measures extend beyond proper scientific accuracy and have been shown to have utility as an economic index (Ernst et al. 1997; Barnett et al., 2014). With the growing emphasis on the early detection of dementia and delirium, the need for standardized and reliable outcome measures is warranted (Woods, 2006; Frick et al., 2013).

To develop an optimal programme for rehabilitation in delirium, factors that determine its potential efficacy must be considered. In previous programmes, cognitive impairment and functional disability have been the classical foci of efforts directed at improving long term outcomes for patients (Flanagan & Spencer, 2015). For example, the literature is growing with regards to cognitive rehabilitation programmes aimed at post ICU patients with the view to improving long term outcomes (Brummel & Girard, 2013). Previous reviews of the literature have identified the inconsistent definition of cognitive based intervention as leading to low numbers of comparable studies. Other factors include the investigation of these interventions on either healthy cohorts or cohorts with mild cognitive impairment in an effort to identify their utility in mild cognitive impairment states and their possible use as preventive strategies (Gauthier et al., 2006; Jean et al., 2010; Albert et al., 2011; Martin et al., 2011). There is considerable diversity in study design and intervention employed. While some studies only used a non-intervention group as control cohort, other studies such as De Vreese et al., (1998) and Davis et al., (2001) included a placebo group of simulating the intervention. Overall sample numbers are small and range from n= 11 to n= 103, and the duration and intervals of intervention vary from 5 weeks to 24 weeks, and many had followed up assessment at 3 to 9 months (Quayhagen et al., 1995; Davis et al., 2001; Galante et al., 2007). In addition, the media of delivery considerably differed from simple pencil and paper methods to computerized formats (Beck et al., 1988; Loewenstein et al., 2004).

The setting from which these participants were recruited included a broad range of sources including research clinics with the majority from the community setting (Cahn-Weiner et al., 2003; Clare et al., 2010). The aim and content of the interventions also varied and were composed of methods to enhance memory, attention, orientation, and general cognitive functioning. While others included extra benefits such as improvements of carer and daily functioning. On-going reviews of these studies have reported that the cognitive training studies did not differ from controls and the existence of only one cognitive rehabilitation study render it currently impossible to conduct a meta-analysis of the efficacy of this form of intervention (Bahar-Fuchs et al., 2013). However, it has been suggested that high quality non RCT be included to increase the evidence base of these interventions (Reeves et al., 2011).

Well defined interventions comprising physical rehabilitation with goal management training were found to have significantly improved executive cognition in a target group relative to the control group (Jackson et al., 2012). In the context of delirium, the success of multicomponent interventions such as HELP is based upon the flexibility, feasibility and focus of two dimensions, the first is amenable interventions that are based upon standardized protocols and the targeting of specific modifiable risk factors, while the second is the use of standardized outcome measures. The targeting of modifiable risk factors for delirium is complex given the wide variety of factors that increase the risk of delirium. Strategies aimed at sleep enhancement have sought to tackle environmental factors, including the minimization of disturbances of sleep by staff during the night and general reductions in environmental noise. However, there is a significant limit one can impose upon the environment, even in the most dutiful clinical setting. Therefore, it is reasonable to propose that enhancing the patients' sleep by using non pharmacological methods used for nightmares and insomnia may be of benefit. Hypnosis has seen a significant beneficial impact upon insomnia. Apart from its name, hypnosis shares many commonalities with sleep, including deep muscular relaxation. But the benefit of hypnosis as an inducer of sleep may come from the ability for enhanced imagination and concentration to overcome the many environmental noise sources that may otherwise disrupt sleep (Sebin et al., 2013; Becker, 2015).

However, the factor that has received the least amount of focus has to be the role of cognitive impairment and more precisely how modifying it would protect vulnerable patients from delirium. Initial strategies aimed at improving or maintaining cognitive status have focused upon reorientation strategies, including discussions on personal concerns, games, and current events as well as environmental modification to reduce the amount of disorientating factors such as high staff turnover (Gillis & MacDonald, 2006). In general, orientation strategies have been used in patient cohorts with either or both dementia and delirium, with such strategies regularly integrated into methods of communicating with these older patients (Woods, 1999; Patton 2006b). In an effort to understand the theoretical framework for orientation strategies, a parallel has been drawn between orientation strategies outlined by established delirium guidelines and the reality orientation approach, which has its origin in rehabilitation interventions for war veterans with mental health problems (Woods, 1999; Spector et al., 2000). The aims of this particular approach are to reduce the occurrence of inappropriate behaviour, cognitive impairment, and confusion (Woods, 1999; Spector et al., 2000, Patton 2006a, O'Connell et al., 2007). In nursing homes it is often delivered throughout the day as part of informal communication to empower patients with a sense of control over their environment (Spector et al., 2000, Patton 2006a, b; Ski & O'Connell, 2006). It is interesting to note that these orientation strategies can sometimes induce distrust, anxiety, and withdrawal due to the fact that these individuals are being confronted by a reality that is different to the one they are currently experiencing (Andersson et al., 1993, Fagerberg & Jonhagen, 2002, McCurren & Cronin, 2003, Stenwall et al., 2008). Based upon the findings from the reality orientation approach, a more individualised validation therapy has been developed to enable health care professionals to engage with patients in an effort to support and validate their current experience of reality (Feil, 1982, 1993, Neal & Barton Wright, 2003; Ski & O'Connell, 2006). Both these approaches have primarily been utilized in patients with existing dementia, and who have become confused. Understanding the patients underlying needs should be the key component of the intervention (Spector et al., 2000; Patton, 2006a). According to Fagerberg and Jonhagen (2002), there exists an implicit power relationship when the reality of the health care professional supersedes the experience of the patient. The unilateral privileging of the experience of the health care professional can distance them from the patient and their experience. Such a disconnection can reduce trust and disrupt the therapeutic alliance. The integrity of the therapeutic alliance is fragile and contingent upon health care professionals not having a prosecutorial attitude towards the experiences of the patient (McCurren & Cronin, 2003, Stenwall et al., 2008). A breakdown in trust leads inevitably to withdrawal and alienation from carers and family members. In contrast, when carers and family demonstrate support, empathy, and mutual understanding in an effort to bring comfort to the patient, patients overwhelmingly report positive feelings of safety and reduced discomfort (McCurren & Cronin, 2003; Stenwall et al., 2008). Therefore, orientation strategies must be considered in line with the current evidence and be reflective of an improved communication between carers and patients rather than an imposition of reality upon the patient (Day et al., 2011).

Despite the most stringent protocol aimed at reducing delirium risk being implemented, patients may still develop delirium and therefore post delirium management is also a critical component of a robust rehabilitation programme. In addition, mental health problems as a result of delirium and critical illness could easily be integrated with modalities and strategies aimed at sleep and cognitive dysfunction. Perhaps solutions can be drawn from psychotherapy because it 'facilitates the remission of symptoms and improves functioning. It not only speeds up the natural healing process, but also often provides additional coping strategies and methods for dealing with future problems. Providers as well as patients can be assured that a broad range of therapies, when offered by skilful, wise, and stable therapists, are likely to result in appreciable gains for the client' (Lambert and Ogles, 2004: 180). In general the accumulated evidence of the last half century has indicated a consistently large demonstrable effect size (0.8-1.2.) across various clinical populations (Asay & Lambert, 1999; Wampold, 2001; Lambert & Ogles, 2004). Psychotherapy also reduces general health care expenditure in the range of 60% to 90% and has a significant positive impact upon measures of interaction with health care services, use of medication and reduced extended care by friends and family (Chiles et al., 1999; Law et al., 2003; Kraft et al., 2006; Cummings, 2007). Investigative attempts at identifying factors that are involved in successful psychotherapy have established core therapeutic factors that impact upon the process (Hubble et al., 1999; Lambert & Barely, 2001). The largest is the extra-therapeutic factors and are typically independent of therapy itself. Such factors include socioeconomic elements such as support systems, resources, and access to services. Other factors are to be attributed to the individual themselves and examples of these include premorbid functioning and motivation (Duncan et al., 2010). These extra-therapeutic factors impact upon the process in the range of 80% to 87% when comparing samples that have been treated to untreated controls (Wampold, 2001). The remainder of the clinical outcome, i.e. 13% to 20%, is based upon the integrity of the treatment itself and is composed of various elements. These intra therapeutic factors have been investigated to highlight their efficacy and a number of ostensibly striking findings have been yielded. The first and most influential is the role of the therapist themselves and the therapeutic alliance that they build with the patient. A robust therapeutic alliance enhances patient engagement with the therapy and is a crucial index for positive change

(Brown et al., 2005; Wampold & Brown, 2005; Baldwin et al., 2007). In addition to the therapeutic alliance, the structure and focus of the therapy has positive effects on efficacy. The most surprising factor is the lack of impact and or efficacy of the theoretical modality, i.e. the way in which the therapist comprehends the therapeutic process upon patient's behavioural change (Lambert & Bergin, 1994). This of course has resonated with other health care professionals who understand that regardless of how we understand medicine, it still works if it is based upon evidence rather than opinion. Theoretical orientation serves the therapist not the patient in an attempt to enable the catalysis for transformation and the growth towards a new mode of behaviour. Therefore, merely lecturing a patient about it is insufficient and is analogous to the effect of reading a menu/recipe versus preparing and eating a meal (Wampold, 2007; Imel & Wampold, 2008; Anderson et al., 2010). In psychotherapy there is an emerging trend towards routine outcome measures. According to the American Psychological Association (APA) Task Force on Evidence-Based Practice (2006), 'providing clinicians with real-time patient feedback to benchmark progress in treatment and clinical support tools to adjust treatment as needed' is one of the 'most pressing research needs' (APA, 2006: 278). The use of feedback informed treatment has emerged with the view to providing real time outcomes for patients measuring the effect of what works and identify what does not improve the situation. However, longitudinal assessment of outcomes must be undertaken and its function analysed statistically. The use of routine outcome measurements can also be utilized in quantitative studies using single-subject research designs (SSRD) (Borkardt et al., 2008; Borkardt & Nash, 2008). Use of such SSRDs have been used to investigate the efficacy of a number of psychotherapeutic modalities including, psychoanalysis, cognitive-behavioural therapy (CBT), and hypnotherapy (Borkardt & Nash, 2002; Frankel & Macfie, 2010).

In accordance with previous work, the outcomes for neurocognitive failure can be categorized into three main domains (Bahar-Fuchs et al., 2013). The first is the effects of the intervention on the trajectory of dementia/delirium such as the rates of residential care admission and/or dementia severity. The second is the outcome assessment based on cognitive and non-cognitive domains of patients receiving the intervention and included measures of cognitive function and quality of life, the third category included measures of outcome for primary caregivers such as quality of life and well-being. The first domain of measuring delirium severity is currently well established with the development and consistent validation of standardised severity scales for delirium with the most well established measure being the revised delirium rating scale (DRS-R98) (Adamis et al., 2013). This scale measures a wide range of phenomenological features including their severity, temporal onset, and fluctuating pattern. It has also been shown to be able to distinguish delirium from mixed neuropsychiatric cohorts which are reflective of the clinical setting (Meagher et al., 2014). The second domain of outcome assessment of cognitive and non-cognitive domains, also benefits from the translation of many measures from the literature on dementia. The majority of studies found currently aim at improving general cognitive function, attention, orientation, and memory functions which all have relevance for cohorts with delirium. Moreover, many of the delirium scales of cognitive and non-cognitive domains (such as the Revised delirium rating scale [DRS-R98] and Memorial Delirium Assessment Scale [MDAS]) can easily replace the measures for dementia with future work examining how both these types of measures may be suitable for delirium outcome studies. Attention is a major deficit in delirium and therefore strategies aimed at improving this deficit would greatly enhance methods of alleviating or preventing delirium. To aid in this campaign, recent work has provided researchers with a wide variety of bed side attention tests (Tieges et al., 2014). Beck et al., (1988) all reported that there were no significant differences between the intervention group and the control group in terms of attention enhancement, but did report that there was a significant improvement of one domain of memory, namely recall of digits. These findings are further confirmed by Quayhagan et al., (1995), Davis et al., (2004) Loewenstein et al., (2004), and Clare et al., (2010). These studies suggest that attention may be amenable to intervention, but more robust evidence is required to substantiate these initial findings. Another key domain that has not been emphasised in these studies is orientation, however, it could be argued that measures such as the mini mental state exam (MMSE) aimed at measuring cognitive impairment the conceptualisation factor on Dementia Rating Scale, and the Geriatric Coping Schedule aimed at executive functioning (problem solving) may provide indirect measures of orientation (Quayhagen et al., 1995; Loewenstein et al., 2004). Previous methods using orientation strategies in reducing the onset of confusion in patients with dementia have yielded conflicting results (Day et al., 2011). More detailed analysis of the conceptual framework has identified an improper application of orientation strategies. Subsequent developments have indicated that a more supportive format for orientation strategies may yield more positive benefits (reduced distress, trust, and fostering a robust therapeutic alliance) may be further bolstered by the use of measures of executive function (McCurren & Cronin, 2003, Stenwall et al., 2008). Furthermore, two such measures, namely Outcome Rating Scale (ORS) and Session Rating Scale (SRS) have been established in psychotherapy, according to the APA recommendations for evidence based practice, to reliably measure clinical session outcomes and the therapeutic alliance (APA, 2006; Hafkensheid et al., 2010; Reese et al., 2013). Therefore, future orientation strategies highlight the importance of outcome measures focused upon the therapeutic alliance, the quality of the session, and executive functioning (Day et al., 2011). The third category for outcome assessment of caregiver well-being and quality of life (QOL) has been used by a number of studies found. Given the extra demand delirium places upon health care professionals, appropriate cognitive focused interventions may be a welcome adjuvant in delirium management. In particular, it has been demonstrated that an intervention format administered by caregivers yielded positive benefits for caregivers. In addition, other studies have highlighted the importance of cognitive focused interventions as relieving the burden of cognitive impairment on primary caregivers (Quayhagen et al., 2000; Neely et al., 2009; Clare et al., 2010).

In addition to the three categories of outcome measures, particular attention should be made to the format of these outcomes. For example, Heiss et al., (1994) demonstrates the utility of using EEG and PET while Clare et al., (2010) report the usefulness of fMRI in measuring outcomes of cognitive based interventions. Many authors also demonstrate the utility of using computer based interventions for cognitively impaired cohorts (Loewenstein et al., 2004; Zhuang et al., 2013). In the context of delirium, computer and app based outcome measures are being developed with recent work exploring the use of actigraphy and eye tracking technology (Godfrey et al., 2010; Morandi et al., 2012; Weir et al., 2014).

Finally, it must also be recognized that defining recovery from delirium is a major challenge in determining the appropriate use of any of the outcome measures for interventions aimed at tackling this complex syndrome. It has been proposed that delirium recovery should be based upon a significant decrease in delirium features as assessed by validated severity scales (Trzepacz et al., 2008). According to Adamis et al., there is inconsistent use of nomenclature to describe recovery from delirium and therefore, operationalized and validated criteria for recovery should be used. A distinction should also be emphasized between related terms such as response (initial reduction in symptom load), remission (a sustained initial period without major symptoms), and resolution (complete symptom reduction) from the recovery. As such, outcome measures should focus on temporal outcomes (long term versus short term) and phenomenological outcomes (general versus feature/domain based recovery) (Adamis et al., 2014).

Taken together key components of a viable optimum rehabilitation intervention have been recognized. Future studies exploring the applicability of outcome measures for interventions for delirium must take into account the setting of these interventions, namely settings that have a high occurrence of delirium e.g. general medical/surgical wards, critical care units and palliative care settings. Each of these settings has challenges and barriers to the successful delirium detection and management (Leonard et al., 2014). But particular focus will have to be on the individual context of delirium as an experience of the alienated psyche.

9.3. Understanding the impact of delirium

Despite the advances in medicine, many chronic conditions associated with the ageing population are emerging to challenge successful health care delivery. Amongst these are dementia and delirium which are predominantly associated with advanced age. The convergence between the increasing aged population and neurocognitive failure may render it a public health emergency. Indeed, the current worldwide incidence rate of dementia is estimated to be 7.7 million and is projected to double every 20 years (ADI, 2009). In contrast to dementia, delirium is an acute onset brain failure that is characterized by a heterogeneous manifestation of fluctuating features such as attention deficits, cognitive impairment, sleep-wake cycle fragmentation, motor behavioural disturbances, and often experiences of psychosis (Gupta et al., 2008; Trzepacz et al., 2010). Delirium is therefore considered a medical emergency and is associated with significant morbidity and mortality. The consequences of this condition also include reduced socio-adaptive function and an increased risk of developing mental health problems (Witlox et al., 2010). With contemporary research delirium is estimated to have a prevalence of 20% in the general hospital setting, almost 50% in the elderly patient population, and up to 80% in ICU and palliative care settings (Hosie et al., 2013; O'Hanlon et al., 2013). Delirium is estimated to cost the United States approximately US$164 billion per year, with similar estimates being derived from Europeon nations (Leslie et al., 2008; OECD, 2012; WHO, 2012).

There must be something special about the boundary between illness and life, and what could be more so than the absence of any definite boundaries. The association of delirium and terminal illness can often exacerbate stress and coping with a loved one in crisis. In qualitative studies investigating the experiences of families with a loved one experiencing delirium, they have reported distress in up to 70% of cases. Other associated emotional problems included exhaustion, anxiety, guilt, and a feeling of helplessness (Namba et al., 2007). Other studies have found that frustration and fear can often dominate in the context of delirium in advanced cancer

(Cohen et al., 2009). Other studies have reported that family members can develop psychological disorders such as post traumatic stress disorder (PTSD) as a result of experiencing loved ones in confused, agitated, and critical states, especially in the context of the ICU (Partridge et al., 2013). Carers are also exposed to the challenges of delirium and it has been reported that there is a 12-fold increase in developing generalized anxiety disorder when caring for a patient who has recently had a delirious episode (Buss et al., 2007). Qualitative analysis of nursing staff experiences with delirious patients has yielded unfortunate findings. Themes such as difficulties in communication with patients, stress associated with the unpredictability of delirium itself, challenging behaviour from patients and frustration that the clinical setting is not equipped to deal with the special needs of elderly patients (O'Malley et al., 2008, Partridge et al., 2013).

Ongoing campaigns to alter the course of this crisis in the clinical setting such as the implementation of delirium detection protocols and multi-component interventions have been highlighted (Inouye et al., 2014). But despite the burgeoning crisis, several obstacles exist that may hinder a successful implementation of strategies to tackle delirium. Education is by far the most common obstacle to overcome. Educational interventions have focused upon the key groups relevant to delirium such as nurses, physicians, patients, and their close family (Rockwood, 1999). Successful educational interventions have been shown to have a positive effect upon delirium detection and clinical practice (Rockwood et al., 1994; Gesin et al., 2012). Interactive workshops have also been proposed as a novel way of delivering education without resorting to didactic lectures. One such method of an interactive educational workshop on delirium was through the format of a television game show (Meagher, 2010). While, several studies have highlighted the washout period that follows the introduction of delirium detection protocols, other studies have drawn attention to the existence of ageism and stigma in the context of neurocognitive failure (Burgener et al., 2013; Mailhot et al., 2014). Perhaps the last of these obstacles may turn out to be the most difficult to overcome because it is the foundation for our perception of the problem, our paradigm. To successfully tackle the problem of neurocognitive failure novel theory and innovative practices must be developed. In Kuhn's *The Structure of Scientific Revolutions,* the conceptualization of a scientific paradigm is outlined as the worldwide/model that represents reality and the ultimate truth through the prism of principles and problems held by a community of researchers. New paradigms emerge when the existing paradigms do not account for the problems of that time, e.g. Newtonian physics versus Einsteinian physics or Lamarckian evolutionary biology versus Darwinian. According to Kuhn, 'successive transition from one paradigm to another via a revolution is the usual developmental pattern of mature science.' Moreover, a scientific paradigm can also be understood as a 'universally recognized scientific achievements that, for a time, provide model problems and solutions to a community of researchers' (Kuhn, 1970). However, this model has been altered to include a combination of a gradualist accumulation of knowledge and progress integreted with significant revolutionary transitions (Kindi, & Arabatzis, 2013).

The current leaders in medicine and nursing are themselves entering old age, and they will be faced with one of two positions, either they will consider the campaign as virtuous and further revolutionize health care by bringing in the much needed reforms to tackle these issues at a national level or they can do it for purely selfish reasons because it will be their generation who will be largely affected by the burgeoning crisis of neurocognitive failure. The choice is for them to make. They have the option of doing their duty and leading healthcare through this crisis or they can hold themselves back, stifle progress, and find themselves on the wrong side of history. Hopefully they will choose the former and not the latter to avoid the prospect of their generation being used as a cautionary tale of hubris, pettiness, and lassitude; the elements of a tragedy.

9.4. Towards a progressive research programme

According to the *Studies to Understand Delirium In Palliative Settings* (SUNDIPS), a progressive delirium research programme is based upon a proposed analytical framework depicting the clinical care pathway of delirium in palliative care. The application of such a framework to delirium research seeks to 'minimize investigator bias in the conception of research, reveals previous beliefs and assumptions that are not evidence-based and imparts patient-centred dimension to the research and associated decision-making' (Lawlor et al., 2014).

Fig. 1 Contributory elements to a scientific account of delirium pathogenesis.

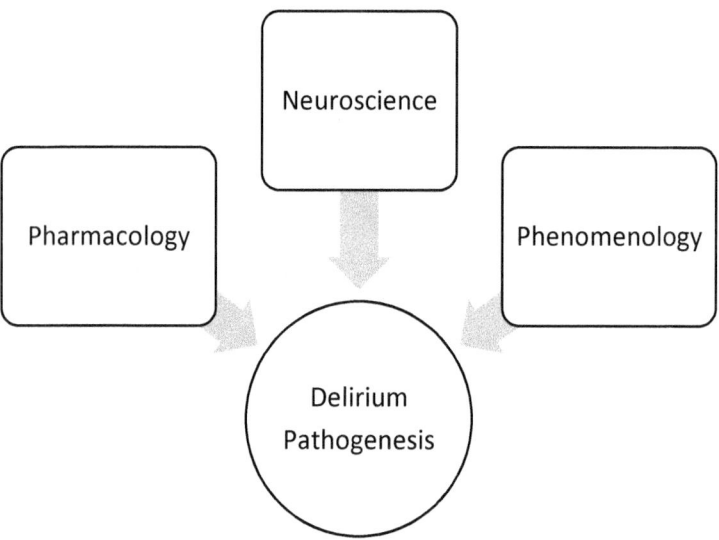

The combined complexities of the delirium syndrome and the palliative care setting pose significant challenges for future research (Sweet et al., 2014). However, addressing the gaps in clinical research may provide insight into how to improve outcomes for patients and their families. At the centre of addressing this initiative is the creation of a foundation for predictive models pertaining to delirium, and an understanding of the reciprocal manner by which precipitating factors (i.e. illness severity) and predisposing factors (i.e. baseline risk) interact (Inouye & Carpentier, 1996, Vasilevskis et al., 2012). Previous work examining precipitating elements using biomarkers (e.g. IGF-1, cortisol, and C-reactive protein) have yielded inconsistent results (MacLullich et al., 2013). Future studies would have to establish more detailed links between the phenomenology of delirium and the underlying neural substrate. Currently, there is a paucity of research pertaining to screening methods for delirium in the palliative care setting (Hosie et al., 2013). Future efforts would benefit from emphasizing less burdensome screening methods (Wong et al., 2010). More recent work has found that caregiver observations pertaining to sleep disturbances has yielded promising results, however detailed investigation is warranted (Kerr et al., 2014). The analysis of archetypal motifs of the experiences of critically ill patients has been largely an understudied, yet promising area. However, methodological challenges remain. For example, there is a disconnect between quantitative methods (e.g. DRS-R98) and qualitative methods (e.g. semi-structured interviews and text analysis) of analysing the phenomenology of delirium (Partridge et al., 2013). This is further complicated by inconsistencies regarding the time frame of the interviews, with some being performed after a considerable amount of time after the patients stay in hospital (Granberg et al., 1998, Magarey & McCutcheon,

2005). Further research should have a more stringent diagnosis of delirium which may integrate a qualitative (e.g. semi-structured interviews) with a quantitative (e.g. DRS-R98) phenomenological analysis of this syndrome in order to enhance our understanding of it (Wright et al., 2014). Another solution may become apparent from detailed studies of the dreams of patients at risk of developing delirium. Such studies may yield novel methods of identifying prodromal features of delirium.

In the context of end of life experiences (ELE), the analysis of archetypal motifs and images may also enable health care professionals to facilitate a more meaningful and comfortable death for the patient. As an analytical technique to understanding symbolism from the unconscious, amplification sets out a method to explicitly establish the parallels between archetypal symbols and mythological motifs. In contrast to free association which would enable the patient to link these images and symbols to personal experiences, amplification would link these to myths, legends, and cultural symbols. Such a dynamic has the dual function of strengthening the therapeutic alliance between therapist and patient, and catalysing the personal growth of the patient through their engagement with aspects of their life that are often *greater* than the mundane details of everyday struggle (Samuels et al., 1986; Cambray, 2001). In the context of the post delirium state, such a method may be integrated into attempts to alleviate the often traumatic experiences of delirium. This method would empower patients with the ability to understand their experience and assist healthcare professionals with the broader goal of reducing psychological morbidity from sleep disturbances including nightmares. Standardized and flexible methods of eliciting dream reports from patients may enable therapists and researchers to yield more comprehensive data for dream analysis (Goelitz, 2007). Recent work applying speech graph analysis software to dream reports has yielded potentially suitable methods for analysing the dreams of patients with severe neuropsychiatric disturbances (Mota et al., 2014).

Further studies may conduct more detailed investigations into the pronounced features of both full-syndromal delirium (FSD) and sub-syndromal delirium (SSD). Particular features would include inattention, disorientation, sleep-wake cycle disturbances, and dysfunctional motor activity. Unfortunately, the real world conditions of the hospital setting render a complete neurocognitive assessment untenable. A multi-centred approach, whereby pooled elderly medical inpatient data using an operationalised diagnostic algorithm and advanced longitudinal analysis (e.g. the GEE method) may further enhance our understanding of the phenotype of subsyndromal delirium (SSD) and its development either into full syndromal delirium (FSD) or resolution. Detailed investigation of key domains of delirium phenomenology may be complemented with bioelectronic devices (e.g. actigraphy and polysomnography). This pairing may further enable the revelation of robust targets for strategies to detect the prodromal phases of either SSD or FSD. In particular, detailed investigation of SSD may enable researchers to determine the impact of co-morbid dementia and depression. Finally, future studies may focus upon the location of neurocognitive assessment (e.g. emergency department versus general medical ward) in order to discover the impact of specific clinical settings on delirium status. Such findings may challenge the current status quo about the optimal structure and function of a hospital.

9.5. Permanent revolution

Despite all the contemporary theory and research, we are still in a similar position to our ancestors who tried to interpret the phenomenology of dreaming and delirium through various forms of divination. Over a century has passed since Jung first published his *The Psychology of Dementia Praecox,* and since that time recurrent scientific revolutions have rendered medicine beyond anything that has ever existed. Domains such as clinical neuroscience, cellular biology, and genome wide research studies all form the foundation of a collaborative scientific enterprise. All fields of medicine have benefited from the advances in the biomedical sciences and have given birth to evidence based research strategies. However, the most neglected aspects of medicine, psychotherapy and behavioural medicine, have remained as hypothetical and controversial since the formulation of the first scientific attempt, psychoanalysis. The proposals first presented in Jungs work did not inevitably lead to the developments now seen in schizophrenia research, because the history of science is not an inevitable accumulation of ideas. Instead, it was his method of departing from rigid paradigms that enabled him to identify new concepts. Such concepts anticipated the subsequent developments in schizophrenia research many decades later (Silverstein, 2014).

The dreams of our ancestors are the same as ours today for they are part of an indestructible pattern of growth. The literature continues to inform us that the psychological and spiritual needs of the dying are neglected (Kendall et al., 2007). Prolonged suffering and distress are often the result of physicians neglecting this dimension of the patient's psyche (Curtis et al., 2004; Kaldjian et al., 2009; Granda-Cameron & Houldin, 2012). The value of the dying experience, the fears, and the confusion continues to be regarded with limited attention or open disregard for the patient. Dying as a part of life is not an epiphenomena of merely coping, but reflective of a transition of meaning (Chochinov, 2012). The notion that life had a meaning sparked Freud, Jung and many earlier generations of physicians to analyse the psyche and enable the patient to have a life of meaning. But their apparent failure to permanently apply such methods to neurocognitive disorders should not dissuade us, but rather reignite the inspiratory flame for a permanent theoretical revolution in psychiatry. According to Marx, 'men make their own history, but they do not make it just as they please; they do not make it under circumstances chosen by themselves, but under circumstances directly encountered, given and transmitted from the past. The tradition of all dead generations weighs like a nightmare on the brain of the living.' (Marx, 1963). Thus, history is not a passive unfolding, it is a mode of behaviour.

We must not succumb to cynicism. We must remain keenly aware of the many advances that have been made and become more mindful still of what needs to be done. Many discoveries and health care advances will have to be fought for, and both the psyche and delirium will have to be understood in the context of a meaningful life. However, the most radical advance has thus far been made, the recasting of the therapeutic alliance and with it the view that delirium is no longer perceived through a fatalistic fog. The highest goal of medicine is to prevent delirium.

References

Abe, M., & Bonini, N. M. (2013). MicroRNAs and neurodegeneration: role and impact. Trends in cell biology, 23(1), 30-36.

Abe, M., Herzog, E. D., Yamazaki, S., Straume, M., Tei, H., Sakaki, Y., Menekar, M. & Block, G. D. (2002). Circadian rhythms in isolated brain regions. The Journal of Neuroscience, 22(1), 350-356.

Adamis D (2009). Statistical methods for analysing longitudinal data in delirium studies. International Review of Psychiatry 21: 74-85.

Adamis, D., Lunn, M., Martin, F. C., Treloar, A., Gregson, N., Hamilton, G., & Macdonald, A. J. (2009). Cytokines and IGF-I in delirious and non-delirious acutely ill older medical inpatients. Age and ageing, 38(3), 326-332.

Adamis, D., Sharma, N., Whelan, P. J. P., & Macdonald, A. J. D. (2010). Delirium scales : A review of current evidence, 14(5), 543–555.

Adamis, D., Slor, C. J., Leonard, M., Witlox, J., de Jonghe, J. F. M., Macdonald, A. J. D., Trzepacz, P. & Meagher, D. (2013). Reliability of delirium rating scale (DRS) and delirium rating scale-revised-98 (DRS-R98) using variance-based multivariate modelling. Journal of psychiatric research, 47(7), 966–71.

Adamis, D., Treloar, A., Martin, F. C. & Macdonald, A. J. D. (2007). A brief review of the history of delirium as a mental disorder. History of Psychiatry, 18(4), 459–469.

Agargun, M. Y., Boysan, M. & Hanoglu, L. (2004). Sleeping position, dream emotions, and subjective sleep quality. Sleep and Hypnosis, 6, 8-13.

Ahn, H. J., Seo, S. W., Chin, J., Suh, M. K., Lee, B. H., Kim, S. T., Im, K. & Na, D. L. (2011). The cortical neuroanatomy of neuropsychological deficits in mild cognitive impairment and Alzheimer's disease: A surface-based morphometric analysis. Neuropsychologia, 49(14), 3931-3945.

Akunne, A., Murthy, L. & Young, J. (2012). Cost-effectiveness of multi-component interventions to prevent delirium in older people admitted to medical wards. Age and ageing, afr147.

Al-Aama, T., Brymer, C., Gutmanis, I., Woolmore-Goodwin, S. M., Esbaugh, J. & Dasgupta, M. (2011). Melatonin decreases delirium in elderly patients: A randomized, placebo-controlled trial. International journal of geriatric psychiatry, 26(7), 687-694.

Albert, M. S., DeKosky, S. T., Dickson, D., Dubois, B., Feldman, H. H., Fox, N. C., Gamst, A. & Phelps, C. H. (2011). The diagnosis of mild cognitive impairment due to Alzheimer's disease: Recommendations from the National Institute on Aging-Alzheimer's Association workgroups on diagnostic guidelines for Alzheimer's disease. Alzheimer's & Dementia, 7(3), 270-279.

Albus, H., Vansteensel, M. J., Michel, S., Block, G. D., & Meijer, J. H. (2005). A GABAergic mechanism is necessary for coupling dissociable ventral and dorsal regional oscillators within the circadian clock. Current Biology, 15(10), 886-893.

Alexander, M. P., Stuss, D. T., & Benson, D. F. (1979). Capgras syndrome A reduplicative phenomenon. Neurology, 29(3), 334-334.

Allard, S., Gosein, V., Cuello, A. C., & Ribeiro-da-Silva, A. (2011). Changes with aging in the dopaminergic and noradrenergic innervation of rat neocortex. Neurobiology of aging, 32(12), 2244-2253.

Alzheimer's Disease International (2009).World Alzheimer Report 2009. Alzheimer's Disease International, London.

Amat, J., Baratta, M. V., Paul, E., Bland, S. T., Watkins, L. R., & Maier, S. F. (2005). Medial prefrontal cortex determines how stressor controllability affects behavior and dorsal raphe nucleus. Nature neuroscience, 8(3), 365-371.

Ambros, V. (2004). The functions of animal microRNAs. Nature, 431(7006), 350-355.

American Academy of Sleep Medicine. (2005). International classification of sleep disorders: diagnostic and coding manual. 2nd. Westchester, IL: The Academy:189-92.

American Psychiatric Association. (2013). DSM 5. American Psychiatric Association.

Amodio, D. M. & Frith, C. D. (2006). Meeting of minds: the medial frontal cortex and social cognition. Nature Reviews Neuroscience, 7(4), 268-277.

Anderson, B. & Rutledge, V. (1996). Age and hemisphere effects on dendritic structure. Brain, 119(6), 1983-1990.

Anderson, T., Lunnen, K. M. & Ogles, B. M. (2010). Putting models and techniques in context. The heart and soul of change: Delivering what works in therapy (2nd ed.)., (pp. 143-166). Washington, DC, US: American Psychological Association, xxix, 455.

Andersson, E., Knutsson, I., Hallberg, I. & Norberg, A. (1993). The experience of being confused: a case study. Geriatric Nursing 14, 242–247.

Andersson, E. M., Hallberg, I. R., Norberg, A. & Edberg, A. K. (2002). The meaning of acute confusional state from the perspective of elderly patients. International journal of geriatric psychiatry, 17(7), 652-663.

Ankri, J. & Poupard, M. (2003). [Prevalence and incidence of dementia among the very old. Review of the literature]. Revue d'epidemiologie et de sante publique, 51(3), 349-360.

Annas, J. (1986). Classical Greek Philosophy. In Boardman, John; Griffin, Jasper; Murray, Oswyn (ed.). The Oxford History of the Classical World. Oxford University Press: New York.

Antle, M. C. & Silver, R. (2005). Orchestrating time: arrangements of the brain circadian clock. Trends in neurosciences, 28(3), 145-151.

Antrobus, J., Kondo, T., Reinsel, R. & Fein, G. (1995). Dreaming in the late morning: Summation of REM and diurnal cortical activation. Consciousness and Cognition, 4(3), 275-299.

APA (1980) Diagnostic and Statistical Manual of Mental Disorders, Third Edition (Washington, DC: American Psychiatric Association).

APA (2000). Diagnostic and Statistical Manual of Mental Disorders, Fourth Edition: DSM-IV-TR®. American Psychiatric Pub.

APA Presidential Task Force on Evidence-Based Practice. (2006). Evidence-based practice in psychology. American Psychologist, 61.

Archer, S.N., Robilliard, D.L., Skene, D.J., Smits, M., Williams, A., Arendt, J. & von Schantz, M. (2003). A Length Polymorphism in the Circadian Clock Gene Per3 is Linked to Delayed Sleep Phase Syndrome and Extreme Diurnal Preference. Sleep, 26, 413-415.

Arendt, A. (1995). Melatonin and the mammalian pineal gland. London: Chapman & Hall.

Ariëns-kappers, J. (1979). Short history of pineal discovery and research. In: Ariëns-Kappers J, Pévet P, editors. The pineal gland of vertebrates including man. Progress in brain research, vol. 52. Amsterdam, New York: Elsevier; p.1–22.

Aristotle (1990). On Dreams. In Aristotle on sleep and dreams, D. Gallop, Perterborough, Ontario: Broadview Press.

Aron, A. R., Robbins, T. W., & Poldrack, R. A. (2004). Inhibition and the right inferior frontal cortex. Trends in cognitive sciences, 8(4), 170-177.

Aronin, N., & DiFiglia, M. (2014). Huntingtin-lowering strategies in Huntington's disease: Antisense oligonucleotides, small RNAs, and gene editing. Movement Disorders, 29(11), 1455-1461.

Arrigoni, E., Mochizuki, T., & Scammell, T. E. (2010). Activation of the basal forebrain by the orexin/hypocretin neurones. Acta physiologica, 198(3), 223-235.

Arroyo, S., Bennett, C. & Hestrin, S. (2014). Nicotinic modulation of cortical circuits. Frontiers in neural circuits, 8.

Artemidorus (1990).The Interpretation of Dreams: Oneirocritica. White, R., trans., Torrance, CA: Original Books, 2nd Edition.

Artinian, L. R., Ding, J. M., & Gillette, M. U. (2001). Carbon monoxide and nitric oxide: interacting messengers in muscarinic signaling to the brain's circadian clock. Experimental neurology, 171(2), 293-300.

Asay, T. P. & Lambert, M. J. (1999). The empirical case for the common factors in therapy: Quantitative findings.

Asendorpf, J. B., Warkentin, V. & Baudonnière, P. M. (1996). Self-awareness and other-awareness. II: Mirror self-recognition, social contingency awareness, and synchronic imitation. Developmental Psychology, 32(2), 313.

Aserinsky, E. & Kleitman, N. (1953). Regularly occurring periods of eye motility, and concomitant phenomena, during sleep. Science, 118(3062), 273-274.

Ashby, W. R. (1947). Principles of the self-organizing dynamic system. The Journal of general psychology, 37(2), 125-128.

Asher, G., & Schibler, U. (2011). Crosstalk between components of circadian and metabolic cycles in mammals. Cell metabolism, 13(2), 125-137.

Aston-Jones, G., & Bloom, F. E. (1981). Activity of norepinephrine-containing locus coeruleus neurons in behaving rats anticipates fluctuations in the sleep-waking cycle. The Journal of Neuroscience, 1(8), 876-886.

Aston-Jones, G., & Cohen, J. D. (2005). An integrative theory of locus coeruleus-norepinephrine function: adaptive gain and optimal performance. Annu. Rev. Neurosci., 28, 403-450.

Atkinson, G., Edwards, B., Reilly, T., & Waterhouse, J. (2007). Exercise as a synchroniser of human circadian rhythms: an update and discussion of the methodological problems. European journal of applied physiology, 99(4), 331-341.

Atkinson, J. R. (2006). The perceptual characteristics of voice-hallucinations in deaf people: insights into the nature of subvocal thought and sensory feedback loops. Schizophrenia bulletin, 32(4), 701-708.

Aurora, R. N., Zak, R. S., Auerbach, S. H., Casey, K. R., Chowdhuri, S., Karippot, A., ... & Standards of Practice Committee. (2010). Best practice guide for the treatment of nightmare disorder in adults. Journal of clinical sleep medicine: JCSM: official publication of the American Academy of Sleep Medicine, 6(4), 389.

Axelrod, J. & Weissbach, H. (1960). Enzymatic O-methylation of N-acetylserotonin to melatonin. Science; 131: 1312.

Axelsen, P. H., Komatsu, H., & Murray, I. V. (2011). Oxidative stress and cell membranes in the pathogenesis of Alzheimer's disease. Physiology, 26(1), 54-69.

Aybek, S., Nicholson, T. R., Zelaya, F., O'Daly, O. G., Craig, T. J., David, A. S., & Kanaan, R. A. (2013). THE NEURAL CORRELATES OF FREUDIAN "REPRESSION" IN CONVERSION DISORDER. Journal of Neurology, Neurosurgery & Psychiatry, 84(9), e1-e1.

Azama, T., Yano, M., Oishi, K., Kadota, K., Hyun, K., Tokura, H., Nishimura, S., Matsunaga, T., Iwanaga, H., Miki, H., Okada, K., Hiraoka, N., Miyata, H., Takiguchi, S., Fujiwara, Y., Yasuda, T., Ishida, N. & Monden, M. 2007. Altered expression profiles of clock genes hPer1 and hPer2 in peripheral blood mononuclear cells of cancer patients undergoing surgery. Life Sci, 80, 1100-8.

Azouz, R., & Gray, C. M. (2003). Adaptive coincidence detection and dynamic gain control in visual cortical neurons in vivo. Neuron, 37(3), 513-523.

Baddeley, A. (1991). The episodic buffer: A new component of working memory? Trends in Cognitive Sciences, 4, 417–423.

Badre, D., & Wagner, A. D. (2007). Left ventrolateral prefrontal cortex and the cognitive control of memory. Neuropsychologia, 45, 2883–2901.

Bahar-Fuchs, A., Clare, L., & Woods, B. (2013). Cognitive training and cognitive rehabilitation for persons with mild to moderate dementia of the Alzheimer's or vascular type: a review. Alzheimers. Res. Ther, 5, 35.

Bai, L., Hof, P. R., Standaert, D. G., Xing, Y., Nelson, S. E., Young, A. B., & Magnusson, K. R. (2004). Changes in the expression of the NR2B subunit during aging in macaque monkeys. Neurobiology of aging, 25(2), 201-208.

Baker, D. (1985). La apertura del tercer ojo. Madrid: Ed. EDAF, S.A.; p. 155.

Baker, E. L., & Nash, M. R. (2008). Psychoanalytic approaches to clinical hypnosis. The Oxford handbook of hypnosis: Theory, research and practice, 439-456.

Bal, M. (1985). Narratology: Introduction to the theory of narrative. Toronto: University of Toronto Press.

Balan, S., Leibovitz, A., Zila, S. O., Ruth, M., Chana, W., Yassica, B., Rahel, B., Goldstein, R., Neumann, E., Blagman, B. & Habot, B. (2003). The relation between the clinical subtypes of delirium and the urinary level of 6-SMT. The Journal of neuropsychiatry and clinical neurosciences, 15(3), 363-366.

Balan, S., Leibovitz, A., Zila, S. O., Ruth, M., Chana, W., Yassica, B., Rahel, B., Goldstein, R., Neumann, E., Blagman, B. & Habot, B. (2014). The relation between the clinical subtypes of delirium and the urinary level of 6-SMT. The Journal of neuropsychiatry and clinical neurosciences.

Balas, M. C., Vasilevskis, E. E., Olsen, K. M., Schmid, K. K., Shostrom, V., Cohen, M. Z., Peitz, G., Gannon, D.E., Sisson, J., Sullivan, J., Stothert, J.C., Lazure, J., Nuss, S.L., Jawa, R.S., Freihaut, F., Wesley, E. & Burke, W. J. (2014). Effectiveness and safety of the awakening and breathing coordination, delirium monitoring/management, and early exercise/mobility (ABCDE) bundle. Critical care medicine, 42(5), 1024.

Balduzzi, D., & Tononi, G. (2009). Qualia: the geometry of integrated information. PLoS computational biology, 5(8), e1000462.

Baldwin, S. A., Wampold, B. E., & Imel, Z. E. (2007). Untangling the alliance-outcome correlation: Exploring the relative importance of therapist and patient variability in the alliance. Journal of Consulting and Clinical Psychology, 75(6), 842.

Ballard, C., Corbett, A., & Howard, R. (2014). Prescription of antipsychotics in people with dementia. The British Journal of Psychiatry, 205(1), 4-5.

Ballard, C., Holmes, C., McKeith, I., Neill, D., O'Brien, J., Cairns, N., Lantos, P., Perry, E., Ince, P. & Perry, R. (1999). Psychiatric morbidity in dementia with Lewy bodies: a prospective clinical and neuropathological comparative study with Alzheimer's disease. American Journal of Psychiatry, 156(7), 1039-1045.

Balsalobre, A., Brown, S. A., Marcacci, L., Tronche, F., Kellendonk, C., Reichardt, H. M., Schutz, G. & Schibler, U. (2000a). Resetting of circadian time in peripheral tissues by glucocorticoid signaling. Science, 289, 2344-7.

Balsalobre, A., Maracci, L. & Schibler, U. (2000b). Multiple signaling pathways elicit circadian gene expression in cultured Rat-1 fibroblasts. Curr Biol, 10, 1291-4.

Barbato, M. (2009). Reflections of a Setting Sun: Healing Experiences Around Death. Michael Barbato.

Barlow, H. (1990). Conditions for versatile learning, Helmholtz's unconscious inference, and the task of perception. Vision research, 30(11), 1561-1571.

Barnes, D. E., Blackwell, T., Stone, K. L., Goldman, S. E., Hillier, T., & Yaffe, K. (2008). Cognition in older women: the importance of daytime movement. Journal of the American Geriatrics Society, 56(9), 1658-1664.

Barnett, J. H., Lewis, L., Blackwell, A. D., & Taylor, M. (2014). Early intervention in Alzheimer's disease: a health economic study of the effects of diagnostic timing. BMC Neurology, 14(1), 101.

Barrett, D. (1992). Just how lucid are lucid dreams?. Dreaming, 2(4), 221.

Barrett, D. (2001). The committee of sleep: How artists, scientists, and athletes use dreams for creative problem-solving–and how you can too. Crown House Publishing Limited.

Barrett, D. (Ed.). (2001). Trauma and dreams. Harvard University Press.

Barrett, D., & McNamara, P. (Eds.). (2012). Encyclopedia of sleep and dreams: the evolution, function, nature, and mysteries of slumber (Vol. 1). ABC-CLIO.

Barrett, T. R., & Ekstrand, B. R. (1972). Effect of sleep on memory: III. Controlling for time-of-day effects. Journal of experimental psychology, 96(2), 321.

Barrett, W. (1926). Death-bed Visions: The Psychical Experiences of the Dying. London: Aquarian Press.

Barthes, R. (1994). The semiotic challenge. Berkeley and Los Angeles: University of California Press. Trans. Richard Howard. [Originally published in French as L'aventure sémiologique, 1985, Paris, Éditions du Seuil.]

Baskett, J. J., Broad, J. B., Wood, P. C., Duncan, J. R., Pledger, M. J., English, J., & Arendt, J. (2003). Does melatonin improve sleep in older people? A randomised crossover trial. Age and ageing, 32(2), 164-170.

Baskett, J. J., Wood, P. C., Broad, J. B., Duncan, J. R., English, J. & Arendt, J. 2001. Melatonin in older people with age-related sleep maintenance problems: a comparison with age matched normal sleepers. Sleep, 24, 418-24.

Baudisch, A. (2011). The pace and shape of ageing. Methods in Ecology and Evolution, 2(4), 375-382.

Beck, A. T. (1967). Depression: Causes and treatment. Philadelphia, PA: University of Pennsylvania Press.

Beck, C., Heacock, P., Mercer, S., Thatcher, R., & Sparkman, C. (1988). The impact of cognitive skills remediation training on persons with Alzheimer's disease or mixed dementia. Journal of Geriatric Psychiatry.

Becker, P. M. (2015). Hypnosis in the Management of Sleep Disorders. Sleep Medicine Clinics, 10(1), 85-92.

Beebe, J. (2004). Can there be a science of the symbolic?. Journal of analytical psychology, 49(2), 177-191.

Behn, C. G. D., Klerman, E. B., Mochizuki, T., Lin, S. C., & Scammell, T. E. (2010). Abnormal sleep/wake dynamics in orexin knockout mice. Sleep, 33(3), 297.

Belicki, D., & Belicki, K. (1982). Nightmares in a university population. Sleep Research, 11, 116.

Bellelli, G., Speciale, S., Morghen, S., Torpilliesi, T., Turco, R., & Trabucchi, M. (2011). Are fluctuations in motor performance a diagnostic sign of delirium?. Journal of the American Medical Directors Association, 12(8), 578-583.

Belli, H. (2014). Dissociative symptoms and dissociative disorders comorbidity in obsessive compulsive disorder: Symptom screening, diagnostic tools and reflections on treatment. World Journal of Clinical Cases: WJCC, 2(8), 327.

Beloosesky, Y., Hendel, D., Weiss, A., Hershkovitz, A., Grinblat, J., Pirotsky, A., & Barak, V. (2007). Cytokines and C-reactive protein production in hip-fracture-operated elderly patients. The Journals of Gerontology Series A: Biological Sciences and Medical Sciences, 62(4), 420-426.

Benson, K.L. & Zarcone, V.P. (2000). Schizophrenia. In: Kryger MH, Roth T, Dement WC, eds. Principles and Practice of Sleep Medicine. 3rd ed. Philadelphia, Pa: WB Saunders Company; 1159–1167.

Bentov, I. (1977). Stalking the Wild Pendulum. New York, E.P. Dutton Co.

Berchtold, N. C., Coleman, P. D., Cribbs, D. H., Rogers, J., Gillen, D. L., & Cotman, C. W. (2013). Synaptic genes are extensively downregulated across multiple brain regions in normal human aging and Alzheimer's disease. Neurobiology of aging, 34(6), 1653-1661.

Bergamaschi, S., Arcara, G., Calza, A., Villani, D., Orgeta, V., & Mondini, S. (2013). One-year repeated cycles of cognitive training (CT) for Alzheimer's disease. Aging clinical and experimental research, 25(4), 421-426.

Bergbom--Engberg, I., & Haljanae, H. (1989). Assessment of patients' experience of discomforts during respirator therapy. Critical care medicine, 17(10), 1068-1072.

Berger, H. (1929). Über das elektroenkephalogramm des menschen. Arch Psychiatr Nervenkr; 97: 6–26.

Berkeley, W. (1914). The use of pineal gland in the treatment of certain classes of defective children. Med Rec; 85: 513–5.

Bernstein, E., Kim, S. Y., Carmell, M. A., Murchison, E. P., Alcorn, H., Li, M. Z., Mills, A. A., Elledge, S. J., Anderson, K. V. & Hannon, G. J. (2003). Dicer is essential for mouse development. Nature genetics, 35(3), 215-217.

Bernstein, M. J., Young, S. G., Brown, C. M., Sacco, D. F., & Claypool, H. M. (2008). Adaptive responses to social exclusion social rejection improves detection of real and fake smiles. Psychological Science, 19(10), 981-983.

Berridge, C. W., & Waterhouse, B. D. (2003). The locus coeruleus–noradrenergic system: modulation of behavioral state and state-dependent cognitive processes. Brain Research Reviews, 42(1), 33-84.

Berrios, G. E. (1981). Delirium and confusion in the 19th century: a conceptual history. The British Journal of Psychiatry, 139(5), 439-449.

Berrios, G., & Porter, R. (1995). A History of Clinical Psychiatry. The Origin and History of Mental Disorders. London: Athlone.

Berson, D. M., Dunn, F. A., & Takao, M. (2002). Phototransduction by retinal ganglion cells that set the circadian clock. Science, 295(5557), 1070-1073.

Bertoni-Freddari, C., Fattoretti, P., Ricciuti, R., Vecchioni, S., Casoli, T., Solazzi, M., & Ducati, A. (2002). Morphometry of E-PTA stained synapses at the periphery of pathological lesions. Micron, 33(5), 447-451.

Betty, L.S. (2006). Are they hallucinations or are they real? The spirituality of deathbed and near-death visions. Omega; 53:1–2.

Bichot, N. P., Rossi, A. F., & Desimone, R. (2005). Parallel and serial neural mechanisms for visual search in macaque area V4. Science, 308(5721), 529-534.

Bigelow, L. (1975). Some effects of aqueous pineal extract administration on schizophrenia symptoms. In: Altschule MD, editor. Frontiers on pineal physiology. Cambridge: Mild Press. p. 225–63.

Bina, K. G., Rusak, B., & Semba, K. (1993). Localization of cholinergic neurons in the forebrain and brainstem that project to the suprachiasmatic nucleus of the hypothalamus in rat. Journal of Comparative Neurology, 335(2), 295-307.

Binder, J. R., Desai, R. H., Graves, W. W., & Conant, L. L. (2009). Where is the semantic system? A critical review and meta-analysis of 120 functional neuroimaging studies. Cerebral Cortex, 19, 2767–2796.

Bixler, E. O., Kales, A., Soldatos, C. R., Kales, J. D., & Healy, S. (1979). Prevalence of sleep disorders in the Los Angeles metropolitan area. American Journal of Psychiatry, 136, 1257– 1262.

Blackwell, T., Yaffe, K., Ancoli-Israel, S., Redline, S., Ensrud, K. E., Stefanick, M. L., Laffen, A. & Stone, K. L. (2011). Associations between Sleep Architecture and Sleep-Disordered Breathing and Cognition in Older Community-Dwelling Men: The Osteoporotic Fractures in Men Sleep Study. Journal of the American Geriatrics Society, 59(12), 2217-2225.

Blagrove, M., & Pace-Schott, E. F. (2010). Trait and neurobiological correlates of individual differences in dream recall and dream content. International review of neurobiology, 92, 155-180.

Blais, M. A., Conboy, C. A., Wilcox, N. & Norman, D. K. (1996). An empirical study of the DSM-IV defensive functioning scale in personality disordered patients. Comprehensive Psychiatry, 37, 435-440.

Blatter, K., & Cajochen, C. (2007). Circadian rhythms in cognitive performance: methodological constraints, protocols, theoretical underpinnings. Physiology & behavior, 90(2), 196-208.

Bleuler, E. Dementia Praecox or the Group of Schizophrenias. New York, NY: International Universities Press; 1966. (originally published in 1911).

Bo, J., Borza, V., & Seidler, R (2009). Age-related declines in visuospatial working memory correlate with deficits in explicit motor sequence learning. Journal of Neurophysiology, 102, 2744–2754.

Boag, S. (2012). Freudian repression, the unconscious, and the dynamics of inhibition. Karnac Books.

Boeters, V. (1971). Die oneiroiden Emotionspsychosen (Basel: Karger).

Boettger, S., & Breitbart, W. (2011). Phenomenology of the subtypes of delirium: Phenomenological differences between hyperactive and hypoactive delirium. Palliative and Supportive Care, 9(02), 129-135.

Boissard, R., Gervasoni, D., Schmidt, M.H., Barbagli, B., Fort, P. & Luppi, P.H. (2002). The rat ponto-medullary network responsible for paradoxical sleep onset and maintenance: a combined microinjection and functional neuroanatomical study. Eur. J. Neurosci., 16, 1959–1973.

Bókkon, I. (2005). Dreams and neuroholography: an interdisciplinary interpretation of development of homeotherm state in evolution. Sleep and Hypnosis, 7(2), 61-76.

Bókkon, I., & Mallick, B. N. (2012). Activation of Retinotopic Visual Areas is Central to REM Sleep Associated Dreams: Visual Dreams and Visual Imagery Possibly Co-emerged in Evolution. ANS: The Journal for Neurocognitive Research, 54(1-2).

Bollobás, B. (1998). Springer-Verlag, editor. Modern Graph Theory. Modern Graph Theory. Berlin, New York: pp. 103–144.

Boly, M., Seth, A. K., Wilke, M., Ingmundson, P., Baars, B., Laureys, S., Edeleman, D. & Tsuchiya, N. (2013). Consciousness in humans and non-human animals: recent advances and future directions. Frontiers in psychology, 4.

Bond M. & Perry J. C. (2004). Long-term changes in defense style with psychodynamic psychotherapy for depressive, anxiety and personality disorders. American Journal of Psychiatry, 161:1665-1671.

Bond, S. M., Dietrich, M. S., Shuster Jr, J. L., & Murphy, B. A. (2012). Delirium in patients with head and neck cancer in the outpatient treatment setting. Supportive Care in Cancer, 20(5), 1023-1030.

Bonhoeffer, K. (1907). Klinische Beiträge zur Lehre von den Degenerationspsychosen (Halle: Marhold).

Borbély, A. A. (1982). A two process model of sleep regulation. Human neurobiology.

Borckardt, J. J., & Nash, M. R. (2002). How practitioners (and others) can make scientifically viable contributions to clinical-outcome research using the single-case time-series design. International Journal of Clinical and Experimental Hypnosis, 50(2), 114-148.

Borkardt, J. J., & Nash, M. R. (Eds.). (2008). Making a contribution to the clinical literature: Time-series designs. Oxford, UK: Oxford University Press.

Borkardt, J. J., Nash, M. R., Murphy, M. D., Moore, M., Shaw, D., & O'Neil, P. (2008). Clinical practice as natural laboratory for psychotherapy research: A guide to case-based time-series analysis. American Psychologist, 63, 77-95.

Borkovec, T. D., Newman, M. G., Pincus, A. L., & Lytle, R. (2002). A component analysis of cognitive-behavioral therapy for generalized anxiety disorder and the role of interpersonal problems. Journal of Consulting and Clinical Psychology, 70(2), 288.

Boschen, K. E., Fadel, J. R., & Burk, J. A. (2009). Systemic and intrabasalis administration of the orexin-1 receptor antagonist, SB-334867, disrupts attentional performance in rats. Psychopharmacology, 206(2), 205-213.

Bouckoms, A., Martuza, R. & Henderson, M. (1986). Capgras syndrome with subarachnoid hemorrhage. The Journal of nervous and mental disease, 174(8), 484-488.

Bourdel-Marchasson, I., Vincent, S., Germain, C., Salles, N., Jenn, J., Rasoamanarivo, E., Emeriau, J.P., Muriel Rainfray, M. & Richard-Harston, S. (2004). Delirium symptoms and low dietary intake in older inpatients are independent predictors of institutionalization: a 1-year prospective population-based study. The Journals of Gerontology Series A: Biological Sciences and Medical Sciences, 59(4), M350-M354.

Bourget, D., & Whitehurst, L. (2004). Capgras syndrome: a review of the neurophysiological correlates and presenting clinical features in cases involving physical violence. Can J Psychiatry, 49(11), 719-725.

Bowers, B. (2007). S. ed. The Medieval Hospital and Medical Practice. Ashgate.

Bowins, B. (2004). Psychological defense mechanisms: A new perspective. Americam Journal of Psychoanalysis, 64, 1-26.

Bowlby, J. (1980). Attachment and loss: Volume 3. Loss. New York: Basic.

Bowlby, J. (1988). A Secure Base. Clinical Applications of Attachment Theory. London: Routledge.

Braak, H., & Braak, E. (1997). Frequency of stages of Alzheimer-related lesions in different age categories. Neurobiology of aging, 18(4), 351-357.

Braak, H., & Del Tredici, K. (2011). Alzheimer's pathogenesis: is there neuron-to-neuron propagation?. Acta neuropathologica, 121(5), 589-595.

Bracken, P., & Thomas, P. (2002). Time to move beyond the mind-body split: The "mind" is not inside but "out there" in the social world. BMJ: British Medical Journal, 325(7378), 1433.

Braun, A. R., Balkin, T. J., Wesenten, N. J., Carson, R. E., Varga, M., Baldwin, P., Belenky, S. G. & Herscovitch, P. (1997). Regional cerebral blood flow throughout the sleep-wake cycle. An H2 (15) O PET study. Brain, 120(7), 1173-1197.

Brayne, S., Farnham, C., & Fenwick, P. (2006). Deathbed phenomena and their effect on a palliative care team: a pilot study. American Journal of Hospice and Palliative Medicine, 23(1), 17-24.

Breen, N., Caine, D., & Coltheart, M. (2000). Models of face recognition and delusional misidentification: A critical review. Cognitive Neuropsychology, 17(1-3), 55-71.

Breitbart, W., Marotta, R., Platt, M. M., Weisman, H., et al (1996). A double-blind trial of haloperidol, chlorpromazine, and lorazepam in the treatment of delirium in hospitalized AIDS patients. American Journal of Psychiatry 153:231–237.

Breitbart, W., Tremblay, A., & Gibson, C. (2002). An open trial of olanzapine for the treatment of delirium in hospitalized cancer patients. Psychosomatics, 43(3), 175-182.

Bremner, J. D. (2010). Cognitive processes in dissociation: comment on Giesbrecht et al.(2008).

Brennan, M., Welsh, M., & Fisher, D. (1997). Aging and executive function skills: An examination of a community dwelling older adult populations. Perceptual and Motor Skills, 84, 1187–1197.

Brent, S. (1978). Prigogine's model for self organisation in non equilibrium systems- its elevance for developmental psychology. Hum Dev: 21: 374-387.

Bretherton, I. (1995). A communication perspective on attachment relationships and internal working models. Monographs of the Society for Research in Child Development, 60(2-3), 310-329.

Brewin, C. R., Dalgleish, T., & Joseph, S. (1996). A dual representation theory of posttraumatic stress disorder. Psychological review, 103(4), 670.

Broad, W. J. (2007). The Oracle: Ancient Delphi and the Science behind Its Lost Secrets, New York, Penguin Press.

Brooke, R. (1991). Jung and phenomenology. London: Routledge.

Brown, G. S., Jones, E., Lambert, M. J., & Minami, T. (2005). Evaluating the effectiveness of psychotherapist in a managed care environment. American Journal of Managed Care, 2(8), 513-520.

Brown, L. J., Fordyce, C., Zaghdani, H., Starr, J. M., & MacLullich, A. M. (2011). Detecting deficits of sustained visual attention in delirium. Journal of Neurology, Neurosurgery & Psychiatry, 82(12), 1334-1340.

Brown, P. (2012). The rise of Western Christendom: triumph and diversity, AD 200-1000 (Vol. 1). John Wiley & Sons.

Brown, T. M. (2000). Basic mechanisms in the pathogenesis of delirium. Psychiatric Care of the Medical Patient. Second Ed. New York, NY: Oxford University Press, Inc, 571-580.

Brummel, N. E., & Girard, T. D. (2013). Preventing delirium in the intensive care unit. Critical care clinics, 29(1), 51-65.

Bubenik, G. A., Blask, D. E., Brown, G. M., Maestroni, G. J., Pang, S. F., Reiter, R. J., Viswanathan, M. & Zisapel, N. (1998). Prospects of the clinical utilization of melatonin. Neurosignals, 7(4), 195-219.

Bucci, W. (1985). Dual coding: A cognitive model for psychoanalytic research. Journal of the American Psychoanalytic Association, 33, 571–607.

Bucci, W. (1997). Psychoanalysis & cognitive science: A multiple code theory. New York, NY: Guilford.

Bucci, W. (2001). Pathways of emotional communication. Psychoanalytic Inquiry, 21, 40–70.

Bucci, W. (2002). The referential process, consciousness, and the sense of self. Psychoanalytic Inquiry, 22, 766–793.

Bucci, W. (2004). Multiple memory systems and the representation of the self: A view from cognitive science. Paper presented at the Fourth Annual AAPI Conference, New York, NY.

Bucci, W. (2011). The role of subjectivity and intersubjectivity in the reconstruction of dissociated schemas; converging perspectives from psychoanalysis, cognitive science and affective neuroscience. Psychoanalytic Psychology, 28(2), 247.

Buchanan, T. W. & Lovallo, W. R. (2001). Enhanced memory for emotional material following stress-level cortisol treatment in humans. Psychoneuroendocrinology 26, 307–317.

Buck, M. L. (2003). The use of melatonin in children with sleep disorders. Pediatr Pharm 2003; 9 (11).

Buckley, T. M., & Schatzberg, A. F. (2010). A pilot study of the phase angle between cortisol and melatonin in major depression–A potential biomarker?. Journal of psychiatric research, 44(2), 69-74.

Buckner, R. L., & Carroll, D. C. (2007). Self-projection and the brain. Trends in cognitive sciences, 11(2), 49-57.

Buckner, R. L., Andrews-Hanna, J. R., & Schacter, D. L. (2008). The brain's default network. Annals of the New York Academy of Sciences, 1124(1), 1-38.

Buckner, R. L., Goodman, J., Burock, M., Rotte, M., Koutstaal, W., Schacter, D., Rosen, B. & Dale, A. M. (1998). Functional-anatomic correlates of object priming in humans revealed by rapid presentation event-related fMRI. Neuron, 20(2), 285-296.

Buckner, R. L., Raichle, M. E., Miezin, F. M., & Petersen, S. E. (1996). Functional anatomic studies of memory retrieval for auditory words and visual pictures. The Journal of Neuroscience, 16(19), 6219-6235.

Buckner, R. L., Sepulcre, J., Talukdar, T., Krienen, F. M., Liu, H., Hedden, T., Sperling, R. A. & Johnson, K. A. (2009). Cortical hubs revealed by intrinsic functional connectivity: mapping, assessment of stability, and relation to Alzheimer's disease. The Journal of Neuroscience, 29(6), 1860-1873.

Buijs, R. M., & Kalsbeek, A. (2001). Hypothalamic integration of central and peripheral clocks. Nature Reviews Neuroscience, 2(7), 521-526.

Bullmore E. & Sporns, O. (2009). Complex brain networks: graph theoretical analysis of structural and functional systems. Nat Rev Neurosci 10: 186–198.

Bureau, J. F., Martin, J., & Lyons-Ruth, K. (2010). Attachment dysregulation as hidden trauma in infancy: Early stress, maternal buffering and psychiatric morbidity in young adulthood. The impact of early life trauma on health and disease: the hidden epidemic, 48-56.

Burrows, B. E., & Moore, T. (2009). Influence and limitations of popout in the selection of salient visual stimuli by area V4 neurons. The Journal of Neuroscience, 29(48), 15169-15177.

Burton, R. (1927 [1620]). The anatomy of melancholy (ed. F. Dell & P. Jordon-Smith). New York: Farrar & Rinehart.

Bury, J. B. (1958). History of the Later Roman Empire from the Death of Theodosius I. to the Death. Dover Publications

Buschman, T. J., & Miller, E. K. (2009). Serial, covert shifts of attention during visual search are reflected by the frontal eye fields and correlated with population oscillations. Neuron, 63(3), 386-396.

Bush, S. H., Leonard, M. M., Agar, M., Spiller, J. A., Hosie, A., Wright, D. K., Meagher, D.J., Currow, D.C. Bruera, E. & Lawlor, P. G. (2014). End-of-life delirium: issues regarding recognition, optimal management, and the role of sedation in the dying phase. Journal of pain and symptom management, 48(2), 215-230.

Buss, A. H. (1980). Self-consciousness and social anxiety (p. 22). San Francisco: WH freeman.

Buss, M. K., Vanderwerker, L. C., Inouye, S. K., Zhang, B., Block, S. D., & Prigerson, H. G. (2007). Associations between caregiver-perceived delirium in patients with cancer and generalized anxiety in their caregivers. Journal of palliative medicine, 10(5), 1083-1092.

Bussière, T., Giannakopoulos, P., Bouras, C., Perl, D. P., Morrison, J. H., & Hof, P. R. (2003). Progressive degeneration of nonphosphorylated neurofilament protein-enriched pyramidal neurons predicts cognitive impairment in Alzheimer's disease: Stereologic analysis of prefrontal cortex area 9. Journal of Comparative Neurology, 463(3), 281-302.

Butt, A. J. (1961). Symbolism and Ritual among the Akawaio of British Guyana. Nieuwe West-Indische Gids 2: 141–161.

Butz, M., Van Ooyen, A., & Wörgötter, F. (2009). A model for cortical rewiring following deafferentation and focal stroke. Frontiers in computational neuroscience, 3.

Buysse, D. J., Monk, T. H., Carrier, J., & Begley, A. (2005). Circadian patterns of sleep, sleepiness, and performance in older and younger adults. Sleep, 28(11), 1365-1376.

Buzsaki, G. (1998). Memory consolidation during sleep: a neurophysiological perspective. J. Sleep Res. 7(Suppl.), 17–23.

Bymaster, F. P., McKinzie, D. L. & Felder, C. C. (2004). New evidence for the involvement of muscarinic cholinergic receptors in psychoses. In: Silman I, Soreq H, Anglister L, Michaelson D, Fisher A, eds. Cholinergic Mechanisms: Function and Dysfunction. London: Taylor & Francis: 331–343.

Bynum, B. (2000). Phrenitis: what's in a name?. The Lancet, 356(9245), 1936.

Byrne, B. M. (2005). Factor analytic models: viewing the structure of an assessment instrument from three perspectives. J Pers Assess; 85:17–32.

Cabeza, R., & Moscovitch, M. (2013). Memory systems, processing modes, and components functional neuroimaging evidence. Perspectives on Psychological Science, 8(1), 49-55.

Cabeza, R., & Nyberg, L. (1997). Imaging cognition: An empirical review of PET studies with normal subjects. Cognitive Neuroscience, Journal of, 9(1), 1-26.

Cabeza, R., & St Jacques, P. (2007). Functional neuroimaging of autobiographical memory. Trends in cognitive sciences, 11(5), 219-227.

Caelius Aurelianus, Treatise on acute disease; Treatise on chronic disease (1950). In Caelius Aurelianus: on acute disease and on chronic diseases, I.E. Drabkin. Chicago: University Press.

Cahn-Weiner, D. A., Malloy, P. F., Rebok, G. W., & Ott, B. R. (2003). Results of a randomized placebo-controlled study of memory training for mildly impaired Alzheimer's disease patients. Applied Neuropsychology, 10(4), 215-223.

Cambray, J. (2001). Enactments and amplification. Journal of Analytical Psychology, 46(2), 275-303.

Campbell, J. (1976). Masks of the Gods: Primitive Mythology. Souvenir Press.

Campbell, J. (2002). The inner reaches of outer space: Metaphor as myth and as religion (Vol. 2). New World Library.

Camus, V., Gonthier, R., Dubos, G., Schwed, P., & Simeone, I. (2000). Etiologic and outcome profiles in hypoactive and hyperactive subtypes of delirium. Journal of geriatric psychiatry and neurology, 13(1), 38-42.

Cantero, J. L., Atienza, M., & Salas, R. M. (2000). Spectral features of EEG alpha activity in human REM sleep: two variants with different functional roles?. SLEEP-NEW YORK-, 23(6), 746-754.

Caplan, G. A., & Harper, E. L. (2007). Recruitment of volunteers to improve vitality in the elderly: the REVIVE* study. Internal medicine journal, 37(2), 95-100.

Caputo, F., & Bernardi, M. (2010). Medications acting on the GABA system in the treatment of alcoholic patients. Current pharmaceutical design, 16(19), 2118-2125.

Capuzzo, M., Valpondi, V., Cingolani, E., De Luca, S., Gianstefani, G., Grassi, L., & Alvisi, R. (2003). Application of the Italian version of the Intensive Care Unit Memory tool in the clinical setting. Critical Care, 8(1), R48.

Cardinali, D. P., Brusco, L. I., Liberczuk, C. & Furio, A. M. (2002). The use of melatonin in Alzheimer's disease. Neuro Endocrinol Lett 23(Suppl 1): 20–23.

Carhart-Harris, R. L., & Friston, K. J. (2010). The default-mode, ego-functions and free-energy: a neurobiological account of Freudian ideas. Brain, awq010.

Carpenter, M. (2014). Acute Brain Failure: Delirium in the ICU. In NURSING RESEARCH (Vol. 63, No. 2, pp. E24-E24). 530 WALNUT ST, PHILADELPHIA, PA 19106-3621 USA: LIPPINCOTT WILLIAMS & WILKINS.

Carver, C. S., & Scheier, M. F. (2001). On the self-regulation of behavior. Cambridge University Press.

Caton, R. (1875). The electric currents of the brain. Br Med J; 2: 278.

Caumo, W., Torres, F., Moreira Jr, N. L., Auzani, J. A., Monteiro, C. A., Londero, G., Ribeiro, F. & Hidalgo, M. P. L. (2007). The clinical impact of preoperative melatonin on postoperative outcomes in patients undergoing abdominal hysterectomy. Anesthesia & Analgesia, 105(5), 1263-1271.

Cave, C. B., & Squire, L. R. (1992). Intact and long-lasting repetition priming in amnesia. Journal of Experimental Psychology: Learning, Memory, and Cognition, 18(3), 509.

Celsus (1935). On Medicine. Books I–IV, translated by W. G. Spencer (Cambridge, MA: Harvard University Press).

Chafe, W. (1990). Some things that narratives tell us about the mind. In B. K. Britton & A.D. Pellegrini (Eds.), Narrative thought and narrative language (pp. 79-98). Hillsdale, NJ: Lawrence Erlbaum.

Chalmers, D. J. (2003). Consciousness and its place in nature. Blackwell guide to the philosophy of mind, 102-142.

Chantraine, P. (1977). Dictionnaire etymologique de la langue grecgue. Paris: Klincksieck.

Chaslin, P. (1895). La confusione mentale primitive, Asselin et Houzzeau, Paris.

Chasseguet-Smirgel, J. (1985). The ego ideal: A psychoanalytic essay on the malady of the ideal. London: Free Association Books

Chatman, S. (1978). Story and discourse: Narrative structure in fiction and film. Ithaca and London: Cornell University Press.

Cheetham, C. E., Hammond, M. S., McFarlane, R., & Finnerty, G. T. (2008). Altered sensory experience induces targeted rewiring of local excitatory connections in mature neocortex. The Journal of Neuroscience, 28(37), 9249-9260.

Chellappa, S. L., Steiner, R., Blattner, P., Oelhafen, P., Götz, T., & Cajochen, C. (2011). Non-visual effects of light on melatonin, alertness and cognitive performance: can blue-enriched light keep us alert?. PLoS One, 6(1), e16429.

Cheung, C. Z., Alibhai, S. M., Robinson, M., Tomlinson, G., Chittock, D., Drover, J., & Skrobik, Y. (2008). Recognition and labeling of delirium symptoms by intensivists: does it matter?. Intensive care medicine, 34(3), 437-446.

Chiles, J. A., Lambert, M. J., & Hatch, A. L. (1999). The Impact of Psychological Interventions on Medical Cost Offset: A Meta-analytic Review. Clinical Psychology: Science and Practice, 6(2), 204-220.

Chochinov, H. M. (2012). Dignity therapy: Final words for final days. Oxford University Press.

Chou, Y.-H., Chen, N.-K., & Madden, D. J. (2013). Functional brain connectivity and cognition: effects of adult age and task demands. Neurobiology of aging, 34(8), 1925–34.

Christoff K., Gordon A. M. & Smith R. (2011). The role of spontaneous thought in human cognition, in Neuroscience of Decision Making, eds Vartanian O., Mandel D. R., editors. (New York, NY: Psychology Press;), 259–284

Christoff, K. (2012). Undirected thought: neural determinants and correlates. Brain research, 1428, 51-59.

Christoff, K., Gordon, A. M., Smallwood, J., Smith, R., & Schooler, J. W. (2009). Experience sampling during fMRI reveals default network and executive system contributions to mind wandering. Proceedings of the National Academy of Sciences, 106(21), 8719-8724.

Christoff, K., Ream, J. M., & Gabrieli, J. D. (2004). Neural basis of spontaneous thought processes. Cortex, 40(4), 623-630.

Chun, M. M., & Phelps, E. A. (1999). Memory deficits for implicit contextual information in amnesic subjects with hippocampal damage. Nature neuroscience, 2(9), 844-847.

Clare, L. & Woods, R.T. (2004). Cognitive training and cognitive rehabilitation for people with early-stage Alzheimer's disease: a review. Neuropsychol Rehabil; 14:385-401.

Clare, L. (2003). Cognitive training and cognitive rehabilitation for people with early-stage dementia. Rev Clin Gerontol; 13:75-83.

Clare, L., Bayer, A., Burns, A., Corbett, A., Jones, R., Knapp, M., & Whitaker, R. (2013). Goal-oriented cognitive rehabilitation in early-stage dementia: study protocol for a multi-centre single-blind randomised controlled trial (GREAT). Trials, 14(1), 152.

Clare, L., Lin den, D. E., Woods, R. T., Whitaker, R., Evans, S. J., Parkinson, C. H., van Paasschen, J., Nelis, S. M., Hoare, Z., Yuen, K. S. & Rugg, M. D. (2010). Goal-oriented cognitive rehabilitation for people with early-stage Alzheimer disease: a single-blind randomized controlled trial of clinical efficacy. The American journal of geriatric psychiatry, 18(10), 928-939.

Clare, L., Woods, R. T., Moniz-Cook, E. D., Orrell, M. & Spector, A. (2003). Cognitive rehabilitation and cognitive training for early-stage Alzheimer's disease and vascular dementia. Cochrane Database Syst Rev; (4):CD003260.

Clarke, H. F., Horst, N. K., & Roberts, A. C. (2015). Regional inactivations of primate ventral prefrontal cortex reveal two distinct mechanisms underlying negative bias in decision making. Proceedings of the National Academy of Sciences, 112(13), 4176-4181.

Clarke, J. D., & Coleman, G. J. (1986). Persistent meal-associated rhythms in SCN-lesioned rats. Physiology & behavior, 36(1), 105-113.

Clemens, Z., Fabo, D., & Halasz, P. (2005). Overnight verbal memory retention correlates with the number of sleep spindles. Neuroscience, 132(2), 529-535.

Climacus, J. L. (1982). In Jogn Climacus: the ladder of divine ascent (trans. C. Luibheid & N. Russell). Mahwah, N.J.: Paulist Press.

Coffey, B. J., & Park, K. S. (1997). Behavioral and emotional aspects of Tourette syndrome. Neurologic clinics, 15(2), 277-289.

Cohen, M. Z., Pace, E. A., Kaur, G., & Bruera, E. (2009). Delirium in advanced cancer leading to distress in patients and family caregivers. Journal of palliative care, 25(3), 164.

Cohen, R. A. (2014). Consciousness and self-directed attention. In The Neuropsychology of Attention (pp. 721-734). Springer US.

Cole, M. G., McCusker, J., Ciampi, A., & Belzile, E. (2008). The 6-and 12-Month Outcomes of Older Medical Inpatients Who Recover from Subsyndromal Delirium. Journal of the American Geriatrics Society, 56(11), 2093-2099.

Cole, M. G., McCusker, J., Voyer, P., Monette, J., Champoux, N., Ciampi, A., & Belzile, E. (2013). The course of subsyndromal delirium in older long-term care residents. The American Journal of Geriatric Psychiatry, 21(3), 289-296.

Cole, M., McCusker, J., Dendukuri, N., & Han, L. (2003). The prognostic significance of subsyndromal delirium in elderly medical inpatients. Journal of the American Geriatrics Society, 51(6), 754-760.

Collier, K., Bickel, B., van Schaik, C. P., Manser, M. B., & Townsend, S. W. (2014). Language evolution: syntax before phonology?. Proceedings of the Royal Society B: Biological Sciences, 281(1788), 20140263.

Collins, M. N., Hawthorne, M. E., Gribbin, N., & Jacobson, R. (1990). Capgras' syndrome with organic disorders. Postgraduate medical journal, 66(782), 1064-1067.

Collins, N., Blanchard, M. R., Tookman, A., & Sampson, E. L. (2010). Detection of delirium in the acute hospital. Age and ageing, 39(1), 131-135.

Coltheart, M. (2015). Phenomenological and neurocognitive perspectives on polythematic and monothematic delusions. World Psychiatry, 14(2), 186-188.

Coltheart, M., Langdon, R., & McKay, R. (2011). Delusional belief. Annual review of psychology, 62, 271-298.

Colwell, C. S., Michel, S., Itri, J., Rodriguez, W., Tam, J., Lelievre, V., Hu, Z., Liu, X. & Waschek, J. A. (2003). Disrupted circadian rhythms in VIP-and PHI-deficient mice. American Journal of Physiology-Regulatory, Integrative and Comparative Physiology, 285(5), R939-R949.

Compton, P. (1991). Critical illness and intensive care: what it means to the client. Critical Care Nurse, 11(1), 50-56.

Conduit, R., Crewther, S. G., & Coleman, G. (2004). Poor recall of eye-movement signals from Stage 2 compared to REM sleep: Implications for models of dreaming. Consciousness and cognition, 13(3), 484-500.

Connors, M. H., & Coltheart, M. (2011). On the behaviour of senile dementia patients vis-à-vis the mirror: Ajuriaguerra, Strejilevitch and Tissot (1963). Neuropsychologia, 49(7), 1679-1692.

Connors, M. H., Barnier, A. J., Coltheart, M., Cox, R. E., & Langdon, R. (2012). Mirrored-self misidentification in the hypnosis laboratory: recreating the delusion from its component factors. Cognitive neuropsychiatry, 17(2), 151-176.

Connors, M. H., Barnier, A. J., Coltheart, M., Langdon, R., Cox, R. E., Rivolta, D., & Halligan, P. W. (2014). Using hypnosis to disrupt face processing: mirrored-self misidentification delusion and different visual media. Frontiers in human neuroscience, 8.

Constantinople, C. M., & Bruno, R. M. (2011). Effects and mechanisms of wakefulness on local cortical networks. Neuron, 69(6), 1061-1068.

Contelmo, G., Hart, J., & Levine, E. H. (2013). Dream orientation as a function of hyperactivating and deactivating attachment strategies. Self and Identity, 12(4), 357-369.

Cooke, J. R., Loredo, J. S., Liu, L., Marler, M., Corey-Bloom, J., Fiorentino, L., Harrison, T. & Ancoli-Israel, S. (2006). Acetylcholinesterase inhibitors and sleep architecture in patients with Alzheimer's disease. Drugs & aging, 23(6), 503-511.

Cordi, M. J., Hirsiger, S., Mérillat, S., & Rasch, B. (2015). Improving sleep and cognition by hypnotic suggestion in the elderly. Neuropsychologia, 69, 176-182.

Corlett, P. R., Frith, C. D., & Fletcher, P. C. (2009). From drugs to deprivation: a Bayesian framework for understanding models of psychosis. Psychopharmacology, 206(4), 515-530.

Cornoldi, C., & Vecchi, T. (2003). Visuo-spatial working memory and individual differences. New York, USA: Psychology Press.

Corrada, M. M., Brookmeyer, R., Paganini-Hill, A., Berlau, D., & Kawas, C. H. (2010). Dementia incidence continues to increase with age in the oldest old: the 90+ study. Annals of neurology, 67(1), 114-121.

Corti, M. (1978). An introduction to literary semiotics. Bloomington: Indiana University Press.

Cosmides, L., & Tooby, J. (1992). Cognitive adaptations for social exchange. The adapted mind, 163-228.

Cowan, N. in Models of Working Memory: Mechanisms of Active Maintenance and Executive Control (eds Miyake, A. & Shah, P.) 62–101 (Cambridge Univ. Press, New York, 1999).

Cramer, P. (1998). Defensiveness and defense mechanisms. Journal of Personality. 66, 879–894.

Crerand, C. E., & Sarwer, D. B. (2010). Body dysmorphic disorder. Corsini Encyclopedia of Psychology.

Crick, F., & Mitchison, G. (1983). The function of dream sleep. Nature, 304(5922), 111-114.

Crick, F., & Mitchison, G. (1995). REM sleep and neural nets. Behavioural brain research, 69(1), 147-155.

Crone, J. S., Höller, Y., Bergmann, J., Golaszewski, S., Trinka, E., & Kronbichler, M. (2013). Self-related processing and deactivation of cortical midline regions in disorders of consciousness. Frontiers in human neuroscience, 7.

Crowley, K. (2011). Sleep and sleep disorders in older adults. Neuropsychology review, 21(1), 41-53.

Cruts, M., Theuns, J., & Van Broeckhoven, C. (2012). Locus-specific mutation databases for neurodegenerative brain diseases. Human mutation, 33(9), 1340-1344.

Cummings, N. A. (2007). Treatment and assessment take place in an economic setting, always. The great ideas of clinical science, 163-184.

Cunningham, C. & Maclullich, A. M. J. (2013). At the extreme end of the psychoneuroimmunological spectrum: Delirium as a maladaptive sickness behaviour response. Brain, Behavior, and Immunity 28 (2013) 1–13

Curtis, J. R., Engelberg, R. A., Nielsen, E. L., Au, D. H., & Patrick, D. L. (2004). Patient-physician communication about end-of-life care for patients with severe COPD. European Respiratory Journal, 24(2), 200-205.

Curtiss, G., Vanderploeg, R. D., Spencer, J., & Salazar, A. M. (2001). Patterns of verbal learning and memory in traumatic brain injury. Journal of the International Neuropsychological Society, 7(5), 574–585.

Cutler, D. J., Haraura, M., Reed, H. E., Shen, S., Sheward, W. J., Morrison, C. F., Harmar, A. & Piggins, H. D. (2003). The mouse VPAC2 receptor confers suprachiasmatic nuclei cellular rhythmicity and responsiveness to vasoactive intestinal polypeptide in vitro. European Journal of Neuroscience, 17(2), 197-204.

Cutting, J. (1987). The phenomenology of acute organic psychosis. Comparison with acute schizophrenia. The British Journal of Psychiatry, 151(3), 324-332.

Czech, B., & Hannon, G. J. (2010). Small RNA sorting: matchmaking for Argonautes. Nature Reviews Genetics, 12(1), 19-31.

Czeisler, C. A., Dumont, M., Duffy, J. F., Steinberg, J. D., Richardson, G. S., Brown, E. N., Sanchez, D., Rio, A. & Ronda, J. M. (1992). Association of sleep-wake habits in older people with changes in output of circadian pacemaker. The lancet, 340(8825), 933-936.

D'Argembeau, A. (2013). On the role of the ventromedial prefrontal cortex in self-processing: the valuation hypothesis. Frontiers in human neuroscience, 7.

Daan, S., Albrecht, U., Van der Horst, G. T. J., Illnerova, H., Roenneberg, T., Wehr, T. A., & Schwartz, W. J. (2001). Assembling a clock for all seasons: are there M and E oscillators in the genes?. Journal of biological rhythms, 16(2), 105-116.

Daan, S., Beersma, D. G., & Borbély, A. A. (1984). Timing of human sleep: recovery process gated by a circadian pacemaker. American Journal of Physiology-Regulatory, Integrative and Comparative Physiology, 246(2), R161-R183.

Daffurn, K., Bishop, G. F., Hillman, K. M., & Bauman, A. (1994). Problems following discharge after intensive care. Intensive and Critical Care Nursing, 10(4), 244-251.

Dalvi, A., Lyons, K. E., & Pahwa, R. (2014). Parkinson's Disease: An Overview of Etiology, Clinical Manifestations, and Treatment. In Inflammation in Parkinson's Disease (pp. 1-24). Springer International Publishing.

Damasio, A. (2012). Self comes to mind: Constructing the conscious brain. Random House LLC.

Damiani, D., Alexander, J. J., O'Rourke, J. R., McManus, M., Jadhav, A. P., Cepko, C. L., & Strettoi, E. (2008). Dicer inactivation leads to progressive functional and structural degeneration of the mouse retina. The Journal of Neuroscience, 28(19), 4878-4887.

Danesi, M. (1999). Of cigarettes, high heels, and other interesting things. New York: St. Martin's Press.

Dang-Vu, T. T., Desseilles, M., Peigneux, P., & Maquet, P. (2006). A role for sleep in brain plasticity. Developmental Neurorehabilitation, 9(2), 98-118.

d'Aquili, E. G., & Newberg, A. B. (1999). The mystical mind: Probing the biology of religious experience. Fortress Press.

Darko, D. F., Miller, J. C., Gallen, C., White, J., Koziol, J., Brown, S. J., Hayduk, R. Atkinson, J.H., Assmus, J. & Munnell, D. T. (1995). Sleep electroencephalogram delta-frequency amplitude, night plasma levels of tumor necrosis factor alpha, and human immunodeficiency virus infection. Proceedings of the National Academy of Sciences, 92(26), 12080-12084.

Datta, S., Li, G., & Auerbach, S. (2008). Activation of phasic pontine-wave generator in the rat: a mechanism for expression of plasticity-related genes and proteins in the dorsal hippocampus and amygdala. European Journal of Neuroscience, 27(7), 1876-1892.

Davidson, E. H. (2010). The regulatory genome: gene regulatory networks in development and evolution. Academic Press.

Davidson, J., Lee-Archer, S., & Sanders, G. (2005). Dream Imagery and Emotion. Dreaming, 15(1), 33.

Davis, B. (2013). Dementia: From Diagnosis to Management—a Functional Approach, by Michelle S. Bourgeois and Ellen M. Hickey: New York, NY: Psychology Press, 2009, 429 pages, hardcover, Activities, Adaptation & Aging, 37(3), 265-266.

Davis, D. H., Terrera, G. M., Keage, H., Rahkonen, T., Oinas, M., Matthews, F. E., Cunningham, C. & Brayne, C. (2012). Delirium is a strong risk factor for dementia in the oldest-old: a population-based cohort study. Brain, 135(9), 2809-2816.

Davis, T. H., Cuellar, T. L., Koch, S. M., Barker, A. J., Harfe, B. D., McManus, M. T., & Ullian, E. M. (2008). Conditional loss of Dicer disrupts cellular and tissue morphogenesis in the cortex and hippocampus. The Journal of Neuroscience, 28(17), 4322-4330.

Davydow, D.S., Gifford, J.M., Desai, S.V., Needham, D.M. & Bienvenu, O.J., (2008). Posttraumatic stress disorder in general intensive care unit survivors: a systematic review. Gen. Hosp. Psychiatry 30, 421–434.

Dawson, D., & Encel, N. (1993). Melatonin and sleep in humans. Journal of pineal research, 15(1), 1-12.

Day, J., Higgins, I., & Keatinge, D. (2011). Orientation strategies during delirium: are they helpful?. Journal of clinical nursing, 20(23-24), 3285-3294.

De Boer, J. Z. & Hale, J. R. (2000). "The Geological Origins of the Oracle of Delphi, Greece," in W.G. McGuire, D.R. Griffiths, P Hancock, and I.S. Stewart, eds. The Archaeology of Geological Catastrophes. Geological Society of London.

De Jonghe, A., Korevaar, J. C., van Munster, B. C., & de Rooij, S. E. (2010). Effectiveness of melatonin treatment on circadian rhythm disturbances in dementia. Are there implications for delirium? A systematic review. International journal of geriatric psychiatry, 25(12), 1201-1208.

De Kloet, E. R., Vreugdenhil, E., Oitzl, M. S., & Joels, M. (1998). Brain Corticosteroid Receptor Balance in Health and Disease 1. Endocrine reviews, 19(3), 269-301.

De Koninck, J., Christ, G., Hebert, G., & Rinfret, N. (1990). Language learning efficiency, dreams and REM sleep. Psychiatric Journal of the University of Ottawa: Revue De Psychiatrie De l'Universite d'Ottawa, 15(2), 9192.

De Koninck, J., Lorrain, D., Christ, G., Proulx, G., & Coulombe, D. (1989). Intensive language learning and increases in rapid eye movement sleep: Evidence of a performance factor. International Journal of Psychophysiology, 8(1), 4347.

De Lecea, L., Kilduff, T. S., Peyron, C., Gao, X. B., Foye, P. E., Danielson, P. E., ... & Sutcliffe, J. G. (1998). The hypocretins: hypothalamus-specific peptides with neuroexcitatory activity. Proceedings of the National Academy of Sciences, 95(1), 322-327.

De Negreiros, D. P. D., Meleiro, A. M. A. D. S., Furlanetto, L. M., & Trzepacz, P. T. (2008). Portuguese version of the Delirium Rating Scale-Revised-98: reliability and validity. International journal of geriatric psychiatry, 23(5), 472-477.

De Rooij, S. E., van Munster, B. C., & de Jonghe, A. (2014). Melatonin prophylaxis in delirium: panacea or paradigm shift?. JAMA psychiatry, 71(4), 364-365.

De Rooij, S. E., van Munster, B. C., Korevaar, J. C., Casteelen, G., Schuurmans, M. J., van der Mast, R. C., & Levi, M. (2006). Delirium subtype identification and the validation of the Delirium Rating Scale—Revised-98 (Dutch version) in hospitalized elderly patients. International journal of geriatric psychiatry, 21(9), 876-882.

de Rooij, S.E., Van Munster, B.C., Korevaar, J.C. & Levi, M.(2007). Cytokines and acute phase response in delirium. J Psychosom Res; 62: 521–5.

De Simone, R., Ajmone-Cat, M. A., Carnevale, D., & Minghetti, L. (2005). Activation of $\alpha7$ nicotinic acetylcholine receptor by nicotine selectively up-regulates cyclooxygenase-2 and prostaglandin E2 in rat microglial cultures. Journal of neuroinflammation, 2(1), 4.

De Vreese L, Verlato C, Emiliani S, Schioppa S, Belloi L, Salvioli G, Neri M: Effect size of a three-month drug treatment in AD when combined with individual cognitive retraining: preliminary results of a pilot study. Neurobiol Aging 1998, 19:S213.

DeCoursey, P. J., & Buggy, J. (1988). Restoration of circadian locomotor activity in arrhythmic hamsters by fetal SCN transplants. Comp Endocrinol, 7, 49-54.

Deely, J. (1990). Basics of semiotics. Bloomington: Indiana University Press.

Del Gobbo, V., Libri, V., Villani, N., Caliō, R., & Nisticō, G. (1989). Pinealectomy inhibits interleukin-2 production and natural killer activity in mice. International journal of immunopharmacology, 11(5), 567-573.

Dement, W.C. & Kleitman, N. (1957). Cyclic variations in EEG during sleep and their relation to eye movements, body motility and dreaming. Electroencephalogr Clin Neurophysiol; 9:673–90.

Demertzi, A., Soddu, A., & Laureys, S. (2013). Consciousness supporting networks. Current Opinion in Neurobiology, 23(2), 239-244.

Desan, P.H., Oren, D.A., Malison, R., Price, L.H., Rosenbaum, J., Smoller, J., Charney, D.S. and Gelernter, J. (2000) Genetic Polymorphism at the CLOCK Gene Locus and Major Depression. Neuropsychiatr Genet, 96, 418-421.

Descartes, R. (1641[1996]). Meditations on First Philosophy, translated by John Cottingham (Cambridge: Cambridge University Press.

Devan, B. D., Pistell, P. J., Duffy, K. B., Kelley-Bell, B., Spangler, E. L., & Ingram, D. K. (2014). Phosphodiesterase inhibition facilitates cognitive restoration in rodent models of age-related memory decline. NeuroRehabilitation, 34(1), 101-111.

Devinsky, O. (2000). Right cerebral hemisphere dominance for a sense of corporeal and emotional self. Epilepsy Behav; 1(1):60-73.

Devinsky, O. (2009) Delusional misidentifications and duplications: right brain lesions, left brain delusions. Neurology; 72(1):80-87.

Devlin, J. W., Roberts, R. J., Fong, J. J., Skrobik, Y., Riker, R. R., Hill, N. S., Robbins, T. & Garpestad, E. (2010). Efficacy and safety of quetiapine in critically ill patients with delirium: A prospective, multicenter, randomized, double-blind, placebo-controlled pilot study*. Critical care medicine, 38(2), 419-427.

Devue, C., Collette, F., Balteau, E., Degueldre, C., Luxen, A., Maquet, P., & Brédart, S. (2007). Here I am: the cortical correlates of visual self-recognition. Brain research, 1143, 169-182.

Dew, I. T., & Cabeza, R. (2011). The porous boundaries between explicit and implicit memory: Behavioral and neural evidence. Annals of the New York Academy of Sciences, 1224, 174–190.

Di Stefano, A., Sozio, P., Serafina Cerasa, L., & Iannitelli, A. (2011). L-Dopa prodrugs: an overview of trends for improving Parkinson's disease treatment. Current pharmaceutical design, 17(32), 3482-3493.

Dickerson, B. C., Bakkour, A., Salat, D. H., Feczko, E., Pacheco, J., Greve, D. N., ... & Buckner, R. L. (2009). The cortical signature of Alzheimer's disease: regionally specific cortical thinning relates to symptom severity in very mild to mild AD dementia and is detectable in asymptomatic amyloid-positive individuals. Cerebral cortex, 19(3), 497-510.

Dickstein, D. L., Weaver, C. M., Luebke, J. I., & Hof, P. R. (2013). Dendritic spine changes associated with normal aging. Neuroscience, 251, 21-32.

Diekelmann, S., & Born, J. (2010). The memory function of sleep. Nature Reviews Neuroscience, 11(2), 114-126.

Dietrich R. (2006). Modularity and the tic-toc of language. In Fuss SG (ed.) Form, structure and grammar: A Festschrift presented to Gu"nther Grewendorf on the occasion of his 60th birthday. Berlin: Akademie Verlag, pp. 299–311.

Dietrich, B. C. (1992). Divine Madness and Conflict at Delphi. Kernos. Revue internationale et pluridisciplinaire de religion grecque antique, (5).

Dijk, D. J., & Cajochen, C. (1997). Melatonin and the circadian regulation of sleep initiation, consolidation, structure, and the sleep EEG. Journal of biological rhythms, 12(6), 627-635.

Dijk, D. J. & Czeisler, C.A. (1994) Paradoxical timing of the circadian rhythm of sleep

Dobbs, B. M., Dobbs, A. R., & Kiss, I. (2001). Working memory deficits associated with chronic fatigue syndrome. Journal of the International Neuropsychological Society, 7(3), 285–293.

Dolan, M. M., Hawkes, W. G., Zimmerman, S. I., Morrison, R. S., Gruber-Baldini, A. L., Hebel, J. R., & Magaziner, J. (2000). Delirium on Hospital Admission in Aged Hip Fracture Patients Prediction of Mortality and 2-Year Functional Outcomes. The

Journals of Gerontology Series A: Biological Sciences and Medical Sciences, 55(9), M527-M534.

Domhoff, G. W. (2001). A new neurocognitive theory of dreams. Dreaming, 11(1), 13-33.

Domhoff, G. W. (2005). Refocusing the neurocognitive approach to dreams: A critique of the Hobson versus Solms debate. Dreaming, 15(1), 3.

Domhoff, G. W., & Hall, C. S. (1996). Finding meaning in dreams: A quantitative approach. Springer.

Domhoff, G.W. (2011). The neural substrate for dreaming: is it a subsystem of the default network?. Consciousness and cognition, 20(4), 1163-1174.

Doran, A. R., LaBarca, R., Wolkowitz, O. M., Roy, A., Douillet, P. & Pickar, D. (1990). Circadian variation of plasma homovanillic acid levels is attenuated by fluphenazine in patients with schizophrenia. Arch Gen Psychiatry, 47, 558-63.

Dosa, D., Intrator, O., McNicoll, L., Cang, Y., & Teno, J. (2007). Preliminary derivation of a nursing home confusion assessment method based on data from the minimum data set. Journal of the American Geriatrics Society, 55(7), 1099-1105.

Dozier, M., Stoval, K. C., Albus, K. E., & Bates, B. (2001). Attachment for infants in foster care: The role of caregiver state of mind. Child development, 72(5), 1467-1477.

Drazen, D. L., Bilu, D., Bilbo, S. D., & Nelson, R. J. (2001). Melatonin enhancement of splenocyte proliferation is attenuated by luzindole, a melatonin receptor antagonist. American Journal of Physiology-Regulatory, Integrative and Comparative Physiology, 280(5), R1476-R1482.

Drews, T., Franck, M., Radtke, F. M., Weiss, B., Krampe, H., Brockhaus, W. R., Winterer, G. & Spies, C. D. (2014). Postoperative delirium is an independent risk factor for posttraumatic stress disorder in the elderly patient: A prospective observational study. European Journal of Anaesthesiology (EJA).

Duan, H., Wearne, S. L., Rocher, A. B., Macedo, A., Morrison, J. H., & Hof, P. R. (2003). Age-related dendritic and spine changes in corticocortically projecting neurons in macaque monkeys. Cerebral Cortex, 13(9), 950-961.

Duffy, J. F., & Wright, K. P. (2005). Entrainment of the human circadian system by light. Journal of Biological Rhythms, 20(4), 326-338.

Duffy, J. F., Zeitzer, J. M., Rimmer, D. W., Klerman, E. B., Dijk, D. J., & Czeisler, C. A. (2002). Peak of circadian melatonin rhythm occurs later within the sleep of older subjects. American Journal of Physiology-Endocrinology and Metabolism, 282(2), E297-E303.

Duncan, B. L., Miller, S. D., Wampold, B. E., & Hubble, M. A. (2010). The heart and soul of change: Delivering what works in therapy. American Psychological Association.

Dunlap, J.C. (1999) Molecular Bases for Circadian Clocks. Cell, 96, 271-290.

Dunn, G. (1989). Design and analysis of reliability studies: The statistical evaluation of measurement errors. Edward Arnold Publishers.

Duntley, J. D., & Buss, D. M. (2011). Homicide adaptations. Aggression and Violent Behavior, 16(5), 399-410.

Duppils, G.S., & Wikblad, K. (2007). Patients' experiences of being delirious. Journal of Clinical Nursing, 16(5), 810-818.

Eadie, M. J. (2003) A pathology of the animal spirits – the clinical neurology of Thomas Willis (1621–1675). Part II – disorders of intrinsically abnormal animal spirits. Journal of Clinical Neuroscience, 10, 146–57.

Ebersoldt, M., Sharshar, T., & Annane, D. (2007). Sepsis-associated delirium. Intensive care medicine, 33(6), 941-950.

Edelman, G. (2006). "From Brain Dynamics to Consciousness: A Prelude to the Future of Brain-Based Devices", Video, IBM Lecture on Cognitive Computing, June 2006.

Edelman, G. (2014). Gerald Edelman. NATURE, 510.

Edelman, G. M. (1993). Neural Darwinism: selection and reentrant signaling in higher brain function. Neuron, 10(2), 115-125.

Edelman, G. M. (2003). Naturalizing consciousness: a theoretical framework. Proceedings of the National Academy of Sciences, 100(9), 5520-5524.

Edelman, G. M. (2004). Wider than the sky: The phenomenal gift of consciousness. Yale University Press.

Edelman, G. M., & Gally, J. A. (2013). Reentry: a key mechanism for integration of brain function. Frontiers in integrative neuroscience, 7.

Edelman, G. M., & Tononi, G. (2013). Consciousness: How matter becomes imagination. Penguin UK.

Edelman, G. M., Gally, J. A., & Baars, B. J. (2011). Frontiers: Biology of Consciousness. Frontiers in Consciousness Research, 2.

Edlund, A., Lundström, M., Brännström, B., Bucht, G., & Gustafson, Y. (2001). Delirium before and after operation for femoral neck fracture. Journal of the American Geriatrics Society, 49(10), 1335-1340.

Eisenberg, D. P., Kohn, P. D., Baller, E. B., Bronstein, J. A., Masdeu, J. C., & Berman, K. F. (2010). Seasonal effects on human striatal presynaptic dopamine synthesis. The Journal of Neuroscience, 30(44), 14691-14694.

El Mansari M, Sakai K, Jouvet M (1989). Unitary characteristics of presumptive cholinergic tegmental neurons during the sleepwaking cycle in freely moving cats. Exp Brain Res 76:5 19-529.

Eliade, Mircea (1972). Shamanism: Archaic Techniques of Ecstasy. Bollingen 76. Princeton University Press.

Elkins, G., White, J., Patel, P., Marcus, J., Perfect, M. M., & Montgomery, G. H. (2006). Hypnosis to manage anxiety and pain associated with colonoscopy for colorectal cancer screening: Case studies and possible benefits. International Journal of Clinical and Experimental Hypnosis, 54(4), 416-431.

Ellenbogen, J. M., Hu, P. T., Payne, J. D., Titone, D., & Walker, M. P. (2007). Human relational memory requires time and sleep. Proceedings of the National Academy of Sciences, 104(18), 7723-7728.

Ellenbogen, J. M., Payne, J. D., & Stickgold, R. (2006). The role of sleep in declarative memory consolidation: passive, permissive, active or none?. Current opinion in neurobiology, 16(6), 716-722.

Elliott, D. (1999). Fallen bodies: pollution, sexuality and demonology. Philadelphia: University of Pennsylvania Press.

Ellis, H. 1936(1898). Studies in the psychology of sex, vol. 1,pt 1.(Revised edition). New York: Randon House.

Engel, G. L., & Rosenbaum, M. (1945). Delirium: III. Electroencephalographic changes associated with acute alcoholic intoxication. Archives of Neurology & Psychiatry, 53(1), 44-50.

Erickson, M. H. (1970). Hypnosis: Its renaissance as a treatment modality. American Journal of Clinical Hypnosis, 13(2), 71-89.

Ernst, R., Hay, J. W., Fenn, C., Tinklenberg, J., & Yesavage, J. A. (1997). Cognitive function and the costs of alzheimer disease: an

Escames, G., López, L. C., Ortiz, F., Ros, E., & Acuña-Castroviejo, D. (2006). Age-dependent lipopolysaccharide-induced iNOS expression and multiorgan failure in rats: effects of melatonin treatment. Experimental gerontology, 41(11), 1165-1173.

Esquirol, E. (1814). Article 'Demence', in Dictionnaire des sciences Medicale en 60 vol. (1812-1822), sous le dir. De Panckoucke, vol 8. P280-294.

Eubank, K. J., & Covinsky, K. E. (2014). Delirium Severity in the Hospitalized Patient: Time to Pay Attention. Annals of internal medicine, 160(8), 574-575.

Evagrius of Pontus, Praktikos, (1971). In Evagre le poutique: traite pratique, ou le moine, vol. 2 (ed.) Guillaumont, A. & Guillaumont, C. (Sources Chretiennes, 171). Paris: Cerf.

Evans, D. (2006). An introductory dictionary of Lacanian psychoanalysis. Routledge.

Everitt, B. J., & Robbins, T. W. (1997). Central cholinergic systems and cognition. Annual review of psychology, 48(1), 649-684.

Ey, H. (1973). Traite des hallucinations: I-II.

Fadel, J., & Burk, J. A. (2010). Orexin/hypocretin modulation of the basal forebrain cholinergic system: Role in attention. Brain research, 1314, 112-123.

Fadel, J., & Frederick-Duus, D. (2008). Orexin/hypocretin modulation of the basal forebrain cholinergic system: insights from in vivo microdialysis studies. Pharmacology Biochemistry and Behavior, 90(2), 156-162.

Fagerberg I & Jonhagen ME (2002). Temporary confusion: a fearful experience. Journal of Psychiatric & Mental Health Nursing 9, 339–346.

Fann, J. R., Alfano, C. M., Burington, B. E., Roth-Roemer, S., Katon, W. J., & Syrjala, K. L. (2005). Clinical presentation of delirium in patients undergoing hematopoietic stem cell transplantation. Cancer, 103(4), 810-820.

Farrer, C., & Frith, C. D. (2002). Experiencing oneself vs another person as being the cause of an action: the neural correlates of the experience of agency. Neuroimage, 15(3), 596-603.

Faymonville, M. E., Boly, M., & Laureys, S. (2006). Functional neuroanatomy of the hypnotic state. Journal of Physiology-Paris, 99(4), 463-469.

Feil, N. (1982). V/F Validation: The Feil Method: How to Help Disoriented Old-Old. Edward Feil Productions, Cleveland, OH.

Feil, N. (1993). The Validation Breakthrough: Simple Techniques for Communicating with People with Alzheimer's Type Dementia. Health Professions Press, Cleveland, OH.

Feinberg, T. E. (2011). Neuropathologies of the self: clinical and anatomical features. Consciousness and cognition, 20(1), 75-81.

Feinberg, T. E., & Shapiro, R. M. (1989). Misidentification-reduplication and the right hemisphere. Neuropsychiatry, Neuropsychology, & Behavioral Neurology.

Feinberg, T. E., Eaton, L. A., Roane, D. M., & Giacino, J. T. (1999). Multiple Fregoli delusions after traumatic brain injury. Cortex, 35(3), 373-387.

Feinberg, T.E., Deluca, J., Giacino, J.T., Roane, D.M. & Solms, M. (2005). Righthemisphere pathology and the self: delusional misidentification and reduplication. In: Feinberg TE, Keenan JP, eds. The Lost Self. New York, NY: Oxford University Press; 100-130.

Fenwick, P., & Brayne, S. (2010). End-of-life experiences: Reaching out for compassion, communication, and connection—Meaning of deathbed visions and coincidences. American Journal of Hospice and Palliative Medicine.

Fenwick, P., Lovelace, H., & Brayne, S. (2007). End of life experiences and their implications for palliative care. International journal of environmental studies, 64(3), 315-323.

Fick, D. M., Agostini, J. V., & Inouye, S. K. (2002). Delirium superimposed on dementia: a systematic review. Journal of the American Geriatrics Society, 50(10), 1723-1732.

Fick, D. M., McDowell, J., Mion, L., Kolanowski, A., DiMeglio, B., Kitt-Lewis, E., ... & Inouye, S. K. (2014). Facilitating person-centered care for the prevention of delirium in hospitalized persons with dementia. Alzheimer's & Dementia: The Journal of the Alzheimer's Association, 10(4), P530-P531.

Fick, D. M., Steis, M. R., Waller, J. L., & Inouye, S. K. (2013). Delirium superimposed on dementia is associated with prolonged length of stay and poor outcomes in hospitalized older adults. Journal of Hospital Medicine, 8(9), 500-505.

Finch, C. E., Pike, M. C., & Witten, M. (1990). Slow mortality rate accelerations during aging in some animals approximate that of humans. Science, 249(4971), 902-905.

Fink, B. (1997). The Lacanian subject: Between language and jouissance. Princeton University Press.

Fink, B. (2011). Fundamentals of psychoanalytic technique: A Lacanian approach for practitioners. WW Norton & Company.

Fisk, A., Rogers, W., Cooper, B., & Gilbert, D. (1996). Automatic category search and its transfer: Aging, type of search, and level of learning. Journal of Gerontology, 52(2), 91–102.

Fiske, V.M., Bryant, G.K. & Putnam, J. (1960). Effect of light in the weight of the pineal in the rat. Endocrinology; 66:489–91.

Fitzgerald, J. M., Adamis, D., Trzepacz, P. T., O'Regan, N., Timmons, S., Dunne, C., & Meagher, D. J. (2013). Delirium: A disturbance of circadian integrity?. Medical hypotheses, 81(4), 568-576.

Fjell, A. M., Amlien, I. K., Sneve, M. H., Grydeland, H., Tamnes, C. K., Chaplin, T. A., Rosa, M.J. & Walhovd, K. B. (2014). The Roots of Alzheimer's Disease: Are High-Expanding Cortical Areas Preferentially Targeted?. Cerebral Cortex, bhu055.

Flacker, J. M., & Lipsitz, L. A. (1999). Serum anticholinergic activity changes with acute illness in elderly medical patients. The Journals of Gerontology Series A: Biological Sciences and Medical Sciences, 54(1), M12-M16.

Flacker, J. M., & Wei, J. Y. (2001). Endogenous anticholinergic substances may exist during acute illness in elderly medical patients. The Journals of Gerontology Series A: Biological Sciences and Medical Sciences, 56(6), M353-M355.

Flacker, J. M., Cummings, V., Mach Jr, J. R., Bettin, K., Kiely, D. K., & Wei, J. (1999). The association of serum anticholinergic activity with delirium in elderly medical patients. The American Journal of Geriatric Psychiatry, 6(1), 31-41.

Flaherty, J. H., Tariq, S. H., Raghavan, S., Bakshi, S., Moinuddin, A., & Morley, J. E. (2003). A model for managing delirious older inpatients. Journal of the American Geriatrics Society, 51(7), 1031-1035.

Flammer, E., & Bongartz, W. (2003). On the efficacy of hypnosis: a meta-analytic study. Contemporary Hypnosis, 20(4), 179-197.

Flanagan, N. M., & Spencer, G. (2015). Family Recognition of Delirium in Post-acute Care: Implications for the Rehabilitation Team. Topics in Geriatric Rehabilitation, 31(2), 129-134.

Fleiss JL. Statistical methods for rates and proportions. 2nd ed. New York: Wiley/ John and Sons, Inc; 1981.

Fleiss, J. L., Levin, B., & Paik, M. C. (2013). Statistical methods for rates and proportions. John Wiley & Sons.

Fletcher, P. C., & Henson, R. N. A. (2001). Frontal lobes and human memory: Insights from functional neuroimaging. Brain, 124, 849–881.

Fodor, J. A. (1983). The modularity of mind: An essay on faculty psychology. MIT press.

Fogassi, L., & Ferrari, P. F. (2007). Mirror neurons and the evolution of embodied language. Current directions in psychological science, 16(3), 136-141.

Folkard, S. (1975). Diurnal variation in logical reasoning. Br. J. Psych. 66:1–8.

Folkard, S., & Åkerstedt, T. (2004). Trends in the risk of accidents and injuries and their implications for models of fatigue and performance. Aviation, space, and environmental medicine, 75(Supplement 1), A161-A167.

Fonagy, P. & Tallindini-Shallice, M. (1993) 'Problems of psychanalytical research in practice', Bulletin pf the Anna Freud Centre, 16(1):5-22.

Fonagy, P. (1999). 'Memory and Therapeutic Action'. In International Journal of Psycho-Analysis, 80, 215.

Fong, T. G., Hshieh, T. T., Wong, B., Tommet, D., Jones, R. N., Schmitt, E. M., Puelle, M.R., Saczynski, J.S., Marcantonio, E.R. & Inouye, S. K. (2015). Neuropsychological Profiles of an Elderly Cohort Undergoing Elective Surgery and the Relationship Between Cognitive Performance and Delirium. Journal of the American Geriatrics Society, 63(5), 977-982.

Fong, T.G., Jones, R.N., Shi, P., Marcantonio, E.R., Yap, L., Rudolph, J.L., Yang, F.M., Kiely, D.K. & Inouye, S.K. (2009). Delirium accelerates cognitive decline in Alzheimer disease. Neurology 72:1570-1575.

Fonseca, F., Bulbena, A., Navarrete, R., Aragay, N., Capo, M., Lobo, A., & Trzepacz, P. T. (2005). Spanish version of the Delirium Rating Scale-Revised-98: reliability and validity. Journal of psychosomatic research, 59(3), 147-151.

Fontenrose, J. E. (1959). Python: a study of Delphic myth and its origins. Univ of California Press.

Forbes, D., Blake, C. M., Thiessen, E. J., Peacock, S., & Hawranik, P. (2014). Light therapy for improving cognition, activities of daily living, sleep, challenging behaviour, and psychiatric disturbances in dementia. The Cochrane Library.

Ford, J. (1999). Samuel Taylor Coleridge and the pains of sleep. History Workshop Journal: 48, 169-86.

Forrest, W.G. (1957). "Colonisation and the Rise of Delphi" (Historia: Zeitschrift für Alte Geschichte Bd. 6, H. 2 (Apr., 1957), pp. 160-175)

Fosse M. J., Fosse R., Hobson J. A., Stickgold R. J. (2003). Dreaming and episodic memory: a functional dissociation? J. Cogn. Neurosci. 15, 1–9.

Fosse R. &Domhoff G. W. (2007). Dreaming as non-executive orienting: a conceptual framework for consciousness during sleep, in The New Science of Dreaming: Content, Recall, and Personality Correlates, Vol. 2, eds Barrett D., McNamara P., editors. (Westport, CT: Praeger), 49–78

Fosse R., Stickgold R. & Hobson J. A. (2004). Thinking and hallucinating: reciprocal changes in sleep. Psychophysiology 41, 298–305

Fosse, M. J., Fosse, R., Hobson, J. A., & Stickgold, R. J. (2003). Dreaming and episodic memory: a functional dissociation?. Journal of Cognitive Neuroscience, 15(1), 1-9.

Foster, J., & Lehoux, D. (2007). The Delphic Oracle and the ethylene-intoxication hypothesis*. Clinical Toxicology, 45(1), 85-89.

Foulkes D. & Fleisher S. (1975). Mental activity in relaxed wakefulness. J. Abnorm. Psychol. 84, 66–75.

Foulkes D. & Scott E. (1973). An above-zero baseline for the incidence of momentarily hallucinatory mentation. Sleep Res. 2:108.

Foulkes, D. (1982). Children's dreams: Longitudinal studies. New York: Wiley.

Foulkes, D. (1993). Dreaming and REM sleep. Journal of sleep research, 2(4), 199-202.

Foulkes, D. (1999). Children's dreaming and the development of consciousness. Harvard University Press; Cambridge, MA.

Foulkes, D., & Fleisher, S. (1975). Mental activity in relaxed wakefulness. Journal of Abnormal Psychology, 84(1), 66.

Foulkes, D., & Scott, E. (1973). An above-zero waking baseline for the incidence of momentarily hallucinatory mentation. In M. H. Chase, W. C. Stern, & P. L. Walter (Eds.), Sleep research (Vol. 2). Los Angeles: Brain Information Service/Brain ResearchInstitute. (Abstract).

Foulkes, D., Meier, B., Strauch, I., Ken, N. H., Bradley, L., & Hollifield, M. (1993). Linguistic phenomena and language selection in the REM dreams of German-English bilinguals. International Journal of Psychology, 28(6), 871.

Foulkes, W. D. (1982). Children's Dreams: Longitudinal Studies. New York: Wiley & Sons.

Fowler, M. J., Sullivan, M. J., & Ekstrand, B. R. (1973). Sleep and memory. Science 179, 302–304.

Fox, R.L. (2008). Travelling Heroes in the Epic Age of Homer. Knopf.

Fraisse, P. (1963). The Psychology of Time, trans. By J. Leith, New York, Harper and Row.

Fraley, R. C., & Shaver, P. R. (2000). Adult romantic attachment: Theoretical developments, emerging controversies, and unanswered questions. Review of general psychology, 4(2), 132.

Franceschi, C., Capri, M., Monti, D., Giunta, S., Olivieri, F., Sevini, F., ... & Salvioli, S. (2007). Inflammaging and anti-inflammaging: a systemic perspective on aging and longevity emerged from studies in humans. Mechanisms of ageing and development, 128(1), 92-105.

Franco, J. G., Trzepacz, P. T., Meagher, D. J., Kean, J., Lee, Y., Kim, J.-L., Kisha, Y., de Pablo, J. (2013). Three core domains of delirium validated using exploratory and confirmatory factor analyses. Psychosomatics, 54(3), 227–38.

Franco, J. G., Trzepacz, P. T., Mejía, M. A., & Ochoa, S. B. (2009). Factor analysis of the Colombian translation of the Delirium Rating Scale (DRS), Revised–98. Psychosomatics, 50(3), 255-262.

Frank, M. G. (2011). The ontogeny and function (s) of REM sleep. Rapid Eye Movement Sleep: Regulation and Function, 49.

Frank, M. G., Issa, N. P., & Stryker, M. P. (2001). Sleep enhances plasticity in the developing visual cortex. Neuron, 30(1), 275-287.

Frank, M.G., Barrientos, R.M., Hein, A.M., Biedenkapp, J.C., Watkins, L.R. & Maier, S.F. (2010). IL-1RA blocks E. coli-induced suppression of Arc and long-term memory

Frankel, M. R., & Macfie, J. (2010). Psychodynamic psychotherapy with adjunctive hypnosis for social and performance anxiety in emerging adulthood. Clinical Case Studies, 9(4), 294-308.

Fransson, P., & Marrelec, G. (2008). The precuneus/posterior cingulate cortex plays a pivotal role in the default mode network: Evidence from a partial correlation network analysis. Neuroimage, 42(3), 1178-1184.

Fraser, P. M. (1969). "The Career of Erasistratus of Ceos". Istituto Lombardo, Rendiconti 103: 518–537.

Fratiglioni, L., Wang, H. X., Ericsson, K., Maytan, M., & Winblad, B. (2000). Influence of social network on occurrence of dementia: a community-based longitudinal study. The lancet, 355(9212), 1315-1319.

Frayling, C. (1996). Nightmare: the birth of horror. London: BBC Books.

Freeman, D., Garety, P. A., Kuipers, E., Fowler, D., & Bebbington, P. E. (2002). A cognitive model of persecutory delusions. British Journal of Clinical Psychology, 41(4), 331-347.

French, R. K. (2003). Medicine before science: The business of medicine from the Middle Ages to the Enlightenment. Cambridge University Press.

Freter, S. H., Dunbar, M. J., MacLeod, H., Morrison, M., MacKnight, C., & Rockwood, K. (2005). Predicting post-operative delirium in elective orthopaedic patients: the Delirium Elderly At-Risk (DEAR) instrument. Age and ageing, 34(2), 169-171.

Freud, A. (1937). The Ego and the Mechanisms of Defence. London: Hogarth Press and Institute of Psycho-Analysis.

Freud, S. (1908). Creative writers and day-dreaming. Standard Edn. 9, 143–153

Freud, S. (1926). Inhibition, Symptùmes et Angoisse. Presses Universitaires de France, Paris.

Freud, S. Psychoanalytic notes on an autobiographical account of a case of paranoia. In: Strachey J, ed. Standard Edition of the Complete Psychological Works of Sigmund Freud Vol. 12. London: Hogarth Press; 1958. (originally published in 1911). pp. 1–82.

Freud, S. (1900). The Interpretation of dreams. In: Strachey J, ed. Standard Edition of the Complete Psychological Works of Sigmund Freud Vol. 3 & 4. London: Hogarth Press; 1958. (originally published in 1900)

Freud, S. (1908). Creative writers and day-dreaming. Standard edition, 9, 143-153.

Freud, S. (1920). Beyond the Pleasure Principle. The Standard Edition of the Complete Psychological Works of Sigmund Freud, Volume XVIII (1920-1922).

Freud, S. (1923). The Ego and the ID. In J. Strachey (Ed. and Trans.),The standard edition of the complete psychological works of Sigmund Freud (Vol. XIX). London: Hogarth Press.

Freud, S. (1962). The aetiology of hysteria. In The Standard Edition of the Complete Psychological Works of Sigmund Freud, Volume III (1893-1899): Early Psycho-Analytic Publications (pp. 187-221).

Fried, I., Katz, A., McCarthy, G., Sass, K. J., Williamson, P., Spencer, S. S., & Spencer, D. D. (1991). Functional organization of human supplementary motor cortex studied by electrical stimulation. The Journal of neuroscience, 11(11), 3656-3666.

Fries, P., Womelsdorf, T., Oostenveld, R., & Desimone, R. (2008). The effects of visual stimulation and selective visual attention on rhythmic neuronal synchronization in macaque area V4. The Journal of Neuroscience, 28(18), 4823-4835.

Friston, K. (2010). The free-energy principle: a unified brain theory?. Nature Reviews Neuroscience, 11(2), 127-138.

Frith, C. D., & Frith, U. (2006). The neural basis of mentalizing. Neuron, 50(4), 531-534.

Frith, C. D., Blakemore, S. J., & Wolpert, D. M. (2000). Explaining the symptoms of schizophrenia: abnormalities in the awareness of action. Brain Research Reviews, 31(2), 357-363.

Fuchs, J. L., & Hoppens, K. S. (1987). Alpha-bungarotoxin binding in relation to functional organization of the rat suprachiasmatic nucleus. Brain Res, 407(1), 9-16.

Fuller, P. M., Gooley, J. J., & Saper, C. B. (2006). Neurobiology of the sleep-wake cycle: sleep architecture, circadian regulation, and regulatory feedback. Journal of biological rhythms, 21(6), 482-493.

Gachon, F., Nagoshi, E., Brown, S. A., Ripperger, J., & Schibler, U. (2004). The mammalian circadian timing system: from gene expression to physiology. Chromosoma, 113(3), 103-112.

Gagnon, J. F., Petit, D., & Fantini, M. L. (2006). REM sleep behavior disor-der and REM sleep without flatonia in probable Alzheimer disease. Sleep, 29, 1321-1325.

Gagnon, J. F., Postuma, R. B., Mazza, S., Doyon, J., & Montplaisir, J. (2006). Rapid-eye-movement sleep behaviour disorder and neurodegenerative diseases. The Lancet Neurology, 5(5), 424-432.

Galante, E., Venturini, G. & Fiaccadori, C. (2007). Computer-based cognitive intervention for dementia: preliminary results of a randomized clinical trial. G Ital Med Lav Ergon, 29:26-32.

Gallagher, H. L., & Frith, C. D. (2003). Functional imaging of 'theory of mind'. Trends in cognitive sciences, 7(2), 77-83.

Gallagher, M., & Rapp, P. R. (1997). The use of animal models to study the effects of aging on cognition. Annual review of psychology, 48(1), 339-370.

Gallagher, S. (2000). Philosophical conceptions of the self: implications for cognitive science. Trends in cognitive sciences, 4(1), 14-21.

Gallese, V. (2013). Bodily Self, Affect, Consciousness, and the Cortex. Neuropsychoanalysis, 15(1), 42-45.

Gallese, V., Lakoff, G. (2005). 'The brain's concepts: the role of the sensory-motor system in conceptual knowledge'. Cognitive Neuropsychology, 21.

Gamillsches, E. (1969). Etymologisches Woterbuch der franzosischen Sprache. Heidelberg: Carl Winter.

Gannon, R. L., & Millan, M. J. (2011). Positive allosteric modulators at GABA< sub> B</sub> receptors exert intrinsic actions and enhance the influence of baclofen on light-induced phase shifts of hamster circadian activity rhythms. Pharmacology Biochemistry and Behavior, 99(4), 712-717.

Gannon, R. L., & Millan, M. J. (2011). Positive and negative modulation of circadian activity rhythms by mGluR5 and mGluR2/3 metabotropic glutamate receptors. Neuropharmacology, 60(2), 209-215.

García Ballester L. (1972a). Galeno. In: Lain Entralgo P, editor. dir. Historia universal de la medicina. Antigüedad clásica, vol. 2. Barcelona: Salvat Editores, S.A. p. 209–67.

García Ballester, L. (1972 b) Alma y enfermedad en la obra de Galeno. Traducción y comentario del escrito Quod animi mores corporis temperamenta sequantur. Valencia: Cuadernos Hispánicos de Historia de la Medicina y de la Ciencia, Serie A (Monografías), n. XII.

Garden, G. A., & Möller, T. (2006). Microglia biology in health and disease. Journal of Neuroimmune Pharmacology, 1(2), 127-137.

Gates, N., Sachdev, P. & Singh, M.F. (2011). Valenzuela M: Cognitive and memory training in adults at risk of dementia: a systematic review. BMC Geriatr; 11:55.

Gaudreau, J. D., Gagnon, P., Roy, M. A., Harel, F., & Tremblay, A. (2007). Opioid medications and longitudinal risk of delirium in hospitalized cancer patients. Cancer, 109(11), 2365-2373.

Gaughwin, P. M., Ciesla, M., Lahiri, N., Tabrizi, S. J., Brundin, P., & Björkqvist, M. (2011). Hsa-miR-34b is a plasma-stable microRNA that is elevated in pre-manifest Huntington's disease. Human molecular genetics, ddr111.

Gauthier, S., Reisberg, B., Zaudig, M., Petersen, R.C., Ritchie, K., Broic, K., Belleville, S., Brodaty, H., Bennett, D., Chertkow, H., Cummings, J.L., de Leon, M., Feldman, H., Ganguli, M., Hampel, H., Scheltens, P., Tierney, M.C., Whitehouse, P. & Winblad, B. (2006). International Psychogeriatric Association Expert Conference on mild cognitive impairment: Mild cognitive impairment. Lancet, 367:1262-1270.

Gay, M. C., Philippot, P., & Luminet, O. (2002). Differential effectiveness of psychological interventions for reducing osteoarthritis pain: a comparison of Erickson hypnosis and Jacobson relaxation. European Journal of Pain, 6(1), 1-16.

George, A. trans. (2003). The Babylonian Gilgamesh Epic: Critical Edition and Cuneiform Texts. Oxford, UK: Oxford University Press.

Georget, E. J. (1820) De la Folie. Considérations sur cette maladie (Paris: Crevot).

Gergely, G., & Watson, J. S. (1996). The social biofeedback theory of parental affect-mirroring: The development of emotional self-awareness and self-control in infancy. The International Journal of Psychoanalysis.

Gerkema, M.P. (2002). Ultradian Rhythms. in: Biological Rhythms, Edited by V. Kumar,

Germain, A., Krakow, B., Faucher, B., Zadra, A., Nielsen, T., Hollifield, M., Warner, T.D. & Koss, M. (2004). Increased Mastery Elements Associated With Imagery Rehearsal Treatment for Nightmares in Sexual Assault Survivors With PTSD. Dreaming, 14(4), 195.

Gerrans, P. (2013). Delusional attitudes and default thinking. Mind & Language, 28(1), 83-102.

Gesin, G., Russell, B. B., Lin, A. P., Norton, H. J., Evans, S. L., & Devlin, J. W. (2012). Impact of a delirium screening tool and multifaceted education on nurses' knowledge of delirium and ability to evaluate it correctly. American Journal of Critical Care, 21(1), e1-e11.

Getz, F. (1998). Medicine in the English Middle Ages. Princeton University Press.

Ghali, L.M. (1996). 'Rest-activity pattern changes in Alzheimer's disease', Dissertation Abstracts International: Section B; The Sciences & Engineering, 55(1-B): 6727.

Gibbs, S. E. B., & D'Esposito, M. (2006). A functional magnetic resonance imaging study of the effects of pergolide, a dopamine receptor agonist, on component processes of working memory. Neuroscience, 139(1), 359-371.

Gibson, G. E., & Peterson, C. (1981). Aging decreases oxidative metabolism and the release and synthesis of acetylcholine. Journal of neurochemistry, 37(4), 978-984.

Gibson, G. E., & Peterson, C. (1983). Acetylcholine and oxidative metabolism in septum and hippocampus in vitro. Journal of Biological Chemistry, 258(2), 1142-1145.

Gibson, G. E., Peterson, C., & Jenden, D. J. (1981). Brain acetylcholine synthesis declines with senescence. Science, 213(4508), 674-676.

Giebel, C., & Challis, D. (2014). Translating cognitive and everyday activity deficits into cognitive interventions in mild dementia and mild cognitive impairment. International journal of geriatric psychiatry, 30(1), 21-31.

Gilbert, P. (2001). Evolutionary approaches to psychopathology: The role of natural defences. Australian and New Zealand Journal of Psychiatry, 35(1), 17-27.

Gilbert, S.J. & Burgess, P.W. (2008). Social and non-social functions of rostral prefrontal cortex: implications for education. Mind, Brain and Education, 2, 148-156.

Gillette, M. U., & Mitchell, J. W. (2002). Signaling in the suprachiasmatic nucleus: selectively responsive and integrative. Cell and tissue research, 309(1), 99-107.

Gillis, A. J., & MacDonald, B. (2006). Unmasking delirium. The Canadian Nurse, 102(9), 18-24.

Ginzburg, C. (1990). Freud, the wolf-man, and the werewolves. In Myths, emblems, clues, C. Ginzburg, 146-55. London: Hutchinson Radius.

Gobbini, M.I., Leibenluft, E., Santiago, N., & Haxby, J. V. (2004). Social and emotional attachment in the neural representation of faces. Neuroimage, 22(4), 1628-1635.

Godfrey, A., Leonard, M., Donnelly, S., Conroy, M., ÓLaighin, G., & Meagher, D. (2010). Validating a new clinical subtyping scheme for delirium with electronic motion analysis. Psychiatry research, 178(1), 186-190.

Goelitz, A. (2007). Exploring dream work at end of life. Dreaming, 17(3), 159.

Goldstone, S. (1967). The human clock: A framework for the study of health and deviant time perception. Ann NY Acad Sci 138: 767- 783.

Golinger, R. C., & Tune, L. E. (1987). Association of Elevated Plasma Anticholinergic Activity. Am J Psychiatry, 144, 1218-1220.

Goodwyn, E. (2013). Recurrent motifs as resonant attractor states in the narrative field: a testable model of archetype. Journal of Analytical Psychology, 58(3), 387-408.

Goodwyn, E. D. (2012). The Neurobiology of the Gods: How Brain Physiology Shapes the Recurrent Imagery of Myth and Dreams. Taylor & Francis.

Gottesmann, C. (2002). The neurochemistry of waking and sleeping mental activity: The disinhibition-dopamine hypothesis. Psychiatry and Clinical Neurosciences, 56(4), 345-354.

Gottesmann, C. (2006). The dreaming sleep stage: a new neurobiological model of schizophrenia?. Neuroscience, 140(4), 1105-1115.

Gottfried, J. A., & Haber, S. N. (2011). Neuroanatomy of Reward: A View from the Ventral Striatum.

Gotthelf, A. (2012). Teleology, First Principles, and Scientific Method in Aristotle's Biology. Oxford University Press.

Graham, T. F. (1967). Medieval minds: mental health in the middle ages. Allen & Unwin.

Granberg, A., Bergborn Engberg, I., & Lundberg, D. (1999). Acute confusion and unreal experiences in intensive care patients in relation to the ICU syndrome. Part II. Intensive and Critical Care Nursing, 15(1), 19-33.

Granberg, A., Engberg, I. B., & Lundberg, D. (1998). Patients' experience of being critically ill or severely injured and cared for in an intensive care unit in relation to the ICU syndrome. Part I. Intensive and Critical Care Nursing, 14(6), 294-307.

Granda-Cameron, C., & Houldin, A. (2012). Concept analysis of good death in terminally ill patients. American Journal of Hospice and Palliative Medicine, 29(8), 632-639.

Greenberg, R. & Pearlman, C. (1967). Delirium tremens and dreaming. Am J Psychiatry; 124: 133–142.

Greenberg, R., Pearlman, C. A., & Gampel, D. (1972). War neuroses and the adaptive function of REM sleep. British Journal of Medical Psychology, 45(1), 27-33.

Gregoriou, G. G., Gotts, S. J., Zhou, H., & Desimone, R. (2009). High-frequency, long-range coupling between prefrontal and visual cortex during attention. Science, 324(5931), 1207-1210.

Greicius, M. D., Supekar, K., Menon, V., & Dougherty, R. F. (2009). Resting-state functional connectivity reflects structural connectivity in the default mode network. Cerebral cortex, 19(1), 72-78.

Greiner, G. F. C. (1817). Der Traum und das fi eberhafte Irreseyn. Ein physiologisch-psychologischer Versuch (Altenburg und Leipzig: F. A. Brockhaus).

Grigoleit, J.S., Kullmann, J.S., Wolf, O.T., Hammes, F., Wegner, A., Jablonowski, S., Engler, H., Gizewski, E., Oberbeck, R., Schedlowski, M., (2011). Dose-dependent effects of endotoxin on neurobehavioral functions in humans. PLoS ONE 6, e28330.

Grigoleit, J.S., Oberbeck, J.R., Lichte, P., Kobbe, P., Wolf, O.T., Montag, T., del Rey, A., Gizewski, E.R., Engler, H., Schedlowski, M., (2010). Lipopolysaccharide-induced experimental immune activation does not impair memory functions in humans. Neurobiol. Learn. Mem. 94, 561–567.

Grill-Spector, K., Henson, R., & Martin, A. (2006). Repetition and the brain: neural models of stimulus-specific effects. Trends in cognitive sciences, 10(1), 14-23.

Grima, B., Chélot, E., Xia, R., & Rouyer, F. (2004). Morning and evening peaks of activity rely on different clock neurons of the Drosophila brain. Nature, 431(7010), 869-873.

Gritton, H. J., Sutton, B. C., Martinez, V., Sarter, M., & Lee, T. M. (2009). Interactions between cognition and circadian rhythms: attentional demands modify circadian entrainment. Behavioral neuroscience, 123(5), 937.

Grover, S., & Shah, R. (2011). Distress due to delirium experience. General hospital psychiatry, 33(6), 637-639.

Grover, S., Chakrabarti, S., Shah, R. & Kumar, V. (2011). A factor analytic study of the delirium Rating Scale-Revised-98 in untreated patients with delirium. J Psychosom Res; 70:473–478.

Grover, S., Ghosh, A., & Ghormode, D. (2014). Experience in Delirium: Is It Distressing?. The Journal of neuropsychiatry and clinical neurosciences.

Guido, M. E., Garbarino-Pico, E., Contin, M. A., Valdez, D. J., Nieto, P. S., Verra, D. M., Acosta-Rodriguez,V.A., De Zavalia,N. & Rosenstein, R. E. (2010). Inner retinal circadian clocks and non-visual photoreceptors: novel players in the circadian system. Progress in neurobiology, 92(4), 484-504.

Gunther, M. L., Jackson, J. C., & Wesley Ely, E. (2007). Loss of IQ in the ICU brain injury without the insult. Medical hypotheses, 69(6), 1179-1182.

Gupta, N., de Jonghe, J., Schieveld, J., Leonard, M., & Meagher, D. (2008). Delirium phenomenology: what can we learn from the symptoms of delirium?. Journal of psychosomatic research, 65(3), 215-222.

Gurney, E., Myers, F.W.H. & Podmore, F. (1886). Phantasms of the Living. London: Rooms of the Society for Psychical Research, Tru¨bner and Company.

Gusnard, D. A., & Raichle, M. E. (2001). Searching for a baseline: functional imaging and the resting human brain. Nature Reviews Neuroscience, 2(10), 685-694.

Guzman-Marin, R., Ying, Z., Suntsova, N., Methippara, M., Bashir, T., Szymusiak, R., Gomez-Pinilla, F. & McGinty, D. (2006). Suppression of hippocampal plasticity-related gene expression by sleep deprivation in rats. The Journal of physiology, 575(3), 807-819.7

Haber, S. N. (2011). Neuroanatomy of reward: a view from the ventral striatum. Gottfried JA, editor. Boca Raton (FL): CRC Press.

Hackforth, R. (tr. and ed.). Plato's Phaedrus. Cambridge: Cambridge University Press, 1972 (orig. Vers. 1952).

Hafkenscheid, A., Duncan, B. L., & Miller, S. D. (2010). The outcome and session rating scales. A cross-cultural examination of the psychometric properties of the Dutch translation. Journal of Brief Therapy, 7(1), 1-12.

Haggard, P. & Chambon, V. (2012). Sense of agency. Curr Biol 22: R390–R392.

Haggard, P., & Clark, S. (2003). Intentional action: conscious experience and neural prediction. Consciousness and cognition, 12(4), 695-707.

Haggard, P., Clark, S., & Kalogeras, J. (2002). Voluntary action and conscious awareness. Nature Neuroscience, 5(4), 382–385.

Hagmann, P., Cammoun, L., Gigandet, X., Meuli, R., Honey, C. J., Wedeen, V. J., & Sporns, O. (2008). Mapping the structural core of human cerebral cortex. PLoS biology, 6(7), e159.

Halberg, F. (1958). [Physiologic 24-hour periodicity; general and procedural considerations with reference to the adrenal cycle]. Internationale Zeitschrift fur Vitaminforschung. Beiheft, 10, 225-296.

Hall, C. S., & Van de Castle, R. L. (1966). The content analysis of dreams. East Norwalk, CT, US: Appleton-Century-Crofts. (1966). xiv 320 pp.

Hall, R. J., Ferguson, K. J., Andrews, M., Green, A. J., White, T. O., Armstrong, I. R., & MacLullich, A. M. (2013). Delirium and cerebrospinal fluid S100B in hip fracture patients: a preliminary study. The American Journal of Geriatric Psychiatry, 21(12), 1239-1243.

Hall, R. J., Meagher, D. J., & MacLullich, A. M. (2012). Delirium detection and monitoring outside the ICU. Best Practice & Research Clinical Anaesthesiology, 26(3), 367-383.

Hall, R. J., Shenkin, S. D., & MacLullich, A. M. (2011). A systematic literature review of cerebrospinal fluid biomarkers in delirium. Dementia and geriatric cognitive disorders, 32(2), 79-93.

Hall, T.S. (1975). History of general physiology. 600 B.C. to A.D. 1900. From pre-socratic times to the enlightenment, vol. 1. London: The University of Chicago Press.

Hallanger, A. & Wainer, B.H. (1988). Ascending projections from the pedunculopontine tegmental nucleus and the adjacent mesopontine tegmentum in the rat. J Comp Neurol 274:483-5 15.

Hampe, B., & Grady, J. E. (2005). From perception to meaning: Image schemas in cognitive linguistics (Vol. 29). Walter de Gruyter.

Hampel, H. (2013). Amyloid-β and cognition in aging and Alzheimer's disease: molecular and neurophysiological mechanisms. Journal of Alzheimer's Disease, 33, S79-S86.

Han, V. Z., & Shi, J. H. (2013). [Current understanding of sleep, dreaming and related memory consolidation]. Sheng li ke xue jin zhan [Progress in physiology], 44(6), 409-414.

Hanania, M., & Kitain, E. (2002). Melatonin for treatment and prevention of postoperative delirium. Anesthesia & Analgesia, 94(2), 338-339.

Hannibal, J., Ding, J. M., Chen, D., Fahrenkrug, J., Larsen, P. J., Gillette, M. U., & Mikkelsen, J. D. (1997). Pituitary adenylate cyclase-activating peptide (PACAP) in the retinohypothalamic tract: a potential daytime regulator of the biological clock. The Journal of neuroscience, 17(7), 2637-2644.

Haque, Amber (2004), "Psychology from Islamic Perspective: Contributions of Early Muslim Scholars and Challenges to Contemporary Muslim Psychologists", Journal of Religion and Health 43 (4): 357–377

Harrington, D. L., Liu, D., Smith, M. M., Mills, J. A., Long, J. D., Aylward, E. H., & Paulsen, J. S. (2014). Neuroanatomical correlates of cognitive functioning in prodromal Huntington disease. Brain and behavior, 4(1), 29-40.

Harris, G. C., & Aston-Jones, G. (2006). Arousal and reward: a dichotomy in orexin function. Trends in neurosciences, 29(10), 571-577.

Harris-McCoy D. E. (2012). Artemidorus' Oneirocritica: Text, Translation, and Commentary. New York, NY: Oxford University Press.

Harrison, N. A., Brydon, L., Walker, C., Gray, M. A., Steptoe, A., & Critchley, H. D. (2009a). Inflammation causes mood changes through alterations in subgenual cingulate activity and mesolimbic connectivity. Biological psychiatry, 66(5), 407-414.

Harrison, N. A., Brydon, L., Walker, C., Gray, M. A., Steptoe, A., Dolan, R. J., & Critchley, H. D. (2009b). Neural origins of human sickness in interoceptive responses to inflammation. Biological psychiatry, 66(5), 415-422.

Hart, B.L., (1988). Biological basis of the behavior of sick animals. Neurosci. Biobehav. Rev. 12, 123–137.

Hartmann, E. (1984). The nightmare: the psychology and biology of terrifying dreams. Basic Books.New York

Hartmann, E. (1995). Making connections in a safe place: Is dreaming psychotherapy?. Dreaming, 5(4), 213.

Hartmann, E. (1996). Outline for a theory on the nature and functions of dreaming. Dreaming, 6(2), 147.

Hartmann, E. (1998). Dreams and nightmares: The new theory on the origin and meaning of dreams. Plenum Trade.

Hartmann, E. (1998a). Nightmare after trauma as paradigm for all dreams: A new approach to the nature and functions of dreaming. Psychiatry: Interpersonal and Biological Processes.

Hartmann, E. (1998b). Dreams and nightmares: The new theory on the origin and meaning of dreams. Plenum Trade.

Hartmann, E. (2007). The nature and functions of dreaming. The New Science of Dreaming: Content, Recall and Personality Correlates, 171-192.

Hartmann, E. (2011). The nature and functions of dreaming. New York: Oxford University Press.

Hartmann, E., & Kunzendorf, R. G. (2006). The Central image (CI) in recent dreams, dreams that stand out, and earliest dreams: relationship to boundaries. Imagination, Cognition and Personality, 25(4), 383-392.

Hartmann, E., Elkin, R., & Garg, M. (1991). Personality and dreaming: The dreams of people with very thick or very thin boundaries. Dreaming, 1(4), 311.

Hartmann, E., Kunzendorf, R., Rosen, R., & Grace, N. G. (2001). Contextualizing images in dreams and daydreams. Dreaming, 11(2), 97-104.

Hartmann, E., Rosen, R., & Grace, N. (1998). Contextualizing images in dreams: more frequent and more intense after trauma. Sleep S, 21, 284.

Hartmann, E., Zborowski, M., & Kunzendorf, R. (2001a). The emotion pictured by a dream: An examination of emotions contextualized in dreams. Sleep and Hypnosis.

Hartmann, E., Zborowski, M., Rosen, R., & Grace, N. (2001b). Contextualizing images in dreams: More intense after abuse and trauma. Dreaming, 11(3), 115.

Hassani, O. K., Lee, M. G., & Jones, B. E. (2009). Melanin-concentrating hormone neurons discharge in a reciprocal manner to orexin neurons across the sleep–wake cycle. Proceedings of the National Academy of Sciences, 106(7), 2418-2422.

Hastings, M. H., & Herzog, E. D. (2004). Clock genes, oscillators, and cellular networks in the suprachiasmatic nuclei. Journal of biological rhythms, 19(5), 400-413.

Hastings, M. H., Reddy, A. B., Garabette, M., King, V. M., Chahad-Ehlers, S., O'Brien, J., & Maywood, E. S. (2004, June). Expression of clock gene products in the suprachiasmatic nucleus in relation to circadian behaviour. In Novartis Found Symp (Vol. 253, pp. 203-217).

Haule, J. (2011). Jung in the 21st century, volume one: Evolution and archetype.

Haus, E., & Smolensky, M. (2006). Biological clocks and shift work: circadian dysregulation and potential long-term effects. Cancer Causes Control, 17(4), 489-500.

Hauser, M. D., Chomsky, N., & Fitch, W. T. (2002). The faculty of language: What is it, who has it, and how did it evolve?. science, 298(5598), 1569-1579.

Hauser, M. D., Yang, C., Berwick, R. C., Tattersall, I., Ryan, M. J., Watumull, J., ... & Lewontin, R. C. (2014). The mystery of language evolution. Frontiers in psychology, 5.

Havens, R. A., & Walters, C. (2002). Hypnotherapy scripts: A neo-Ericksonian approach to persuasive healing. Psychology Press.

Haynes, S. N., & Mooney, D. K. (1975). Nightmares: Etiological, theoretical, and behavioral treatment considerations. Psychological Record, 25, 225– 236.

Hébert, S. S., Horré, K., Nicolaï, L., Papadopoulou, A. S., Mandemakers, W., Silahtaroglu, A. N., ... & De Strooper, B. (2008). Loss of microRNA cluster miR-29a/b-1 in sporadic Alzheimer's disease correlates with increased BACE1/β-secretase expression. Proceedings of the National Academy of Sciences, 105(17), 6415-6420.

Hedges, C. (2002). War is a force that gives us meaning. Random House LLC.

Hedreen, J. C., Struble, R. G., Whitehouse, P. J., & Price, D. L. (1984). Topography of the magnocellular basal forebrain system in human brain. Journal of Neuropathology & Experimental Neurology, 43(1), 1-21.

Heilman, M. K. M., & Valenstein, E. (Eds.). (2011). Clinical neuropsychology. Oxford University Press.

Hein, A. M., Stutzman, D. L., Bland, S. T., Barrientos, R. M., Watkins, L. R., Rudy, J. W. & Maier, S. F. (2007). Prostaglandins are necessary and sufficient to induce contextual fear learning impairments after interleukin-1 beta injections into the dorsal hippocampus. Neuroscience 150, 754–763.

Hein, C., Forgues, A., Piau, A., Sommet, A., Vellas, B., & Nourhashémi, F. (2014). Impact of polypharmacy on occurrence of delirium in elderly emergency patients. Journal of the American Medical Directors Association, 15(11), 850-e11.

Heiss, W. D., Kessler, J., Slansky, I., Mielke, R., Szelies, B., & Herholz, K. (1993). Activation PET as an Instrument to Determine Therapeutic Efficacy in Alzheimer's Diseasea. Annals of the New York Academy of Sciences, 695(1), 327-331.

Heller, S. S., Frank, K. A., Malm, J. R., Bowman Jr, F. O., Harris, P. D., Charlton, M. H., & Kornfeld, D. S. (1970). Psychiatric complications of open-heart surgery: a re-examination. New England Journal of Medicine, 283(19), 1015-1020.

Henke, K. (2010). A model for memory systems based on processing modes rather than consciousness. Nature Reviews Neuroscience, 11, 523–532.

Herodotus (1998). History. (trans. D. Grene.) Chicago: University Press.

Herzog, E.D. & Muglia, L. J. (2006). You are when you eat. Nat. Neurosci. 9:300–302.

Heun, R., Ahokas, A., Boyer, P., Giménez-Montesinos, N., Pontes-Soares, F., & Olivier, V. (2013). The efficacy of agomelatine in elderly patients with recurrent major depressive disorder: a placebo-controlled study. The Journal of clinical psychiatry, 74(6), 587-594.

Heynick, F. (1983). Theoretical and empirical investigation into verbal aspects of the Freudian model of dream generation (M.D.). University of Groningen, Groningen.

Hilker, R., Schweitzer, K., Coburger, S., Ghaemi, M., Weisenbach, S., Jacobs, A. H., ... & Heiss, W. D. (2005). Nonlinear progression of Parkinson disease as determined by serial positron emission tomographic imaging of striatal fluorodopa F 18 activity. Archives of neurology, 62(3), 378-382.

Hirayama J, Saurabh S, Grimaldi B, Tamaru T, Takamatsu K, Yasukaza N, Sassone-Corsi P. (2007). Clock-mediated acetylation of Bmal1 controls circadian function. Nature 450:1086–1091.

Hirni, D. I., Kivisaari, S. L., Monsch, A. U., & Taylor, K. I. (2013). Distinct neuroanatomical bases of episodic and semantic memory performance in Alzheimer's disease. Neuropsychologia, 51(5), 930-937.

Hirshkowitz, M., & Sharafkhaneh, A. (2005). The physiology of sleep. Guilleminault C. Clinical neurophysiology of sleep disorder. Handbook of clinical neurophysiology, 6, 3-20.

Hoagland, H. (1933). The psychological control of judgement of duration: evidence for a chemical clock. J Gen Psychology: 9: 267-287.

Hoagland, H. (1966). Some biochemical considerations of time. In The Voices of Time. Ed. By J.T. Fraser, New York, George Braziller pp 312-329.

Hobson, A. (2004). A model for madness?. Nature, 430(6995), 21-21.

Hobson, A. (2009). The neurobiology of consciousness: lucid dreaming wakes up. International Journal of Dream Research, 2(2), 41-44.

Hobson, A., & Voss, U. (2011). A mind to go out of: Reflections on primary and secondary consciousness. Consciousness and cognition, 20(4), 993-997.

Hobson, A., Hong, C. C. H., & Friston, K. (2014). Virtual reality in waking and dreaming consciousness. Cognitive Science, 0.

Hobson, J. A. (1997). Dreaming as delirium: a mental status analysis of our nightly madness. In Seminars in Neurology (Vol. 17, No. 02, pp. 121-128). © 1997 by Thieme Medical Publishers, Inc..

Hobson, J. A. (2009). REM sleep and dreaming: towards a theory of protoconsciousness. Nature Reviews Neuroscience, 10(11), 803-813.

Hobson, J. A. (2014). Introduction. In Dream Consciousness (pp. 3-7). Springer International Publishing.

Hobson, J. A., & Friston, K. J. (2012). Waking and dreaming consciousness: Neurobiological and functional considerations. Progress in neurobiology, 98(1), 82-98.

Hobson, J. A., & Pace-Schott, E. F. (2002). The cognitive neuroscience of sleep: neuronal systems, consciousness and learning. Nature Reviews Neuroscience, 3(9), 679-693.

Hobson, J. A., McCarley, R. W., & Wyzinski, P. W. (1975). Sleep cycle oscillation: reciprocal discharge by two brainstem neuronal groups. Science, 189(4196), 55-58.

Hobson, J. A., Pace-Schott, E. F., & Stickgold, R. (2000). Dreaming and the brain: toward a cognitive neuroscience of conscious states. Behavioral and brain sciences, 23(06), 793-842.

Hobson, J. A., Stickgold, R., & Pace-Schott, E. F. (1998). The neuropsychology of REM sleep dreaming. Neuroreport, 9(3), R1-R14.

Hobson, J.A. & Voss, U. (2011). A mind to go out of: Reflections on primary and secondary consciousness. Consciousness and Cognition 20 (2011) 993–997.

Hobson, J.A. (1999). Dreaming as Delirium: How the Brain Goes Out of Its Mind. MIT Press.

Hobson, J.A., & Robert, M. (1977). The brain as a dream state generator: an activation-synthesis hypothesis of the dream process. Am J Psychiatry, 134(12).

Hof, P. R., & Morrison, J. H. (2004). The aging brain: morphomolecular senescence of cortical circuits. Trends in neurosciences, 27(10), 607-613.

Hofle, N., Paus, T., Reutens, D., Fiset, P., Gotman, J., Evans, A. C., & Jones, B. E. (1997). Regional cerebral blood flow changes as a function of delta and spindle activity during slow wave sleep in humans. The Journal of Neuroscience, 17(12), 4800-4808.

Hofman, M. A., & Swaab, D. F. (2006). Living by the clock: the circadian pacemaker in older people. Ageing research reviews, 5(1), 33-51.

Hogan, R. E. and Kaiboriboon, K. (2003) The "dreamy state": John Hughlings-Jackson's ideas of epilepsy and consciousness. American Journal of Psychiatry, 160, 1740–7.

Hogenson, G. B. (2001). The Baldwin effect: a neglected influence on CG Jung's evolutionary thinking. Journal of Analytical Psychology, 46(4), 591-611.

Hogenson, G.B. (2004). 'Archetypes: emergence and the psyche's deep structure'. In Analytical Psychology: Contemporary Perspectives in Jungian Analysis, eds. J. Cambray & L. Carter. New York: Brunner-Routledge.

Hogenson, G. B. (2009). 'Archetypes as action patterns'. Journal of Analytical Psychology, 54, 3, 325–37.

Honma, S., & Honma, K. I. (2003).The biological clock: Ca2+ links the pendulum to the hands. Trends Neurosci, 26, 650-3.

Hoppál, Mihály (1987). Shamanism: An Archaic and/or Recent System of Beliefs. Nicholson, Shirley, "Shamanism", Quest Books; 1st edition

Horwitz, A. R. (2012). The origins of the molecular era of adhesion research. Nature Reviews Molecular Cell Biology, 13(12), 805-811.

Hosie, A., Davidson, P. M., Agar, M., Sanderson, C. R., & Phillips, J. (2013). Delirium prevalence, incidence, and implications for screening in specialist palliative care inpatient settings: a systematic review. Palliative medicine, 27(6), 486-498.

Houran, J. & Lange, R. (1997). Hallucinations that comfort: Contextual mediation of deathbed visions. Percept Mot Skills;84: 1491–1504.

Hu, K., Scheer, F. A., Ivanov, P. C., Buijs, R. M., & Shea, S. A. (2007). The suprachiasmatic nucleus functions beyond circadian rhythm generation. Neuroscience, 149(3), 508-517.

Huang, M. C., Lee, C. H., Lai, Y. C., Kao, Y. F., Lin, H. Y., & Chen, C. H. (2009). Chinese version of the Delirium Rating Scale-Revised-98: reliability and validity. Comprehensive psychiatry, 50(1), 81-85.

Huang, Y., & Mucke, L. (2012). Alzheimer mechanisms and therapeutic strategies. Cell, 148(6), 1204-1222.

Hubble, M. A., Duncan, B. L., & Miller, S. D. (1999). Introduction. American Psychological Association.

Hunter, R. M. & Macalpine, I. (eds) (1963). Three Hundred Years of Psychiatry, 1535–1860. A History Presented in Selected English Texts (London: Oxford University Press).

Hurley, K. M., Herbert, H., Moga, M. M., & Saper, C. B. (1991). Efferent projections of the infralimbic cortex of the rat. Journal of Comparative Neurology, 308(2), 249-276.

Hurley, L. M., Devilbiss, D. M., & Waterhouse, B. D. (2004). A matter of focus: monoaminergic modulation of stimulus coding in mammalian sensory networks. Current opinion in neurobiology, 14(4), 488-495.

Imel, Z., & Wampold, B. (2008). The importance of treatment and the science of common factors in psychotherapy. Handbook of counseling psychology, 249-262.

Inagaki, T.K., Muscatell, K.A., Irwin, M.R., Cole, S.W. & Eisenberger, N.I., (2012). Inflammation selectively enhances amygdala activity to socially threatening images. Neuroimage 59, 3222–3226.

Innouye, S. K., Dyck, C. H. V., Alessi, C. A., Balkin, S., Siegal, A. P., & Horwitz, R. I. (1990). Clarifying confusion: the confusion assessment method. Ann Intern Med, 113, 941-948.

Inouye, S. K. (2006). Delirium in older persons. New England Journal of Medicine, 354(11), 1157-1165.

Inouye, S. K., & Charpentier, P. A. (1996). Precipitating factors for delirium in hospitalized elderly persons: predictive model and interrelationship with baseline vulnerability. Jama, 275(11), 852-857.

Inouye, S. K., Bogardus Jr, S. T., Charpentier, P. A., Leo-Summers, L., Acampora, D., Holford, T. R., & Cooney Jr, L. M. (1999). A multicomponent intervention to prevent delirium in hospitalized older patients. New England journal of medicine, 340(9), 669-676.

Inouye, S. K., Westendorp, R. G., & Saczynski, J. S. (2014). Delirium in elderly people. The Lancet, 383(9920), 911-922.

Iranzo, A., Santamaria, J., & Tolosa, E. (2009). The clinical and pathophysiological relevance of REM sleep behavior disorder in neurodegenerative diseases. Sleep medicine reviews, 13(6), 385-401.

Iranzo, A., Santamaria, J., Rye, D. B., Valldeoriola, F., Marti, M. J., Munoz, E., Vilaseca, I. & Tolosa, E. (2005). Characteristics of idiopathic REM sleep behavior disorder and that associated with MSA and PD. Neurology, 65(2), 247-252.

Itoi, K., & Sugimoto, N. (2010). The brainstem noradrenergic systems in stress, anxiety and depression. Journal of neuroendocrinology, 22(5), 355-361.

Ivanov, P. C., Hu, K., Hilton, M. F., Shea, S. A., & Stanley, H. E. (2007). Endogenous circadian rhythm in human motor activity uncoupled from circadian influences on cardiac dynamics. Proceedings of the National Academy of Sciences, 104(52), 20702-20707.

Iwashyna, T.J., Ely, E.W., Smith, D.M. & Langa, K.M. (2010). Long-term cognitive impairment and functional disability among survivors of severe sepsis. JAMA 304, 1787–1794.

Izuma, K., Saito, D. N., & Sadato, N. (2008). Processing of social and monetary rewards in the human striatum. Neuron, 58(2), 284-294.

Izuma, K., Saito, D. N., & Sadato, N. (2010). The roles of the medial prefrontal cortex and striatum in reputation processing. Social neuroscience, 5(2), 133-147.

Jaccard, R. (1975). L'exil interieure. Paris: PUF. James, R. (1745) A Medicinal Dictionary; including Physic, Surgery, Anatomy, Chymistry, and Botany, in all their Branches Relative to Medicine. Together with a History of Drugs. and an Introductory

Preface, Tracing the Progress of Physic, and Explaining the Theories which have. Prevail'd in all Ages (London: T. Osborne).

Jack Jr, C. R., Knopman, D. S., Jagust, W. J., Petersen, R. C., Weiner, M. W., Aisen, P. S., ... & Trojanowski, J. Q. (2013). Tracking pathophysiological processes in Alzheimer's disease: an updated hypothetical model of dynamic biomarkers. The Lancet Neurology, 12(2), 207-216.

Jackendoff, R. (2002). Foundations of language: Brain, meaning, grammar, evolution. Oxford University Press.

Jackson, J. C., Pandharipande, P. P., Girard, T. D., Brummel, N. E., Thompson, J. L., Hughes, C. G., Pun, P.T. & Ely, E. (2014). Depression, post-traumatic stress disorder, and functional disability in survivors of critical illness in the BRAIN-ICU study: a longitudinal cohort study. The Lancet Respiratory Medicine, 2(5), 369-379.

Jacobi, J., Fraser, G. L., Coursin, D. B., Riker, R. R., Fontaine, D., Wittbrodt, E. T., Donald B. Chalfin ... & Lumb, P. D. (2002). Clinical practice guidelines for the sustained use of sedatives and analgesics in the critically ill adult. Critical care medicine, 30(1), 119-141.

Jacobs, M. (2010). Psychodynamic Counselling in Action, 4th edn, Sage, London.

Jacobsen, A. M., Beardslee, W., Hauser, S. T., Noam, G. G., Powers, S. I., Houlihan, J. & Rider, E. (1986). Evaluating ego defense mechanisms using clinical interviews: an empirical study of adolescent diabetic and psychiatric patients. J Adolesc, 9:303-319.

Jacobson, L., & Sapolsky, R. (1991). The Role of the Hippocampus in Feedback Regulation of the Hypothalamic-Pituitary-Adrenocortical Axis*. Endocrine reviews, 12(2), 118-134.

Jacobson, S. & Jerrier, H. (2000). EEG in delirium. Sem Clin Neuropsychiatry;5: 86–92.

Jacobson, S. A., Dwyer, P. C., Machan, J. T., & Carskadon, M. A. (2008). Quantitative analysis of rest-activity patterns in elderly postoperative patients with delirium: support for a theory of pathologic wakefulness. Journal of clinical sleep medicine: JCSM: official publication of the American Academy of Sleep Medicine, 4(2), 137.

Jaeggi, S. M., Studer-Luethi, B., Buschkuehl, M., Su, Y. F., Jonides, J., & Perrig, W. J. (2010). The relationship between n-back performance and matrix reasoning—implications for training and transfer. Intelligence, 38(6), 625-635.

Jagota, A., Horacio, O., & Schwartz, W. J. (2000). Morning and evening circadian oscillations in the suprachiasmatic nucleus in vitro. Nature neuroscience, 3(4), 372-376.

James, I. A., Reichelt, F. K., Freeston, M. H., & Barton, S. B. (2007). Schemas as memories: Implications for treatment. Journal of Cognitive Psychotherapy, 21(1), 51-57.

James, W. (1890). The Principles of Psychology, 2 vols. (1890) Dover Publications (1950).

Jan, J. & O'Donnell, M. (1996). Use of melatonin in the treatment of paediatric sleep disorders. J Pineal Res; 21:193–9.

Jansson, A., Olin, K., Yoshitake, T., Hagman, B., Herrington, M. K., Kehr, J., & Permert, J. (2004). Effects of isoflurane on prefrontal acetylcholine release and hypothalamic Fos response in young adult and aged rats. Experimental neurology, 190(2), 535-543.

Javedan, H., & Tulebaev, S. (2014). Management of Common Postoperative Complications: Delirium. Clinics in geriatric medicine, 30(2), 271-278.

Jean, L., Bergeron, M. È., Thivierge, S., & Simard, M. (2010). Cognitive intervention programs for individuals with mild cognitive impairment: systematic review of the literature. The American Journal of Geriatric Psychiatry, 18(4), 281-296.

Jewett, M. E., Rimmer, D. W., Duffy, J. F., Klerman, E. B., Kronauer, R. E., & Czeisler, C. A. (1997). Human circadian pacemaker is sensitive to light throughout subjective day without evidence of transients. American Journal of Physiology-Regulatory, Integrative and Comparative Physiology, 273(5), R1800-R1809.

Jicha, G. A., & Rentz, D. M. (2013). Cognitive and brain reserve and the diagnosis and treatment of preclinical Alzheimer disease. Neurology, 80(13), 1180-1181.

Jiménez-Capdeville, M. E., & Dykes, R. W. (1993). Daily changes in the release of acetylcholine from rat primary somatosensory cortex. Brain research, 625(1), 152-158.

Johanson, M., Revonsuo, A., Chaplin, J., & Wedlund, J. E. (2003). Level and contents of consciousness in connection with partial epileptic seizures. Epilepsy & Behavior, 4(3), 279-285.

Johnson, C. H., Stewart, P. L., & Egli, M. (2011). The cyanobacterial circadian system: from biophysics to bioevolution. Annual review of biophysics, 40, 143.

Johnson, M. (1987). The Body in the mind: The bodily basis of meaning, reason and Imagination. Chicago: Chicago University Press.

Johnson, S. (1755 [2003]). Samuel Johnson's Dictionary. Walker & Company.

Jones, B. E. (2003). Arousal systems. Front Biosci, 8(5), 438-451.

Jones, C., Griffiths, R. D., & Humphris, G. (2000). Disturbed memory and amnesia related to intensive care. Memory, 8(2), 79-94.

Jones, C., Griffiths, R. D., Humphris, G., & Skirrow, P. M. (2001). Memory, delusions, and the development of acute posttraumatic stress disorder-related symptoms after intensive care. Critical care medicine, 29(3), 573-580.

Jones, E. (1971[1931]). On the Nightmare. New York: Liveright

Jones, E. (1974[1932]). Beliefs concerning the nightmare. In Psycho-myth, psycho-history, E.Jones, 110-13. New York: Hillstone.

Jones, R. A. (2003). Jung's view on myth and post-modern psychology. Journal of Analytical Psychology, 48(5), 619-628.

Jones, R. N., Fong, T. G., Metzger, E., Tulebaev, S., Yang, F. M., Alsop, D. C., Edward R. Marcantonio, L. Adrienne Cupples, Gary Gottlieb... & Inouye, S. K. (2010). Aging, brain disease, and reserve: implications for delirium. The American Journal of Geriatric Psychiatry, 18(2), 117-127.

Jorm, A. F., & Jolley, D. (1998). The incidence of dementia A meta-analysis. Neurology, 51(3), 728-733.

Jouvet, M., & Delorme, F. (1965). Locus coeruleus et sommeil paradoxal. Comptes Rendus des Seances de la Societe de Biologie et de ses Filiales, 159(4), 895-+.

Jung, C. G. (1904). 'Studies in word association'. Collected Works Vol. 2. Trans R.F.C. Hull, Routledge.

Jung, C. G. (1921/1971). 'Definitions'. CW 6. Trans R.F.C. Hull, Routledge.

Jung, C. G. (1934). The practical use of dream-analysis. Collected works, 16, 139-162. Trans R.F.C. Hull, Routledge.

Jung, C. G. (1945). On the nature of dreams. Collected works, 8, 363-379. Trans R.F.C. Hull, Routledge.

Jung, C. G. (1951). The ego. Aion: Researches into the Phenomenology of the Self, 9(pt 2), 3-7. Trans R.F.C. Hull, Routledge.

Jung, C. G. (1956). Symbols of Transformation. Collected Works, vol. 5, Bollingen Series XX. Pantheon, New York.

Jung, C. G. (1957). The Undiscovered Self (Present and Future). Collected Works Vol. 10. Trans R.F.C. Hull, Routledge.

Jung, C. G. (1959). Collected works. Vol. IX, Pt. I. The archetypes and the collective unconscious.

Jung, C. G. (1974). Dreams. From The collected works of C.G. Jung, vols. 4,8,12,16. Trans. R.F.C. Hull. Princeton: Princeton University Press.

Jung, C. G. (1907). 'Psychophysical researches'. Collected Works Vol. 2. Trans R.F.C. Hull, Routledge.

Jung, C. G. (1907). The psychology of dementia praecox. In: Jung CG, ed. Collected Works Vol. 3—The Psychogenesis of Mental Disease. New York, NY: Nervous and Mental Disease Publ. Co.; 1936. (originally published in 1907). pp. 1–184.

Jurgens, H. A., Amancherla, K. & Johnson, R.W. (2012). Influenza infection induces neuroinflammation, alters hippocampal neuron morphology, and impairs cognition in adult mice. J. Neurosci. 32, 3958–3968.

Karlsson, K. & Blumberg, M. S. (2003). Hippocampal theta in the newborn rat is revealed under conditions that promote REM sleep. J Neurosci, 23, pp. 1114–1118

Kahn, I., Davachi, L., & Wagner, A. D. (2004). Functional-neuroanatomic correlates of recollection: implications for models of recognition memory. The Journal of Neuroscience, 24(17), 4172-4180.

Kain, Z. N., Caldwell-Andrews, A. A., Maranets, I., McClain, B., Gaal, D., Mayes, L. C., ... & Zhang, H. (2004). Preoperative anxiety and emergence delirium and postoperative maladaptive behaviors. Anesthesia & Analgesia, 99(6), 1648-1654.

Kain, Z. N., MacLaren, J. E., Herrmann, L., Mayes, L., Rosenbaum, A., Hata, J., & Lerman, J. (2009). Preoperative melatonin and its effects on induction and emergence in children undergoing anesthesia and surgery. Anesthesiology, 111(1), 44-49.

Kakuma, R., Fort, D., Galbaud, G., Arsenault, L., Perrault, A., Platt, R. W., ... & Wolfson, C. (2003). Delirium in older emergency department patients discharged home: effect on survival. Journal of the American Geriatrics Society, 51(4), 443-450.

Kaldjian, L. C., Curtis, A. E., Shinkunas, L. A., & Cannon, K. T. (2009). Review article: Goals of care toward the end of life: A structured literature review. American Journal of Hospice and Palliative Medicine, 25(6), 501-511.

Káli, S., & Dayan, P. (2004). Off-line replay maintains declarative memories in a model of hippocampal-neocortical interactions. Nature neuroscience, 7(3), 286-294.

Kaneko, T., Takahashi, S., Naka, T., Hirooka, Y., Inoue, Y., & Kaibara, N. (1997). Postoperative delirium following gastrointestinal surgery in elderly patients. Surgery today, 27(2), 107-111.

Kang, J. E., Lim, M. M., Bateman, R. J., Lee, J. J., Smyth, L. P., Cirrito, J. R., Fujiki, N., Nishino, S. & Holtzman, D. M. 2009. Amyloid-beta dynamics are regulated by orexin and the sleep-wake cycle. Science, 326, 1005-7.

Karasek, M. (1999). Melatonin in humans. Where we are 40 years after its discovery. Neuroendocrinol Lett; 20:179–88.

Karasek, M. (2007). Does melatonin play a role in aging processes?. JOURNAL OF PHYSIOLOGY AND PHARMACOLOGY, 58(6), 105-113.

Kato, M., Kishi, Y., Okuyama, T., Trzepacz, P. T., & Hosaka, T. (2010). Japanese version of the Delirium Rating Scale, Revised–98 (DRS-R98–J): reliability and validity. Psychosomatics, 51(5), 425-431.

Kaufmann, C., Wehrle, R., Wetter, T. C., Holsboer, F., Auer, D. P., Pollmächer, T., & Czisch, M. (2006). Brain activation and hypothalamic functional connectivity during human non-rapid eye movement sleep: an EEG/fMRI study. Brain, 129(3), 655-667.

Kean, J., Trzepacz, P. T., Murray, L. L., Abell, M., & Trexler, L. (2010). Initial validation of a brief provisional diagnostic scale for delirium. Brain injury, 24(10), 1222-1230.

Kellehear, A., Pogonet, V., Mindruta-Stratan, R., & Gorelco, V. (2011). Deathbed visions from the Republic of Moldova: A content analysis of family observations. OMEGA--Journal of Death and Dying, 64(4), 303-317.

Kendall, M., Harris, F., Boyd, K., Sheikh, A., Murray, S. A., Brown, D., Mallinson, I., Kearney, N. & Worth, A. (2007). Key challenges and ways forward in researching the "good death": qualitative in-depth interview and focus group study. BMJ, 334(7592), 521.

Kennedy, S. (1994). Melatonin disturbances in anorexia nervosa and bulimia nervosa. International Journal of Eating Disorders, 16(3), 257-265.

Kernberg, O. F. (1967). Borderline personality organization. J. Am. Psychoanal. Assoc.; 15: 641–685.

Kerr, C. W., Donnelly, J. P., Wright, S. T., Kuszczak, S. M., Banas, A., Grant, P. C., & Luczkiewicz, D. L. (2014). End-of-life dreams and visions: a longitudinal study of hospice patients' experiences. Journal of palliative medicine, 17(3), 296-303.

Kessler, B. A., Stanley, E. M., Frederick-Duus, D., & Fadel, J. (2011). Age-related loss of orexin/hypocretin neurons. Neuroscience, 178, 82-88.

Khaldun, I., Rosenthal, F. & Dawood, N. J. (1967), The Muqaddimah, trans., p. 338, Princeton University Press.

Kiely, D. K., Jones, R. N., Bergmann, M. A., & Marcantonio, E. R. (2007). Association between psychomotor activity delirium subtypes and mortality among newly admitted postacute facility patients. The Journals of Gerontology Series A: Biological Sciences and Medical Sciences, 62(2), 174-179.

Kiely, D. K., Marcantonio, E. R., Inouye, S. K., Shaffer, M. L., Bergmann, M. A., Yang, F. M., Fering, M.A. & Jones, R. N. (2009). Persistent delirium predicts greater mortality. Journal of the American Geriatrics Society, 57(1), 55-61.

Killingsworth M. A., Gilbert D. T. (2010). A wandering mind is an unhappy mind. Science 330, 932

Kilroe, P. (1997). Toward a semiotics of dreams. Paper presented at the 22nd annual meeting of the Semiotic Society of America, Louisville, Kentucky.

Kilroe, P. (1998). Freudian artifacts and imprints of imagination: Signification in language and dreaming, presented at the 23rd annual meeting of the Semiotic Society of America, Toronto, October 18, 1998.

Kilroe, P. (1999a). What is a play on words without words? Consider the dream pun. Ms. under review.

Kilroe, P. (1999b). The role of language in dreaming. Paper presented through the University of Louisiana-Lafayette Mind & Matter colloquium series, November 5, 1999.

Kim, K., & Johnson, M. K. (2014). Activity in ventromedial prefrontal cortex during self-related processing: Positive subjective value or personal significance?. Social cognitive and affective neuroscience, nsu078.

Kindi, V., & Arabatzis, T. (Eds.). (2013). Kuhn's the structure of scientific revolutions revisited. Routledge.

Kinsey, A.C., Pomeroy, W.B. & Martin, C.E. (1948). Sexual behaviour in the human male. Philadelphia: W.B. Saunders.

Kirkwood, T. B. (1977). Evolution of ageing. Nature, 270(5635), 301-304.

Kirkwood, T. B. (2002). Evolution of ageing. Mechanisms of ageing and development, 123(7), 737-745.

Kirsch, I. (1997). Suggestibility or hypnosis: What do our scales really measure?. International Journal of Clinical and Experimental Hypnosis, 45(3), 212-225.

Kishi, Y., Kato, M., Okuyama, T., Hosaka, T., Mikami, K., Meller, W., ... & Kathol, R. (2007). Delirium: patient characteristics that predict a missed diagnosis at psychiatric consultation. General hospital psychiatry, 29(5), 442-445.

Kitay, J. I. & Altschule, M. D. (1954). The pineal gland. A review of the physiologic literature. Cambridge: Harvard University Press.

Klein, M. (1973). The Psychoanalysis of Children. Hogarth Press, London.

Kleist, K. (1924). Über die gegenwärtigen Strömungen in der klinischen Psychiatrie. Allgemeine Zeitschrift für Psychiatrie, 81, 389–93.

Kleist, K. (1928). Über cycloide, paranoide und epileptoide Psychosen und über die Frage der Degenerationspsychosen. Schweizer Archiv für Neurologie, Neurochirurgie und Psychiatrie, 23, 3–37.

Klinger, E. (2008). Daydreaming and fantasizing: thought flow and motivation, in Handbook of Imagination and Mental Simulation, eds Markman K. D., Klein W. M. P., Suhr J. A., editors. (New York, NY: Psychology Press; 225–239.

Klinger, E. (2009). Daydreaming and fantasizing: Thought flow and motivation. In K. Markman, W. Klein & J. Suhr (Eds.), Handbook of imagination and mental simulation (pp. 225-239). New York: Psychology Press.

Klinger, E., & Cox, W. M. (1987). Dimensions of thought flow in everyday life. Imagination, Cognition and Personality, 7(2), 105-128.

Kluger, H. Y. (1975). Archetypal dreams and" everyday" dreams: a statistical investigation into Jung's theory of the collective unconscious. Israel Annals of Psychiatry & Related Disciplines.

Knowlton, B. J., & Squire, L. R. (1994). The information acquired during artificial grammar learning. Journal of Experimental Psychology: Learning, Memory, and Cognition, 20(1), 79.

Knowlton, B. J., Mangels, J. A., & Squire, L. R. (1996). A neostriatal habit learning system in humans. Science, 273, 1399–1402.

Knox, J. (2003). Archetype, Attachment, Analysis. London: Routledge.

Knox, J. (2004). From archetypes to reflective function. Journal of Analytical Psychology, 49(1), 1-19.

Knox, J. (2009). Mirror neurons and embodied simulation in the development of archetypes and self-agency. Journal of Analytical Psychology, 54(3), 307-323.

Knox, J. (2010). Responses to Erik Goodwyn's 'Approaching archetypes: reconsidering innateness'. Journal of Analytical Psychology, 55(4), 522-533.

Knox, J. (2013). The Mind in Fragments: The Neuroscientific, Developmental, and Traumatic Roots of Dissociation and Their Implications for Clinical Practice. Psychoanalytic Inquiry, 33(5), 449-466.

Knox, J. (1997). 'Internal objects: a theoretical analysis of Jungian and Kleinian models'. Journal of Analytical Psychology, 42, 4,653–66.

Knutsson, A. (2003). Health disorders of shift workers. Occup Med (Lond), 53(2), 103-108.

Kocsis, B., Varga, V., Dahan, L., & Sik, A. (2006). Serotonergic neuron diversity: identification of raphe neurons with discharges time-locked to the hippocampal theta rhythm. Proceedings of the National Academy of Sciences of the United States of America, 103(4), 1059-1064.

Koehler, R., Wilhelm, E. & Shoulson, I. (2011). Cognitive Rehabilitation Therapy for Traumatic Brain Injury Cognitive Rehabilitation Therapy for Traumatic Brain Injury: Evaluating the Evidence. Washington, DC: The National Academies Press.

Koepping, K. P. (1983). Adolf Bastian and the psychic unity of mankind. Adolf Bastian and the Psychic Unity of Mankind.

Kohen, D. P., & Olness, K. (2012). Hypnosis and hypnotherapy with children. Routledge.

Köhler, S., Moscovitch, M., Winocur, G., Houle, S., & McIntosh, A. R. (1998). Networks of domain-specific and general regions involved in episodic memory for spatial location and object identity. Neuropsychologia, 36(2), 129-142.

Kohut, H. (2013). The analysis of the self: A systematic approach to the psychoanalytic treatment of narcissistic personality disorders. University of Chicago Press.

Kojima, T., Shimazono, Y., Ichise, K., Atsumi, Y., Ando, H. & Ando, K. (1981). Eye movement as an indicator of brain function. Fol Psychiatr Neurol; 35: 425–436.

Kolanowski, A. M., Fick, D. M., Yevchak, M. A. M., Hill, M. N. L., Mulhall, M. P. M., & McDowell, M. J. A. (2012). Pay Attention!: The Critical Importance of Assessing Attention in Older Adults with Dementia. Journal of gerontological nursing, 38(11), 23.

Koltai, D. C., Welsh-Bohmer, K. A. & Smechel, D. E. (2001). Influence of anosognosia on treatment outcome among dementia patients. Neuropsychol Rehabil, 11:455-475.

Korczak, A. L., D'Almeida, V. and Pedrazzoli, M. (2005). Association of the length polymorphism in the human Per3 gene with the delayed sleep-phase syndrome: does latitude have an influence upon it. Sleep, 28(1), 29-32.

Kordasiewicz, H. B., Stanek, L. M., Wancewicz, E. V., Mazur, C., McAlonis, M. M., Pytel, K. A., ... & Cleveland, D. W. (2012). Sustained therapeutic reversal of Huntington's disease by transient repression of huntingtin synthesis. Neuron, 74(6), 1031-1044.

Korkmaz, A., Topal, T., Tan, D. X., & Reiter, R. J. (2009). Role of melatonin in metabolic regulation. Reviews in endocrine and metabolic disorders, 10(4), 261-270.

Koster, S., Hensens, A. G., Schuurmans, M. J., & van der Palen, J. (2012). Consequences of delirium after cardiac operations. The Annals of thoracic surgery, 93(3), 705-711.

Kotz, C. M., Mullett, M. A., & Wang, C. (2005). Diminished feeding responsiveness to orexin A (hypocretin 1) in aged rats is accompanied by decreased neuronal activation. American Journal of Physiology-Regulatory, Integrative and Comparative Physiology, 289(2), R359-R366.

Kraepelin, E. (1893). Psychiatrie. Ein kurzes Lehrbuch für Studirende und Aerzte. 4., vollständig

Kraepelin, E. (1896). Psychiatrie. Ein Lehrbuch für Studirende und Aerzte. 5., vollständig umgearbeitete Auflage (Leipzig: Barth).

Kraepelin, E. (1899). Psychiatrie. Ein Lehrbuch für Studirende und Aerzte. 6., vollständig umgearbeitete Auflage (Leipzig: Barth).

Kraepelin, E. (1904). Psychiatrie. Ein Lehrbuch für Studirende und Aerzte. 7, vielfach umgearbeitete Auflage (Leipzig: Barth).

Kraepelin, E. (1913). Psychiatrie. Ein Lehrbuch für Studierende und Ärzte. 8. Auflage, Band III, II. Teil (Leipzig: Barth).

Kraepelin, E. (1920). Die Erscheinungsformen des Irrescins. Zeitschrift für die gesamte Neurologie und Psychiatrie, 62, 1–29.

Kraft, S., Puschner, B., Lambert, M. J., & Kordy, H. (2006). Medical utilization and treatment outcome in mid-and long-term outpatient psychotherapy. Psychotherapy Research, 16(02), 241-249.

Kramer, H. & Sprenger, J.(1970[1486]). Malleus maleficarum (trans. M. Summers). (Second edition). New York: Benjamin Blom.

Kramer, M. (1993). The selective mood regulatory function of dreaming: An update and revision.

Kramer, M. (2006). The dream experience: a systematic exploration. Routledge.

Kramer, M., Kinney, L., & Scharf, M. (1983). Sex differences in dreams. Psychiatric Journal of the University of Ottawa.

Kramer, M., Roth, T., & Trinder, J. (1975). Dreams and dementia: A laboratory exploration of dream recall and dream content in chronic brain syndrome patients. The International Journal of Aging and Human Development, 6(2), 169-178.

Kripke, D. F., Youngstedt, S. D., Elliott, J. A., Tuunainen, A., Rex, K. M., Hauger, R. L., & Marler, M. R. (2005). Circadian Phase in Adults of Contrasting Ages*. Chronobiology international, 22(4), 695-709.

Krol, J., Loedige, I., & Filipowicz, W. (2010). The widespread regulation of microRNA biogenesis, function and decay. Nature Reviews Genetics, 11(9), 597-610.

Krueger, J. M., Fang, J., Taishi, P., Chen, Z., Kushikata, T., & Gardi, J. (1998). Sleep: A Physiologic Role for IL-1β and TNF-αa. Annals of the New York Academy of Sciences, 856(1), 148-159.

Kuberski, P. (2008). Kubrick's Odyssey: Myth, Technology, Gnosis. Arizona Quarterly: A Journal of American Literature, Culture, and Theory, 64(3), 51-73.

Kudlien, F. (1972). Medicina helenística y helenístico-romana. In: Lain Entralgo P, editor. dir. Historia universal de la medicina. Antigüedad clásica, vol. 2. Barcelona: Salvat Editores, S.A. p. 153- 9.

Kudo, T. (2011). [Behavioral pathology in Alzheimer's Disease Rating Scale (Behave -AD)]. Nihon Rinsho, 69 Suppl 8, 464-70.

Kudoh, A., Takase, H., Katagai, H., & Takazawa, T. (2005). Postoperative interleukin-6 and cortisol concentrations in elderly patients with postoperative confusion. Neuroimmunomodulation, 12(1), 60-66.

Kuhn, T. S. (1970). The Structure of Scientific Revolutions. Enlarged (2nd ed.). University of Chicago Press.

Kunzendorf, R. G., Hartmann, E., Cohen, R., & Cutler, J. (1997). Bizarreness of the dreams and daydreams reported by individuals with thin and thick boundaries. Dreaming, 7(4), 265.

Kuriyama, A., Honda, M., & Hayashino, Y. (2014). Ramelteon for the treatment of insomnia in adults: a systematic review and meta-analysis. Sleep medicine, 15(4), 385-392.

Kussé, C., Muto, V., Mascetti, L., Matarazzo, L., Foret, A., Bourdiec, A. S. L., & Maquet, P. (2010). Neuroimaging of dreaming: state of the art and limitations. International review of neurobiology, 92, 87-99.

Labouvie-Vief, G., DeVoe, M., & Bulka, D. (1989). Speaking about feelings: Conceptions of emotion across the life span. Psychology and Aging, 4, 425–437.

Labrecque, G., & Vanier, M. C. (1995). Biological rhythms in pain and in the effects of opioid analgesics. Pharmacology & therapeutics, 68(1), 129-147.

Lacan, J. (1953). "Some Reflections on the Ego," Int. J. Psycho-Anal., vol. 34,: p. 11

Lacan, J. (1977). Ecrits: A selection, translated by Alan Sheridan. London: Tavistock.

Lacan, J. (1988). The Seminar of Jacques Lacan: Book II: The Ego in Freud's Theory and in the Technique of Psychoanalysis. CUP Archive.

Lacasse, H., Perreault, M. M., & Williamson, D. R. (2006). Systematic review of antipsychotics for the treatment of hospital-associated delirium in medically or surgically III patients. Annals of Pharmacotherapy, 40(11), 1966-1973.

Lakoff, G. & Johnson, M. (1980). Metaphors We Live By. Chicago: University of Chicago Press.

Lakoff, G. (1987). Women, Fire and Dangerous Things: What Categories Reveal about the Mind. Chicago: University of Chicago press.

Lakoff, G. & Turner, M. (1989). More Than Cool Reason: A Field Guide to Poetic Metaphor. Chicago: University of Chicago Press.

Lakoff, G., & Johnson, M. (1999). Philosophy in the flesh: The embodied mind and its challenge to western thought. Basic books

Lambe, E. K., Olausson, P., Horst, N. K., Taylor, J. R., & Aghajanian, G. K. (2005). Hypocretin and nicotine excite the same thalamocortical synapses in prefrontal cortex: correlation with improved attention in rat. The Journal of neuroscience, 25(21), 5225-5229.

Lambert, M. J., & Barley, D. E. (2001). Research summary on the therapeutic relationship and psychotherapy outcome. Psychotherapy: Theory, Research, Practice, Training, 38(4), 357.

Lambert, M. J., & Bergin, A. E. (1994). The effectiveness of psychotherapy. Bergin, Allen E. (Ed); Garfield, Sol Louis (Ed), (1994). Handbook of psychotherapy and behavior change (4th ed.). , (pp. 143-189). Oxford, England: John Wiley & Sons, xvi, 864 pp.

Lamme, V. A., & Roelfsema, P. R. (2000). The distinct modes of vision offered by feedforward and recurrent processing. Trends in neurosciences, 23(11), 571-579.

Langdon, R., & Coltheart, M. (2000). The cognitive neuropsychology of delusions. Mind & Language, 15(1), 184-218.

Lange, T., Dimitrov, S., & Born, J. (2010). Effects of sleep and circadian rhythm on the human immune system. Annals of the New York Academy of Sciences, 1193(1), 48-59.

Lanius, R. A., Vermetten, E., Loewenstein, R. J., Brand, B., Schmahl, C., Bremner, J. D., & Spiegel, D. (2010). Emotion modulation in PTSD: Clinical and neurobiological evidence for a dissociative subtype. American Journal of Psychiatry, 167(6), 640-647.

Lanius, R. A., Williamson, P. C., Boksman, K., Densmore, M., Gupta, M., Neufeld, R. W., ... & Menon, R. S. (2002). Brain activation during script-driven imagery induced dissociative responses in PTSD: a functional magnetic resonance imaging investigation. Biological psychiatry, 52(4), 305-311.

Lansky, M. R., & Bley, C. R. (1995). Posttraumatic nightmares: Psychodynamic explorations. Analytic Press, Inc.

Large, M. C., Reichard, C., Williams, J. T., Chang, C., Prasad, S., Leung, Y., ... & Steinberg, G. D. (2013). Incidence, risk factors, and complications of postoperative delirium in elderly patients undergoing radical cystectomy. Urology, 81(1), 123-129.

Larøi, F., & Woodward, T. S. (2007). Hallucinations from a cognitive perspective. Harvard review of psychiatry, 15(3), 109-117.

Latreille, V., Carrier, J., Lafortune, M., Postuma, R. B., Bertrand, J. A., Panisset, M., ... & Gagnon, J. F. (2014). Sleep spindles in Parkinson's disease may predict the development of dementia. Neurobiology of Aging.

Laub, D., & Lee, S. (2003). Thanatos and massive psychic trauma: The impact of the death instinct on knowing, remembering, and forgetting. Journal of the American Psychoanalytic Association, 51(2), 433-464.

Laughlin, C. D. (1996). The properties of neurognosis. Journal of Social and Evolutionary Systems, 19(4), 363-380.

Laughlin, C. D., & Loubser, J. H. (2010). Neurognosis, the development of neural models, and the study of the ancient mind. Time and Mind, 3(2), 135-158.

Laughlin, C. D., & Tiberia, V. A. (2012). Archetypes: Toward a Jungian anthropology of consciousness. Anthropology of Consciousness, 23(2), 127-157.

Laurila JV, Pitkala KH, Strandberg TE, Tilvis RS (2004). Delirium among patients with and without dementia: does the diagnosis according to the DSM-IV differ from the previous classifications? International Journal of Geriatric Psychiatry. 19:271-7.

Law, D. D., Crane, D. R., & Berge, J. M. (2003). The influence of individual, marital, and family therapy on high utilizers of health care. Journal of Marital and Family Therapy, 29(3), 353-363.

Lawlor, P. G., Davis, D. H., Ansari, M., Hosie, A., Kanji, S., Momoli, F., ... & Stewart, D. J. (2014). An analytical framework for delirium research in palliative care settings:

integrated epidemiologic, clinician-researcher, and knowledge user perspectives. Journal of pain and symptom management, 48(2), 159-175.

Lawlor, P. G., Gagnon, B., Mancini, I. L., Pereira, J. L., Hanson, J., Suarez-Almazor, M. E., & Bruera, E. D. (2000). Occurrence, causes, and outcome of delirium in patients with advanced cancer: a prospective study. Archives of Internal Medicine, 160(6), 786-794.

Le Goff, J. (1988). Christianity and dreams (second to seventh century). In The medieval imagination, J. Le Goff, 193-231. Chicago: University of Chicago Press.

Le Strat, Y., & Gorwood, P. (2008). Agomelatine, an innovative pharmacological response to unmet needs. Journal of Psychopharmacology, 22(7 suppl), 4-8.

Leavitt, M.L., Trzepacz, P.T. & Ciongoli, K. (1994). Rat model of delirium: atropine dose-response relationships. J Neuropsychiatry Clin Neurosci; 6: 279–84.

Lecea, L. D., Sutcliffe, G. J., & Fabre, V. (2002). Hypocretins/orexins as integrators of physiological information: lessons from mutant animals. Neuropeptides, 36(2), 85-95.

Lee, G. J., Lu, P. H., Mather, M. J., Shapira, J., Jimenez, E., Leow, A. D., Thompson, P. & Mendez, M. F. (2014). Neuroanatomical Correlates of Emotional Blunting in Behavioral Variant Frontotemporal Dementia and Early-Onset Alzheimer's Disease. Journal of Alzheimer's disease: JAD, 41(3), 793.

Lee, G., Lu, P., Meghpara, M., Shapira, J., Mather, M., Kaiser, N., Jimenez, E., Thompson, P. & Mendez, M. (2013). Neuroanatomical Correlates of Symptoms on the Frontal Systems Behavior Scale in Frontotemporal Dementia and Early-Onset Alzheimer's Disease. In NEUROLOGY (Vol. 80). 530 WALNUT ST, PHILADELPHIA, PA 19106-3621 USA: LIPPINCOTT WILLIAMS & WILKINS.

Lee, H. S., Billings, H. J., & Lehman, M. N. (2003). The suprachiasmatic nucleus: a clock of multiple components. Journal of biological rhythms, 18(6), 435-449.

Lee, K. S., Chung, J. H., Choi, T. K., Suh, S. Y., Oh, B. H., Hong, C. H. (2009). Peripheral cytokines and chemokines in Alzheimer's disease. Dement. Geriatr. Cogn. Disord. 28, 281–287.

Lee, Y., Ryu, J., Lee, J., Kim, H. J., Shin, I. H., Kim, J. L., & Trzepacz, P. T. (2011). Korean version of the delirium rating scale-revised-98: reliability and validity. Psychiatry investigation, 8(1), 30-38.

Leger, D., Laudon, M., & Zisapel, N. (2004). Nocturnal 6-sulfatoxymelatonin excretion in insomnia and its relation to the response to melatonin replacement therapy. The American journal of medicine, 116(2), 91-95.

Lehoux D.R. (2007). Drugs and the Delphic Oracle. Classical World, 101, 1, 41-56.

Leichsenring, F. (2005). Are psychodynamic and psychoanalytic therapies effective?: A review of empirical data. The International Journal of Psychoanalysis, 86(3), 841-868.

Leonard, M. M., Nekolaichuk, C., Meagher, D. J., Barnes, C., Gaudreau, J. D., Watanabe, S., Agar, M., Bush, S.H. & Lawlor, P. G. (2014). Practical assessment of delirium in palliative care. Journal of pain and symptom management.

Leonard, M., Adamis, D., Saunders, J., Trzepacz, P., & Meagher, D. (2013). A longitudinal study of delirium phenomenology indicates widespread neural dysfunction. Palliative and Supportive Care, 1-10.

Leonard, M., Spiller, J., Keen, J., MacLullich, A., Kamholtz, B., & Meagher, D. (2009). Symptoms of depression and delirium assessed serially in palliative-care inpatients. Psychosomatics, 50(5), 506-514.

Leslie, D. L., Marcantonio, E. R., Zhang, Y., Leo-Summers, L., & Inouye, S. K. (2008). One-year health care costs associated with delirium in the elderly population. Archives of internal medicine, 168(1), 27-32.

Leslie, D. L., Zhang, Y., Holford, T. R., Bogardus, S. T., Leo-Summers, L. S., & Inouye, S. K. (2005). Premature death associated with delirium at 1-year follow-up. Archives of Internal Medicine, 165(14), 1657-1662.

Levens, S. M., Larsen, J. T., Bruss, J., Tranel, D., Bechara, A., & Mellers, B. A. (2014). What might have been? The role of the ventromedial prefrontal cortex and lateral orbitofrontal cortex in counterfactual emotions and choice. Neuropsychologia, 54, 77-86.

Levin, R. (1994). Sleep and dream characteristics of frequent nightmare subjects in a university population. Dreaming 4: 127–137.

Levin, R., & Basile, R. (2003). Psychopathological correlates of contextualized images in dreams. Perceptual and motor skills, 96(1), 224-226.

Levin, R., & Nielsen, T. (2009). Nightmares, bad dreams, and emotion dysregulation a review and new neurocognitive model of dreaming. Current Directions in Psychological Science, 18(2), 84-88.

Levin, R., Heresco-Levy, U., Edelman, S., Shapira, H., Ebstein, R. P., & Lichtenberg, P. (2011). Hypnotizability and sensorimotor gating: a dopaminergic mechanism of hypnosis. International Journal of Clinical and Experimental Hypnosis, 59(4), 399-405.

Levkoff, S. E., Liptzin, B., Cleary, P. D., Wetle, T., Evans, D. A., Rowe, J. W., & Lipsitz, L. A. (1996). Subsyndromal delirium. The American Journal of Geriatric Psychiatry, 4(4), 320-329.

Lewis, C. T., Short, C. & Andrews, E. A. (1879) Harpers' Latin dictionary. A New Latin Dictionary Founded on the Translation of Freund's Latin-German Lexicon, edited by E. A. Andrews

Lewis, S. W. (1987). Brain imaging in a case of Capgras syndrome. Br J Psychiatry; 150: 117-121.

Li, F., Wang, F., & Jia, J. (2013). Evaluating the prevalence of dementia in hospitalized older adults and effects of comorbid dementia on patients' hospital course. Aging clinical and experimental research, 25(4), 393-401.

Liang, C., Zhu, H., Xu, Y., Huang, L., Ma, C., Deng, W., ... & Qin, C. (2012). MicroRNA-153 negatively regulates the expression of amyloid precursor protein and amyloid precursor-like protein 2. Brain research, 1455, 103-113.

Lim, S. Y., & Lang, A. E. (2010). The nonmotor symptoms of Parkinson's disease—an overview. Movement Disorders, 25(S1), S123-S130.

Lincoln, J. S. (1935). The dream in primitive cultures. Landmarks in anthropology. Johnson Reprint Corp. University of Michigan.

Lindsley, D. B., Bowden, J. W., & Magoun, H. W. (1949). Effect upon the EEG of acute injury to the brain stem activating system. Electroencephalography and clinical neurophysiology, 1(1), 475-486.

Lipourlis, D. (1983). Ιπποκρατικη Ιατρικη [Hippocratic Medicine] (Thessalonika: Paratiritis).

Lipowski, Z. J. (1980). Delirium: acute brain failure in man (No. 1028). Charles C. Thomas Publisher.

Lipowski, Z. J. (1990) Delirium: Acute Confusional States (New York: Oxford University Press).

Lipowski, Z. J. (1991) Delirium: how its concept has developed. International Psychogeriatrics, 3, 115–20.

Liu, L.C. & Hedeker, D. (2006). A mixed effects regression model for longitudinal multivariate ordinal data. Biometrics 62, 261-268.

Liu, C. & Reppert, S. M. (2000). GABA synchronizes clock cells within the suprachiasmatic circadian clock. Neuron, 25(1), 123-128.

Liu, C., Weaver, D. R., Jin, X., Shearman, L. P., Pieschl, R. L., Gribkoff, V. K., & Reppert, S. M. (1997). Molecular dissection of two distinct actions of melatonin on the suprachiasmatic circadian clock. Neuron, 19(1), 91-102.

Llinás, R. R. (1988). The intrinsic electrophysiological properties of mammalian neurons: insights into central nervous system function. Science, 242(4886), 1654-1664.

Lockley, S. W., Brainard, G. C., & Czeisler, C. A. (2003). High sensitivity of the human circadian melatonin rhythm to resetting by short wavelength light. J Clin Endocrinol Metab, 88(9), 4502-4505.

Loewenstein, D. A., Acevedo, A., Czaja, S. J. & Duara, R. (2004). Cognitive rehabilitation of mildly impaired Alzheimer disease patients on cholinesterase inhibitors. Am J Geriatric Psychiatry, 12: 395.

Loewenstein, R., & Welzant, V. (2010). Pragmatic approaches to stage-oriented treatment for early life trauma-related complex post-traumatic stress and dissociative disorders. The impact of early life trauma on health and disease: The hidden epidemic, 257-267.

Long, A. A. & Sedley, D. N. (1987). The Hellenistic philosophers. 2 vols. Cambridge: University Press.

Long, J. M., & Lahiri, D. K. (2011). MicroRNA-101 downregulates Alzheimer's amyloid-β precursor protein levels in human cell cultures and is differentially expressed. Biochemical and biophysical research communications, 404(4), 889-895.

Long, J. M., Ray, B., & Lahiri, D. K. (2012). MicroRNA-153 physiologically inhibits expression of amyloid-β precursor protein in cultured human fetal brain cells and is dysregulated in a subset of Alzheimer disease patients. Journal of Biological Chemistry, 287(37), 31298-31310.

Loomis, A.L., Harvey, E.N. & Hobart, G.A. (1937). Cerebral states during sleep as studied by human brain potentials. J Exper Psychol; 21:127–44.

Lu, J. X., Qiang, W., Yau, W. M., Schwieters, C. D., Meredith, S. C., & Tycko, R. (2013). Molecular structure of β-amyloid fibrils in Alzheimer's disease brain tissue. Cell, 154(6), 1257-1268.

Lu, J., Greco, M. A., Shiromani, P., & Saper, C. B. (2000). Effect of lesions of the ventrolateral preoptic nucleus on NREM and REM sleep. The Journal of Neuroscience, 20(10), 3830-3842.

Lu, J., Jhou, T. C., & Saper, C. B. (2006). Identification of wake-active dopaminergic neurons in the ventral periaqueductal gray matter. The Journal of neuroscience, 26(1), 193-202.

Luchsinger, J. A., & Mayeux, R. (2004). Dietary factors and Alzheimer's disease. The Lancet Neurology, 3(10), 579-587.

Lupien, S. J., McEwen, B. S., Gunnar, M. R., & Heim, C. (2009). Effects of stress throughout the lifespan on the brain, behavior, and cognition. Nat. Rev. Neurosci. 10, 434–445.

Luppi, P. H., Clément, O., Sapin, E., Gervasoni, D., Peyron, C., Léger, L., Salvert, M. & Fort, P. (2011). The neuronal network responsible for paradoxical sleep and its dysfunctions causing narcolepsy and rapid eye movement (REM) behavior disorder. Sleep medicine reviews, 15(3), 153-163.

Lustig, C., Snyder, A. Z., Bhakta, M., O'Brien, K. C., McAvoy, M., Raichle, M. E., ... & Buckner, R. L. (2003). Functional deactivations: change with age and dementia of the Alzheimer type. Proceedings of the National Academy of Sciences, 100(24), 14504-14509.

Lutgendorf, S. K., Lang, E. V., Berbaum, K. S., Russell, D., Berbaum, M. L., Logan, H., . Eric G. Benotsch, Sebastian Schulz-Stubner, Turesky, D. & Spiegel, D. (2007). Effects of age on responsiveness to adjunct hypnotic analgesia during invasive medical procedures. Psychosomatic medicine, 69(2), 191-199.

Macchi, M. M., & Bruce, J. N. (2004). Human pineal physiology and functional significance of melatonin. Frontiers in neuroendocrinology, 25(3), 177-195.

Macfarlane, J. W. (1962). A development study of the behavior problems of normal children between twenty-one months and fourteen years (Vol. 2). Univ of California Press.

Maclullich, A. M., Ferguson, K. J., Miller, T., de Rooij, S. E. & Cunningham, C. (2008). Unravelling the pathophysiology of delirium: a focus on the role of aberrant stress responses. J Psychosom Res; 65: 229–38.

Maclullich, A. M., Anand, A., Davis, D. H., Jackson, T., Barugh, A. J., Hall, R. J., Ferguson, J., Meagher, D. J. & Cunningham, C. (2013). New horizons in the pathogenesis, assessment and management of delirium. Age and ageing, aft148

Maclullich, A. M., Anand, A. & Davis, D. H. J. (2013). New horizons in the pathogenesis, assessment and management of delirium. Age and Ageing 2013; 42: 667–674.

MacLullich, A.M., Beaglehole, A., Hall, R.J. & Meagher, D.J. (2009). Delirium and longterm cognitive impairment. Int Rev Psychiatry 21, 30–42.

MacNish, R. (1830). The philosophy of sleep. Glasgow: W.R. McPhun.

Maestroni, G. J. (1993). The immunoneuroendocrine role of melatonin. Journal of pineal research, 14(1), 1-10.

Maffei, C., Fossati, A., Lingiardi, V., & Madeddu, F. (1995). Personality maladjustment, defenses, and psychopathological symptoms in nonclinical subjects. Journal of Personality Disorders , 9, 330-345.

Magarey, J. M., & McCutcheon, H. H. (2005). 'Fishing with the dead'—Recall of memories from the ICU. Intensive and Critical Care Nursing, 21(6), 344-354.

Mahlberg, R., Kunz, D., Sutej, I., Kühl, K. P., & Hellweg, R. (2004). Melatonin treatment of day-night rhythm disturbances and sundowning in Alzheimer disease: an open-label pilot study using actigraphy. Journal of clinical psychopharmacology, 24(4), 456-459.

Mailhot, T., Cossette, S., Bourbonnais, A., Côté, J., Denault, A., Côté, M. C., Lamarche, Y. & Guertin, M. C. (2014). Evaluation of a nurse mentoring intervention to family caregivers in the management of delirium after cardiac surgery (MENTOR_D): a study protocol for a randomized controlled pilot trial. Trials, 15(1), 306.

Maldonado, J. R. (2008). Pathoetiological model of delirium: a comprehensive understanding of the neurobiology of delirium and an evidence-based approach to prevention and treatment. Critical care clinics, 24(4), 789-856.

Maldonado, J. R. (2013). Neuropathogenesis of delirium: review of current etiologic theories and common pathways. The American Journal of Geriatric Psychiatry, 21(12), 1190-1222.

Maldonado, J., Key, R. G., & Kamholz, B. (2013). Delirium Updates: Pathophysiology and Biomarkers; Strategies to Manage DTs; and Delirium in Patients With Cancer. The American Journal of Geriatric Psychiatry, 21(3), S10-S11.

Malhotra, S., Sawhney, G., & Pandhi, P. (2004). The therapeutic potential of melatonin: a review of the science. Medscape General Medicine, 6(2).

Mander, B. A., Rao, V., Lu, B., Saletin, J. M., Lindquist, J. R., Ancoli-Israel, S. & Walker, M. P., (2013). Prefrontal atrophy, disrupted NREM slow waves and impaired hippocampal-dependent memory in aging. Nature Neurosci. 16 (3), 357–364.

Mandler, G. (1975). Mind and Body: Psychology of Emotion and Stress, New York and London: W.W. Norton.

Manning, K. A., Wilson, J. R., & Uhlrich, D. J. (1996). Histamine-immunoreactive neurons and their innervation of visual regions in the cortex, tectum, and thalamus in the primate Macaca mulatta. Journal of Comparative Neurology, 373(2), 271-282.

Mano, M. M. & Kime. C. R. (2004). Logic And Computer Design Fundamentals (Third Edition) Pearson Education International, Upper Saddle River, NJ.

Maquet, P. (2001). The Role of Sleep in Learning and Memory. Science, 294, 1048-1052.

Maquet, P., Péters, J. M., Aerts, J., Delfiore, G., Degueldre, C., Luxen, A., & Franck, G. (1996). Functional neuroanatomy of human rapid-eye-movement sleep and dreaming. Nature, 383(6596), 163-166.

Maquet, P., Ruby, P., Maudoux, A., Albouy, G., Sterpenich, V., Dang-Vu, T., Desailles, M. & Laureys, S. (2005). Human cognition during REM sleep and the activity profile within frontal and parietal cortices: a reappraisal of functional neuroimaging data. Progress in brain research, 150, 219-595.

Marcantonio, E. R. (2011). Delirium. Annals of internal medicine, 154(11), ITC6-1.

Marcantonio, E. R., Kiely, D. K., Simon, S. E., John Orav, E., Jones, R. N., Murphy, K. M., & Bergmann, M. A. (2005). Outcomes of older people admitted to postacute facilities with delirium. Journal of the American Geriatrics Society, 53(6), 963-969.

Marcantonio, E. R., Simon, S. E., Bergmann, M. A., Jones, R. N., Murphy, K. M., & Morris, J. N. (2003). Delirium symptoms in post-acute care: Prevalent, persistent, and associated with poor functional recovery. Journal of the American Geriatrics Society, 51(1), 4-9.

Marcantonio, E., Ta, T., Duthie, E., & Resnick, N. M. (2002). Delirium severity and psychomotor types: their relationship with outcomes after hip fracture repair. Journal of the American Geriatrics Society, 50(5), 850-857.

Markowitsch, H. J., & Staniloiu, A. (2013). The spaces left over between REM sleep, dreaming, hippocampal formation, and episodic autobiographical memory. Behavioral and Brain Sciences, 36(06), 622-623.

Markus, H. R., & Kitayama, S. (1991). Culture and the self: Implications for cognition, emotion, and motivation. Psychological review, 98(2), 224.

Marr, D. (1982). Vision: a computational approach. Freeman, San Francisco.

Marrosu, F., Portas, C., Mascia, M. S., Casu, M. A., Fà, M., Giagheddu, M., Imperato, A. & Gessa, G. L. (1995). Microdialysis measurement of cortical and hippocampal acetylcholine release during sleep-wake cycle in freely moving cats. Brain research, 671(2), 329-332.

Marshall, L. & Born, J. (2007). The contribution of sleep to hippocampus-dependent memory consolidation. Trends Cogn. Sci. 11, 442–450.

Martin, J. C., Liley, D. T., Harvey, A. S., Kuhlmann, L., Sleigh, J. W., & Davidson, A. J. (2014). Alterations in the functional connectivity of frontal lobe networks preceding emergence delirium in children. Anesthesiology, 121(4), 740-752.

Martin, M., Clare, L., Altgassen, A.M., Cameron, M.H. & Zehnder, F. (2011). Cognition-based interventions for healthy older people and people with mild cognitive impairment. Cochrane Database Syst Rev. (1):CD006220.

Marx, K. (1963). The Eighteenth Brumaire of Louis Bonaparte (New York).

Mason, M. F., Norton, M. I., Van Horn, J. D., Wegner, D. M., Grafton, S. T., & Macrae, C. N. (2007). Wandering minds: the default network and stimulus-independent thought. Science, 315(5810), 393-395.

Mason, S. F. (1956). A History of the Sciences. Collier Books: New York.

Matsuki, T., Nomiyama, M., Takahira, H., Hirashima, N., Kunita, S., Takahashi, S., ... & Sakurai, T. (2009). Selective loss of GABAB receptors in orexin-producing neurons results in disrupted sleep/wakefulness architecture. Proceedings of the National Academy of Sciences, 106(11), 4459-4464.

Matsushima, E., Nakajima, K., Moriya, H., Matsuura, M., Motomiya, T., & Kojima, T. (1997). A psychophysiological study of the development of delirium in coronary care units. Biological psychiatry, 41(12), 1211-1217.

Mattern, S. P. (1999). Physicians and the Roman imperial aristocracy: the patronage of therapeutics. Bulletin of the History of Medicine, 73(1), 1-18.

Matthews, F., & Brayne, C. (2005). The incidence of dementia in England and Wales: findings from the five identical sites of the MRC CFA Study. PLoS medicine, 2(8), e193.

Mattoo, S. K., Grover, S., Chakravarty, K., Trzepacz, P. T., Meagher, D. J., & Gupta, N. (2012). Symptom Profile and Etiology of Delirium in a Referral Population in Northern India: Factor Analysis of the DRS–R98. The Journal of neuropsychiatry and clinical neurosciences, 24(1), 95-101.

Mayr, E. (1982). The Growth of Biological Thought: Diversity, Evolution, and Inheritance. The Belknap Press of Harvard University Press: Cambridge, Massachusetts.

Mazzarino-Willett, A. (2009). Deathbed phenomena: its role in peaceful death and terminal restlessness. American Journal of Hospice and Palliative Medicine.

Mc Lellan, D. L. (1991). Functional recovery and the principles of disability medicine. In Clinical Neurology. Edited by Swash M. London: Churchill Livingstone; 768-790.

McClelland, J. L., McNaughton, B. L., & O'Reilly, R. C. (1995). Why there are complementary learning systems in the hippocampus and neocortex: insights from the successes and failures of connectionist models of learning and memory. Psychological review, 102(3), 419.

McCurren, C., & Cronin, S. N. (2003). Delirium: elders tell their stories and guide nursing practice. Medsurg nursing: official journal of the Academy of Medical-Surgical Nurses, 12(5), 318-323.

McDowell, M. J. (2001). 'Principle of organization: a dynamic-systems view of the

McEwen, B. (2007). Physiology and neurobiology of stress and adaptation: Central role of the brain. Physiol. Rev. 87, 873–904.

McEwen, B. S. (2000). The neurobiology of stress: From serendipity to clinical relevance. Brain Res. 866, 172–189.

McGaugh, J. L. (2000). Memory—A century of consolidation. Science 287, 248–251.

McGuire, B.E., Basten, C.J., Ryan, C.J. & Gallagher, J. (2000). Intensive care unit syndrome. A dangerous misnomer. Archives of InternalMedicine; 160: 906–909.

McGuire, P. K., Silbersweig, D. A., & Frith, C. D. (1996). Functional neuroanatomy of verbal self-monitoring. Brain, 119(3), 907-917.

McIntyre, I. (1990). Plasma concentrations of melatonin in panic disorder. Am J Psychiatry; 147: 462–4.

McLoughlin, H. S., Fineberg, S. K., Ghosh, L. L., Tecedor, L., & Davidson, B. L. (2012). Dicer is required for proliferation, viability, migration and differentiation in corticoneurogenesis. Neuroscience, 223, 285-295.

McNamara, P., McLaren, D., & Durso, K. (2007). Representation of the Self in REM and NREM Dreams. Dreaming, 17(2), 113.

Meagher, D. & Leonard, M. (2008). The active management of delirium: improving detection and treatment. Advances in Psychiatric Treatment (2008), vol. 14, 292–301

Meagher, D. (2001) Delirium: optimising management. BMJ, 7279, 144–149.

Meagher, D. (2009). Motor subtypes of delirium: past, present and future. International Review of Psychiatry, 21(1), 59-73.

Meagher, D. J. (2010). Impact of an educational workshop upon attitudes towards pharmacotherapy for delirium. International Psychogeriatrics, 22(06), 938-946.

Meagher, D. J., Leonard, M., Donnelly, S., Conroy, M., Adamis, D., & Trzepacz, P. T. (2011). A longitudinal study of motor subtypes in delirium: relationship with other phenomenology, etiology, medication exposure and prognosis. Journal of psychosomatic research, 71(6), 395-403.

Meagher, D. J., Leonard, M., Donnelly, S., Conroy, M., Saunders, J., & Trzepacz, P. T. (2010). A comparison of neuropsychiatric and cognitive profiles in delirium, dementia, comorbid delirium-dementia and cognitively intact controls. Journal of Neurology, Neurosurgery & Psychiatry, 81(8), 876-881.

Meagher, D. J., McLoughlin, L., Leonard, M., Hannon, N., Dunne, C., & O'Regan, N. (2013). What do we really know about the treatment of delirium with antipsychotics? Ten key issues for delirium pharmacotherapy. The American Journal of Geriatric Psychiatry, 21(12), 1223-1238.

Meagher, D. J., Moran, M., Raju, B., Gibbons, D., Donnelly, S., Saunders, J., & Trzepacz, P. T. (2007). Phenomenology of delirium Assessment of 100 adult cases using standardised measures. The British Journal of Psychiatry, 190(2), 135-141.

Meagher, D. J., Morandi, A., Inouye, S. K., Ely, W., Adamis, D., Maclullich, A. J., ... & Trzepacz, P. T. (2014). Concordance between DSM-IV and DSM-5 criteria for delirium diagnosis in a pooled database of 768 prospectively evaluated patients using the delirium rating scale-revised-98. BMC medicine, 12(1), 164.

Meagher, D., Adamis, D., Trzepacz, P., & Leonard, M. (2012). Features of subsyndromal and persistent delirium. The British Journal of Psychiatry, 200(1), 37-44.

Meagher, D., Moran, M., Raju, B., Leonard, M., Donnelly, S., Saunders, J., & Trzepacz, P. (2008). A new data-based motor subtype schema for delirium. The Journal of neuropsychiatry and clinical neurosciences, 20(2), 185-193.

Meagher, D., O'Regan, N., Ryan, D., Connolly, W., Boland, E., O'Caoimhe, R., Clare, J. & Timmons, S. (2014). Frequency of delirium and subsyndromal delirium in an adult acute hospital population. The British Journal of Psychiatry, 205(6), 478-485.

Meagher, D. J. & Trzepacz, P. T. (2009) Delirium. In: Gelder M, Andreasen N, Lopez-Ibor JJ, Geddes J, Eds. Oxford Textbook of Psychiatry. Oxford: Oxford University Press; pp 325–332.

Meagher, D. J., O'Hanlon, D., O'Mahony, E., Casey, P. R. & Trzepacz, P. T. (1996). The use of environmental strategies and psychotropic medications in the management of delirium. British Journal of Psychiatry 168: 512-5.

Mentis, M. J., Weinstein, E. A., Horwitz, B., McIntosh, A. R., Pietrini, P., Alexander, G. E., Furey, M. & Murphy, D. G. (1995). Abnormal brain glucose metabolism in the delusional misidentification syndromes: a positron emission tomography study in Alzheimer disease. Biological psychiatry, 38(7), 438-449.

Merleau-Ponty, M. (1962). Phenomenology of perception (C. Smith, Trans.). London: Routledge Kegan Paul.

Metzler-Baddeley, C. (2007). A review of cognitive impairments in dementia with Lewy bodies relative to Alzheimer's disease and Parkinson's disease with dementia. Cortex, 43(5), 583-600.

Meyer, D., Wood, S., & Stanley, B. (2013). Nurture Is Nature Integrating Brain Development, Systems Theory, and Attachment Theory. The Family Journal, 21(2), 162-169.

Meyer, J. P. (2010). Reliability. Oxford: Oxford University Press.

Meyer-Massetti, C., Vaerini, S., Bravo, A. E. R., Meier, C. R., & Guglielmo, B. J. (2011). Comparative safety of antipsychotics in the WHO pharmacovigilance database: the haloperidol case. International journal of clinical pharmacy, 33(5), 806-814.

Middleton, L. E., Grinberg, L. T., Miller, B., Kawas, C., & Yaffe, K. (2011). Neuropathologic features associated with Alzheimer disease diagnosis Age matters. Neurology, 77(19), 1737-1744.

Mieda, M., Williams, S. C., Richardson, J. A., Tanaka, K., & Yanagisawa, M. (2006). The dorsomedial hypothalamic nucleus as a putative food-entrainable circadian pacemaker. Proceedings of the National Academy of Sciences, 103(32), 12150-12155.

Migliore, L., & Coppedè, F. (2009). Genetics, environmental factors and the emerging role of epigenetics in neurodegenerative diseases. Mutation Research/Fundamental and Molecular Mechanisms of Mutagenesis, 667(1), 82-97.

Milling, L. S., Coursen, E. L., Shores, J. S., & Waszkiewicz, J. A. (2010). The predictive utility of hypnotizability: The change in suggestibility produced by hypnosis. Journal of consulting and clinical psychology, 78(1), 126.

Mindell, J. A., & Barrett, K. M. (2002). Nightmares and anxiety in elementary-aged children: is there a relationship?. Child: care, health and development, 28(4), 317-322.

Minkowski, E. (1997). La schizophre´nie. Paris, France: Editions Payot & Rivages. (originally published in 1927).

Miñones-Moyano, E., Porta, S., Escaramís, G., Rabionet, R., Iraola, S., Kagerbauer, B., ... & Martí, E. (2011). MicroRNA profiling of Parkinson's disease brains identifies early downregulation of miR-34b/c which modulate mitochondrial function. Human molecular genetics, 20(15), 3067-3078.

Mintz, E. M., Jasnow, A. M., Gillespie, C. F., Huhman, K. L., & Albers, H. E. (2002). GABA interacts with photic signaling in the suprachiasmatic nucleus to regulate circadian phase shifts. Neuroscience, 109(4), 773-778.

Mirabella, G., Bertini, G., Samengo, I., Kilavik, B. E., Frilli, D., Della Libera, C., & Chelazzi, L. (2007). Neurons in area V4 of the macaque translate attended visual features into behaviorally relevant categories. Neuron, 54(2), 303-318.

Mishra, J., & Gazzaley, A. (2014). Harnessing the neuroplastic potential of the human brain & the future of cognitive rehabilitation. Frontiers in human neuroscience, 8.

Mistraletti, G., Carloni, E., Cigada, M., Zambrelli, E., Taverna, M., Sabbatici, G., Ombrello, M., lia, G., Destrebecq, A.L.L. & Iapichino, G. (2008). Sleep and delirium in the intensive care unit. Minerva anestesiologica, 74(6), 329-334.

Miyauchi, S., Misaki, M., Kan, S., Fukunaga, T., & Koike, T. (2009). Human brain activity time-locked to rapid eye movements during REM sleep. Experimental brain research, 192(4), 657-667.

Modai, I., Malmgren, R., Wetterberg, L., Eneroth, P., Valevski, A., & Åsberg, M. (1992). Blood levels of melatonin, serotonin, cortisol, and prolactin in relation to the circadian rhythm of platelet serotonin uptake. Psychiatry research, 43(2), 161-166.

Modinos, G., Ormel, J., & Aleman, A. (2009). Activation of anterior insula during self-reflection. PLoS One, 4(2), e4618.

Monaco, T., Silvestre, D., & Silveira, P. S. (2012). Senescence in Animals: Why Evolutionary Theories Matter. INTECH Open Access Publisher.

Money, E. A., Kirk, R. C., & McNaughton, N. (1992). Alzheimer's dementia produces a loss of discrimination but no increase in rate of memory decay in delayed matching to sample. Neuropsychologia, 30(2), 133–143.

Monk, T. H. (2005). Aging human circadian rhythms: conventional wisdom may not always be right. Journal of Biological Rhythms, 20(4), 366-374.

Monteleone, P., Catapano, F., Buono, G., & Maj, M. (1994). Circadian rhythms of melatonin, cortisol and prolactin in patients with obsessive-compulsive disorder. Acta Psychiatrica Scandinavica, 89(6), 411-415.

Montiel L. (1998). La medicina de la mente en el periodo moderno. In: López-Muñoz F, Alamo C, editors. Historia de la neuropsicofarmacología. Una nueva aportación a la terapéutica farmacológica de los trastornos del sistema nervioso central. Madrid: Ediciones Eurobook S.L. p. 39–50.

Moor, B.G., Güroğlu, B., Op de Macks, Z. A., Rombouts, S. A., Van der Molen, M. W., & Crone, E. A. (2012). Social exclusion and punishment of excluders: neural correlates and developmental trajectories. Neuroimage, 59(1), 708-717.

Moore, R. Y. & Lenn, N. J. (1972).A retinohypothalamic projection in the rat. J Comp Neurol; 146: 1–14.

Moore, R. Y. (1997). Circadian rhythms: basic neurobiology and clinical applications. Annual review of medicine, 48(1), 253-266.

Moore, R. Y., Speh, J. C., & Leak, R. K. (2002). Suprachiasmatic nucleus organization. Cell and tissue research, 309(1), 89-98.

Moore, R. Y. & Eichler, V. (1972). Loss of a circadian adrenal corticosterone rhythm following suprachiasmatic lesions in the rat. Brain Res; 42: 201–6.

Moores, K. A., Clark, C. R., McFarlane, A. C., Brown, G. C., Puce, A., & Taylor, D. J. (2008). Abnormal recruitment of working memory updating networks during maintenance of trauma-neutral information in post-traumatic stress disorder. Psychiatry Research: Neuroimaging, 163(2), 156-170.

Moraes, W. D. S., Poyares, D. R., Guilleminault, C., Ramos, L. R., Bertolucci, P. H., & Tufik, S. (2006). The effect of donepezil on sleep and REM sleep EEG in patients with Alzheimer disease: a double-blind placebo-controlled study. Sleep, 29(2), 199-205.

Moran, J. M., Kelley, W. M., & Heatherton, T. F. (2013). What can the organization of the brain's default mode network tell us about self-knowledge?. Frontiers in human neuroscience, 7.

Morandi, A., McCurley, J., Vasilevskis, E. E., Fick, D. M., Bellelli, G., Lee, P., Jackson, J.C. & MacLullich, A. (2012). Tools to detect delirium superimposed on dementia: a systematic review. Journal of the American Geriatrics Society, 60(11), 2005-2013.

Morandi, A., Rogers, B. P., Gunther, M. L., Merkle, K., Pandharipande, P., Girard, T. D., Jackson, J.C. & Cannistraci, C. J. (2012). The Relationship between Delirium Duration, White Matter Integrity, and Cognitive Impairment in Intensive Care Unit Survivors as Determined by Diffusion Tensor Imaging. Critical care medicine, 40(7), 2182.

Morgan, C. (1990). Athletes and Oracles, Cambridge.

Morita, T., Tanabe, H. C., Sasaki, A. T., Shimada, K., Kakigi, R., & Sadato, N. (2013). The anterior insular and anterior cingulate cortices in emotional processing for self-face recognition. Social cognitive and affective neuroscience, nst011.

Morone, N. E., & Greco, C. M. (2007). Mind–body interventions for chronic pain in older adults: A structured review. Pain Medicine, 8(4), 359-375.

Morris, R. G. (1994). Working memory in Alzheimer-type dementia. Neuropsychology, 8, 544–554.

Morrish, E., King, M. A., Smith, I. E., & Shneerson, J. M. (2004). Factors associated with a delay in the diagnosis of narcolepsy. Sleep medicine, 5(1), 37-41.

Morrison, J. H., & Hof, P. R. (1997). Life and death of neurons in the aging brain. Science, 278(5337), 412-419.

Morton LL, Diubaldo D. (1995). Circadian differences in hemisphere-linked spelling proficiencies. Int. J. Neurosci. 81:101–110.

Moruzzi, G., & Magoun, H. W. (1949). Brain stem reticular formation and activation of the EEG. Electroencephalography and clinical neurophysiology, 1(1), 455-473.

Moss, H. E. (2014). Hallucinations. Neuro-Ophthalmology, (0), 1-1.

Mota, N. B., Furtado, R., Maia, P. P., Copelli, M., & Ribeiro, S. (2014). Graph analysis of dream reports is especially informative about psychosis. Scientific reports, 4.

Mota, N. B., Vasconcelos, N. A., Lemos, N., Pieretti, A. C., Kinouchi, O., Cecchi, G. A., Copelli, M. & Ribeiro, S. (2012). Speech graphs provide a quantitative measure of thought disorder in psychosis. PloS one, 7(4), e34928.

Muckli, L. (2010). What are we missing here? Brain imaging evidence for higher cognitive functions in primary visual cortex V1. International Journal of Imaging Systems and Technology, 20(2), 131-139.

Muller, L., & Destexhe, A. (2012). Propagating waves in thalamus, cortex and the thalamocortical system: experiments and models. Journal of Physiology-Paris, 106(5), 222-238.

Münch, M., Knoblauch, V., Blatter, K., Schröder, C., Schnitzler, C., Kräuchi, K., Wirz-Justice, A. & Cajochen, C. (2005). Age-related attenuation of the evening circadian arousal signal in humans. Neurobiology of aging, 26(9), 1307-1319.

Murkar, A., Smith, C., Dale, A., & Miller, N. (2014). A Neuro-Cognitive Model of Sleep Mentation & Memory. International Journal of Dream Research, 7(1), 85-89.

Murray, C., Sanderson, D.J., Barkus, C., Deacon, R.M., Rawlins, J.N., Bannerman, D.M. & Cunningham, C. (2012). Systemic inflammation induces acute working memory deficits in the primed brain: relevance for delirium. Neurobiol Aging 33, 603– 616 e603.

Murray, J., Ehlers, A., and Mayou, R. A. (2002). Dissociation and post-traumatic stress disorder: two prospective studies of road traffic accident survivors. Br. J. Psychiatry 180, 363–368.

Nagahama, Y., Okina, T., Suzuki, N. & Matsuda, M. (2010). Neural correlates of psychotic symptoms in dementia with Lewy bodies. Brain. 133(pt 2):557-567.

Namba, M., Morita, T., Imura, C., Kiyohara, E., Ishikawa, S., & Hirai, K. (2007). Terminal delirium: families' experience. Palliative Medicine, 21(7), 587-594.

Naumann, A., Bellebaum, C., & Daum, I. (2006). Cognitive deficits in narcolepsy. Journal of sleep research, 15(3), 329-338.

Neal, M. & Barton-Wright, P. (2003). Validation therapy for dementia. Cochrane Database of Systematic Reviews, Issue 3, Art. No.: CD001394.

Neely, A.S., Vikstrom, S. & Josephsson, S. (2009). Collaborative memory intervention in dementia: caregiver participation matters. Neuropsychol Rehabil, 19:696-715.

Neill, D. (2012). Should Alzheimer's disease be equated with human brain ageing?: A maladaptive interaction between brain evolution and senescence. Ageing research reviews, 11(1), 104-122.

Neisser, U., & Winograd, E. (Eds.). (1988). Remembering reconsidered: Ecological and traditional approaches to the study of memory. Cambridge: Cambridge University Press.

Nelson, P. T., Head, E., Schmitt, F. A., Davis, P. R., Neltner, J. H., Jicha, G. A., Abner, E.A. & Scheff, S. W. (2011). Alzheimer's disease is not "brain aging": neuropathological, genetic, and epidemiological human studies. Acta neuropathologica, 121(5), 571-587.

Nesse, R. M. & Lloyd, A. T. (1992) 'The evolution of psychodynamic mechanisms', in J.H. Barkow, L. Cosmides & J. Tooby (eds) The Adapted Mind: Evolutionary

Psychology and the Generation of Culture, New York and Oxford: Oxford University Press.

Newman, M. A. (1995). Toward a theory of health. A developing discipline: Selected works of Margaret Newman, 105.

Newman, M. A. (1999). Health as expanding consciousness. iUniverse.

Nielsen, T. A. (2000). A review of mentation in REM and NREM sleep: "covert" REM sleep as a possible reconciliation of two opposing models. Behavioral and Brain Sciences, 23(06), 851-866.

Nielsen, T. A., Laberge, L., Paquet, J., Tremblay, R. E., Vitaro, F., & Montplaisir, J. (2000). Development of Disturbing Dreams During Adolescence and Their Relatiox to Anxiety Symptoms. SLEEP-NEW YORK-, 23(6), 727-737.

Nielsen, T. A., Stenstrom, P., & Levin, R. (2006). Nightmare frequency as a function of age, gender, and September 11, 2001: Findings from an Internet questionnaire. Dreaming, 16(3), 145.

Nielsen, T., & Levin, R. (2007). Nightmares: a new neurocognitive model. Sleep Medicine Reviews, 11(4), 295-310.

Nietzsche, F. (1917). Thus spake Zarathustra (T. Common, Trans.). *New York: Boni and Liveright.(Original work published in German 1883– 1885).*

Niggemyer, K. A., Begley, A., Monk, T., & Buysse, D. J. (2004). Circadian and homeostatic modulation of sleep in older adults during a 90-minute day study. Sleep, 27(8), 1535-1541.

Nimchinsky, E. A., Sabatini, B. L., & Svoboda, K. (2002). Structure and function of dendritic spines. Annual review of physiology, 64(1), 313-353.

Nir, Y., & Tononi, G. (2010). Dreaming and the brain: from phenomenology to neurophysiology. Trends in cognitive sciences, 14(2), 88-100.

Nishida, M., Nariai, T., Hiura, M., Ishii, K., & Nishikawa, T. (2011). Memory deficits due to brain injury: unique PET findings and dream alterations. BMJ case reports, 2011, bcr0920114845.

Nofzinger, E. A., Mintun, M. A., Wiseman, M., Kupfer, D. J., & Moore, R. Y. (1997). Forebrain activation in REM sleep: an FDG PET study. Brain Research, 770(1), 192-201.

Northoff, G., Heinzel, A., de Greck, M., Bermpohl, F., Dobrowolny, H., & Panksepp, J. (2006). Self-referential processing in our brain—a meta-analysis of imaging studies on the self. Neuroimage, 31(1), 440-457.

Norton, S., Matthews, F. E., Barnes, D. E., Yaffe, K., & Brayne, C. (2014). Potential for primary prevention of Alzheimer's disease: an analysis of population-based data. The Lancet Neurology, 13(8), 788-794.

Noudoost, B., & Moore, T. (2011). The role of neuromodulators in selective attention. Trends in cognitive sciences, 15(12), 585-591.

Noudoost, B., Chang, M. H., Steinmetz, N. A., & Moore, T. (2010). Top-down control of visual attention. Current opinion in neurobiology, 20(2), 183-190.

Novak, S. J. (1997). LSD before Leary: Sidney Cohen's critique of 1950s psychedelic drug research. Isis, 87-110.

Nutton, V. (1973). "The Chronology of Galen's Early Career". Classical Quarterly 23 (1): 158–171.

Nutton, V. (2004). Ancient Medicine. Routledge.

Nyberg, L., Habib, R., McIntosh, A. R., & Tulving, E. (2000). Reactivation of encoding-related brain activity during memory retrieval. Proceedings of the National Academy of Sciences, 97(20), 11120-11124.

Nyberg, L., Petersson, K. M., Nilsson, L. G., Sandblom, J., Åberg, C., & Ingvar, M. (2001). Reactivation of motor brain areas during explicit memory for actions. Neuroimage, 14(2), 521-528.

O'Connell, B., Gradner, A., Takase, M., Hawkins, M., Ostaszkiewicz, J., Ski, C. & Josipovic, P. (2007). Clinical usefulness and feasibility of using reality orientation with patients who have dementia in acute care settings. International Journal of Nursing Practice 13, 182–192.

O'Keeffe, S. T. & Lavan, J. N. (1999). Clinical significance of delirium subtypes in older people. Age Ageing 28:115-119.

Oakley, D. A., & Halligan, P. W. (2011). Using hypnosis to gain insights into healthy and pathological cognitive functioning. Consciousness and cognition, 20(2), 328-331.

Oakley, D. A., & Halligan, P. W. (2013). Hypnotic suggestion: opportunities for cognitive neuroscience. Nature Reviews Neuroscience, 14(8), 565-576.

Obal Jr, F. Opp, M., Cady, A. B., Johannsen, L. A. R. S., Postlethwaite, A. E., Poppleton, H. M., Seyer, J. & Krueger, J. M. (1990). Interleukin 1 alpha and an interleukin 1 beta fragment are somnogenic. American Journal of Physiology-Regulatory, Integrative and Comparative Physiology, 259(3), R439-R446.

Oberhelman, S. (1983). Galen, On diagnosis from dreams. Journal of the History of Medicine and Allied Sciences (38), 36-47.

Ochsner, K. N., Beer, J. S., Robertson, E. R., Cooper, J. C., Gabrieli, J. D., Kihsltrom, J. F., & D'Esposito, M. (2005). The neural correlates of direct and reflected self-knowledge. Neuroimage, 28(4), 797-814.

Ogawa, K., Nittono, H., & Hori, T. (2006). Cortical regions activated after rapid eye movements during REM sleep. Sleep and Biological Rhythms, 4(1), 63-71.

O'Hanlon, S., O'Regan, N., MacLullich, A. M., Cullen, W., Dunne, C., Exton, C., & Meagher, D. (2014). Improving delirium care through early intervention: from bench to bedside to boardroom. Journal of Neurology, Neurosurgery & Psychiatry, 85(2), 207-213.

Ohayon, M. M., & Guilleminault, C. (2005). Epidemiology of sleep disorders. Sleep: A Comprehensive Handbook, 73-82.

Ohayon, M. M., Carskadon, M. A., Guilleminault, C., & Vitiello, M. V. (2004). Meta-analysis of quantitative sleep parameters from childhood to old age in healthy individuals: developing normative sleep values across the human lifespan. SLEEP-NEW YORK THEN WESTCHESTER-, 27, 1255-1274.

Ohayon, M. M., Morselli, P. L., & Guilleminault, C. (1997). Prevalence of nightmares and their relationship to psychopathology and daytime functioning in insomnia subjects. Sleep, 20, 340– 348.

Öhman, A., Flykt, A., & Esteves, F. (2001). Emotion drives attention: detecting the snake in the grass. Journal of experimental psychology: general, 130(3), 466.

Okawa, M. & Honma, K. (2002). Light and health. Matsushita Electric Works Ltd; pp. 5—6.

Okawa, M., Mishima, K., Hishikawa, Y., & Hozumi, S. (1991). Circadian rhythm disorders in sleep-waking and body temperature in elderly patients with dementia and their treatment. Sleep: Journal of Sleep Research & Sleep Medicine.

Olofsson, K., Alling, C., Lundberg, D., & Malmros, C. (2004). Abolished circadian rhythm of melatonin secretion in sedated and artificially ventilated intensive care patients. Acta anaesthesiologica scandinavica, 48(6), 679-684.

Olofsson, S. M., Weitzner, M. A., Valentine, A. D., Baile, W. F., & Meyers, C. A. (1996). A retrospective study of the psychiatric management and outcome of delirium in the cancer patient. Supportive care in cancer, 4(5), 351-357.

Olson, E. J., Boeve, B. F., & Silber, M. H. (2000). Rapid eye movement sleep behaviour disorder: demographic, clinical and laboratory findings in 93 cases. Brain, 123(2), 331-339.

O'Malley, G., Leonard, M., Meagher, D., & O'Keeffe, S. T. (2008). The delirium experience: a review. Journal of psychosomatic research, 65(3), 223-228.

O'Neill, L. A., Sheedy, F. J., & McCoy, C. E. (2011). MicroRNAs: the fine-tuners of Toll-like receptor signalling. Nature Reviews Immunology, 11(3), 163-175.

Onoda, K., Okamoto, Y., Nakashima, K. I., Nittono, H., Yoshimura, S., Yamawaki, S., ... & Ura, M. (2010). Does low self-esteem enhance social pain? The relationship between trait self-esteem and anterior cingulate cortex activation induced by ostracism. Social cognitive and affective neuroscience, 5(4), 385-391.

Orem, J. (Ed.). (2012). Physiology in sleep. Elsevier.

Organisation for Economic Co-operation and Development. OECD health data 2012. Paris: Organisation for Economic Co-operation and Development, 2012.

Ornstein, R. (1969). On the Experience of Time. Baltimore, Penguin Books, 1969.

Osis, K. & Haraldsson, E. (1997). What They Saw…at the Hour of Death: A New Look at Evidence for Life after Death. Norwalk, CT: Hastings House.

Osorio, C., Price, A. I., Gradini, R., Cummings, M., & Sfera, A. (2015). Searching for peripheral markers of sepsis-induced delirium (SID). Frontiers in Psychiatry, 6, 77.

Osse, R. J., Tulen, J. H., Bogers, A. J., & Hengeveld, M. W. (2009). Disturbed circadian motor activity patterns in postcardiotomy delirium. Psychiatry and clinical neurosciences, 63(1), 56-64.

Osse, R. J., Tulen, J. H., Wierdsma, A. I., Bogers, A. J., van der Mast, R. C., Hengeveld, M. W., & Hoogendijk, W. J. (2013). Postoperative delirium in the long-term diminishes attention and executive functioning without affecting memory. Delirium after Cardiac Surgery in Older Patients, 103.

Oudiette, D., Dealberto, M. J., Uguccioni, G., Golmard, J. L., Merino-Andreu, M., Tafti, M., Garma, L., Schwartz, S. & Arnulf, I. (2012). Dreaming without REM sleep. Consciousness and cognition, 21(3), 1129-1140.

Ouimet, S., Riker, R., Bergeon, N., Cossette, M., Kavanagh, B., & Skrobik, Y. (2007). Subsyndromal delirium in the ICU: evidence for a disease spectrum. Intensive care medicine, 33(6), 1007-1013.

Owen, A.M., Hampshire, A., Grahn, J.A., Stenton, R., Dajani, S., Burns, A.S., Howard, R.J. &, Ballard, C.G. (2010). Putting brain training to the test. Nature; 465:775-778.

Oyebode F. The neurology of psychosis. Med Princ Pract. 2008; 17(3):263-269.

Özyurtkan, M. O., Yildizeli, B., Kuşçu, K., Bekiroğlu, N., Bostanci, K., Batirel, H. F., & Yüksel, M. (2010). Postoperative psychiatric disorders in general thoracic surgery: incidence, risk factors and outcomes. European Journal of Cardio-Thoracic Surgery, 37(5), 1152-1157.

Pace-Schott E. (2011). The neurobiology of dreaming, in Principles and Practice of Sleep Medicine, 5th Edn, eds Kryger M., Roth T., Dement W. C., editors. (Philadelphia, PA: Elsevier Saunders), 563–575.

Pace-Schott, E. F. (2007). The frontal lobes and dreaming. The New Science of Dreaming: Content, Recall, and Personality Correlates, 1, 115-154.

Pace-Schott, E. F., & Hobson, J. A. (2002). The neurobiology of sleep: genetics, cellular physiology and subcortical networks. Nature Reviews Neuroscience, 3(8), 591-605.

Pacherie, E., Green, M., & Bayne, T. (2006). Phenomenology and delusions: Who put the 'alien'in alien control?. Consciousness and cognition, 15(3), 566-577.

Page, R. A., & Green, J. P. (2007). An update on age, hypnotic suggestibility, and gender: a brief report. American Journal of Clinical Hypnosis, 49(4), 283-287.

Pagel, J. F. (2000). Nightmares and disorders of dreaming. American family physician, 61(7), 2037-42.

Pagels, E. (1988). Adam, Eve and the serpent. New York: Vintage.

Paille`re-Martinot, M. L., Dao-Castellana, M. H., Masure, M. C., Pillon, B. & Martinot, J. L. (1994). Delusional misidentification: a clinical, neuropsychological and brain imaging case study. Psychopathology; 27 (3-5):200-210.

Pallier, P. N., Maywood, E. S., Zheng, Z., Chesham, J. E., Inyushkin, A. N., Dyball, R., Hastings, M.H. & Morton, A. J. (2007). Pharmacological imposition of sleep slows cognitive decline and reverses dysregulation of circadian gene expression in a transgenic mouse model of Huntington's disease. The Journal of neuroscience, 27(29), 7869-7878.

Pan, X. D., Zhu, Y. G., Lin, N., Zhang, J., Ye, Q. Y., Huang, H. P., & Chen, X. C. (2011). Microglial phagocytosis induced by fibrillar β-amyloid is attenuated by oligomeric β-amyloid: implications for Alzheimer's disease. Molecular neurodegeneration, 6(1), 1-18.

Panda, A., Arjona, A., Sapey, E., Bai, F., Fikrig, E., Montgomery, R. R., ... & Shaw, A. C. (2009). Human innate immunosenescence: causes and consequences for immunity in old age. Trends in immunology, 30(7), 325-333.

Panksepp, J. & G. Northoff. (2009). The trans-species core SELF: The emergence of active cultural and neuroecological agents through self-related processing within subcortical midline networks. Consciousness and Cog., 18: 193–215.

Panksepp, J. (1998), Affective Neuroscience: The Foundations of Human and Animal Emotion. New York: Oxford University Press.

Papp, K.V., Walsh, S.J. & Snyder, P.J. (2009). Immediate and delayed eff ects of cognitive interventions in healthy elderly: a review of current literature and future directions. Alzheimers Dement, 5:50-60.

Pappert, E. J., Goetz, C. G., Niederman, F. G., Raman, R., & Leurgans, S. (1999). Hallucinations, sleep fragmentation, and altered dream phenomena in Parkinson's disease. Movement Disorders, 14(1), 117-121.

Pardo, C., & Saura Antolín, C. A. (2014). New approaches to molecular basis of Huntington's chorea: from disease targets to new treatments.

Paredes, D., Rada, P., Bonilla, E., Gonzalez, L. E., Parada, M., & Hernandez, L. (1999). Melatonin acts on the nucleus accumbens to increase acetylcholine release and modify the motor activity pattern of rats. Brain research, 850(1), 14-20.

Parent, M., & Descarries, L. (2008). Acetylcholine innervation of the adult rat thalamus: distribution and ultrastructural features in dorsolateral geniculate, parafascicular, and reticular thalamic nuclei. Journal of Comparative Neurology, 511(5), 678-691.

Park, H., Quinlan, J., Thornton, E., & Reder, L. M. (2004). The effect of midazolam on visual search: Implications for understanding amnesia. Proceedings of the National Academy of Sciences of the United States of America, 101(51), 17879-17883.

Partinen, M. (1994). Epidemiology of sleep disorders. In M. H.Kryger, T.Roth, & W. C.Dement (Eds.), Principles and practice of sleep medicine (2nd ed., pp. 437–452). Philadelphia: WB Saunders.

Partridge, J. S., Martin, F. C., Harari, D., & Dhesi, J. K. (2013). The delirium experience: what is the effect on patients, relatives and staff and what can be done to modify this?. International journal of geriatric psychiatry, 28(8), 804-812.

Parvizi, J., Van Hoesen, G. W., Buckwalter, J., & Damasio, A. (2006). Neural connections of the posteromedial cortex in the macaque. Proceedings of the National Academy of Sciences of the United States of America, 103(5), 1563-1568.

Patton, D. (2006a). Reality orientation: its use and effectiveness within older person mental health care. Journal of Clinical Nursing 15, 1440–1449.

Patton, D. (2006b). The value of reality orientation with older adults who are mentally ill. Journal of Gerontological Nursing 32, 6–13.

Pavese, N., & Brooks, D. I. (2013). Functional neuroanatomy and physiology in movement disorders. Rehabilitation in Movement Disorders, 1.

Payne, J. D. & Nadel, L. (2004). Sleep, dreams, and memory consolidation: The role of the stress hormone cortisol. Learn. Mem. 11, 671–678.

Payne, J. D., Jackson, E. D., Hoscheidt, S., Ryan, L., Jacobs, W. J., and Nadel, L. (2007). Stress administered prior to encoding impairs neutral but enhances emotional long-term episodic memories. Learn. Mem. 14, 861–868.

Payne, J. D., Jackson, E. D., Ryan, L., Hoscheidt, S., Jacobs, W. J., and Nadel, L. (2006). The impact of stress on memory for neutral vs. emotional aspects of episodic memory. Memory 14(1), 1–16.

Payne, J. D., Nadel, L., Allen, J. J. B., Thomas, K. G. F., and Jacobs, W. J. (2002). The effects of experimentally induced stress on false recognition. Memory 10, 1–6.

Pearson, A., de Vries, A., Middleton, S. D., Gillies, F., White, T. O., Armstrong, I. R., ... & MacLullich, A. M. (2010). Cerebrospinal fluid cortisol levels are higher in patients with delirium versus controls. *BMC research notes*, 3(1), 33.

Pepeu, G., & Giovannini, M. G. (2004). Changes in acetylcholine extracellular levels during cognitive processes. Learning & Memory, 11(1), 21-27.

Peretz, C., Korczyn, A. D., Shatil, E., Aharonson, V., Birnboim, S., & Giladi, N. (2011). Computer-based, personalized cognitive training versus classical computer games: a randomized double-blind prospective trial of cognitive stimulation. *Neuroepidemiology, 36*(2), 91-99.

Perlow, M. (1995). Understanding Mental Objects. London & New York: Routledge.

Perogamvros, L., & Schwartz, S. (2012). The roles of the reward system in sleep and dreaming. Neuroscience & Biobehavioral Reviews, 36(8), 1934-1951.

Perry C. & Cooper S. (1989). An empirical study of defense mechanisms: clinical interview and life vignette ratings. Arch. Gen. Psychiatry; 46: 444–452.

Perry, E., Walker, M., Grace, J., & Perry, R. (1999). Acetylcholine in mind: a neurotransmitter correlate of consciousness?. Trends in neurosciences, 22(6), 273-280.

Perry, J. C. & Cooper, S. H.(1986). What do cross-sectional measures of defenses predict?. Empirical Studies of Ego Mechanisms of Defense Washington, DC, American Psychiatric PressVaillant GE, 32-40.

Perry, V. H. (2004). The influence of systemic inflammation on inflammation in the brain: implications for chronic neurodegenerative disease. Brain, behavior, and immunity, 18(5), 407-413.

Persson, J., & Nyberg, L. (2000). Conjunction analysis of cortical activations common to encoding and retrieval. Microscopy research and technique, 51(1), 39-44.

Pessoa, L. (2008). On the relationship between emotion and cognition. Nature reviews. Neuroscience, 9(2), 148–58.

Petchkovsky, L., Petchkovsky, M., Morris, P., Dickson, P., Montgomery, D., Dwyer, J., & Burnett, P. (2013). fMRI responses to Jung's Word Association Test: implications for theory, treatment and research. Journal of Analytical Psychology, 58(3), 409-431.

Peters, A. (2002). The effects of normal aging on myelin and nerve fibers: a review. Journal of neurocytology, 31(8-9), 581-593.

Peters, A., Morrison, J. H., Rosene, D. L., & Hyman, B. T. (1998). Are neurons lost from the primate cerebral cortex during normal aging?. Cerebral Cortex, 8(4), 295-300.

Peterson, M. J., & Benca, R. M. (2008). Sleep in mood disorders. Sleep Medicine Clinics, 3(2), 231-249.

Peyron, C., Faraco, J., Rogers, W., Ripley, B., Overeem, S., Charnay, Y., ... & Mignot, E. (2000). A mutation in a case of early onset narcolepsy and a generalized absence of hypocretin peptides in human narcoleptic brains. Nature medicine, 6(9), 991-997.

Peyron, C., Tighe, D. K., Van Den Pol, A. N., De Lecea, L., Heller, H. C., Sutcliffe, J. G., & Kilduff, T. S. (1998). Neurons containing hypocretin (orexin) project to multiple neuronal systems. The Journal of Neuroscience, 18(23), 9996-10015.

Phillips, A. J., Robinson, P. A., Kedziora, D. J., & Abeysuriya, R. G. (2010). Mammalian sleep dynamics: how diverse features arise from a common physiological framework. PLoS computational biology, 6(6), e1000826.

Piccardi, L., Monti, C., Vaselli, O., Tassi, F., Gaki-Papanastassiou, K., & Papanastassiou, D. (2008). Scent of a myth: tectonics, geochemistry and geomythology at Delphi (Greece). Journal of the Geological Society, 165(1), 5-18.

Pietikainen, P. (1998). Archetypes as symbolic forms. Journal of Analytical Psychology, 43(3), 325-343.

Piggins, H. D. (2002). Human clock genes. Ann Med, 34, 394-400.

Pihlajamäki, M., O'Keefe, K., Bertram, L., Tanzi, R. E., Dickerson, B. C., Blacker, D., ... & Sperling, R. A. (2010). Evidence of altered posteromedial cortical fMRI activity in subjects at risk for Alzheimer disease. Alzheimer disease and associated disorders, 24(1), 28.

Pinel, P. (1809). Traité mèdico-philosophique sur l'aliénation mentale. 2nd ed. Paris: Brosson.

Pinel, J. P. J. (2001) Biopsychologie, 2. Auflage, Spektrum Verlag.

Pinker, S. (2007). The stuff of thought. London: Allen Lane.

Pittendrigh, C. S., & Daan, S. (1976). A functional analysis of circadian pacemakers in nocturnal rodents. Journal of Comparative Physiology, 106(3), 223-252.

Plaschke, K., Thomas, C., Engelhardt, R., Teschendorf, P., Hestermann, U., Weigand, M. A., Martin, E. & Kopitz, J. (2007). Significant correlation between plasma and CSF anticholinergic activity in presurgical patients. Neuroscience letters, 417(1), 16-20.

Platek, S. M., Wathne, K., Tierney, N. G., & Thomson, J. W. (2008). Neural correlates of self-face recognition: an effect-location meta-analysis. Brain research, 1232, 173-184.

Plato, Republic (1994). (trans. R. Waterfield). Oxford: University Press.

Plutarch (1935). De defectu oraculorum ("On the Decline of Oracles") and De Pythiae Oraculis ("On the Oracles of the Pythia"), in Moralia, vol. 5 (Loeb Library, Harvard University Press).

Popovych, O. V., Hauptmann, C., & Tass, P. A. (2006). Control of neuronal synchrony by nonlinear delayed feedback. Biological cybernetics, 95(1), 69-85.

Popp, J. (2013). Delirium and cognitive decline: more than a coincidence. Current opinion in neurology, 26(6), 634-639.

Porkka-Heiskanen, T., Alanko, L., Kalinchuk, A., & Stenberg, D. (2002). Adenosine and sleep. Sleep medicine reviews, 6(4), 321-332.

Porter, R. (1997). The Greatest Benefit to Mankind: A Medical History of Humanity from Antiquity to the Present. Harper Collins.

Possin, K. L., Laluz, V. R., Alcantar, O. Z., Miller, B. L., & Kramer, J. H. (2011). Distinct neuroanatomical substrates and cognitive mechanisms of figure copy performance in Alzheimer's disease and behavioral variant frontotemporal dementia. Neuropsychologia, 49(1), 43-48.

Post, F. (1962). The significance of affective symptoms in old age: a follow-up study of one hundred patients (No. 10). Oxford University Press.

Postuma, R. B., Bertrand, J. A., Montplaisir, J., Desjardins, C., Vendette, M., Rios Romenets, S., ... & Gagnon, J. F. (2012). Rapid eye movement sleep behavior disorder and risk of dementia in Parkinson's disease: a prospective study. Movement disorders, 27(6), 720-726.

Poulet, J. F., Fernandez, L. M., Crochet, S., & Petersen, C. C. (2012). Thalamic control of cortical states. Nature neuroscience, 15(3), 370-372.

Prauss, K., Varatharajan, R., Joseph, K., & Moser, A. (2014). Transmitter self-regulation by extracellular glutamate in fresh human cortical slices. Journal of Neural Transmission, 1-7.

Preskorn, S. H. & Reveley, A. (1978). Pseudohypoparathyroidism and Capgras'syndrome. Br J Psychiatry; 133:34-37.

Prigogine, I. (1980). From Being to Becoming. San Francisco, W.H. Freeman & Co.

Prince, G. (1982). Narratology: The form and functioning of narrative. Berlin: Mouton.

Prince, M., Bryce, R., Albanese, E., Wimo, A., Ribeiro, W., & Ferri, C. P. (2013). The global prevalence of dementia: a systematic review and metaanalysis. Alzheimer's & Dementia, 9(1), 63-75.

Prince, S. E., Tsukiura, T., Daselaar, S. M., & Cabeza, R. (2007). Distinguishing the neural correlates of episodic memory encoding and semantic memory retrieval. Psychological Science, 18, 144–151.

Provencio, I., Rodriguez, I. R., Jiang, G., Hayes, W. P., Moreira, E. F., & Rollag, M. D. (2000). A novel human opsin in the inner retina. The journal of Neuroscience, 20(2), 600-605.

Prudentius, (1949). The daily round (liber cathimerinon). (trans H.J. Thomson). (Loeb Classical Library). London: Heinemann.

Putnam, R. A. (Ed.). (1997). The Cambridge Companion to William James. Cambridge University Press.

Qin, L., Wu, X., Block, M. L., Liu, Y., Breese, G. R., Hong, J. S., Knapp, D. & Crews, F. T. (2007). Systemic LPS causes chronic neuroinflammation and progressive neurodegeneration. Glia, 55(5), 453-462.

Qin, P., & Northoff, G. (2011). How is our self related to midline regions and the default-mode network?. Neuroimage, 57(3), 1221-1233.

Quan, N., & Banks, W. A. (2007). Brain-immune communication pathways. Brain, behavior, and immunity, 21(6), 727-735.

Quay, W.B. (1963). Circadian rhythm in rat pineal serotonin and its modifications by estrous cycle and photoperiod. Gen Comp Endocrinol; 3: 473–9.

Quayhagen, M. P., Quayhagen, M., Corbeil, R. R., Hendrix, R. C., Jackson, J. E., Snyder, L. & Bower, D. (2000). Coping with dementia: evaluation of four nonpharmacologic interventions. Int Psychogeriatr, 12:249-265.

Quayhagen, M. P., Quayhagen, M., Corbeil, R. R., Roth, P. A. & Rodgers, J. A. (1995). A dyadic remediation program for care recipients with dementia. Nurs Res; 44:153-159.

Quincy, J. (1719). Lexicon Physico-medicum: or, a New Physical Dictionary, Explaining the Difficult Terms used in the Several Branches of the Profession, and in such Parts of Philosophy as are Introductory Thereunto (London: printed for A. Bell, W. Taylor and J. Osborn).

Radenkova, J., Saeva, E., & Saev, V. (2011). Psychoactive substances in different cultures and religious practices.

Raichle, M. E., & Snyder, A. Z. (2007). A default mode of brain function: a brief history of an evolving idea. Neuroimage, 37(4), 1083-1090.

Rainville, P., & Price, D. D. (2003). Hypnosis phenomenology and the neurobiology of consciousness. International Journal of Clinical and Experimental Hypnosis, 51(2), 105-129.

Ralph, M. R., Foster, R. G., Davis, F. C., & Menaker, M. (1990). Transplanted suprachiasmatic nucleus determines circadian period. Science, 247(4945), 975-8.

Raz, A. (2011). Hypnosis: a twilight zone of the top-down variety: Few have never heard of hypnosis but most know little about the potential of this mind–body regulation technique for advancing science. Trends in cognitive sciences, 15(12), 555-557.

Raz, A., Fan, J., & Posner, M. I. (2006). Neuroimaging and genetic associations of attentional and hypnotic processes. Journal of Physiology-Paris, 99(4), 483-491.

Reese, R. J., Gillaspy, J. A., Owen, J. J., Flora, K. L., Cunningham, L. C., Archie, D., & Marsden, T. (2013). The influence of demand characteristics and social desirability on clients' ratings of the therapeutic alliance. Journal of clinical psychology, 69(7), 696-709.

Reeves, B. C., Deeks, J. J., Higgins, J. P. T. & Wells, G. A. (2011). Chapter 13: Includin g nonrandomized studies. In Cochrane Handbook for Systematic Reviews of Interventions Version 510 (updated March 2011). Edited by Higgins JPT. Oxford, UK: The Cochrane Collaboration.

Reghunandanan, V., Reghunandanan, R., & Marya, R. K. (1990). Vasopressin: its possible role in circadian time keeping. Chronobiologia, 18(1), 39-47.

Reichenberg, A., Yirmiya, R., Schuld, A., Kraus, T., Haack, M., Morag, A., & Pollmächer, T. (2001). Cytokine-associated emotional and cognitive disturbances in humans. Archives of general psychiatry, 58(5), 445-452.

Reid, K. J., & Zee, P. C. (2009). Circadian rhythm disorders. In Seminars in neurology (Vol. 29, No. 04, pp. 393-405). © Thieme Medical Publishers.

Reid, K. J., Chang, A. M., & Zee, P. C. (2004). Circadian rhythm sleep disorders. Med Clin North Am, 88(3), 631-651, viii.

Reiman, E. M., Chen, K., Alexander, G. E., Caselli, R. J., Bandy, D., Osborne, D., Saunders, A. & Hardy, J. (2004). Functional brain abnormalities in young adults at genetic risk for late-onset Alzheimer's dementia. Proceedings of the National Academy of Sciences, 101(1), 284-289.

Reinberg, A., Ugolini, C., Motohashi, Y., Dravigny, C., Bicakova-Rocher, A., & Levi, F. (1988). Diurnal rhythms in performance tests of school children with and without language disorders. Chronobiology international, 5(3), 291-299.

Relnoso-Suárez, F., de Andrés, I., Rodrigo-Angulo, M. L., & Garzón, M. (2001). Brain structures and mechanisms involved in the generation of REM sleep. Sleep medicine reviews, 5(1), 63-77.

Reiter, R. J. (2003). Melatonin: clinical relevance. Best practice & research clinical endocrinology & metabolism, 17(2), 273-285.

Reppert, S. M., & Weaver, D. R. (2001). Molecular analysis of mammalian circadian rhythms. Annual review of physiology, 63(1), 647-676.

Reppert, S. M., & Weaver, D. R. (2002). Coordination of circadian timing in mammals. Nature, 418(6901), 935-941.

Resnick, J., Stickgold, R., Pace-Schott, E., Williams, J. & Hobson, J. A. (1994). Self-representation and bizarreness in children's dreams. Conscious Cogn. 3, 30–45.

Resnick, J., Stickgold, R., Rittenhouse, C. D., & Hobson, J. A. (1994). Self-Representation and Bizarreness in Children' s Dream Reports Collected in the Home Setting. Consciousness and Cognition, 3(1), 30-45.

Revonsuo, A. (2000). The reinterpretation of dreams: An evolutionary hypothesis of the function of dreaming. Behavioral and Brain Sciences, 23(06), 877-901.

Revonsuo, A. (2006). Inner presence: Consciousness as a biological phenomenon. MIT Press.

Revonsuo, A. (2014). The Idea, Championed by Your Group, That Dreaming Functions as Threat Avoidance Would Seem to Be Quite Compatible with Protoconsciousness Theory. But Is It Really Dreaming (as Against REM) That Performs That Function? In Other Words, Are You a Dualist or a Neutral Monist?. In Dream Consciousness (pp. 191-194). Springer International Publishing.

Revonsuo, A., & Salmivalli, C. (1995). A content analysis of bizarre elements in dreams. Dreaming, 5(3), 169.

Revonsuo, A., & Valli, K. (2008). How to test the threat-simulation theory. Consciousness and cognition, 17(4), 1292-1296.

Richardson, G. S., Zee, P. C., Wang-Weigand, S., Rodriguez, L., & Peng, X. (2008). Circadian phase-shifting effects of repeated ramelteon administration in healthy adults. Journal of clinical sleep medicine: JCSM: official publication of the American Academy of Sleep Medicine, 4(5), 456.

Rieger, M., Mayer, G., & Gauggel, S. (2003). Attention deficits in patients with narcolepsy. SLEEP-NEW YORK THEN WESTCHESTER-, 26(1), 36-43.

Riemann, D. & Perlis, M. L. (2009). The treatments of chronic insomnia: a review of benzodiazepine receptor agonists and psychological and behavioral therapies. Sleep Med. Rev. 13 (3), 205– 214.

Riemersma-van der Lek, R. F., Swaab, D. F., Twisk, J., Hol, E. M., Hoogendijk, W. J., & Van Someren, E. J. (2008). Effect of bright light and melatonin on cognitive and noncognitive function in elderly residents of group care facilities: a randomized controlled trial. Jama, 299(22), 2642-2655.

Risse, G. B. (1990). Mending bodies, saving souls: a history of hospitals. Oxford University Press. p. 56

Rizzo, J. A., Bogardus Jr, S. T., Leo-Summers, L., Williams, C. S., Acampora, D., & Inouye, S. K. (2001). Multicomponent targeted intervention to prevent delirium in hospitalized older patients: what is the economic value?. Medical care, 39(7), 740-752.

Rizzolatti, G., & Luppino, G. (2001). The cortical motor system. Neuron, 31, 889–901.

Rizzuto, A. M. (2014). Shame in psychoanalysis. Shame and sexuality: Psychoanalysis and visual culture, 53.

Robbins, M. (2013). Affect, emotion and the psychotic mind. Psychosis and Emotion: The Role of Emotions in Understanding Psychosis, Therapy and Recovery, 149.

Robbins, T. W. (2005). Chemistry of the mind: neurochemical modulation of prefrontal cortical function. J. Comp. Neurol. 493, 140–146.

Robbins, T. W. (2013a). Psychopharmacology of Cognition. The Oxford Handbook of Cognitive Neuroscience, Volume 2: The Cutting Edges, 2, 401.

Robbins, T. W., & Arnsten, A. F. (2009). The neuropsychopharmacology of fronto-executive function: monoaminergic modulation. Annual review of neuroscience, 32, 267.

Robbins, T. W., & Cools, R. (2014). Cognitive deficits in Parkinson's disease: A cognitive neuroscience perspective. Movement Disorders, 29(5), 597-607.

Robbins, T. W., James, M., Owen, A. M., Sahakian, B. J., Lawrence, A. D., McInnes, L., & Rabbitt, P. (1998). A study of performance on tests from the CANTAB battery sensitive to frontal lobe dysfunction in a large sample of normal volunteers: Implications for theories of executive functioning and cognitive aging. Journal of the International Neuropsychological Society, 4(05), 474-490.

Robbins, T. W. (1997). Arousal systems and attentional processes, Biol. Psychol. 45; 57–71.

Robert, G., & Zadra, A. (2013). Thematic and content analysis of idiopathic nightmares and bad dreams. Sleep, 37(2), 409-417.

Roberts, M. F., & Wink, M. (Eds.). (1998). Alkaloids: biochemistry, ecology, and medicinal applications. Springer.

Rockwood, K. (1999). Educational interventions in delirium. Dementia and geriatric cognitive disorders, 10(5), 426-429.

Rockwood, K. (2002). Vascular cognitive impairment and vascular dementia. Journal of the neurological sciences, 203, 23-27.

Rockwood, K., Cosway, S., Stolee, P., Kydd, D., Carver, D., Jarrett, P., & O'Brien, B. (1994). Increasing the recognition of delirium in elderly patients. Journal of the American Geriatrics Society, 42(3), 252-256.

Roediger, H. L., (1996). Memory illusions. Journal of Memory and Language, 35, 76–100.

Roemer, L., & Orsillo, S. M. (2007). An open trial of an acceptance-based behavior therapy for generalized anxiety disorder. Behavior therapy, 38(1), 72-85.

Roenneberg, T. (1992). Spatial and temporal environment. The chrono-ecology of biological rhythms. Universitas, 34, 202-210.

Roenneberg, T. & Foster, R. G. (1997). Twilight Times: Light and the circadian system.

Roenneberg, T., Daan, S. & Merrow, M. (2003b). The Art of Entrainment. J Biol Rhythms,

Rofé, Y. (2008). Does repression exist? Memory, pathogenic, unconscious and clinical evidence. Review of General Psychology, 12(1), 63.

Roffwarg, H. P., Dement, W. C., Muzio, J. N., & Fisher, C. (1962). Dream imagery: relationship to rapid eye movements of sleep. Archives of general psychiatry, 7(4), 235-258.

Rogers, T. B., Kuiper, N. A., & Kirker, W. S. (1977). Self-reference and the encoding of personal information. Journal of personality and social psychology, 35(9), 677.

Roper, L. (1994). Oedipus and the Devil. London: Routledge.

Roscher, W. (1900). Ephialtes: eine pathologisch-mythologische Abhandlung uber die Alptraume und Alpdamonen des klassichen Altertums. Leipzig: Teubner. [Pan and the nightmare, trans., abridged J. Hillman, 1979. Irving, Tex.:Spring Publications].

Rose, G. S., & Walters, S. T. (2012). Theories of motivation and addictive behaviour. Treating substance abuse: Theory and technique, 9-27.

Rosenzweig, E. S., & Barnes, C. A. (2003). Impact of aging on hippocampal function: plasticity, network dynamics, and cognition. Progress in neurobiology, 69(3), 143-179.

Roskies, A. L. (2009). Brain-mind and structure-function relationships: A methodological response to Coltheart. Philosophy of Science, 76, 927–939.

Ross, C. A., Peyser, C. E., Shapiro, I., & Folstein, M. F. (1991). Delirium: phenomenologic and etiologic subtypes. International Psychogeriatrics, 3(02), 135-147.

Rossi, L., Mazzitelli, S., Arciello, M., Capo, C. R., & Rotilio, G. (2008). Benefits from dietary polyphenols for brain aging and Alzheimer's disease. Neurochemical research, 33(12), 2390-2400.

Rotondi, A. J., Chelluri, L., Sirio, C., Mendelsohn, A., Schulz, R., Belle, S., ... & Pinsky, M. R. (2002). Patients' recollections of stressful experiences while receiving prolonged mechanical ventilation in an intensive care unit*. Critical care medicine, 30(4), 746-752.

Rubin, F. H., Neal, K., Fenlon, K., Hassan, S., & Inouye, S. K. (2011). Sustainability and scalability of the hospital elder life program at a community hospital. Journal of the American Geriatrics Society, 59(2), 359-365.

Rubin, F. H., Williams, J. T., Lescisin, D. A., Mook, W. J., Hassan, S., & Inouye, S. K. (2006). Replicating the Hospital Elder Life Program in a community hospital and demonstrating effectiveness using quality improvement methodology. Journal of the American Geriatrics Society, 54(6), 969-974.

Rudrabhatla, P. (2014). Regulation of Neuronal Cytoskeletal Protein Phosphorylation in Neurodegenerative Diseases. Journal of Alzheimer's Disease.

Rugg, M. D. (Ed.). (2013). Cognitive neuroscience. Psychology Press.

Ruini, C., & Fava, G. A. (2009). Well-being therapy for generalized anxiety disorder. Journal of clinical psychology, 65(5), 510-519.

Ruiz de Mendoza Ibáñez, F. J. (1998). On the nature of blending as a cognitive phenomenon. Journal of Pragmatics, 30(3), 259-274.

Ruiz de Mendoza Ibáñez, F. J. (2003). The role of mappings and domains in understanding metonymy1. Metaphor and metonymy at the crossroads: A cognitive perspective, 30, 109.

Ruiz de Mendoza Ibáñez, F. J., & Pérez Hernández, L. (2001). Metonymy and the grammar: motivation, constraints and interaction. Language & Communication, 21(4), 321-357.

Rutishauser, U., & Edelman, G. M. (2012). Transmembrane control and cell surface recognition. Differentiation and Development, 15, 211.

Ryman, D. C., Acosta-Baena, N., Aisen, P. S., Bird, T., Danek, A., Fox, N. C., ... & Bateman, R. J. (2014). Symptom onset in autosomal dominant Alzheimer disease A systematic review and meta-analysis. Neurology, 83(3), 253-260.

Saalmann, Y. B., Pigarev, I. N., & Vidyasagar, T. R. (2007). Neural mechanisms of visual attention: how top-down feedback highlights relevant locations. Science, 316(5831), 1612-1615.

Saczynski, J. S., Inouye, S. K., Kosar, C. M., Tommet, D., Marcantonio, E. R., Fong, T., Tammy, H. & SAGES Study Group. (2014). Cognitive and brain reserve and the risk of postoperative delirium in older patients: analysis of data from a prospective observational study. The Lancet Psychiatry, 1(6), 437-443.

Sakai, K., & Jouvet, M. (1980). Brain stem PGO-on cells projecting directly to the cat dorsal lateral geniculate nucleus. Brain research, 194(2), 500-505.

Sakurai, T. (2007). The neural circuit of orexin (hypocretin): maintaining sleep and wakefulness. Nature Reviews Neuroscience, 8(3), 171-181.

Sakurai, T., Amemiya, A., Ishii, M., Matsuzaki, I., Chemelli, R. M., Tanaka, H., Williams, C. & Yanagisawa, M. (1998). Orexins and orexin receptors: a family of hypothalamic neuropeptides and G protein-coupled receptors that regulate feeding behavior. Cell, 92(4), 573-585.

Sakurai, T., Mieda, M., & Tsujino, N. (2010). The orexin system: roles in sleep/wake regulation. Annals of the New York Academy of Sciences, 1200(1), 149-161.

Sala, J. B., Rämä, P., & Courtney, S. M. (2003). Functional topography of a distributed neural system for spatial and nonspatial information maintenance in working memory. Neuropsychologia, 41(3), 341-356.

Salgado-Delgado, R., Angeles-Castellanos, M., Saderi, N., Buijs, R. M., & Escobar, C. (2010). Food intake during the normal activity phase prevents obesity and circadian desynchrony in a rat model of night work. Endocrinology, 151(3), 1019-1029.

Salinas, E., & Sejnowski, T. J. (2001). Correlated neuronal activity and the flow of

Salvio, M. A., Wood, J. M., Schwartz, J., & Eichling, P. S. (1992). Nightmare prevalence in the healthy elderly. Psychology and aging, 7(2), 324.

Sammallahti P, & Aalberg V. (1995). Defense style in borderline patients. An empirical study. Journal of Nervous and Mental Disease, 183, 522-527.

Samuels, A., Shorter, B., & Plaut, F. (1986). A critical dictionary of Jungian analysis. Psychology Press.

Sanchez-Espinosa, M.P., Atienza, M., Cantero, J.L., 2014. Sleep deficits in mild cognitive impairment are associated with increased plasma amyloid-β levels and cortical thinning. NeuroImage 98, 395–404.

Sanders, R. D. (2011). Hypothesis for the pathophysiology of delirium: Role of baseline brain network connectivity and changes in inhibitory tone. Medical hypotheses, 77(1), 140-143.

Sandler, J., Fonagy, P., & Person, E. S. (Eds.). (2012). Freud's on Narcissism: an Introduction. Karnac Books.

Santiago, J. M., Stoker, D. L., Beigel, A., Yost, D., & Spencer, P. (1987). Capgras' syndrome in a myxedema patient. Psychiatric Services, 38(2), 199-201.

Santos, R. X., Correia, S. C., Zhu, X., Smith, M. A., Moreira, P. I., Castellani, R. J., Nunomura, A. & Perry, G. (2013). Mitochondrial DNA oxidative damage and repair in aging and Alzheimer's disease. Antioxidants & redox signaling, 18(18), 2444-2457.

Saper, C. B., Chou, T. C., & Scammell, T. E. (2001). The sleep switch: hypothalamic control of sleep and wakefulness. Trends in neurosciences, 24(12), 726-731.

Sapin, E., Lapray, D., Bérod, A., Goutagny, R., Léger, L., Ravassard, P., O. Clément, L. Hanriot, P. Fort,... & Luppi, P. H. (2009). Localization of the brainstem GABAergic neurons controlling paradoxical (REM) sleep. PLoS One, 4(1), e4272.

Sara, S. J. (2009). The locus coeruleus and noradrenergic modulation of cognition. Nature reviews neuroscience, 10(3), 211-223.

Sarbin, T. R. (1986). The narrative as a root metaphor for psychology. In T.R. Sarbin (Ed.), Narrative psychology: The storied nature of human conduct (pp.3-21). New York: Praeger.

Sarter, M., & Bruno, J. P. (1997). Cognitive functions of cortical acetylcholine: toward a unifying hypothesis. Brain Research Reviews, 23(1), 28-46.

Sarter, M., & Bruno, J. P. (1999). Cortical cholinergic inputs mediating arousal, attentional processing and dreaming: differential afferent regulation of the basal forebrain by telencephalic and brainstem afferents. Neuroscience, 95(4), 933-952.

Sarter, M., Hasselmo, M. E., Bruno, J. P., & Givens, B. (2005). Unraveling the attentional functions of cortical cholinergic inputs: interactions between signal-driven and cognitive modulation of signal detection. Brain Research Reviews, 48(1), 98-111.

Sarter, M., Lustig, C., Howe, W. M., Gritton, H., & Berry, A. S. (2014). Deterministic functions of cortical acetylcholine. European Journal of Neuroscience, 39(11), 1912-1920.

Satlin, A., Volicer, L., Stopa, E.G. & Harper, D. (1996). 'Circadian locomotor activity and core-body temperature rhythms in alzheimer's disease', Neurobiology of Aging, 16; 5: 765-771.

Sato, A., & Yasuda, A. (2005). Illusion of sense of self-agency: discrepancy between the predicted and actual sensory consequences of actions modulates the sense of self-agency, but not the sense of self-ownership. Cognition, 94(3), 241-255.

Satoh, K. & Fibiger, H.C. (1986). Choline@ neurons of the laterodorsal tegmental nucleus: efferent and afferent connections. J Comp Neurol 2531277-302.

Saunders, T. J. (1987). Introduction to Ion. London: Penguin Books, p.39

Scarone, S., Manzone, M. L., Gambini, O., Kantzas, I., Limosani, I., D'Agostino, A., & Hobson, J. A. (2008). The dream as a model for psychosis: an experimental approach using bizarreness as a cognitive marker. Schizophrenia bulletin, 34(3), 515-522.

Schabus, M., Hödlmoser, K., Pecherstorfer, T. & Klösch, G. (2005). Influence of midday naps on declarative memory performance and motivation. Somnologie 9:148–153.

Schabus, M., Gruber, G., Parapatics, S., Sauter, C., Klo¨sch, G., Anderer, P., Klimesch, W., Saletu, B. & Zeitlhofer, J. (2004). Sleep spindles and their significance for declarative memory consolidation. Sleep 27:1479 –1485.

Schacter, D.L. (1995). Memory distortion: How minds, brains and societies reconstruct the past. Cambridge, MA: Harvard University Press.

Schaefer, C. B., Ooi, S. K., Bestor, T. H., & Bourc'his, D. (2007). Epigenetic decisions in mammalian germ cells. Science, 316(5823), 398-399.

Scheff, J. D., Calvano, S. E., Lowry, S. F., & Androulakis, I. P. (2010). Modeling the influence of circadian rhythms on the acute inflammatory response. Journal of theoretical biology, 264(3), 1068-1076.

Schenck, C. H., & Mahowald, M. W. (2002). REM sleep behavior disorder: clinical, developmental, and neuroscience perspectives 16 years after its formal identification in SLEEP. Sleep, 25(2), 120-138.

Schibler, U., & Sassone-Corsi, P. (2002). A web of circadian pacemakers. Cell, 111(7), 919-922.

Schiff, N. D., & Plum, F. (2000). The role of arousal and "gating" systems in the neurology of impaired consciousness. Journal of Clinical Neurophysiology, 17(5), 438-452.

Schmahl, C., Lanius, R. A., Pain, C., & Vermetten, E. (2010). Biological framework for traumatic dissociation related to early life trauma. The impact of early relational trauma on health and disease. The hidden epidemic. Cambridge University Press, Cambridge, 178-188.

Schmidt, C., Peigneux, P., Muto, V., Schenkel, M., Knoblauch, V., Münch, M., Dominique,J.F., Wirz-Justice, A., & Cajochen, C. (2006). Encoding difficulty promotes postlearning changes in sleep spindle activity during napping. The Journal of neuroscience, 26(35), 8976-8982.

Schmitt, E. M., Marcantonio, E. R., Alsop, D. C., Jones, R. N., Rogers, S. O., Fong, T. G., Eran Metzger, Sharon K. Inouye... & SAGES Study Group. (2012). Novel risk markers and long-term outcomes of delirium: the successful aging after elective surgery (SAGES) study design and methods. Journal of the American Medical Directors Association, 13(9), 818-e1.

Schmitz, J. M., Bordnick, P. S., L Kearney, M., Fuller, S. M., & Breckenridge, J. K. (1997). Treatment outcome of cocaine-alcohol dependent patients. Drug and Alcohol Dependence, 47(1), 55-61.

Schofield, I. (1997). A small exploratory study of the reaction of older people to an episode of delirium. Journal of advanced nursing, 25(5), 942-952.

Schonrock, N., Matamales, M., Ittner, L. M., & Götz, J. (2012). MicroRNA networks surrounding APP and amyloid-β metabolism—Implications for Alzheimer's disease. Experimental neurology, 235(2), 447-454.

Schore, A. N. (1994). Affect regulation and the origin of the self. Mahwah, NJ: Erlbaum.

Schore, A. N. (2003a). Affect dysregulation and disorders of the self. New York, NY: Norton.

Schore, A. N. (2003b). Affect regulation and the repair of the self. New York, NY: Norton.

Schore, A. N. (2004). The essential role of the right brain in the implicit self: Development, pathogenesis, and psychotherapy. Paper presented at the Fourth Annual AAPI Conference, New York, NY.

Schredl, M. (2003). Effects of state and trait factors on nightmare frequency. European archives of psychiatry and clinical neuroscience, 253(5), 241-247.

Schredl, M. (2010). Characteristics and contents of dreams. International review of neurobiology, 92, 135-154.

Schredl, M. (2014). You Emphasize the Continuity Between Waking and Dreaming. But What About Continuity in the Other Direction, ie Between Dreaming and Waking? And What About Discontinuity? Do You Deny Its Existence?. In Dream Consciousness (pp. 197-200). Springer International Publishing.

Schredl, M., Kleinferchner, P., & Gell, T. (1996). Dreaming and personality: Thick vs. thin boundaries. Dreaming, 6(3), 219.

Schredl, M., Weber, B., Leins, M. L., & Heuser, I. (2001). Donepezil-induced REM sleep augmentation enhances memory performance in elderly, healthy persons. Experimental Gerontology, 36(2), 353-361.

Schreiber, M., Schweizer, A., Lutz, K., Kalveram, K.T. & Jäncke, L. (1999). Potential of an interactive computer-based training in the rehabilitation of dementia: an initial study. Neuropsychol Rehabil, 9:155-167.

Schröder, P. (1920). Degeneratives Irresein und Degenerationspsychosen. Zeitschrift für die gesamte.

Schröder, P. (1922). Degenerationspsychosen und Dementia praecox. Archiv für Psychiatrie und Nervenkrankheiten, 66, 1–51.

Schröder, P. (1926) Über Degenerationspsychosen (Metabolische Erkrankungen). Zeitschrift für die

Schultes, R. E. & Smith, E.W. (1976). A Golden Guide to Hallucinogenic Plants. Golden Press.

Schulz, P., & Steimer, T. (2009). Neurobiology of circadian systems. CNS drugs, 23(2), 3-13.

Schwartz, J. (1999). Cassandra's Daughter: A History of Psychoanalysis. New York: Viking.

Schwartz, S. (2000). A historical loop of one hundred years: Similarities between 19th century and contemporary dream research. Dreaming, 10(1), 55.

Searcy, W. A., & Nowicki, S. (2005). The evolution of animal communication: reliability and deception in signaling systems. Princeton University Press.

Sehgal, A., & Mignot, E. (2011). Genetics of sleep and sleep disorders. Cell, 146(2), 194-207.

Sei, H., Sano, A., Oishi, K., Fujihara, H., Kobayashi, H., Ishida, N., & Morita, Y. (2003). Increase of hippocampal acetylcholine release at the onset of dark phase is suppressed in a mutant mice model of evening-type individuals. Neuroscience, 117(4), 785-789.

Sellal, F. & Collard, M. (2001). Sindrome confusionale, Encycl Med Chir, Vol. 17-044-C-30,Edition Scientifique et Medicales Elsevier SAS, 2001.

Selmaoui, B., & Touitou, Y. (2003). Reproducibility of the circadian rhythms of serum cortisol and melatonin in healthy subjects: a study of three different 24-h cycles over six weeks. Life sciences, 73(26), 3339-3349.

Selterman, D. F., Apetroaia, A. I., Riela, S., & Aron, A. (2013). Dreaming of You Behavior and Emotion in Dreams of Significant Others Predict Subsequent Relational Behavior. Social Psychological and Personality Science, 1948550613486678.

Selzer, M., Clarke, S., Cohen, L., Kwakkel, G., & Miller, R. (Eds.). (2014). Textbook of neural repair and rehabilitation (Vol. 1). Cambridge University Press.

Semetsky, I. (2004). The complexity of individuation. International Journal of Applied Psychoanalytic Studies, 1(4), 324-346.

Semmler, A., Hermann, S., Mormann, F., Weberpals, M., Paxian, S. A., Okulla, T., Schäfers, M., Kummer, M. P., Klockgether,T. & Heneka, M. T. (2008). Sepsis causes neuroinflammation and concomitant decrease of cerebral metabolism. Journal of neuroinflammation, 5(1), 38.

Serban, I. L., Padurariu, M., Ciobica, A., Cojocaru, D., & Lefter, R. (2013). The role of hypnosis and related techniques in insomnia. Archives of Biological Sciences, 65(2), 507-510.

Sforza, E., Krieger, J., & Petiau, C. (1997). REM sleep behavior disorder: clinical and physiopathological findings. Sleep medicine reviews, 1(1), 57-69.

Shansky, R. M., & Lipps, J. (2013). Stress-induced cognitive dysfunction: hormone-neurotransmitter interactions in the prefrontal cortex. Frontiers in human neuroscience, 7.

Sherin, J. E., Elmquist, J. K., Torrealba, F., & Saper, C. B. (1998). Innervation of histaminergic tuberomammillary neurons by GABAergic and galaninergic neurons in the ventrolateral preoptic nucleus of the rat. The Journal of neuroscience, 18(12), 4705-4721.

Sherrington, C. (1946). The endeavour of Jean Fernel. Cambridge: Cambridge University Press.

Shin, Joong-Sun Lee, O.-S. Han, B.-Y. R., (2005). 'The influence of complexes on implicit learning'. Journal of Analytical Psychology, 50, 175–90.

Siapas, A.G. & Wilson, M. A. (1998). Coordinated interactions between hippocampal ripples and cortical spindles during slow-wave sleep. Neuron 21:1123–1128.

Siddle, R., Haddock, G., Tarrier, N., & Faragher, E. B. (2002). Religious delusions in patients admitted to hospital with schizophrenia. Social psychiatry and psychiatric epidemiology, 37(3), 130-138.

Silverstein, S. M. (2014). Jung's views on causes and treatments of schizophrenia in light of current trends in cognitive neuroscience and psychotherapy research I. Aetiology and phenomenology. Journal of Analytical Psychology, 59(1), 98-129.

Simard, V., Nielsen, T. A., Tremblay, R. E., Boivin, M., & Montplaisir, J. Y. (2008). Longitudinal study of bad dreams in preschool-aged children: prevalence, demographic correlates, risk and protective factors. Sleep, 31(1), 62.

Sinason, V. (Ed.). (2002). Attachment, trauma and multiplicity: Working with dissociative identity disorder. Psychology Press.

Singer, C., Tractenberg, R. E., Kaye, J., Schafer, K., Gamst, A., Grundman, M., Thomas, R. & Thal, L. J. (2003). A multicenter, placebo-controlled trial of melatonin for sleep disturbance in Alzheimer's disease. SLEEP-NEW YORK THEN WESTCHESTER-, 26(7), 893-901.

Sinha, C. (2005). 'Epigenetics, semiotics and the mysteries of the organism'. Biological Theory, 1.2, 1–19.

Sirota, A., Csicsvari, J., Buhl, D., & Buzsáki, G. (2003). Communication between neocortex and hippocampus during sleep in rodents. Proceedings of the National Academy of Sciences, 100(4), 2065-2069.

Sjöberg, F., & Svanborg, E. (2013). How do we know when patients sleep properly or why they do not?. Critical Care, 17(3), 145.

Ski C & O'Connell B (2006) Mismanagement of delirium places patients at risk. The Australian Journal of Advanced Nursing 23, 42–46.

Skirrow, P., Jones, C., Griffiths, R. D., & Kaney, S. (2002). The impact of current media events on hallucinatory content: The experience of the intensive care unit (ICU) patient. British journal of clinical psychology, 41(1), 87-91.

Skocbat, T., Haimov, I., & Lavie, P. (1998). Melatonin-the key to the gate of sleep. Annals of medicine, 30(1), 109-114.

Slor, C. J., Adamis, D., Jansen, R. W., Meagher, D. J., Witlox, J., Houdijk, A. P., & de Jonghe, J. F. (2014). Validation and psychometric properties of the Delirium Motor

Subtype Scale in elderly hip fracture patients (Dutch version). Archives of gerontology and geriatrics, 58(1), 140-144.

Slotnick, S. D., Moo, L. R., Tesoro, M. A., & Hart, J. (2001). Hemispheric asymmetry in categorical versus coordinate visuospatial processing revealed by temporary cortical deactivation. Journal of Cognitive Neuroscience, 13(8), 1088-1096.

Smith, R. C. (1984). The meaning of dreams: the need for a standardized dream report. Psychiatry Research; 13: 267–274.

Smith, T. D., Adams, M. M., Gallagher, M., Morrison, J. H., & Rapp, P. R. (2000). Circuit-specific alterations in hippocampal synaptophysin immunoreactivity predict spatial learning impairment in aged rats. The Journal of Neuroscience, 20(17), 6587-6593.

Smythe, W. E., & Baydala, A. (2012). The hermeneutic background of CG Jung. Journal of Analytical Psychology, 57(1), 57-75.

Snyder, F. (1970). The psychodynamic implications of the physiological studies on dreams. In L. Madow & L. H. Snow (Eds.), The phenomenology of dreaming (pp. 124151). Springfield, IL: C. C. Thomas

Solms, M. (1997). The neuropsychology of dreams. Mahwah, NJ: Lawrence Erlbaum.

Solms, M. (2000). Dreaming and REM sleep are controlled by different brain mechanisms. Behavioral and Brain Sciences, 23(06), 843-850.

Solms, M. (2011). Neurobiology and the neurological basis of dreaming. Handbook of clinical neurology, 98, 519.

Solms, M. (2014). The neuropsychology of dreams: A clinico-anatomical study. Psychology Press.

Son, J. H., Shim, J. H., Kim, K. H., Ha, J. Y., & Han, J. Y. (2012). Neuronal autophagy and neurodegenerative diseases. Experimental & molecular medicine, 44(2), 89-98.

Sørensen, J. (2007). A Cognitive Theory of Magic. New York: Alta Mira Press.

Soto, C. (2013). Protein Misfolding in Neurodegenerative Diseases: The Key Pending Questions. Journal of Neurology & Translational Neuroscience.

Sparkman, N. L., Buchanan, J. B., Heyen, J. R., Chen, J., Beverly, J. L. & Johnson, R. W. (2006). Interleukin-6 facilitates lipopolysaccharide-induced disruption in working memory and expression of other proinflammatory cytokines in hippocampal neuronal cell layers. J. Neurosci. 26, 10709–10716.

Spector, A., Davies, S., Woods, B. & Orrell, M. (2000). Reality orientation for dementia: a systematic review of the evidence of effectiveness from randomized controlled trials. The Gerontologist 40, 206.

Sperber, D. (2000). An objection to the memetic approach to culture. Darwinizing culture: the status of memetics as a science, 163-173.

Sperling, R. A., LaViolette, P. S., O'Keefe, K., O'Brien, J., Rentz, D. M., Pihlajamaki, M., ... & Johnson, K. A. (2009). Amyloid deposition is associated with impaired default network function in older persons without dementia. Neuron, 63(2), 178-188.

Spiegel, D. A. (1991). Neurophysiological correlates of hypnosis and dissociation. The Journal of neuropsychiatry and clinical neurosciences.

Spitzer, M., Mamelak, A., Stickgold, R., Williams, J., Koutstall, W., Rittenhouse, C., Maher, B.A. & Hobson, J. A. (1991). Semantic priming in a lexical decision task on awakenings from REM-sleep: Evidence for a disinhibited semantic network. Sleep Research, 20, 131.

Spreng, R. N., Sepulcre, J., Turner, G. R., Stevens, W. D., & Schacter, D. L. (2013). Intrinsic architecture underlying the relations among the default, dorsal attention, and frontoparietal control networks of the human brain. Journal of cognitive neuroscience, 25(1), 74-86.

Squire, L. R., Knowlton, B., & Musen, G. (1993). The structure and organization of memory. Annual Review of Psychology, 44, 453–495.

Starkstein, S. E., Vazquez, S., Petracca, G., Sabe, L., Migliorelli, R., Teson, A., & Leiguarda, R. (1994). A SPECT study of delusions in Alzheimer's disease. Neurology, 44(11), 2055-2055.

States, B. (1988). The rhetoric of dreams. Ithaca and London: Cornell University Press.

States, B. (1993). Dreaming and storytelling. Ithaca and London: Cornell University Press.

States, B. (1997). Seeing in the dark. New Haven: Yale University Press.

Stawarczyk D., Majerus S., Maj M., Van der Linden M., D'Argembeau A. (2011). Mind-wandering: phenomenology and function as assessed with a novel experience sampling method. Acta Psychol. 136, 370–381.

Stawarczyk, D., Majerus, S., Maquet, P., & D'Argembeau, A. (2011). Neural correlates of ongoing conscious experience: both task-unrelatedness and stimulus-independence are related to default network activity. PLoS One, 6(2), e16997.

SteelFisher, G. K., Martin, L. A., Dowal, S. L., & Inouye, S. K. (2011). Sustaining clinical programs during difficult economic times: a case series from the Hospital Elder Life Program. Journal of the American Geriatrics Society, 59(10), 1873-1882.

Steininger, T. L., Alam, M. N., Gong, H., Szymusiak, R., & McGinty, D. (1999). Sleep–waking discharge of neurons in the posterior lateral hypothalamus of the albino rat. Brain research, 840(1), 138-147.

Stenstrom P. (2006). Dreaming as Madness? An Evaluation of Schizophrenia-Like Cognition in Stage REM and Stage 2 Sleep Mentation Reports. Unpublished M. Sc. Thesis, University of Montreal, Montreal, Canada.

Stenwall, E., Jönhagen, M. E., Sandberg, J., & Fagerberg, I. (2008). The older patient's experience of encountering professional carers and close relatives during an acute confusional state: an interview study. International journal of nursing studies, 45(11), 1577-1585.

Stephan, F. K. (2002). The "other" circadian system: food as a Zeitgeber. Journal of biological rhythms, 17(4), 284-292.

Stephan, F.K. & Zucker, I. (1972). Circadian rhythms in drinking behavior and locomotor activity of rats are eliminated by hypothalamic lesions. Proc Natl Acad Sci USA; 69: 1583–6.

Stephane, M., Thuras, P., Nasrallah, H., & Georgopoulos, A. P. (2003). The internal structure of the phenomenology of auditory verbal hallucinations. Schizophrenia research, 61(2), 185-193.

Steriade, M., & Timofeev, I. (2003). Neuronal plasticity in thalamocortical networks during sleep and waking oscillations. Neuron, 37(4), 563-576.

Steriade, M., McCormick, D. A., & Sejnowski, T. J. (1993). Thalamocortical oscillations in the sleeping and aroused brain. Science, 262(5134), 679-685.

Stern, D. (1985). The Interpersonal World of the Human Infant. New York: Basic Books.

Sterpenich, V., Albouy, G., Darsaud, A., Schmidt, C., Vandewalle, G., Vu, T. T. D., ... & Maquet, P. (2009). Sleep promotes the neural reorganization of remote emotional memory. The Journal of neuroscience, 29(16), 5143-5152.

Stevens, A. & Price, J. (2000). Evolutionary Psychiatry: A New Beginning (2nd edn).Routledge.

Stevens, A. (1997). Private Myths: Dreams and Dreaming. Harvard University Press. Cambridge, Massachusetts.

Stevens, A. (2002). Archetype Revisited: An Updated Natural History of the Self. 2nd Edition. Routledge.

Stevens, A. (2013). Archetype: A natural history of the self. Routledge.

Stickgold, R., & Walker, M. P. (2013). Sleep-dependent memory triage: evolving generalization through selective processing. Nature neuroscience, 16(2), 139-145.

Stickgold, R., Scott, L., Rittenhouse, C., & Hobson, J. A. (1999). Sleep-induced changes in associative memory. Journal of Cognitive Neuroscience, 11(2), 182-193.

Stoleru, D., Peng, Y., Agosto, J., & Rosbash, M. (2004). Coupled oscillators control morning and evening locomotor behaviour of Drosophila. Nature, 431(7010), 862-868.

Stoll, C., Kapfhammer, H. P., Rothenhäusler, H. B., Haller, M., Briegel, J., Schmidt, M., T. Krauseneck, K. Durst... & Schelling, G. (1999). Sensitivity and specificity of a screening test to document traumatic experiences and to diagnose post-traumatic stress disorder in ARDS patients after intensive care treatment. Intensive Care Medicine, 25(7), 697-704.

Störring, G. (1969). Zyklothymie, Emotionspsychosen, Schizophrenie. In G. Huber (ed.), Schizophrenie und Zyklothymie (Stuttgart: Thieme), 68–77.

Störring, G. E., Suchenwirth, R. and Völkel, H. (1962). Emotionalität und cycloide Psychosen. Psychiatrie, Neurologie und Medizinische Psychologie, 14, 85–97.

Strachan, T. and Read, A.P. (2004). Human Molecular Genetics 3. Garland Publishing.

Strauch, I., & Meier, B. (1996). In search of dreams: Results of experimental dream research. SUNY Press.

Strijbos, M. J., Steunenberg, B., van der Mast, R. C., Inouye, S. K., & Schuurmans, M. J. (2013). Design and methods of the Hospital Elder Life Program (HELP), a multicomponent targeted intervention to prevent delirium in hospitalized older patients: efficacy and cost-effectiveness in Dutch health care. BMC geriatrics, 13(1), 78.

Sugiura, M., Sassa, Y., Jeong, H., Wakusawa, K., Horie, K., Sato, S., & Kawashima, R. (2012). Self-face recognition in social context. Human brain mapping, 33(6), 1364-1374.

Sultan, S. S. (2010). Assessment of role of perioperative melatonin in prevention and treatment of postoperative delirium after hip arthroplasty under spinal anesthesia in the elderly. Saudi journal of anaesthesia, 4(3), 169.

Summers, G. (2014). Dynamic ego states: the significance of non-conscious and unconscious patterns, as well as conscious patterns. Co-Creative Transactional Analysis: Papers, Responses, Dialogues, and Developments, 89.

Surmeier, D. J., Graves, S. M., & Shen, W. (2014). Dopaminergic modulation of striatal networks in health and Parkinson's disease. Current opinion in neurobiology, 29, 109-117.

Sveinsson, I. S. (1975). Postoperative psychosis after heart surgery. The Journal of thoracic and cardiovascular surgery, 70(4), 717-726.

Swanson, L. W. (2007). Quest for the basic plan of nervous system circuitry. Brain Res Rev; 55:356–72.

Sweet, D. C., Levine, A. S., Billington, C. J., & Kotz, C. M. (1999). Feeding response to central orexins. Brain research, 821(2), 535-538.

Sweet, L., Adamis, D., Meagher, D. J., Davis, D., Currow, D. C., Bush, S. H., Barnes, C. & Lawlor, P. G. (2014). Ethical challenges and solutions regarding delirium studies in palliative care. Journal of pain and symptom management, 48(2), 259-271.

Symons, C. S., & Johnson, B. T. (1997). The self-reference effect in memory: a meta-analysis. Psychological bulletin, 121(3), 371.

Tacikowski, P., Brechmann, A., Marchewka, A., Jednoróg, K., Dobrowolny, M., & Nowicka, A. (2011). Is it about the self or the significance? An fMRI study of self-name recognition. Social neuroscience, 6(1), 98-107.

Taguchi, T. (2013). Bright light treatment for prevention of perioperative delirium in elderly patients. Journal of Nursing Education and Practice, 3(10), p10.

Tajfel, H. (1982). Social psychology of intergroup relations. Annual review of psychology, 33(1), 1-39.

Takahashi, K., Lin, J. S., & Sakai, K. (2009). Characterization and mapping of sleep–waking specific neurons in the basal forebrain and preoptic hypothalamus in mice. Neuroscience, 161(1), 269-292.

Takahashi, S., Kapás, L., Fang, J., & Krueger, J. M. (1999). Somnogenic relationships between tumor necrosis factor and interleukin-1. American Journal of Physiology-Regulatory, Integrative and Comparative Physiology, 276(4), R1132-R1140.

Tallis, R. (2012). Aping Mankind: Neuromania, Darwinitis and the Misrepresentation of Humanity. Acumen Publishing, Limited.

Tanaka, M., Hayashi, S., Tamada, Y., Ikeda, T., Hisa, Y., Takamatsu, T., & Ibata, Y. (1997). Direct retinal projections to GRP neurons in the suprachiasmatic nucleus of the rat. Neuroreport, 8(9), 2187-2191.

Tatematsu, N., Hayashi, A., Narita, K., Tamaki, A., & Tsuboyama, T. (2011). The effects of exercise therapy on delirium in cancer patients: a retrospective study. Supportive Care in Cancer, 19(6), 765-770.

Taub, J., M. Kramer, D. Arand, & G. Jacobs. (1978). Nightmare dreams and nightmare confabulations. Comprehensive Psychiatry, 19, 285-91.

Taylor, K., Mandon, S., Freiwald, W. A., & Kreiter, A. K. (2005). Coherent oscillatory activity in monkey area v4 predicts successful allocation of attention. Cerebral Cortex, 15(9), 1424-1437.

Teeling, J. L., & Perry, V. H. (2009). Systemic infection and inflammation in acute CNS injury and chronic neurodegeneration: underlying mechanisms. Neuroscience, 158(3), 1062-1073.

Teman, P. T., Tippmann-Peikert, M., Silber, M. H., Slocumb, N. L., & Auger, R. R. (2009). Idiopathic rapid-eye-movement sleep disorder: associations with antidepressants, psychiatric diagnoses, and other factors, in relation to age of onset. Sleep medicine, 10(1), 60-65.

Terzaghi, M., Sartori, I., Rustioni, V., & Manni, R. (2014). Sleep disorders and acute nocturnal delirium in the elderly: A comorbidity not to be overlooked. European journal of internal medicine, 25(4), 350-355.

Thaipisuttikul, P., Lobach, I., Zweig, Y., Gurnani, A., & Galvin, J. E. (2012). Capgras syndrome in dementia with Lewy bodies. International Psychogeriatrics, 25(05), 843-849.

Thal, D. R., Rüb, U., Orantes, M., & Braak, H. (2002). Phases of Aβ-deposition in the human brain and its relevance for the development of AD. Neurology, 58(12), 1791-1800.

Thapan, K., Arendt, J., & Skene, D. J. (2001). An action spectrum for melatonin suppression: evidence for a novel non-rod, non-cone photoreceptor system in humans. The Journal of physiology, 535(1), 261-267.

Thompson, J. M., Hamilton, C. J., Gray, J. M., Quinn, J. G., Mackin, P., Young, A. H., & Nicol Ferrier, I. (2006). Executive and visuospatial sketchpad resources in euthymic bipolar disorder: Implications for visuospatial working memory architecture. Memory, 14(4), 437-451.

Thompson, R. (1930). The Epic of Gilgamesh. Oxford: Oxford University Press.

Tieges, Z., Brown, L. J., & MacLullich, A. M. (2014). Objective assessment of attention in delirium: a narrative review. International journal of geriatric psychiatry.

Tiesinga, P., Fellous, J. M., & Sejnowski, T. J. (2008). Regulation of spike timing in

Tillhagen, C. H. (1960). The conception of the nightmare in Sweden. Humanioria: Essays in Literature, Folklore and Bibliography Honoring Archer Taylor, 317-29.

Timofeev, I., Grenier, F., & Steriade, M. (2001). Disfacilitation and active inhibition in the neocortex during the natural sleep-wake cycle: an intracellular study. Proceedings of the National Academy of Sciences, 98(4), 1924-1929.

Tittle, A., & Burgess, G. H. (2011). Relative contribution of attention and memory toward disorientation or post-traumatic amnesia in an acute brain injury sample. Brain Injury, 25(10), 933-942.

Todorov, T. (1986). Structural analysis of narrative. In R.C. Davis (Ed.), Contemporary literary criticism: Modernism through poststructuralism. New York: Longman.

Tom, S. E., Hubbard, R. A., Crane, P. K., Haneuse, S. J., Bowen, J., McCormick, W. C., McCurry, M. C. & Larson, E. B. (2014). Characterization of Dementia and Alzheimer's Disease in an Older Population: Updated Incidence and Life Expectancy With and Without Dementia. American journal of public health, (0), e1-e6.

Tononi, G., & Cirelli, C. (2003). Sleep and synaptic homeostasis: a hypothesis. Brain research bulletin, 62(2), 143-150.

Toolan, M. J. (1988). Narrative: A critical linguistic introduction. London and New York: Routledge.

Tracey, K. J. (2002). The inflammatory reflex. Nature, 420(6917), 853-859.

Trevarthen, C. (1998). The concept and foundations of infant intersubjectivity. Intersubjective communication and emotion in early ontogeny, 15-46.

Trompeo, A. C., Vidi, Y., Locane, M. D., Braghiroli, A., Mascia, L., Bosma, K., & Ranieri, V. M. (2011). Sleep disturbances in the critically ill patients: role of delirium and sedative agents. Minerva anestesiologica, 77(6), 604-612.

Trzepacz, P. T., Baker, R. W., & Greenhouse, J. (1988). A symptom rating scale for delirium. Psychiatry research, 23(1), 89-97.

Trzepacz, P. T. (1994). The neuropathogenesis of delirium: a need to focus our research. Psychosomatics, 35(4), 374-391.

Trzepacz, P. T. (1999). Update on the neuropathogenesis of delirium. Dementia and geriatric cognitive disorders, 10(5), 330-334.

Trzepacz, P. T. (2000). Is there a final common neural pathway in delirium? Focus on acetylcholine and dopamine. In Seminars in clinical neuropsychiatry (Vol. 5, No. 2, pp. 132-148).

Trzepacz, P. T., Bourne, R. & Zhang, S. (2008). Designing clinical trials for the treatment of delirium. J Psychosom Res; 65: 299–307.

Trzepacz, P. T., Mittal, D., Torres, R., Kanary, K., Norton, J. & Jimerson, N. (2001). Validation of the Delirium Rating Scale-Revised-98 (DRS-R-98). Journal of Neuropsychiatry and Clinical Neurosciences 13:229-242.

Trzepacz, P. T., Mittal, D., Torres, R., Kanary, K., Norton, J., Jimerson, N. (2002). Delirium vs dementia symptoms: Delirium Rating Scale-Revised (DRS-R-98) and Cognitive Test for Delirium (CTD) item comparisons. Psychosomatics 43: 156-7.

Trzepacz, P.T. & Meagher, D.J. (2008). Neuropsychiatric aspects of delirium. In: Yudofsky SC, Hales RE, Eds. American Psychiatric Publishing Textbook of Neuropsychiatry. Washington, DC: American Psychiatric Publishing; pp 445–517.

Trzepacz, P.T., Meagher, D., Leonard, M. (2010). Delirium. In: Levenson J, editor. Textbook of Psychosomatic Medicine. Washington (DC): American Psychiatric Press, Inc.

Trzepacz, P. T., Meagher, D. J., & Leonard, M. (2011). Delirium. The American Psychiatric Publishing Textbook of Psychosomatic Medicine. 2nd ed. Washington, DC: American Psychiatric Publishing.

Trzepacz, P. T., Franco, J. G., Meagher, D. J., Lee, Y., Kim, J. L., Kishi, Y., Furlanetto, L. & Leonard, M. (2012). Phenotype of subsyndromal delirium using pooled multicultural Delirium Rating Scale—Revised-98 data. Journal of psychosomatic research, 73(1), 10-17.

Tsakiris, M., Haggard, P., Franck, N., Mainy, N., & Sirigu, A. (2005). A specific role for efferent information in self-recognition. Cognition, 96, 215-231.

Turner, J. (2013). Human Psychology as Seen Through the Dream (Vol. 34). Routledge.

Turner, R. P., Lukoff, D., Barnhouse, R. T. & Lu, F. G. (1995) Religious or Spiritual Problem. A Culturally Sensitive Diagnostic Category in the DSM-IV. Journal of Nervous and Mental Disease, Vol.183, No. 7, pp. 435-444.

Turner, M. (1996). The literary mind: The origins of thought and language. New York: Oxford University Press.

Tussey, C. M., Broshek, D. K., & Marcopulos, B. A. (2010). Delirium Assessment in Older Adults. Handbook of Assessment in Clinical Gerontology, 179.

Uddin, L. Q., Iacoboni, M., Lange, C., & Keenan, J. P. (2007). The self and social cognition: the role of cortical midline structures and mirror neurons. Trends in cognitive sciences, 11(4), 153-157.

Ullman, M. (1969). Dreaming as metaphor in motion. Archives of General Psychiatry, 21, 696-703.

Uspenskij, B.A., et al. (1973). Theses on the semiotic study of cultures. In J. van der Eng & M. Grygar (Eds.), Structure of texts and semiotics of culture (pp. 1-28).The Hague: Mouton.

Vaidya, C. J., Zhao, M., Desmond, J. E., & Gabrieli, J. D. (2002). Evidence for cortical encoding specificity in episodic memory: memory-induced re-activation of picture processing areas. Neuropsychologia, 40(12), 2136-2143.

Vaillant, G. (2012). Lifting the Field's "Repression" of Defenses. Am J Psychiatry, 169: 9.

Vaillant, G. E. & Battista, J. R. (1982). Empirical test of Vaillant's hierarchy of ego functions. Am J Psychiatry, 139:356-357.

Vaillant, G. E. & Drake, R. E. (1985). Maturity of ego defense in relation to DSM-III Axis II personality disorders. Arch Gen Psychiatry, 42:597-601.

Vaillant, G. E. (1977). Adaptation to Life. Boston, Little, Brown.

Vaillant, G. E. (1976). Natural history of male psychological health: the relation of choice of ego mechanisms of defense to adult adjustment. Arch Gen Psychiatry, 33:535-545.

Vaillant, G. E., & Vaillant, C. O. (1990). Natural history of male psychological health XII: a 45-year study of predictors of successful aging at 65. American Journal of Psychiatry, 147, 31-37.

Vaillant, G. E., Bond, M. & Vaillant, C. O. (1986). An empirically validated hierarchy of defense mechanisms. Arch Gen Psychiatry, 43:786-794.

Van der Cammen, T. J., Tiemeier, H., Engelhart, M. J., & Fekkes, D. (2006). Abnormal neurotransmitter metabolite levels in Alzheimer patients with a delirium. International journal of geriatric psychiatry, 21(9), 838-843.

Van der Hart, O., Nijenhuis, E. R., & Steele, K. (2006). The haunted self: Structural dissociation and the treatment of chronic traumatization. WW Norton & Company.

Van der Kolk, B. A., & d'Andrea, W. (2010). Towards a developmental trauma disorder diagnosis for childhood interpersonal trauma. The impact of early life trauma on health and disease: The hidden epidemic, 57-68.

Van der Kolk, B. A. & Fisler, R. (1995). Dissociation and the fragmentary nature of traumatic memories: Overview and exploratory study. Journal of traumatic stress, 8(4), 505-525.

Van der Kolk, B. A., McFarlane, A. C., & Weisaeth, L. (Eds.). (2012). Traumatic stress: The effects of overwhelming experience on mind, body, and society. Guilford Press.

Van der Kolk, B., Blitz, R., Burr, W., Sherry, S., & Hartmann, E. (1984). Nightmares and trauma: a comparison of nightmares after combat with lifelong nightmares in veterans. Am J Psychiatry, 141(2), 187-90.

Van der Linden (1998). The relationships between working memory and long-term memory. Comptes Rendus de l Acadamie des Sciences, Serie III, Sciences de la vie (Paris), 321(2-3), 175–177.

Van Munster, B. C., Korse, C. M., de Rooij, S. E., Bonfrer, J. M., Zwinderman, A. H. & Korevaar, J. C. (2009). Markers of cerebral damage during delirium in elderly patients with hip fracture. BMC Neurology 9:21.

Van Munster, B. C., Korevaar, J. C., De Rooij, S. E., Levi, M., & Zwinderman, A. H. (2007). Genetic polymorphisms related to delirium tremens: a systematic review. Alcoholism: Clinical and Experimental Research, 31(2), 177-184.

Van Munster, B. C., Bisschop, P. H., Zwinderman, A. H., Korevaar, J. C., Endert, E., Wiersinga, W. J., Oosten, H. E., Goslings, J. C. & de Rooij, S.E. (2010). Cortisol, interleukins and S100B in delirium in the elderly. Brain Cogn. 74, 18–23.

Van Someren, E. J. W. (2000). Circadian and sleep disturbances in the elderly. Experimental gerontology, 35(9), 1229-1237.

Vanhaudenhuyse, A., Laureys, S., & Faymonville, M. E. (2014). Neurophysiology of hypnosis. Neurophysiologie Clinique/Clinical Neurophysiology, 44(4), 343-353.

Vanhaudenhuyse, A., Noirhomme, Q., Tshibanda, L. J. F., Bruno, M. A., Boveroux, P., Schnakers, C., Soddu, A., Perlbarg, V., Ledoux, D., Brichant, J.F., Moonen, G., Maquet, P., Greicius, M.D., Laureys, S. & Boly, M. (2010). Default network connectivity reflects the level of consciousness in non-communicative brain-damaged patients. Brain, 133(1), 161-171.

Vasilevskis, E. E., Han, J. H., Hughes, C. G., & Ely, E. W. (2012). Epidemiology and risk factors for delirium across hospital settings. Best Practice & Research Clinical Anaesthesiology, 26(3), 277-287.

Vaughan, S., Spitzer, R., Davies, M. & Roose, S. (1997). 'The definition and assesment of analytical process: can analysts agree?', International Journal of Psychoanalysis, 78 (5): 959-74.

Venero, J. L., Revuelta, M., Atiki, L., Santiago, M., Toms-Camardiel, M. C., Cano, J., & Machado, A. (2003). Evidence for dopamine-derived hydroxyl radical formation in the nigrostriatal system in response to axotomy. Free Radical Biology and Medicine, 34(1), 111-123.

Vergauwen, R. (2014). Consciousness, Recursion and Language. In Language and Recursion (pp. 169-179). Springer New York.

Verret, L., Fort, P., Gervasoni, D., Leger, L. & Luppi, P-H. (2006). Localization of the neurons active during paradoxical (REM) sleep and projecting to the locus coeruleus noradrenergic neurons in the rat. J. Comp. Neurol., 495, pp. 573–586.

Victor, M. & Adams, R.D. (1962). The acute confusional states. In: Principles of internal medicine (eds T.R. Harrison et al.,) McGraw-Hill, New York.

Vlassenko, A. G., Mintun, M. A., Xiong, C., Sheline, Y. I., Goate, A. M., Benzinger, T. L., & Morris, J. C. (2011). Amyloid-beta plaque growth in cognitively normal adults: Longitudinal [11C] Pittsburgh compound B data. Annals of neurology, 70(5), 857-861.

Vogeley, K., Bussfeld, P., Newen, A., Herrmann, S., Happé, F., Falkai, P. Maier, W. Shah, N. J. M, Fink, G. R. & Zilles, K. (2001). Mind reading: neural mechanisms of theory of mind and self-perspective. Neuroimage, 14(1), 170-181.

Volicer, L., Harper, D. G., Manning, B. C., Goldstein, R., & Satlin, A. (2001). Sundowning and circadian rhythms in Alzheimer's disease. American Journal of Psychiatry, 158(5), 704-711.

Von der Malsburg, C. & Singer, W. (1988). Principles of cortical network organization. Neurobiology of neocortex, 69, 99.

Von Franz, M. L. (1964). The process of individuation. Man and his symbols, 164.

Von Franz, M. L. (1974). Shadow and evil in fairy tales:[comprised text from 2 lectures]. Spring Publications (Zürich).

Von Franz, M. L. (1985). Projection and re-collection in Jungian psychology: Reflections of the soul. Open Court Publishing.

Von Franz, M. L. (1999). Archetypal dimensions of the psyche. Shambhalla PUB Incorporated.

Von Helmholtz, H. (1971). Selected writings of Hermann von Helmholtz. Wesleyan Univ Pr.

Von Staden, H. (1989). Herophilus: the art of medicine in early Alexandria. Cambridge: University Press.

Voyer, P., Richard, S., Doucet, L., & Carmichael, P. H. (2009). Detecting delirium and subsyndromal delirium using different diagnostic criteria among demented long-term care residents. Journal of the American Medical Directors Association, 10(3), 181-188.

Waage, S., Moen, B. E., Pallesen, S., Eriksen, H. R., & Ursin, H. (2009). Shift work disorder among oil rig workers in the North Sea. Sleep, 32(4), 558.

Wacker, P., Nunes, P. V., Cabrita, H., Forlenza, O. V. (2006). Post-operative delirium is associated with poor cognitive outcome and dementia. Dementia and Geriatric Cognitive Disorders 21:221-7.

Wager, T. D., Waugh, C. E., Lindquist, M., Noll, D. C., Fredrickson, B. L., & Taylor, S. F. (2009). Brain mediators of cardiovascular responses to social threat: part I: Reciprocal dorsal and ventral sub-regions of the medial prefrontal cortex and heart-rate reactivity. Neuroimage, 47(3), 821-835.

Wagner, A. D., Shannon, B. J., Kahn, I., & Buckner, R. L. (2005). Parietal lobe contributions to episodic memory retrieval. Trends in cognitive sciences, 9(9), 445-453.

Wagner, U., Gais, S., & Born, J. (2001). Emotional memory formation is enhanced across sleep intervals with high amounts of rapid eye movement sleep. Learning & Memory, 8(2), 112-119.

Wakefulness, N. (2012). Neuroanatomy and neurobiology of sleep. ERS Handbook of Respiratory Sleep Medicine, 1.

Walker, M. P. (2009). The role of sleep in cognition and emotion. Ann. N. Y. Acad. Sci. 1156, 168–197.

Walker, M. P., Liston, C., Hobson, J. A., & Stickgold, R. (2002). Cognitive flexibility across the sleep–wake cycle: REM-sleep enhancement of anagram problem solving. Cognitive Brain Research, 14(3), 317-324.

Walker, S. (2014). Jung and the Jungians on Myth. Routledge.

Waller, J. (1816). Treatise on the incubus, or night-mare, disturbed sleep, terrific dreams, and nocturnal visions: with the means of removing these distressing complaints. London: E. Cox & Son.

Wampold, B. E. (2001). Contextualizing psychotherapy as a healing practice: Culture, history, and methods. Applied and Preventive Psychology, 10(2), 69-86.

Wampold, B. E., & Brown, G. S. J. (2005). Estimating variability in outcomes attributable to therapists: a naturalistic study of outcomes in managed care. Journal of consulting and clinical psychology, 73(5), 914.

Wamsley, E. J., Hirota, Y., Tucker, M. A., Smith, M. R., & Antrobus, J. S. (2007). Circadian and ultradian influences on dreaming: a dual rhythm model. Brain research bulletin, 71(4), 347-354.

Wamsley, E. J., Perry, K., Djonlagic, I., Reaven, L. B., & Stickgold, R. (2010). Cognitive replay of visuomotor learning at sleep onset: temporal dynamics and relationship to task performance. Sleep, 33(1), 59.

Wamsley, E. J., Tucker, M., Payne, J. D., Benavides, J. A., & Stickgold, R. (2010). Dreaming of a learning task is associated with enhanced sleep-dependent memory consolidation. Current Biology, 20(9), 850-855.

Wang, D., Cui, L. N., & Renaud, L. P. (2003). Pre-and postsynaptic gaba< sub> b</sub> receptors modulate rapid neurotransmission from suprachiasmatic nucleus to parvocellular hypothalamic paraventricular nucleus neurons. Neuroscience, 118(1), 49-58.

Wang, Y. (2013). Gene Regulatory Networks. In Encyclopedia of Systems Biology (pp. 801-805). Springer New York.

Wardlaw, J. M., Smith, E. E., Biessels, G. J., Cordonnier, C., Fazekas, F., Frayne, R., Lindley, R. A. & Dichgans, M. (2013). Neuroimaging standards for research into small vessel disease and its contribution to ageing and neurodegeneration. The Lancet Neurology, 12(8), 822-838.

Waring, J. D., Payne, J. D., Schacter, D. L., & Kensinger, E. (2010). Impact of individual differences upon emotion-induced memory trade-offs. Cognition & emotion, 24(1), 150–167.

Warman, V. L., Dijk, D. J., Warman, G. R., Arendt, J., & Skene, D. J. (2003). Phase advancing human circadian rhythms with short wavelength light. Neuroscience letters, 342(1), 37-40.

Watson, D. C. (2002). Predicting psychiatric symptomatology with the Defense Style Questionnaire-40. International Journal of Stress Management, 9, 275-287.

Webster, H. H., & Jones, B. E. (1988). Neurotoxic lesions of the dorsolateral pontomesencephalic tegmentum-cholinergic cell area in the cat. II. Effects upon sleep-waking states. Brain research, 458(2), 285-302.

Weinberger, D. R., & McClure, R. K. (2002). Neurotoxicity, neuroplasticity, and magnetic resonance imaging morphometry: what is happening in the schizophrenic brain?. Archives of General Psychiatry, 59(6), 553-558.

Weinhouse, G. L., Schwab, R. J., Watson, P. L., Patil, N., Vaccaro, B., Pandharipande, P., & Ely, E. W. (2009). Bench-to-bedside review: delirium in ICU patients-importance of sleep deprivation. Crit Care, 13(6), 234.

Weintraub, D., Doshi, J., Koka, D., Davatzikos, C., Siderowf, A. D., Duda, J. E., Wolk,D.A, Moberg,P.J., Xie, S.X. & Clark, C. M. (2011). Neurodegeneration across stages of cognitive decline in Parkinson disease. Archives of Neurology, 68(12), 1562-1568.

Weir, A. J., Paterson, C. A., Tieges, Z., MacLullich, A. M., Parra-Rodriguez, M., Della Sala, S., & Logie, R. H. (2014, August). Development of Android apps for cognitive assessment of dementia and delirium. In Engineering in Medicine and Biology Society (EMBC), 2014 36th Annual International Conference of the IEEE (pp. 2169-2172). IEEE.

Weiskrantz, L., & Carey, D. P. (1998). Consciousness lost and found. Trends in Neurosciences, 21(1), 49-49.

Weitzman, E. D., Moline, M. L., Czeisler, C. A., & Zimmerman, J. C. (1983). Chronobiology of aging: temperature, sleep-wake rhythms and entrainment. Neurobiology of aging, 3(4), 299-309.

Welsh, D. K., Logothetis, D. E., Meister, M., & Reppert, S. M. (1995). Individual neurons dissociated from rat suprachiasmatic nucleus express independently phased circadian firing rhythms. Neuron, 14(4), 697-706.

West, M. L. (1983).The Orphic Poems, Oxford: Clarendon Press.

West, M. L. (2006). Homeric Hymns, Classical Quarterly 56 (331-48).

Westra, H. A., Arkowitz, H., & Dozois, D. J. (2009). Adding a motivational interviewing pretreatment to cognitive behavioral therapy for generalized anxiety disorder: A preliminary randomized controlled trial. Journal of Anxiety Disorders, 23(8), 1106-1117.

Wever, R. (1969). [Strength of a light-dark cycle as a time determiner for circadian rhythm in man]. Pflugers Archiv: European journal of physiology, 321(2), 133-142.

Weyer, J. (1991 [1583]). Witches, devils and doctors in the Renaissance. Johann Wyer: De praestigiis daemonum (ed. G. Mora). Binghamton, N.Y.: Center for Medieval & Renaissance Studies.

Wheeler, M. E., Petersen, S. E., & Buckner, R. L. (2000). Memory's echo: vivid remembering reactivates sensory-specific cortex. Proceedings of the National Academy of Sciences, 97(20), 11125-11129.

Whitehead, N. (2002). Dark Shamans: Kanaima and the Poetics of

Whitewell, J. R. (1927). Historical notes on psychiatry. Philadelphia.Blaldsten.

Whitmont, E. C. (1969). The symbolic quest: Basic concepts of analytical psychology.

WHO Regional Office for Europe. European hospital morbidity database. Copenhagen: World Health Organization, 2012.

Willard, B., Hauss-Wegrzyniak, B., & Wenk, G. L. (1999). Pathological and biochemical consequences of acute and chronic neuroinflammation within the basal forebrain cholinergic system of rats. Neuroscience, 88(1), 193-200.

Wille, L. (1888). Die Lehre von der Verwirrtheit. Archives für Psychiatrie, (19), 328-51.

Williams, J., Merritt, J., Rittenhouse, C., & Hobson, J. A. (1992). Bizarreness in dreams and fantasies: implications for the activation-synthesis hypothesis. Consciousness and Cognition, 1(2), 172-185.

Wills-Brandon, C. (2000). One Last Hug Before I Go: The Mystery and Meaning of Deathbed Visions. Deerfield Beach, FL: Lightning Source Incorporated.

Wilson, B. A. (2002). Towards a comprehensive model of cognitive rehabilitation. neuropsychological rehabilitation, 12(2), 97-110.

Wilson, E. O. (1998). Consilience: the unity of knowledge. New York: Knopf.

Wilson, K., Broadhurst, C., Driver, M., Jackson, M. & Mottram, P. (2005). Plasma insulin growth factor-1 and incident delirium in older people. Int J Geriatr Psychiatry; 20: 154–9.

Wilson, R. S., Nag, S., Boyle, P. A., Hizel, L. P., Yu, L., Buchman, A. S., Schneider, J.A. & Bennett, D. A. (2013). Neural reserve, neuronal density in the locus ceruleus, and cognitive decline. Neurology, 80(13), 1202-1208.

Windt, J. M. (2014). How Can the Protoconsciousness Hypothesis Contribute to Philosophical Theories of Consciousness and the Self?. In Dream Consciousness (pp. 225-230). Springer International Publishing.

Wingo, T. S., Rosen, A., Cutler, D. J., Lah, J. J., & Levey, A. I. (2012). Paraoxonase-1 polymorphisms in Alzheimer's disease, Parkinson's disease, and AD-PD spectrum diseases. Neurobiology of aging, 33(1), 204-e13.

Winkler, J. (1990). Unnatural acts: erotic protocols in Artemidoros' Dream analysis. In The constraints of desire, J Winkler, 17-44. London: Routledge.

Winson, J. (1985). Brain and psyche: The biology of the unconscious. Anchor Press/Doubleday, Garden City, NY.

Winson, J. (2002). The meaning of dreams. Sci. Am. 12: 54–61.

Winson, J. (2004). To sleep, perchance to dream. Learn. Mem. (11).

Wisor, J. P., Edgar, D. M., Yesavage, J., Ryan, H. S., McCormick, C. M., Lapustea, N., & Murphy Jr, G. M. (2005). Sleep and circadian abnormalities in a transgenic mouse model of Alzheimer's disease: a role for cholinergic transmission. Neuroscience, 131(2), 375-385.

Witlox, J., Eurelings, L. S., de Jonghe, J. F., Kalisvaart, K. J., Eikelenboom, P., & Van Gool, W. A. (2010). Delirium in elderly patients and the risk of postdischarge mortality, institutionalization, and dementia: a meta-analysis. Jama, 304(4), 443-451.

Wolkove, N., Elkholy, O., Baltzan, M., & Palayew, M. (2007). Sleep and aging: 1. Sleep disorders commonly found in older people. Canadian Medical Association Journal, 176(9), 1299-1304.

Womelsdorf, T., Fries, P., Mitra, P. P., & Desimone, R. (2005). Gamma-band synchronization in visual cortex predicts speed of change detection. Nature, 439(7077), 733-736.

Wong, C. L., Holroyd-Leduc, J., Simel, D. L., & Straus, S. E. (2010). Does this patient have delirium?: value of bedside instruments. Jama, 304(7), 779-786.

Wood, J. M., & Bootzin, R. R. (1990). The prevalence of nightmares and their independence from anxiety. Journal of Abnormal Psychology, 99(1), 64.

Wood, J. M., Bootzin, R. R., Quan, S. F., & Klink, M. E. (1993). Prevalence of nightmares among patients with asthma and chronic obstructive airways disease. Dreaming, 3(4), 231.

Woodruff, C. C., Johnson, J. D., Uncapher, M. R., & Rugg, M. D. (2005). Content-specificity of the neural correlates of recollection. Neuropsychologia, 43(7), 1022-1032.

Woods, R. T. & Clare, L: (2006). Cognition-based therapies and mild cognitive impairment. In Perspectives on Mild Cognitive Impairment. international Perspectives. Edited by Tuokko H, Hultsch D. New York: Taylor & Francis:245-264.

Woods, B. (1999). The person in dementia care. Generations, 23(3), 35.

Woods, B., Aguirre, E., Spector, A. E., & Orrell, M. (2012). Cognitive stimulation to improve cognitive functioning in people with dementia. Cochrane Database Syst Rev, 2.

Woody, E. Z., & Szechtman, H. (2011). Adaptation to potential threat: the evolution, neurobiology, and psychopathology of the security motivation system. Neuroscience & Biobehavioral Reviews, 35(4), 1019-1033.

World Health Organization (1993). International Statistical Classification of Diseases

Wright, D. K., Brajtman, S., & Macdonald, M. E. (2014). A relational ethical approach to end-of-life delirium. Journal of pain and symptom management, 48(2), 191-198.

Wurtman, R. J., Altschule, M. D., & Holmgren, U. (1959). Effects of pinealectomy and of a bovine pineal extract in rats. Amer. J. Physiol, 197, 108-110.

Xie, A., Gao, J., Xu, L., & Meng, D. (2014). Shared Mechanisms of Neurodegeneration in Alzheimer's Disease and Parkinson's Disease. BioMed Research International, 2014.

Yang, F. M., Inouye, S. K., Fearing, M. A., Kiely, D. K., Marcantonio, E. R., & Jones, R. N. (2008). Participation in activity and risk for incident delirium. Journal of the American Geriatrics Society, 56(8), 1479-1484.

Yang, F. M., Jones, R. N., Inouye, S. K., Tommet, D., Crane, P. K., Rudolph, J. L., ... Marcantonio, E. R. (2013). Selecting optimal screening items for delirium: an application of item response theory. BMC Medical Research Methodology, 13(1), 8.

Yang, F. M., Marcantonio, E. R., Inouye, S. K., Kiely, D. K., Rudolph, J. L., Fearing, M. A., & Jones, R. N. (2009). Phenomenological subtypes of delirium in older persons: patterns, prevalence, and prognosis. Psychosomatics, 50(3), 248-254.

Yang, J. J., Wang, Y. T., Cheng, P. C., Kuo, Y. J., & Huang, R. C. (2010). Cholinergic modulation of neuronal excitability in the rat suprachiasmatic nucleus. Journal of neurophysiology, 103(3), 1397-1409.

Yaretsky, A., Arzi, T. & Ashkenazi, I. (1996). Diurnal variation in language tests and relevance to early detection of dementia: Disruption of time dependency in dementing subjects. J. Am. Geriatr. Soc. 44:882–883.

Yaroush, R., Sullivan, M. J. et al. (1971). Effect of sleep on memory. II: Differential effect of first and second half of the night. J. Exp. Psychol. 88, s361–366.

Yirmiya, R. & Goshen, I. (2011). "Immune modulation of learning, memory, neural plasticity and neurogenesis," Brain, Behavior, and Immunity, vol. 25, no. 2, pp. 181–213.

Yoo, S. H., Yamazaki, S., Lowrey, P. L., Shimomura, K., Ko, C. H., Buhr, E. D., Spieka, S.M. & Takahashi, J. S. (2004). PERIOD2:: LUCIFERASE real-time reporting of circadian dynamics reveals persistent circadian oscillations in mouse peripheral tissues. Proceedings of the National Academy of Sciences of the United States of America, 101(15), 5339-5346.

Yoon, I. Y., Kripke, D. F., Elliott, J. A., Youngstedt, S. D., Rex, K. M., & Hauger, R. L. (2003). Age-related changes of circadian rhythms and sleep-wake cycles. Journal of the American Geriatrics Society, 51(8), 1085-1091.

Yoshida, K., McCormack, S., España, R. A., Crocker, A., & Scammell, T. E. (2006). Afferents to the orexin neurons of the rat brain. Journal of Comparative Neurology, 494(5), 845-861.

Young, A.W., Hellawell, D., Wright, S. & Ellis, H.D. (1994). Reduplication of visual stimuli. Behav Neurol.; 7 (3-4): 135-142.

Young, G. (2008). Capgras delusion: an interactionist model. Consciousness and cognition, 17(3), 863-876.

Young, J., & Inouye, S. K. (2007). Delirium in older people. Bmj, 334(7598), 842-846.

Zadra A. & Domhoff G. W. (2011). The content of dreams: methods and findings, in Principles and Practices of Sleep Medicine, 5th Edn., eds Kryger M., Roth T., Dement W., editors. (Philadelphia, PA: Elsevier Saunders), 585–594

Zadra, A., & Domhoff, G. W. (2011). Dream content: quantitative findings. Principles and Practice of Sleep Medicine, Elsevier Saunders, St. Louis MO, 585-594.

Zadra, A., & Donderi, D. C. (1993). Variety and intensity of emotions in bad dreams and nightmares. Can Psychol, 34, 294.

Zadra, A., & Donderi, D. C. (2000). Nightmares and bad dreams: their prevalence and relationship to well-being. Journal of abnormal psychology, 109(2), 273.

Zadra, A., Pilon, M., & Donderi, D. C. (2006). Variety and intensity of emotions in nightmares and bad dreams. The Journal of nervous and mental disease, 194(4), 249-254.

Zanasi, M., De Persis, S., Caporali, M., & Siracusano, A. (2005). Dreams and age 1. Perceptual and motor skills, 100(3c), 925-938.

Zanetti, O., Zanieri, G., di Giovanni, G., de Vreese, L.P., Pezzini, A., Metitieri, T., Trabucchi, M. (2001). Effectiveness of procedural memory stimulation in mild Alzheimer's disease patients: a controlled study. Neuropsychol Rehabil; 11:263-272.

Zatz, M., & Brownstein, M. J. (1979). Intraventricular carbachol mimics the effects of light on the circadian rhythm in the rat pineal gland. Science, 203(4378), 358-361.

Zatz, M., & Herkenham, M. A. (1981). Intraventricular carbachol mimics the phase-shifting effect of light on the circadian rhythm of wheel-running activity. Brain research, 212(1), 234-238.

Zhang, B., Gaiteri, C., Bodea, L. G., Wang, Z., McElwee, J., Podtelezhnikov, A. A., Zhang, C. & Emilsson, V. (2013). Integrated systems approach identifies genetic nodes and networks in late-onset Alzheimer's disease. Cell, 153(3), 707-720.

Zhang, D., Wang, Y., Zhou, L., Yuan, H., & Shen, D. (2011). Multimodal classification of Alzheimer's disease and mild cognitive impairment. Neuroimage, 55(3), 856-867.

Zhang, T., Zhu, Y., & Wu, Y. (2014). Losing oneself upon placement in another's position: The influence of perspective on self-referential processing. Consciousness and cognition, 27, 53-61.

Zhang, Y., Zee, P. C., Kirby, J. D., Takahashi, J. S., & Turek, F. W. (1993). A cholinergic antagonist, mecamylamine, blocks light-induced Fos immunoreactivity in specific regions of the hamster suprachiasmatic nucleus. Brain research, 615(1), 107-112.

Zhdanova, I. V., Wurtman, R. J., Regan, M. M., Taylor, J. A., Shi, J. P., & Leclair, O. U. (2001). Melatonin treatment for age-related insomnia. The Journal of Clinical Endocrinology & Metabolism, 86(10), 4727-4730.

Zhuang, J-P., Fang, R., Feng, X., Xu, X-H., Liu, L-H., Bai, Q-K., Tang, H-D., Zhao, Z-G. & Chen, S-D. (2013). The impact of human-computer interaction-based comprehensive training on the cognitive functions of cognitive impairment elderly individuals in a nursing home. Journal of Alzheimer's Disease; 36(2): 245-251.

Zisapel, N. (2001). Melatonin–dopamine interactions: from basic neurochemistry to a clinical setting. Cellular and molecular neurobiology, 21(6), 605-616.

Zrenner, C. (1985). Early theories of pineal functions. Pineal Res Rev; 3:1–40.

www.ingramcontent.com/pod-product-compliance
Lightning Source LLC
Chambersburg PA
CBHW071327280526
45787CB00001B/22